Public Investment, Growth and Fiscal Constraints

Public Investment, Growth and Fiscal Constraints

Challenges for the EU New Member States

Edited by

Massimo Florio

Professor of Public Economics and Jean Monnet Chair of Economics of European Integration and Head, Dipartimento di Scienze Economiche, Aziendali e Statistiche, Università di Milano, Italy

Edward Elgar

Cheltenham, UK • Northampton, MA, USA

Published by
Edward Elgar Publishing Limited
The Lypiatts
15 Lansdown Road
Cheltenham
Glos GL50 2JA
UK

Edward Elgar Publishing, Inc.
William Pratt House
9 Dewey Court
Northampton
Massachusetts 01060
USA

A catalogue record for this book
is available from the British Library

Library of Congress Control Number: 2010929043

MIX
Paper from responsible sources
FSC® C018575

ISBN 978 1 84980 457 8

Typeset by Servis Filmsetting Ltd, Stockport, Cheshire
Printed and bound by MPG Books Group, UK

Contents

Contributors

Giuseppe Bognetti, University of Milan, Italy. Professor Bognetti holds a degree in law from Università degli Studi di Milano, and a BA in Economics from Cambridge University. He has taught at the Universities of Urbino and Milano, Italy, where he has been teaching public finance since 1980. Director of the Department of Economics at the Faculty of Political Sciences from 1992 to 1995, he was appointed again from 1998 to 2004. Formerly Vice President of Ciriec International (1992–1994) he is currently chief editor of the journal *Economia Pubblica*. His research interests include taxation theory, public enterprise theory, public services and regulation, history of public finance and public finance doctrines.

Ángel Catalina Rubianes, European Commission, Brussels, Belgium. Rubianes is a policy analyst in the Unit for Economic and Quantitative Analysis in the Directorate General for Regional Policy at the European Commission. He is responsible for the analysis of interactions between national policies and the EU cohesion policy and for the verification of the principle of additionality. Of Spanish nationality, he joined the Commission five years ago to work in the European Anti-Fraud Office (OLAF) where he was responsible for drafting the annual report on the protection of the EU financial interests. Before, he spent four years working as an official representative of the Galicia region in Brussels. He is now part of the team that will draft the Fifth Report on economic and social cohesion. He holds university degrees in economics and political science and a postgraduate degree in European economy.

Massimo Cingolani, European Investment Bank, Luxembourg. Cingolani is deputy head of division in the Directorate for Lending Operations in Europe at the European Investment Bank in Luxembourg. His research interests are in the modelling and evaluation of economic policy, in particular in the fields of macroeconomics, finance, regional economics, infrastructure and growth. Recent publications are: 'Per il rilancio della politica economica in Europa', *MondOperaio*, D 2006; 'Full employment as a possible objective for EU policy – I. A perspective from the point of view of the monetary circuit', and 'II. Review of some empirical aspects', *Panoeconomicus*, 2008, volumes 1 and 2. Since 2006 he has been an EIB tutor for the STAREBEI research on 'Evolutions des agrégats macro-financiers dans les Nouveaux Pays Membres et dans les Pays Candidats à l'UE: une lecture par la théorie du circuit monétaire'.

Chiara Del Bo, University of Milan, Italy. Del Bo is a researcher at Università degli Studi di Milano. She holds a PhD in Economics from the same university, with the dissertation 'Essays on investment and growth in an international setting'. She earned a Master's degree in Economics (MEc) at Università Commerciale Luigi Bocconi in 2003. She graduated in economics at Università Cattolica del Sacro Cuore, Milan with a dissertation on 'Research joint ventures in the semiconductor industry'. Between August 2005 and December 2006 she was a visiting student at the Economics Department of Boston College, USA. In 2009, she was a visiting researcher at the Department of Spatial Economics, Vrije Universiteit, Amsterdam. Her research interests are in applied economics, with a specific focus on regional, growth and international issues.

Massimo Florio, University of Milan, Italy. Florio is Head of the Department of Economics, Università degli Studi di Milano, Professor of Public Economics, and Jean Monnet Chair in Economics of European Integration. His main research interests are in welfare economics, cost–benefit analysis, industrial and regional policies, infrastructure and growth, regulation and privatization. Recent publications include: *The Great Divestiture: Evaluating the Welfare Impact of the British Privatizations, 1979–1997*, MIT Press (2004), *Cost–Benefit Analysis and Incentives in Evaluation. The Structural Funds of the European Union*, Edward Elgar (2007) and the EC *Guide to Cost–Benefit Analysis of Investment Projects* (2008).

Jan Hanousek, CERGE-EI Prague, Czech Republic. Hanousek has a PhD in Probability and Statistics from Charles University, Prague, Czech Republic. He is Professor of Economics at CERGE-EI, a joint workplace of Charles University and the Academy of Sciences of the Czech Republic, Prague, and Professor of Economics at Charles University, Prague. He is a co-ordinator for PHARE projects on the informal sector in transitional economies. He is also member of the National Discussion Group Ministry of Finance, advisory body of the Ministry of Finance, Czech Republic. He is currently working on the effects of privatization in transition economies.

Evžen Kočenda, CERGE-EI Prague, Czech Republic. Kočenda graduated in 1985 from the Prague School of Economics with a degree in international trade management. He received an MA in Economics from the University of Toledo, Ohio, USA in 1992, and a PhD in Economics from the University of Houston, Texas, USA, in 1996. From 1996 to 1998 he was Deputy Director for Research at CERGE, Charles University, Prague, Czech Republic, and the Economics Institute of the Academy of Sciences of the Czech Republic. Since 2004 he has been Professor of Economics at CERGE. He is a Research Fellow of the William Davidson Institute at the University of Michigan Business School and Research Affiliate of CEPR, London, and EABCN. He was Economic Advisor to the Minister of Foreign Affairs of the Czech Republic in 1997. Since 1998 he has been a member of the editorial board of the journal *Finance a uver*. From 1998 to 1999 he was a member of the Scientific Council of the Ministry of Transport and Communications. Since 1999 he has been a member of the CERGE Scientific Council.

Luigi Moretti, University of Florence, Italy. Moretti holds a degree in political sciences from the University of Florence and earned a PhD in Economics, Markets and Institutions at IMT Institute for Advanced Studies, Lucca, Italy. He has been a PhD visiting student at the Centre for Finance and Credit Markets, School of Economics, University of Nottingham, UK and at the Universidad Carlos III de Madrid, Spain. His main research areas are the analysis of the real effects of banking market development and the assessment of the impact of European Regional Policy.

Aleksandra Parteka, Gdansk University of Technology, Poland. Parteka works as an Assistant Professor at Gdansk University of Technology, Faculty of Management and Economics, Poland. She completed her PhD in Economics at Università Politecnica delle Marche, Ancona, Italy in 2007. She completed her MA studies in economics at the Gdansk University of Technology and Università Politecnica delle Marche, and in Contemporary European Studies at the University of Sussex. Her research interests include international economics, with a particular focus on trade issues, European integration and economics of transition.

Giorgio Ragazzi, University of Bergamo, Italy. Ragazzi is Associate Professor of Public Finance. He worked at the IMF as an economist and at the World Bank as Executive Director, he was financial manager in a multinational company and served as a consultant for several government and private institutions. He taught finance at the LUISS University in Rome, Italy and macroeconomic policy in Bergamo. His research interests are public sector accounts, fiscal policy, regulation of natural monopolies and public services.

Malcolm Sawyer, University of Leeds, UK. With a Masters in Economics from the University of London and a BA in Mathematics from Oxford, Sawyer is a member of the Council of the Royal Economic Society, Senior Visiting Fellow at the J. Levy Economics Institute, USA, Co-editor of *International Papers in Political Economy* and Managing Editor of *International Review of Applied Economics*, and a consultant to the OECD, the EU and the National Institute for Economic and Social Research. His main research interests involve the intellectual and institutional obstacles to full employment, the development of post-Keynesian macroeconomics, the nature and role of markets and the economics of Michal Kalecki.

Emanuela Sirtori, CSIL, Italy. Sirtori graduated with honours in Economics from the Bicocca University of Milan, Italy. After attending a post-degree training course on methods of cooperation and development, she started her research fellowship at CSIL. Her field of expertise is econometrics, poverty and inequality analysis, mainly applied to issues of regional development. Recently she presented a paper at the Third Annual Conference of the Political Economy in the International Organization (PEIO) in Washington DC, on the impact of collaboration between the World Bank and the IMF on growth in the beneficiary countries.

Silvia Vignetti, CSIL, Italy. Vignetti is currently a CSIL partner and Director of the Development and Evaluation Unit. She holds a degree in economics from Bocconi University, Italy and after a traineeship at UNESCO, Paris, she started her collaboration as a research fellow at CSIL. She has also had teaching appointments at the University of Milan, Italy in macroeconomics, economics of European integration and cost–benefit analysis. She specializes in structural funds interventions and evaluation of projects and programmes, and has gained relevant experience in this field, both at the EU as well as at the national level.

Abbreviations

ANOVA	Analysis of Variance
CA	Current Account
CEE	Central and Eastern European
CERGE-EI	Centre for Economic Research and Graduate Education – Economics Institute
CEPA	Classification of Environmental Protection Activities
CF	Cohesion Fund
COFOG	Classification of the Functions of Government
CPI	Consumer Price Index
EBRD	European Bank for Reconstruction and Development
EC	European Commission
EERP	European Economic Recovery Program
EIB	European Investment Bank
EMU	Economic and Monetary Union
ERDF	European Regional Development Fund
ESF	European Social Fund
ESPON	European Observation Network, Territorial Development and Cohesion
EU	European Union
EUR	Euro Code
FDI	Foreign Direct Investment
GDP	Gross Domestic Product
GFCF	Gross Fixed Capital Formation
GNP	Gross National Product
HICP	Harmonized Index of Consumer Prices
ICT	Information and Communication Technology
IMF	International Monetary Fund
NAIRU	Non-Accelerating Inflation Rate of Unemployment
NMS	New Member States
NPG	No Ponzi Game
NUTS	Nomenclature of Territorial Units for Statistics
OECD	Organisation for Economic Co-operation and Development
OMS	Old Member States
PPI	Producer Price Index

PPS	Purchase Power Standards
PSFNW	Public Sector Net Financial Worth
PWT	Penn World Tables
R&D	Research and Development
RTDI	Research Technology, Development and Innovation
SCF	Structural and Cohesion Fund
SERIEE	Système Europèen de Rassemblement de l'Information Economique sur l'Environment (European System of Collection of Economic Information on the Environment)
SGP	Stability and Growth Pact
SME	Small and Medium Enterprises
TFA	Tangible Fixed Assets
TEN	Trans-European Network
TEN-T	Trans-European Transport Network
TRT	Trasporti e Territorio
UK	United Kingdom
US	United States of America
USD	United States dollar
VAR	Vector Autoregressive
VAT	Value Added Tax

Introduction: public investment, growth and fiscal constraints in the EU

Massimo Florio

The European project, after the recent global financial crisis, faces a difficult challenge. In order to achieve real convergence and sustained growth of the 27 EU Member States, substantial resources should be devoted to investment, particularly in the recently accessed countries. The banking sector, however, is currently not in the position to offer the amount of credit needed by firms. These in turn are facing a weak demand, and have dramatically cut fixed capital formation. At the same time, public finances are under stress because of the sudden increase of government expenditures committed to support private banks, manufacturing firms, and households facing unemployment. This does not look like a favourable scenario for a grand public investment design. Yet, this is still needed, and in fact it was duly planned in ordinary times by the EU governments, as part of their long-term growth strategies. The situation in Europe is perhaps more complex than elsewhere because of the lack of a proper federal budget, the pending rules of the Stability and Growth Pact, the necessity to avoid a loss of confidence in the solidity of the euro, the not yet fully implemented provisions of the Treaty (hence a cumbersome governance of policy making), and the persisting gap between the 'Old' and the 'New' members. The latter were set on a relatively high growth path before the crisis of 2008, with average per capita GDP growth approximately two times higher than in the EU15. In fact, the objective of convergence in Europe depends upon achieving this gap in the long term. The European Commission is right in targeting the Structural Funds (around 350 billion Euro in the programming period 2007–2013) to sustain a positive growth differential in regions and countries that are lagging behind.

What is the potential role of public investment in this context? How is it possible to finance capital accumulation in the present and future conditions of mounting public sector debt? It seems time to re-open a serious discussion on public expenditure as a tool for economic policy making, after perhaps a certain neglect of attention in some quarters because of an excessive confidence in financial markets, public-private partnerships and in general private initiatives. This book offers a selection of papers presented at the Milan European Economy Workshop 2009, and further reviewed after a lively discussion there and in the following months. The Workshop itself was part of a wide research project at the DEAS, Department of Economics, Business and Statistics, University of Milan, sponsored by the European Investment Bank (EIBURS programme). Other material related to the project is available as DEAS working papers at www.economia.unimi.it/, and in a special issue of *Transition Studies Review*, (Florio, 2010).

The book contains nine chapters, assembled in three parts. The first part is more general in scope, and deals with the conceptual issues involved in the role of public expenditure in a growth perspective. It contains three chapters: one by Malcolm Sawyer (Leeds University), who draws from his keynote presentation in Milan; Chiara Del Bo (Università degli Studi di Milano) reviews recent advances in the literature, while Massimo Cingolani (EIB) offers a post-Keynesian viewpoint on the topic. The second part focuses on public investment and fiscal constraints in the NMS. The three chapters included in it offer a sweeping overview of the current fiscal conditions and growth trends in the EU: Ángel Catalina Rubianes (European Commission) looks at the EU scenario as a whole; Giuseppe Bognetti (Università degli Studi di Milano) and Giorgio Ragazzi (Bergamo University) focus on public sector accounts; Jan Hanousek and Evžen Kočenda (Charles University and CERGE-EI, Prague) offer a detailed review of the situation in the NMS, country by country. Finally, the third part looks at the industry-specific and regional dimensions of structural change and public intervention: Aleksandra Parteka (Gdansk University) looks at the determinants of productivity growth in the New Member States (NMS); Luigi Moretti (University of Florence) considers the role of Structural Funds in supporting business growth at the regional level; Emanuela Sirtori and Silvia Vignetti (CSIL Centre for Industrial Studies, Milan) review the evidence on infrastructure needs in the NMS regions. In the rest of this introduction I briefly discuss the issues raised by these contributions. I frame the discussion around three questions: Does public investment matter for growth? Are fiscal conditions in the EU and particularly in the NMS favourable to public investment? What is the role of regional policy?

DOES PUBLIC INVESTMENT MATTER FOR GROWTH?

After two decades of decline of public investment and of decrease of confidence in the government, this is still a simple, but important question.

One consequence of the crisis of confidence has been the return of fiscal rules that have the pre-Keynesian flavour of balanced budget accounting dogmas. Malcolm Sawyer's contribution explains the conceptual underpinnings of the controversy. He identifies two traditions in macroeconomic analysis with regard to budget deficits, that of 'fiscal consolidation and Ricardian equivalence' and the 'functional finance' approach, rooted in Keynes's and Lerner's early ideas. He argues that the deficit/debt position should be approached in terms of 'functional finance', which sets the budget position to be compatible with the highest achievable and sustainable level of economic activity, against an alternative 'rule' for the 'balanced budget over the cycle'. The chapter points to the focus on the size of the public debt, and argues that the government's capital account balance sheet should be viewed in terms of assets and liabilities and not liabilities alone. It also argues that there is no merit in the adoption of a 'golden rule'. Clearly, if we agree with Sawyer, the fiscal framework for public spending is more flexible than the various versions of the balanced budget rules. Moreover, I would also submit the view that savers after the global crisis have suddenly rediscovered worldwide why public debt is different from private debt, for example allowing the US Treasury to pay an extremely limited risk premium on its issues, in face of a huge increase of federal debt and deficit. The same leniency did not apply, of course, to bonds issued for example by Greece, and this shows that the scale of government operations and possibly the institutional quality are also important in shaping governments' credibility.

Do these ideas find support in academic literature? The aim of Chiara Del Bo's chapter is to review to what extent public investment, public capital and fiscal policy in general affect growth, and through which channels this impact is working, according to recent contributions. The first part examines the positive relation between public expenditure and capital on economic growth, highlighting trends and the role of different categories of expenditure. The chapter also surveys a recent and promising research avenue in the explicit analysis of distributional and inequality-reducing effects of increases in productive public investment. The second part focuses instead on fiscal policy, taking into account both the revenue and expenditure side. The role played by fiscal consolidation rules and adjustments is examined and the link between public investment, fiscal consolidation and growth is stressed. The picture here is more nuanced, as the controversy is still open and wide and the chapter concludes with some directions for future research.

Massimo Cingolani offers a 'disequilibrium' view of public finance. Cingolani suggests that, as governments around the world realized in the recent crisis, the standard neoclassical view of macroeconomic equilibrium optimum cannot be the only reference for economic policy. It is argued that the model of the monetary circuit, put into the more general perspective of post-Keynesian analysis, is useful to illustrate policy choices in disequilibrium situations, characterized by underemployment of the labour force and a sub-optimal utilization of the productive capacity. This type of disequilibrium also implies that investment causes savings. According to the 'circuit' view, if the state budget is restricted to previously accumulated savings for financing its expenditures, governments deprive themselves of an important instrument for planning long-term budgetary policies that could stabilize the economy by anchoring the diverging expectations of the private sector. It also gives support to the idea of coordinating European fiscal policy at the continental level through the collective management of investment and other public expenditure. In my view the latter point is particularly important. Going back to my earlier comment, the fact that the US government is able to incur its debt with a strong federal backing is a clear advantage. As a counterfactual, one can think of the fiscal credibility of the US if most of its public debt were issued by its 50 states.

Overall, the three chapters suggest that there are good theoretical and empirical reasons to view productive public expenditure as a leverage mechanism for growth, both in the short run and in the longer term. It seems that the earlier preoccupations about the crowding-out effects of public expenditure were misplaced or exaggerated, because of the overly abstract assumptions needed to support them. This does not amount, of course, to saying that any public investment project is good *per se*. Or that permanent and unsustainable deficit is good. Or that credibility of governments does not play a role. Careful evaluation is needed at the micro level, see below, but at the more macro level there is room for a more optimistic view of the role of public finance in supporting accumulation of fixed or human capital, when private finance is not adequate in meeting the aggregate demand.

DO FISCAL CONDITIONS IN THE EUROPEAN UNION AND IN THE NMS SUPPORT INVESTMENT?

The second part of the book looks into the actual fiscal situation in Europe from the angle of public investment. Ángel Catalina Rubianes' chapter assesses to what extent the budgetary restrictions to which the NMS were and are confronted with are having a negative impact on public expenditure and particularly public investment. Catalina also looks at the composition of total public expenditure and in which functional areas lies the difference between the old EU15 and NMS in public expenditure in terms of gross domestic product (GDP). He observes that the NMS have been confronted in the last decade with a tight restriction of public financial resources compared to their GDP. While public expenditure accounted for more than 52 per cent of GDP in 1999, it was just about 41 per cent in 2007. As a result, total public expenditure in the NMS is about 5 percentage points lower than in the old EU15 countries. The reduction, however, was not in general made at the expense of public investment. While the total expenditure dropped by more than 11 percentage points of GDP, public investment decreased by only 0.4 percentage points of GDP. Moreover, public investment in physical capital is substantially higher in NMS relative to GDP. In the EU at large, public investment seems to appear a determinant for growth and 'catching-up' over the period 1999–2007.

The European cohesion policy supports a very significant part of the public investments made in the NMS. In the area of environmental protection, for example, it accounts on average for about 75 per cent of the total investments in this field. Thus, I would comment that without the Structural Funds probably the working of the EU accession mechanisms would have imposed serious damage on capital accumulation in the NMS. Hence, after all, there is a lesson to be learned here for the future: without substantial capital transfers by the EU to the NMS their investment pattern and growth would be at risk. Moreover, a revision of the Stability and Growth Pact should reconsider the integration with Cohesion Policy (that is, the 'growth' side of the story).

Accounting rules and fiscal guidelines are not as simple and transparent as one would think or wish. Some controversial issues concerning the definition and measurement of deficits and public debt are discussed by Giuseppe Bognetti and Giorgio Ragazzi. The rationality of the two Maastricht targets for public finance is also critically analysed. The economies of six NMS are then considered, from 2003 onwards. All of them experienced a high and steady rate of growth, but also a relatively high rate of inflation, accelerating after 2006. In spite of a high investment ratio by the public sector, national budget deficits were generally low and below the 3 per cent target. Thanks to the rapid expansion of nominal GNP, the public sector debt ratio declined in all countries, with the exception of Hungary.

Moreover, most of them have a positive net financial position. Thus Bognetti and Ragazzi conclude that these countries (except Hungary) have met the convergence criteria for public sector accounts and have followed prudent fiscal policies: the causes for external imbalances and excessive inflation are to be found (with some exception like the Czech Republic) in lax monetary policies and in the large inflow of foreign capital, primarily for direct investment but also on account of bank lending to the private sector.

A closer view of fiscal conditions in each of the NMS is given in Jan Hanousek and Evžen Kočenda's chapter. The overall macroeconomic situation, fiscal reforms and public finance developments are discussed for each Member State with a focus on the developments in growing public investments. Sectors that benefited most are transport systems, general government services, housing and education. Earlier favourable developments in the NMS have been hampered, however, by the recent crisis as external demand for exports fell and capital inflows into the region were reduced, coupled with a lower domestic demand. The crisis has affected all new EU members with a varying impact due to different magnitudes of earlier macroeconomic imbalances as well as differences in the degree of economic integration with the rest of the EU. The future convergence and economic development of the new EU members will depend mainly on maintaining financial stability to regain the credibility of the foreign investors, rational fiscal policies with the support of growth-enhancing public investments and the social networks, and the economic situation in the region's major economic partners.

The common message from the three chapters is that, overall, the NMS have been taking advantage of their economic integration in the EU, and that in spite of cuts in general public expenditure they have been able until now to couple sustained public investment and growth with fiscal consolidation. To this end, capital transfers from the EU were crucial. There are, however, still problems in terms of the speed of change, inflation and specific country imbalances. When compared, however, with earlier preoccupations about the impact of the enlargement shock in former transition economies, the overall assessment is rather optimistic. The recent financial crisis may disturb this development path, but the overall discussion shows that it would be wise to avoid excessive corrections that may cut public investment. It also shows that the Cohesion Policy and the Structural Funds must remain for at least one decade in order to counterbalance the impact of fiscal consolidation on other public expenditure items. This issue is discussed from a different perspective in the next chapters.

WHAT CAN REGIONAL POLICY DO FOR STRUCTURAL CHANGE AND INFRASTRUCTURE NEEDS?

Growth is not an abstract idea; its ingredients are output/input change, industry by industry. This question requires a more detailed look into productivity growth in the NMS. This is done by Aleksandra Parteka, who focuses on the ten NMS (NMS-10) that joined the EU in 2004 and analyses the productivity dynamics of their labour structures between the years 1995 and 2005 in a comparative setting versus EU15 economies. NMS-10 have gone through a rapid process of economic restructuring and its speed has been positively related to economic development. However, shift–share analysis of productivity growth indicates that changes in value added per hour worked were due mainly to positive developments (rising productivity) within single sectors and only to a lower extent to the shift towards higher productivity sectors. The process of a structural change and productivity growth has been characterized by a 'beta' convergence-type mechanism, with public spending (especially on education, social protection, public order and safety) and trade (in particular with more advanced EU15 countries) promoting overall and intra-industry productivity upgrading.

Some answers to the question of how the EU can influence this pattern are given in the last two chapters. Luigi Moretti looks into the capital grants to firms under the Structural and Cohesion Funds (SCF) in the NMS, given their importance (as also discussed by Catalina). These funds are substantial not only as a share of total SCF expenditure but also as a share of GDP. Thus it is particularly important to understand the real effects of SCF business support and its impact on the reallocation of resources and activities across industries. In a related paper, Florio and Moretti (2009) show that the SCF business support to GDP ratio does not have significant average effects on employment growth in manufacturing industries, but the effects are positive and statistically significant for smaller sized and 'higher growth opportunity' industries. Using the estimated coefficients of the relationships between the ratio of SCF business support to GDP and employment growth in manufacturing industries obtained in that study for a sample of German, Italian and Spanish regions, Moretti presents a sensitivity analysis for the effects of SCF business support on employment growth in New Member States. In particular, given the structure and specialization of the regions' manufacturing industries, he shows which regions, country and industries would benefit most from higher SCF business support expenditure

Finally, Emanuela Sirtori and Silvia Vignetti provide a review of the infrastructural gaps in EU transition economies at the national and, as far as possible, regional level for some infrastructure sectors: transport, telecommunication, environment and energy. These gaps are still substantial, and a continued investment effort is needed for at least one decade or two. While infrastructure support should indeed be promoted to foster regional growth as a key priority in the framework of the EU Cohesion Policy, an effort should be made by policy makers to understand how to tailor the features and options of infrastructural policy to regional characteristics and actual long-term needs.

The three chapters remind us that one issue is the macroeconomic environment, but a quite different issue is the actual arena where public intervention can achieve its targets or fall short of them. Specific regions and industries respond differently to EU assistance and to government capital expenditure. This broad message suggests that a combination of flexible and co-ordinated European fiscal policy and of national and EU regional and industrial policies are needed to extract the growth potential for each Euro spent in sustaining capital accumulation in the NMS.

I would close this Introduction with a more personal view about the policy implications of the research contributions offered in this book. There have been wide oscillations in the economic profession about the role of public investment and public expenditure in general. While in the post-war years of the last century there has been perhaps a degree of over-optimism about what governments could do by investment planning, particularly in developing countries, the mood since the 1980s was too pessimistic. At the same time, in the last two decades there was a lot of enthusiasm about the self-regulatory and progressive features of financial markets. After all, if energy, water, schooling, transport, telecoms, hospitals and other important services are needed, why can't private demand simply be matched by private investments, financed by private savings?

This is still a core and controversial issue in economic policy. Do we really need *public* investment? The recent history of the NMS of the EU (as well the possibly more remote and forgotten history of post-war Western Europe) offers a possible answer. The answer is quite positive. In spite of a wide mobilization of private resources in the NMS, including foreign investment, there is a wealth of opportunities that went unexploited by private investors. We cannot ask financial markets to do more than what they are able to do. After all, when most of the dividend of physical and human capital accumulation cannot be efficiently appropriated by private owners, and spills over to the society at large in the form of aggregate growth, markets do fail and governments do have a chance to play a positive role. In fact, there are often strong externalities in any investment, as modern endogenous growth theory has convincingly clarified. Good private finance will offer funds to projects that ensure an adequate return to the investors. Bad private finance will waste resources in betting on unsustainable games.

Public finance of investment can do a similar job. When it is good, it will channel savings towards projects that offer an adequate social dividend, even when there are externalities. If public finance is bad, however, it will waste economic opportunities. The answer is having good government in place, which in turn means having high quality human capital committed to civil service. This book suggests that there is a proper role for public investment, as it can be associated with socially beneficial accumulation channels. From the wide current evidence of mismanagement of savings by global financial markets we need to learn a lesson for public investment as well. We do not live in an abstract equilibrium environment. We live in a real world, where growth opportunities and deep pitfalls are all around us. Public and private investments can be complements, but only under certain conditions. Achieving a fair balance of the two governance mechanisms, with different incentives and tools, is the challenge for the future. Simplistic fiscal rules do not capture the essence of the trade-offs faced by governments. In my reading, the overall message of the book is that there is now a convincing case for public investment as a core driver of convergence and growth in Europe. We need, however, a new international and intergenerational fiscal pact to frame a more optimistic view of the role of government. I hope that this book will contribute to this understanding.

Milano, 6 April, 2010

REFERENCE

Florio, M. (ed.) (2010), 'Infrastructure, convergence and investment decisions in the European Union', *Transition Studies Review*, special issue, **7**(3).

Florio, M. and L. Moretti (2009), 'The effect of business support on employment in manufacturing: evidence from the EU Structural Funds in Germany, Italy and Spain', University of Milan Department of Economics, Business and Statistics working paper 2009–33.

PART I

Public investment and growth: conceptual framework

1. Budget deficits, public debt and the level of public investment

Malcolm Sawyer

INTRODUCTION

There have long been two traditions in macroeconomic analysis with regard to budget deficits: constraints on them and need for them. The first tradition is labelled here 'fiscal consolidation and Ricardian equivalence' and the second 'functional finance'. From the first tradition, the idea of an intertemporal budget constraint is taken as an expression of this approach, and that idea is briefly outlined and examined. From the second tradition, the idea of functional finance is outlined under which there is a presumption that the level of aggregate demand is not balanced with potential supply (usually but not always demand being less than supply), and the need for budget deficits arises to sustain a high level of demand.

The chapter argues for the deficits/debt position to be approached in terms of functional finance, that is seeking to set the budget position to be compatible with the highest achievable and sustainable level of economic activity (which incorporates constraints arising from the level and structure of productive capacity, and balance of payments constraints). This would provide an alternative 'rule' for budget deficits to those such as 'balanced budget over the cycle'. Government accounts should seek to follow the principles that the manner in which public expenditure (and notably public investment) is financed (for example through tax revenues, through borrowing, through public–private partnerships) does not influence the decisions on the level and structure of public investment. Further, any concern over the level of public debt should be tempered by the realisation that much of it is held internally (within the country concerned), and that public debt (government bonds and so on) is an asset for its holders, and provides an associated income stream in the form of interest payments. It should also be tempered by a full consideration of the physical and other assets held by the public sector. It makes little sense to be concerned over liabilities without consideration of assets.

The implications of this view for public investment are that the scale of public expenditure relative to the level of taxation should be set in accordance with functional finance. The division between current expenditure and capital expenditure should be made in accordance with social priorities with due allowance made for the impact of public investment on growth prospects. It leaves open the question of the appropriate rate of discount to be applied to public investment projects. This would, though, suggest a much broader view on what constitutes investment to include, for example, much of education spending. An appropriate division would be between investment which leads to assets owned by the public sector and investment which leads to other 'assets' (for example, human capital). This approach does not, though, support any notion of a 'golden rule' whereby the current budget is balanced with borrowing (over the business cycle) undertaken for capital project purposes.

1. BALANCING THE BOOKS

The first tradition in macroeconomic analysis with regard to the effects of fiscal policy and budget deficits (which has come in several different guises) involves ideas that in market economies there are strong automatic market forces which lead to a situation of full employment of resources.[1] It then follows that public expenditure competes with private expenditure for resources, and that attempts to increase public expenditure will inevitably 'crowd out' private expenditure as the resources of the economy are scarce.

Two sets of arguments have been prominent in recent years with regard to the relationship between the overall level of demand in the economy and the budget position. The first has been the revival of interest in Ricardian equivalence (without here going into whether this corresponds to Ricardo's own views). Starting with Barro (1974), the idea of Ricardian equivalence has been used to argue that any change in government budget deficit will be exactly offset in expenditure terms by changes in private expenditure. The approach focuses on changes in the budget position initiated by the government to which the private sector responds, rather than envisaging that it is changes in the behaviour of the private sector (with regard to investment and savings) which causes change in the budget position (as illustrated by the notion of automatic stabilisers as tax revenue falls, and budget deficits rise in the face of a slowdown in private demand). Ricardian equivalence suggests a constant level of aggregate demand, or at least a level of demand which is not impacted by government expenditure and budget position.

The second set of arguments has been the idea summarised in the expression 'fiscal consolidation' that announced that reductions in budget deficits can have overall expansionary effects. This clearly runs counter to the traditional Keynesian multiplier arguments to the effect that public expenditure 'crowds in' other expenditures leading to an increase of output which is a multiple of the increase in public expenditure, and instead proposes a form of demand 'crowding out'. The key idea is that announcements of policies to reduce budget deficits raise confidence in the private sector, leading to increases in expenditure and notably in investment. The perception of an unsustainable position of a budget deficit, with rising debt and future interest obligations cumulating, is changed. In a paper entitled 'Can budgetary consolidations be expansionary? What the theory says' the European Commission (2003) argues:

> If agents are forward-looking and rational in forming their expectations, they will anticipate that a tax cut today, financed by government debt, will translate into higher taxes at some point in the future. If, in addition, government intervention is non-distortionary, capital markets are perfect and consumers sufficiently long-lived, the so called Ricardian equivalence should hold, namely, permanent income will be unaffected by fiscal policy, and so consumption. Under these abstract circumstances, fiscal multipliers will be zero, since higher government savings obtained through fiscal consolidations will be compensated by an equivalent reduction in private savings.' (p. 140)

The non-Keynesian effects can come through a variety of routes, and it is often argued that whilst Keynesian effects may be observed with low levels of government debt, non-Keynesian ones come at high debt levels. It is argued that if fiscal consolidation is made when there is a high debt level, then there may be an expected increase in permanent income leads to higher consumption. 'The reason is that by consolidating now, the government will not raise taxes too much in the future to pay back the debt. This reduces the dead-weight loss imposed by taxes, thus raising agents' permanent income' (p. 141).

A further argument was proposed by Bertola and Drazen (1993), which is that when public expenditure is in some sense regarded as high, then people start to anticipate that there will be a future major fiscal adjustment.

> This may offset any loosening of fiscal policy. At the same time, a consolidation occurring when public spending is high may then change agents' expectations concerning a future major retrenchment, and the lower expected level of taxes raises permanent income and consumption. A further rationale for possible non-Keynesian effects through the consumption channel emerges if fiscal consolidations are assumed to affect the risk of government insolvency. By reducing their budget deficits, governments will signal to markets their willingness to switch to 'sound finances'. If this signal is taken as credible, interest premiums on government bonds will fall. The consequent reduction in interest rates will

> in turn contribute to raise agents' permanent income, since they will discount future income streams at a lower rate. (European Commission, 2003, p. 141)

Following Alesina et al. (2002) it is argued that the link between fiscal policy and investment behaviour operates via the labour market on the basis that investment decisions are based on the expected present value of investment which is taken to be negatively related with real wages.

> Fiscal consolidation obtained through expenditure cuts may increase short-run investments via reduced wage pressures for a number of reasons. A reduction in the government wage bill will in general contribute to wage moderation in the private sector as well. A similar effect would be obtained by means of reductions in government transfers. The possibility for fiscal consolidations to exhibit non-Keynesian effects through the investment channel will then crucially depend upon the composition of adjustment (expenditure cuts versus tax increases) and on institutional factors, above all the working of the labour market. (European Commission, 2003, pp. 141–2)

These arguments and associated ones have been highly influential in the revival of the use of budgetary rules on the size of budget deficits with the target size of deficit less than recent experience. However the budgetary rules have generally been applied over the course of a business cycle (or equivalent) rather than applying in any single calendar year. Yet these arguments do not indicate reasons for the application of the rules on that basis – crudely why would the budget deficit rule be applied over the cycle rather than on an annual basis? The Ricardian equivalence arguments would suggest that a budget deficit would never have a stimulating effect on the economy. The budgetary rules have included (a) balanced budget or small surplus over the cycle (Stability and Growth Pact) and (b) balanced current budget over the cycle, borrowing to fund capital investment ('golden rule') (UK Code for Fiscal Stability). These have often gone alongside views on the scale of the public debt (60 per cent under SGP, 40 per cent under the Code for Fiscal Stability).

2. FUNCTIONAL FINANCE

The functional finance approach (using the term first applied by Lerner, 1943) could be seen to start from observations of substantial unemployment as the 'norm' in market economies, along with views on the importance of the level of aggregate demand for the level of economic activity and that any market forces pushing the economy towards full employment being weak or non-existent.[2] When applied in the context of an otherwise underemployed economy, public expenditure crowds in rather than crowds out private expenditure. Lerner (1943) put the case for functional finance, which 'rejects completely the traditional doctrines of "sound finance" and the principle of trying to balance the budget over a solar year or any other arbitrary period' (p. 355), including over the business cycle. The arguments of Kalecki (1944a, 1994b) were essentially similar to the effect that a budget deficit is required to correct a deficiency of aggregate demand, that this was more a long-term effect rather than a temporary one, and it is precisely in conditions of deficient aggregate demand that funds will be available to fund the budget deficit.

Functional finance can be represented in terms of a rule which replaces any form of balanced budget rules by: seeking to set a budget deficit (or surplus) to attain the highest level of sustainable output, labelled Y_f. This can be written as seeking to set a budget deficit:

$$G - T = S(Y_f) - I(Y_f) + CA(Y_f) \tag{1.1}$$

where G is government expenditure (including debt interest), T tax revenue, S savings, I investment and CA current account deficit (= financial account surplus).

It should, though, be firmly kept in mind that these variables will depend on other variables, and the distribution of income between wages and profits and the exchange rate would be significant ones, and factors such as the state of expectations and confidence have key roles. The difficulties of making the correct calculations should not be minimised, but similar difficulties arise when striving to meet other rules (such as balanced budget).

A major consideration in the pursuit of a functional finance approach should be that a budget deficit is only required (on the left-hand side of the equation) when there is some combination of net private savings and capital account inflow which can provide the funding of that budget deficit (the extent of borrowing from overseas is an issue to which we return below). A fiscal policy operated along these lines does not run into issues of funding for the deficit. The functional finance approach is immune to the crowding out objection, since the need for a budget deficit arises because there is a lack of demand to crowd out, and also to the 'how is the deficit to be paid for' question. In the absence of a budget deficit the private savings (in excess of private investment) would not actually be able to happen. This approach suggests that there is no essential funding problem (and the question of pressure on interest rates is returned to below).

A budget deficit set according to Equation 1.1 does not raise issues of 'crowding out' nor of inflation, provided that the target for the level of output is beyond the capacity of the economy to produce without inflationary consequences. The functional finance approach recognises that there maybe a requirement for a long-term budget deficit (or conceivably a long-term surplus) which would depend on the propensities and desires to save and to invest (as well as the current account position). A long-term deficit clearly would involve an expanding public debt, which raises issues of sustainability in the face of rising debt and associated interest payments. This is returned to below where it is argued that for the relevant budget deficit, the debt to GDP ratio would converge on a 'steady state' value, which avoids issues of unsustainability though a high debt to GDP ratio could be involved.

The development of budgetary rules can be seen to reflect a general notion that the government has sooner or later to balance the books, and this is formally expressed as the 'intertemporal budget constraint'. The basic idea is, as the name suggests, that the government, like any other economic agent, faces a budget constraint, which is such that borrowing can be undertaken in some periods, but not in all, and that overall the debt position of the government sums to zero.

3. INTERTEMPORAL BUDGET CONSTRAINT

Blanchard and Fischer (1989) suggest that

> Integrating this budget constraint and imposing the NPG [No Ponzi Game[3]] condition this time on the government (that debt not increase faster asymptotically than the interest rate) gives an intertemporal budget constraint for the government
>
> $$b_0 + \int_0^\infty g_t R_t dt = \int_0^\infty \tau_t R_t dt \qquad (1.2)$$
>
> The present values of taxes must be equal to the present value of government spending plus the value of the initial government debt b_0, given the NPG condition. Equivalently, the government must choose a path of spending and taxes such that the present value of $g_t - \tau_t$, which is sometimes referred to as the primary deficit, equals the negative of initial debt, b_0; if the government has positive outstanding debt, it must anticipate running primary surpluses at some point in the future. (p. 55)

Here g is government expenditure (other than interest payments), τ tax revenue and R the discount factor. The particularly significant element comes from the last sentence of the quote with the future involving government tax revenue exceeding government expenditure, though noting that government expenditure here does not include interest payments (as the discounted value of those payments is reflected in the outstanding government debt).

Blanchard and Fischer (1989) go on to argue that

> integrating this budget constraint subject to the NPG condition gives the following intertemporal budget constraint:
>
> $$\int_0^\infty c_t R_t dt = k_0 - b_{p0} + b_0 + \int_0^\infty w_t R_t dt - \int_0^\infty \tau_t R_t dt \tag{1.3}$$
>
> The present value of consumption must be equal to the sum of nonhuman wealth, which is the sum of $k_0 - b_{p0}$ and b_0, and of human wealth, which is the present value of wages minus taxes. The government budget constraint shows that for a given pattern of government spending (and given b_0), the government has to levy taxes of a given present value: equivalently, the government need not run a balanced budget at every moment of time. (p. 55)

Re-writing equations (1.1) and (1.2) above gives:

$$b_0 = \int_0^\infty \tau_t R_t dt - \int_0^\infty g_t R_t dt \tag{1.4}$$

$$b_0 = \int_0^\infty c_t R_t dt - k_0 + b_{p0} - \int_0^\infty w_t R_t dt + \int_0^\infty \tau_t R_t dt \tag{1.5}$$

so that the discounted value of the budget surplus is equal to the discounted value of the private sector deficit. This is essentially the dynamic equivalent of $S - I = G - T$ (S savings, I investment, G government expenditure and T tax revenue) in an *ex ante* sense.

In the present context of a closed economy, a similar-looking equation would hold as an *ex post* accounting identity. But here it is clearly presented as an *ex ante* result, albeit derived from the assumption of a budget constraint imposed on the government. In a closed economy, the counterpart to an intertemporal government budget constraint is an intertemporal private sector budget constraint, of the form that the present value of the difference between private savings and investment summed over the future would also be zero (noting that the same discount rate would have to be used for both constraints).

The fulfilment of the intertemporal private sector budget constraint requires the equality (over time) between *ex ante* savings and investment. It is possible that savings and investment would be equal at a rate of interest linked with the rate of discount used and compatible with a high level of economic activity. In effect if the private sector imposed upon itself the intertemporal budget constraint, then the government would be faced with a corresponding constraint. Similarly, if the private sector operated with a constraint of the form that discounted future investment is greater or equal to discounted future savings, the constraint on the government is that discounted tax revenue would be greater than or equal to government expenditure. But conversely if the private sector did not perform according to that constraint, and specifically if investment tended to fall short of savings, then the budget constraint on the government would have to be amended accordingly. But further the private sector constraint is intended to apply to *ex ante* savings and investment and at the supply side equilibrium level of economic activity.

One of two arguments would usually be invoked to support the view that *ex ante* investment is at least equal to *ex ante* savings. The first would correspond to an appeal to Say's Law to the effect that 'supply creates its own demand'. The second would be to argue that the interest rate was also set such that the condition held. However, in any other circumstances (that is when *ex ante* savings tend to exceed *ex ante* investment at full employment), then adherence to the intertemporal budget constraint would impose on the private sector a requirement of (over time) *ex post* savings equal to *ex post* investment. This would entail low levels of economic activity to reduce savings (below the full employment *ex ante* level), and significant levels of unemployment would be the consequence of meeting the intertemporal budget constraint.

If the private sector seeks to save more than it invests (in a single period or more generally), then the private sector is not imposing (on itself) a budget constraint (intertemporal or otherwise) in terms of equality between *ex ante* savings and *ex ante* investment. If it were indeed the case that (*ex ante*) savings and investment were equal, then that equality would be in effect the budget constraint for the private sector, and hence there would be a budget constraint on the public sector. If there is an intertemporal equality between savings and investment, then similarly there would be an intertemporal budget constraint on the public sector. But then the question arises as to whether households behave in the manner portrayed by the intertemporal budget constraint thesis.

It is relevant to also recall that this approach is embedded within a tradition which is that there is no inherent lack of aggregate demand. In the context of a single interest rate, there is the notion of a 'natural rate of interest' (Wicksell, [1898] 1965). The 'natural rate of interest' is viewed as a 'real side' phenomenon with a separation between the 'real' and the 'monetary' (the classical dichotomy).

> There is a certain rate of interest on loans which is neutral in respect to commodity prices, and tends neither to raise nor to lower them. This is necessarily the same as the rate of interest which would be determined by supply and demand if no use were made of money and all lending were effected in the form of real capital goods. It comes to much the same thing to describe it as the current value of the natural rate of interest on capital. (Wicksell, 1965, p. 102)

The significant elements here are that there is an interest rate which can be set compatible with full employment. How well formulated this is has always been a matter of debate – for example, lack of credit rationing, separation of 'real' and 'monetary', 'capital controversy' issues. The natural rate of interest could be seen to provide the basis for the rate of discount to be used for public investment project evaluation.

The essence of the argument of this section is that if there were a binding constraint on government of the intertemporal budget constraint form, then savings and investment would in effect be in balance at full employment, and there would be no requirement for a budget deficit as there would be no shortfall of aggregate demand. Further, insofar as there was some form of natural rate of interest then that rate of interest would appear to be an appropriate one for use to judge public investment programmes.

The intertemporal budget constraint suggests that there are requirements for future primary budget surpluses (on the assumption of initial public debt). The absence of any reference to public assets and focus only on public liabilities is discussed in the next section. It should, though, be noted here that these arguments rest on the No Ponzi Game condition, which can be linked with relationship between the rate of interest and rate of growth, to which we return below. It can be further noted that constraints on budget deficits would relate to real primary deficits (the requirement for some future primary surpluses), yet discussion on budget deficits is generally undertaken in terms of nominal total deficits. Finally, the intertemporal budget constraint on government involves a corresponding constraint for the private sector, and any tendency for (*ex ante*) savings to exceed (*ex ante*) investment undermines the notion of such a constraint for the private sector.

4. ASSETS AND LIABILITIES

The intertemporal budget constraint above is cast in terms of the financial position of the government. The liabilities of the public sector in the form of public debt are included but there is no mention of any assets. But the public sector does own a wide range of assets often in the form of infrastructure such as roads, other transport facilities, buildings and so on. The recent estimates for the UK for 2007/08 put net worth of public sector at 28.9 per cent of GDP, which can be compared with public debt at 36.5 per cent of GDP. The net worth figure is estimated at 25.5 per cent of GDP in 2008/09 and projected to fall to −2.9 per cent in 2013/14 (reflecting the projected large budget deficits with debt rising to 76.2 per cent, and a reduction in the scale of public investment) (HM Treasury, 2009, Table 2.6).

The intertermporal budget constraint is written by Buiter (2001) in the following forms:

$$\dot{B} = iB + P(G^C + G^I - \theta K^G - T) \quad (1.6)$$

where G^C, G^I are government expenditure on current goods and services and investment respectively, K^G is the government capital stock and θ is the extent to which the capital stock contributes to government revenue (for example through charges, through effects on tax revenue) and T is tax revenue.

The net liability position of the government is then given by:

$$L = B - PK^G \quad (1.7)$$

and the rate of change by:

$$\dot{L} = iL + P(G^C - T) + [r - (\theta - \delta)]PK^G \quad (1.8)$$

and hence

$$L(t) = \int_t^\infty P(s)[T(s) - G^C(s)]e^{-i(s-t)}ds + \int_t^\infty [r - (\theta - \delta)]P(s)K^G(s)e^{-i(s-t)}ds \quad (1.9)$$

where for simplicity the discount rate is assumed constant over time.

There are two interesting aspects of this formulation. First, the intertemporal budget constraint is now expressed in terms of the net liability position of government, which can give a different complexion to that constraint. From equation 1.9 it can be seen that the net liability position is equal to the discounted future budget surplus plus discounted return on public assets. Clearly the net liability position may be positive or negative. In the case where there is positive public sector net worth (and taking the second term on the right-hand side as small or zero), then this constraint indicates that with net liabilities negative then the sum of future surpluses would also be negative. Insofar as there is some form of budget constraint on government which takes assets and liabilities into account, then for an initial position of an excess of assets over liabilities, equation 1.9 points to future possibilities for primary deficits.

Second, Buiter (2001) postulates some financial return to public sector assets. The argument is that these 'cash returns . . . include not only user charges and other revenues obtained by extracting fees from private beneficiaries of the services provided by the public sector capital stock, but also any additions to tax revenues resulting from the positive effects of the public sector capital stock on the tax base' (p. 3, fn. 4), that is by raising national income. In one sense this would appear to involve double counting as the tax revenues are already included in the equations above. However, it would mean that future tax revenues are not independent of the current level of public expenditure. The nature of the budget constraint facing the government is thereby changed in that public expenditure now which raises future income and taxation thereby shifts out the budget constraint on the government. It would also change the budget constraint facing the private sector in that the level of income in the future would be higher than otherwise.

Even where public assets do not generate income flows for the public sector, they generally do retain some potential resale value. There are, of course, numerous valuation issues, and the private sale value of a public asset (for example road) would depend on the future use of that asset (for example lease back to the public sector).

The arguments here could be taken further in two respects. First, expenditure undertaken by government which is treated as current expenditure may still have impacts on future income and taxation, even though that current expenditure does not lead to a tangible asset owned by the public sector. Expenditure on education and health services would be the most notable examples. Second, the effects which public investment and other forms of public expenditure have on the rate of economic growth (positive or negative) should be taken on board.

From this discussion, we would suggest that the theoretical argument on which the intertemporal budget constraint is based appears flawed if it focuses only on liabilities without any recognition that there can be public assets which aid the generation of income and tax revenues and which have a potential resale value. It is then suggested that the capital account position of the government should be viewed in terms of assets and liabilities, rather than liabilities alone.

The use of assets and liabilities, rather than solely liabilities, in the assessment of a government's balance sheet position is dismissed by HM Treasury on the grounds of unreliability of the measurement of government assets. 'Net worth is not used as a key indicator of the public finances, mainly as a result of the difficulties involved in accurately measuring many government assets and liabilities' (HM Treasury, 2009, p. 223). It can be recognised readily that there are severe measurement difficulties in terms of both the theoretical issues involved and empirical ones. It could, for example, be argued that liabilities should include future obligations with respect to pension arrangements and assets future tax streams. We would instead argue for assets to be those which have resulted from what is defined as capital expenditure for budget purposes. The use of assets and liabilities would give a much better sense of the strength (or otherwise) of the government's capital position. It may also lessen the temptations to reduce government debt through the sale of assets when the assets are realised for less than their value to the public sector. It would also lessen the temptation to undertake activities (notably public–private partnerships) which are undertaken because of the way in which they are treated in the public balance sheet.

5. SUSTAINABILITY OF DEFICITS AND DEBTS

The idea of a continuing budget deficit raises issues of sustainability in the face of rising debt and interest payments.[4] Any discussion of sustainability should distinguish whether it is the primary or total deficit which is being discussed and the assumption which is made on the relationship between the rate of interest (on government debt) and the rate of growth of GDP (there can be a further point, namely whether the size of the deficit makes allowance for the effects of inflation on the real value of the outstanding government debt). Attention should also be given as to whether the deficit is calculated in real terms or nominal terms (the main difference arising from the effects of inflation in eroding real value of outstanding public debt).

The basic relationships are straightforward. The growth of government debt B is given by $dB/dt = D + rB$ where D is the primary budget deficit (that is excluding interest payments on debt) and r the rate of interest on government debt.[5] The rate of change of the debt to income ratio is then given by $d(B/Y)/dt = D/B + r - g = d/b + r - g$ where g is the rate of growth of income Y, $d = D/Y$ and $b = B/Y$. For a given primary budget deficit (relative to income), the debt to income ratio would stabilise at $b = d/(g - r)$, which requires $g > r$. Note that in this formula, g and r can either be both in real terms or both in nominal terms, and that the relevant interest rate is the post-tax rate on government bonds.

As Lerner (1943), Domar (1944) and others established, a permanent primary budget deficit would be sustainable provided that the growth rate exceeds the rate of interest. The 'No Ponzi Game' assumption above involves the reverse, namely $g < r$. Indeed if $g > r$ was a general feature, then calculation of the discounted present value of a stream of profits (or other income) which grew in line with GDP could not be made. However the matter is not so clear-cut. First, the relevant rate of interest on government bonds could be taken as the post-tax rate as the net cost of borrowing for the government (with allowance for the degree to which the budget deficit is effectively money funded). Second, in the context of monetary policy (and hence the setting of the key interest rate by the Central Bank), Taylor (1993) developed what has become known as Taylor's rule which has the property that 'the 2-percent "equilibrium" real rate is close to the assumed steady-state growth rate of 2.2 percent' (Taylor, 1993, p. 202). Third, some argue that 'government debt must pay the same rate as capital, if agents are to hold it in their portfolio' (Blanchard and Fischer, 1989, p. 54). Yet, the 'golden rule' of capital accumulation (p. 45) is marginal product of capital equals 'natural' rate of growth and the assumption that the rate of profit equal to the rate of interest is equal to the marginal product of capital. Fourth, the empirical evidence on the relationship between rate of interest and rate of growth is not clear-cut. Some illustrative figures are given in Arestis and Sawyer (2006). A recent example is the UK government's assumption that the nominal rate of interest on government borrowing over the coming years will be around 4.3 per cent in the context of nominal growth rate of around 5 per cent.

The case where rate of interest and growth rate are approximately equal 'represents the "golden rule" of capital accumulation. . . . In this case, the public budget can be permanently in deficit and the public debt can thereby increase indefinitely, but national income increases at the same rate (g) so that the D/Y ratio remains constant. Another way of looking at this case is to say that the government budget has a deficit which is wholly due to interest payments' (Pasinetti, 1997, p. 163). This can be readily seen from $b = d'/g$ (where d' is total budget deficit) $= (d + br)/g$, and hence $d = 0$. This leaves the size of the budget deficit and debt undefined, and could be potentially at any level from a sustainability point of view.

However, it is the total budget deficit including interest payments which is relevant in the sense that it is that type of budget deficit which 'mops up' excess private savings. Further, it is usually the total budget deficit which is mentioned in debates and over which concern is expressed. For a given total budget deficit (relative to income), the debt to income ratio stabilises at $b = (d + br)/g$. In that context, the budget deficit is always sustainable in the sense that the debt to income ratio stabilises rather than continues to grow indefinitely, provided that nominal growth is positive. It must be noted that the primary budget position may well be in surplus though the total budget is in deficit in light of the interest payments, and in some regards it is the primary budget position which indicates the balance between public expenditure on goods and services and taxes (net of income transfers apart from interest payments). Further, when there is inflation, the budget deficit in nominal terms overstates the deficit in real terms to the extent of the decline in the value of the government debt. Whenever the relevant budget deficit is the overall one, there is not (in the absence of negative nominal growth) a sustainability issue for the overall deficit.

The relationship between a continuing deficit and the steady state debt ratio given above can be readily seen to translate for a 5 per cent nominal growth rate into: deficit 3 per cent of GDP, debt ratio 60 per cent (as in the Convergence Criteria); deficit 2 per cent of GDP, debt ratio 40 per cent which broadly corresponds to the (now suspended) Code for Fiscal Stability in the UK.

There are two respects in which a budget deficit and associated public debt could place some upward pressure on the interest rate on government bonds. This is, though, not a general crowding argument in that it is not envisaged that there is a general pressure on interest rates and that interest rates for private borrowers rise thereby reducing investment (indeed the first argument points to perhaps lower interest rates for private borrowers). First, the continuing budget deficit means that government bonds are being sold, and the relative composition of financial assets changing. A higher (than otherwise) budget deficit clearly means that government bonds as a proportion of total financial assets is greater than it would have been, and this could entail lower price/higher interest rate on government bonds. But the other side of that is that non-government bonds carry a higher price/lower interest rate. However, since there is a general balance between demand for and supply of funds, this would not constitute general upward pressure on interest rates. When considering the level of interest rates, the role of the Central Bank has also to be brought into the picture.

Second, it is a general proposition in Keynesian economics that there is strong sense in which investment 'causes' savings rather than savings 'cause' investment. For the moment consider the simple case where there is no government and no foreign sector. The accounting identity ensures that *ex post* savings $S^* =$ *ex post* investment I^*, and let us suppose that in a given period that also corresponds to *ex ante* savings $S+ =$ *ex ante* investment $I+$. Now conduct the thought experiment of increase in intentions to invest. If those intentions are carried through then in the relevant period $S^* = I^*$, and after some adjustments $S+ = I+$, and in that sense corresponding savings will become available. But at the time when there is the intention to invest, those savings do not exist. The realisation of the investment intentions requires availability of finance, and the usual route postulated is by bank lending. Banks in this context have the ability to create loans, and thereby create money and purchasing power. The effect which increased investment intentions have on interest rates depends on the reactions of banks – if (as is often assumed) banks readily supply loans at the going loan interest rate, then there would be no immediate pressure on interest rates.

Now introduce government into the picture. It is rather paradoxical that while private firms have access to loans which thereby change the money supply, governments (here taken to exclude the Central Bank) are not able to 'print money' to finance their spending. If there is a relationship between budget deficit, sale of bonds and the money supply, then it comes through the endogeneity of money at the interface of banks and the Central Bank. That is the Central Bank (in normal times) provides reserves to the banking system in exchange for government bonds, and it is only at the point where government bonds are exchanged in this way for reserves that the government deficit could be said to be money financed or monetised. The immediate effect of a larger government budget deficit is that the government has to borrow for what is at that point in time a pool of savings. If the government deficit is increased then a higher (than otherwise) level of income will result, and subsequently higher tax revenues and higher savings.[6] It could then be anticipated that there will be occasions on which a government finds some difficulty in securing funds, particularly if its 'offering' is not as attractive as it could be.

'Old age is not so bad when you consider the alternatives'[7] (Maurice Chevalier). The situation often with budget deficits is similar. Budget deficits should generally be seen as a sign that an economy is weak, but not that the budget deficit is the cause of the weakness, and attempts to reduce the budget deficit would make the economy weaker.

6. THE INCOHERENCE OF THE STABILITY AND GROWTH PACT

The Stability and Growth Pact seeks to impose two conditions. The first is a balanced budget (in nominal terms) over the cycle, which implies a budget surplus in real terms of around 1 per cent (in conditions of 2 per cent inflation and debt ratio of 60 per cent). The second is a debt ratio of 60 per cent;[8] a persistent budget deficit of around 3 per cent of GDP is consistent with that ratio with nominal growth of 5 per cent.

It is the overall budget deficit which is targeted by the SGP, and it can be readily shown that an *average* 3 per cent budget deficit and a 60 per cent debt ratio are compatible and sustainable (see discussion above), if the rate of growth of money GDP is 5 per cent (which is not an unreasonable assumption and could arise from, for example, 2.5 per cent inflation and 2.5 per cent real growth).

The Stability and Growth Pact, the (on average) balanced budget requirement, the 60 per cent debt to income ratio and an inflation target of 2 per cent implies that the primary budget is in substantial surplus (on average), and that in real terms the total budget is in surplus to around 1.2 per cent (since there is a 2 per cent decline in the real value of the outstanding debt). The SGP is then designed to be net deflationary in fiscal policy terms.

The SGP has sought to impose a 'one size (of straitjacket) fits all' fiscal policy –namely that over the course of the cycle national government budgets should be in balance or slight surplus with a maximum deficit of 3 per cent of GDP. It has *never* been shown (or even argued) that fiscal policy ought to be uniform across countries. 'Private saving propensities can make a public debt–GDP ratio of 60% prudent or unsustainable. A one-size-fits-all figure such as the 60% ceiling of the Maastricht Treaty makes no sense at all' (Buiter, 2001, p. 10)

7. CURRENT EXPENDITURE AND CAPITAL EXPENDITURE

An alternative fiscal policy rule which has been advocated to replace the Stability and Growth Pact and forms the basis of the fiscal rules of the UK government that separates current expenditure and capital expenditure, is the idea of a 'golden rule'.[9] This golden rule of fiscal policy has been described in the following terms: 'over the economic cycle the government will borrow only to invest and not to fund current expenditure' and 'public debt as a proportion of national income will be held over the economic cycle at a stable and prudent level' (HM Treasury, 1998, p. 16).

The appeal of the golden rule arises from the notion that borrowing is not undertaken for current expenditure but is undertaken for capital expenditure, perhaps under the misapprehension that capital expenditure by government generates future income (for government), which can be used to pay off the borrowing. But capital expenditure by general government does not yield any direct future 'profit' to the government. Some forms of capital expenditure (for example roads) may aid national prosperity and thereby raise national income and tax revenue. But that is also true of many forms of expenditure that are recorded as current expenditure, most notably that on education and health services.

Government expenditure can potentially have a range of impacts on the level of output and employment and, of significance here, on tax revenue and hence budget position. The Keynesian perspective would focus on the effects that government expenditure could have on aggregate demand and thereby the level of economic activity. A more supply-side orientation would mention the potential effects that infrastructure investment, education and health expenditures have on the supply potential of the economy, which if realised would add to economic activity and tax revenue.

There is now a substantial body of literature (see for example, Aschauer, 1989; Easterly and Rebelo, 1993; Erenburg and Wohar, 1995; Martinez Lopez, 2006), which argues that public investment, notably on infrastructure, can have a positive supply-side effect on private capital formation and the supply rate of growth. This simple analysis of the budget deficit makes no allowance for any reaction in the willingness and desire of the private sector to hold the public debt.

The focus of the functional finance approach is that budget deficits should be used to stimulate aggregate demand, and from that perspective a euro spent on capital expenditure is the same as a euro spent on current expenditure. The 'functional finance' approach is concerned over the level of public expenditure relative to the level of taxation: it is not particularly concerned over the allocation of public expenditure between different areas. The advocates of 'functional finance' would also advocate that public expenditure is spent wisely. But there is no reason to think that a level of capital expenditure equal (on average) to the budget deficit is the appropriate level of public capital expenditure.

Interestingly Keynes (1980) specified an approach which looks like a golden rule, but in his approach the scale of public investment, and hence the size of the budget deficit, was equal to the excess of private savings over private investment which would be generated at full employment. This is akin to the functional finance rule with the addition that deficit is equal to public investment.

The golden rule of public finance, along with a number of others (such as the balance or small surplus of budget over the cycle as in the Stability and Growth Pact), appears to provide a precise rule, but in practice issues such as the dating of the business cycle and the calculation as to whether deficit in a specific year does or does not meet the rules arise. The golden rule has the shortcomings from the perspective of the intertemporal budget constraint approach in the simple form in that it does not conform to the requirements of that constraint. From the functional finance approach, the golden rule leaves unspecified the size of the budget deficit since the scale of public investment is left unspecified. Whatever rules may be used to decide the scale of public investment, there is no particular reason to think that the resulting deficit is of the relevant size.

8. BUDGET DEFICITS AND THE BALANCE OF PAYMENTS

The issues of sustainability of budget deficit are often considered in the context of a closed economy. In the context of an open economy it is necessary to further discuss the implications of borrowing from overseas and the sustainability issues which that raises.

It is often argued that using fiscal policy, and particularly running a budget deficit, has consequences for and is constrained by balance of payments considerations. Equation 1.1 above can be used to highlight some of the issues. Insofar as private domestic savings and investment are closely related, then the equation suggests a link between two deficits (the 'twin deficit' issue) with a link between budget deficit and current account deficit.

It should first be noted that in general current account deficits pose a much greater constraint on an economy than budget deficits. Both require borrowing and the incurring of future debts and interest (or equivalent) payments. But whilst the public debt is a liability as far as the government and taxpayers are concerned, it is an asset as far the bondholders are concerned. The interest payments on bonds are a domestic transfer between taxpayers and bondholders. The relevant rate of interest on bonds for sustainability of deficits is the post-tax rate of interest, and as argued above the post-tax real rate of interest on government bonds is around the rate of growth.

It can further be argued that what is relevant for fiscal policy and stimulus is the overall budget deficit whereas for the current account it is the trade deficit which is generated from private decisions and relates to production and consumption decisions. Insofar as government debt is denominated in the domestic currency, the government is always in a position to avoid default on the debt, whether that comes from its tax-raising powers or its *in extremis* ability to create the necessary money.

Insofar as equation 1.1 above cannot be satisfied because the resulting current account deficit and the corresponding financial account surplus cannot be achieved, then this should not be seen as an issue for fiscal policy. In effect any policy which sought to achieve income of Y_f would run into essentially the same problems (see caveat below). For example, if monetary policy were the instrument of choice to achieve the desired level of income, a current account deficit would still result. Further, even if there was a strong belief in market forces which would restore income and output to a market-clearing 'full employment' position, there would still be a current account deficit. The current account problems in the case of the use of fiscal policy as compared with other policies may differ in three respects. First, the target level of income may be different. If fiscal policy were used in a more ambitious way, then the target level of income would be greater and the corresponding current account deficit larger. Second, the composition of demand would differ between the different 'solutions', and hence the demand for imports would differ. It could be argued that fiscal policy insofar as it utilised expansion of government expenditure in a directed fashion could have a lower import content than a corresponding expansion of private demand through interest rate reductions. Third, different policy regimes have effects on the exchange rate. For example, a lower interest rate designed to stimulate the domestic economy could well lead to a lower exchange rate, which would (provided the Marshall–Lerner conditions held) ease the current account deficit problem.[10]

It could be argued that issues over the current account deficit could be removed through appropriate changes in the exchange rate (in general subject to Marshall–Lerner conditions holding). It is possible that the necessary change in the exchange rate would lead to intolerable reductions in terms of trade and living standards. But the major difficulty relates to the vagaries of the exchange markets.

The thrust of the argument in this section is that there may be balance of payments constraints on the use of fiscal policy to achieve a high level of demand and income. However, those constraints should not be viewed as specific to fiscal policy but rather constraints on the economy achieving through whatever means a high level of income and output. The policy conclusion (easily stated but only resolved with great difficulty) is to direct policy towards relieving the balance of payments constraints rather than foregoing the use of fiscal policy.

Fiscal policy can itself only address issues of demand deficiency (or excess) aggregate demand, though the composition of government expenditure and the structure of taxation can address other issues (for example, the role of public investment in terms of growth, taxation with respect to income distribution). The effective use of fiscal policy can often be constrained through (as discussed here) balance of payments constraints and through a lack of productive capacity (which we have not addressed here but which may prevent the achievement of high levels of employment through lack of capacity and hence also the achievement of desired levels of output). But those constraints should be viewed as operating on any policy options (including the 'do nothing' policy) and not specific to fiscal policy, and the appropriate response is the development of policy instruments which directly address those constraints.

9. CONCLUDING COMMENTS

The chapter has argued for the adoption of a functional finance approach to fiscal policy and the scale of the budget deficit, rather than the adoption of rules on balancing budgets over some time frame. The aim in setting the size of the budget deficit is to secure the highest sustainable level of economic activity. It is argued that the adoption of a functional finance view means there is no inherent difficulty in funding the resulting budget deficit. It is also argued that from that perspective the relevant budget deficit is the total deficit including interest payments where it can be readily shown that public debt would converge, relative to GDP, to the equivalent of budget deficit divided by nominal growth rate.

The chapter has pointed to the focus on the size of the public debt. It has been first argued that insofar as the public debt has been arrived at through application of the functional finance approach, then the deficit will have enabled savings to occur which would not otherwise have occurred and that the debt will have been willingly acquired and willingly held. It is further argued that the government's capital account balance sheet should be viewed in terms of assets and liabilities and not liabilities alone. Any 'budget constraint' on government should be seen in terms of net assets. Government assets do not in general yield income though they do yield valuable public services and do contribute to the general level of income and thereby tax revenues. However, government assets can in principle be realised by sale to the private sector – say in the context of lease-back arrangements. There are substantial issues of valuation associated with the development of a public sector balance sheet, and also significant debates to be had over which assets and liabilities should be included. Nevertheless we would argue that the use of a public sector balance sheet would put government debt into perspective, and more significantly would mitigate against basing decisions on the effects on public debt when those decisions may harm the position of the government – for example, sale of publicly owned assets at a 'knock-down' price in order to reduce recorded deficit and debt. The chapter also argues that there is no merit in the adoption of a golden rule whereby governments borrow to cover capital expenditure (and balance current expenditure through tax revenues).

NOTES

1. The dominant school in macroeconomics in the past decade has been the 'New Consensus in Macroeconomics'. A notable feature of this approach has been the absence of market forces which would propel the economy to the supply-side equilibrium, whether or not that equilibrium is one of full employment. Instead the achievement of the supply-side equilibrium (often formulated in terms of zero output gap with actual output equal potential, or the NAIRU, non-accelerating inflation rate of unemployment) is taken to come form the operation of administrative forces in the shape of the Central Bank, its operating rules in the setting of interest rates, and the idea of the 'natural rate of interest' at which demand is taken to be equal to the supply-side equilibrium level of economic activity.
2. Although the remark was made in a different context, Keynes's (1936) remark that 'In the long run we are all dead' has been applied to the idea that in the 'long run' there will be full employment to convey the idea that the long run may be far away.
3. Blanchard and Fischer (1989 p. 55) treat the NPG condition as 'that debt does not increase faster asymptotically than the interest rate'.
4. A continuing surplus would also raise issues as a result of the disappearance of government debt. Since government debt plays a key role in monetary policy and open market operations, the nature of monetary policy would need to change. Perhaps more significantly with a continuing surplus after the debt has been paid off the government starts to accumulate assets, that is nationalisation.
5. As in the discussion in the previous section we proceed as though all of the budget deficit is bond financed. Governments typically borrow to fund budget deficit, but through open market operations the Central Bank exchanges money for bonds. When the Central Bank is consolidated into government accounts, then the deficit would be part bond funded and part money funded. The seignorage of the government then reduces to some degree the cost of borrowing to fund budget deficits.
6. Often, as in the present, larger budget deficits arise from a slowdown in the economy which results in lower tax receipts. The government is then faced with the choice of increased borrowing or attempting to raise taxes or reduce expenditure. The point here is that without the increased budget deficit and borrowing, the level of economic activity would continue to decline, and the budget deficit is acting as an 'automatic stabiliser'.
7. http://www.brainyquote.com/quotes/authors/m/maurice_chevalier.html.
8. 'In fact the Maastricht criteria are set in terms of the gross general government debt (for reasons known only to the author of the Maastricht Treaty, and perhaps not even to them)' (Buiter, 2001, p. 12).
9. These rules have, in the face of the financial crisis, recently been suspended until the middle of the next decade.
10. Two further caveats: interest rate parity suggests that a lower domestic interest rate would be associated with a rising exchange rate; if 'sentiment' in the exchange markets responds favourably to the prospect of higher domestic income, then the exchange rate would tend to rise.

REFERENCES

Alesina, A., S. Ardagna, R. Perotti and F. Schiantarelli (2002), 'Fiscal policy, profits and investment', *American Economic Review*, **92**(3), 571–89.

Arestis, P. and M. Sawyer (2006), 'Fiscal policy matters', *Public Finance*, **54**(3), 1–15.

Aschauer, David A. (1989), 'Does public capital crowd out private capital?', *Journal of Monetary Economics*, **24**(2), 171–88.
Barro, R.J. (1974), 'Are government bonds net wealth?', *Journal of Political Economy*, **82**(6), 1095–111.
Bertola, G. and A. Drazen (1993), 'Trigger points and budget cuts: explaining the effects of fiscal austerity', *American Economics Review*, **83**, 1170–88.
Blanchard, Olivier J. and Stanley Fischer (eds) (1989), *Lectures on Macroeconomics*, Cambridge, MA: The MIT Press.
Buiter, Willem H. (2001), 'Notes on "A code for fiscal stability"', *Oxford Economic Papers*, **53**(1), 1–19.
Domar, Evsey D. (1944), 'The "burden of the debt" and the national income', *American Economic Review*, **34**(4), 798–827.
Easterly, W. and S. Rebelo (1993), 'Fiscal policy and economic growth: an empirical investigation', *Journal of Monetary Economics*, **32**(3), 458–93.
Erenburg, S.J. and M.E. Wohar (1995), 'Public and private investment: are there causal linkages?', *Journal of Macroeconomics*, **17**(1), 1–30.
European Commission (2003), 'Public Finances in EMU – 2003', *European Economy – Reports and Studies* 3, Luxembourg: OOPEC.
HM Treasury (1998), *The Code for Fiscal Stability*, London: HM Treasury.
HM Treasury (2009), *Budget 2009, Building Britain's Future*, London: HM Treasury.
Kalecki, M. (1944a), 'The white paper on employment policy', *Bulletin of the Oxford University Institute of Statistics*, **6**(8), 137–44.
Kalecki, M. (1944b), 'Three ways to full employment', in Oxford University Institute of Statistics, *The Economics of Full Employment*, Oxford: Blackwell.
Keynes, John M. (ed.) (1936), *The General Theory of Employment, Interest and Money*, London: Macmillan.
Keynes, John M. (ed.) (1980), *Activities 1940–1946 Shaping the Post-War World: Employment and Commodities, Collected Writings*, vol. 27, London: Macmillan.
Lerner, A. (1943), 'Functional finance and the Federal debt', *Social Research*, **10**, 38–51; reprinted in Max Gerhard Mueller (ed.), *Readings in Macroeconomics*, New York: Holt, Rinehart and Winston, reprint pp. 353–60.
Martinez Lopez, D. (2006), 'Linking public investment to private investment: the case of Spanish regions', *International Review of Applied Economics*, **20**(4), 411–24.
Pasinetti, Luigi L. (1997), 'The social "burden" of high interest rates' in Philip Arestis, Gabriel Palma and Malcolm Sawyer (eds), *Capital Controversy, Post-Keynesian Economics and the History of Economics: Essays in Honour of Geoff Harcourt*, London: Routledge, pp. 161–8.
Taylor, John B. (1993), 'Discretion versus policy rules in practice', *Carnegie-Rochester Conference Series on Public Policy*, **39**(1), 195–214.
Wicksell, Knut (ed.) ([1898] 1965), *Interest and Prices*, New York: Reprints of Economic Classics.

2. Recent advances in public investment, fiscal policy and growth

Chiara Del Bo*

INTRODUCTION

Economic growth is one of the most extensively studied topics in economics and one of the key questions researchers are seeking to answer is 'what is the main determinant of sustained economic growth?'. Different answers have emerged during time and the quest for the ultimate driver is still ongoing. Several factors, including human and physical capital accumulation, institutions and public policies have been singled out in the theoretical and empirical literature as the main forces allowing economies to enjoy long-run growth. The question we are addressing in this review is to what extent public investment, public capital and fiscal policy affect growth, and through which channels this impact is working. The literature on these subjects is vast and growing at a steady rate, forcing us to select contributions that we deemed essential to the understanding of the issue. The focus is mainly on empirical contributions, though important theoretical models, with clear and well-defined policy implications, are also considered.

The issues surveyed in the following sections are especially relevant in countries belonging to the European Union (EU), both because of the existence of the Stability and Growth Pact (SGP) and Maastricht criteria, which set enforceable fiscal targets and rules, and because of the recent and ongoing process of enlargement. The New EU Member States (NMS) are likely to suffer, with respect to Old Member States, from infrastructure gaps in terms of quantity and quality, warranting a need for significant investment, and are characterized by different levels and distribution of GDP and economic and political institutions. Having a clearer picture of the growth effects of public investment and the relation with mandatory fiscal adjustment policies seems a relevant research agenda for NMS and accession countries in the EU.

The first part examines the relation between public investment and capital and economic growth, highlighting trends and the role of different categories of expenditure. We also survey a recent and promising interest in the analysis of distributional and inequality-reducing effects of increases in productive public investment. The second part focuses on fiscal policy (taking into account both the revenue and expenditure side), examines the role played by fiscal consolidation rules and adjustments, and stresses the link between public investment, fiscal consolidation and growth, reviewing influential proposals for a reform of fiscal rules that take these issues explicitly into account. Finally, the concluding section discusses the main findings and derives directions for future research.

1. PUBLIC INVESTMENT AND GROWTH

1.1 Main Findings

The issue of the growth-enhancing effect of public investment and capital has been the focus of a vast theoretical and empirical literature in the past 30 years. Several endogenous growth models have incorporated disaggregated public capital categories as long-run forces promoting economic growth, mainly focusing on investment, and considering government consumption as a force hampering economic growth.[1]

From a formal modelling perspective, the seminal contributions focus on investment in education (Lucas, 1988) and productive public capital (especially infrastructure: Barro, 1990) entering as inputs in the output production process. The role of health public expenditure (Bloom et al., 2003) and R&D investment (Romer, 1990), have also been highlighted as driving forces for capital accumulation and, ultimately, long run growth. In the Lucas (1988) endogenous growth model, investments in human capital generate increasing returns through two mechanisms. First, they directly contribute to GDP formation. Second, they represent a positive externality which individuals do not fully take into account when deciding how much time to devote to human capital accumulation. Both empirics and theory support the view that education makes individuals more productive, thus further accelerating GDP growth (Zagler and Durnecker, 2003).

From an empirical perspective, a vast literature originated from the initial contributions of Aschauer and Munnell. Using US data between 1949 and 1985, Aschauer (1989) estimated a public capital augmented production function, along with labour and private capital inputs, finding that the estimated elasticity of output with respect to public capital was approximately 0.36. Munnell (1990) found that the marginal products of public and private capital were roughly the same and equal to 0.34.[2]

Delorme et al. (1999) estimated an aggregate production function for the US, and found that the positive effect of public capital on output is indirect, working through the complementarity with private capital: public capital affects private productivity by reducing technical inefficiencies.

Given these early empirical findings, the next sections will delve deeper into the analysis of the growth impact of public investment, considering the different categories of expenditure (current vs. capital, aggregate vs. specific items, productive vs. non-productive) to verify if there is homogeneity in terms of growth properties. Finally, welfare is also considered and distributional effects of public spending are accounted for, in order to have a clearer picture of the overall impact on the economy.

1.2 Public Capital and Growth

In Barro's (1990) framework, government expenditure enters the individual firms' production function and increases the rate of return to private capital, thus increasing private investment and growth. As surveyed by Irmen and Kuehnel (2009), the analysis of the effect of productive government expenditure on economic growth has been expanded to include congestion effects (as in Turnovsky, 1996) and adjustment costs from a production function perspective, and by introducing public consumption services in consumers' utility functions thus affecting endogenous labour supply. The long-run growth effects of productive government expenditures have also been analysed in an overlapping generation model (Glomm and Ravikumar, 1997) confirming the main findings of endogenous growth models.

The main contribution of this strand of literature has been to formally analyse the role of public capital, focusing on productive components of government expenditure, on economic activity, productivity and dynamics of private investment and, ultimately, on economic growth, and to highlight the specific channels through which the effect works. These channels have been validated by econometric studies, characterized by different techniques and level of analysis. We will provide a brief and non-exhaustive overview of cross-sectional and single country analyses, which consider the disaggregation in productive and unproductive public expenditure components.

An important aspect of empirical investigations of the effect of public capital on growth rests on the analysis of different components of public expenditure, discriminating between productive and unproductive categories, and by considering initial conditions (Devarajan et al., 1996). Other important issues are linked to the appropriate definition of public capital (Kamps, 2005) and estimation techniques used to assess the growth impact of public capital (Romp and De Haan 2007). As surveyed by Romp and De Haan, the main available techniques are: the production function approach, which is the most commonly used, the cost function approach, which exploits the dual properties of cost and production functions, vector autoregressive (VAR) studies, cross-country or regional cross-section growth regressions and structural econometric models with public investment (see also Sturm (1998) on this issue). By considering results and implications for growth, Romp and De Haan find that there is now more agreement about the positive effect of public capital on growth. They discuss the advantages and shortcomings of the different estimation techniques and remark on the possibility of reverse causation between public capital and productivity using the production function approach. However, according to their evaluation, it is difficult to identify one technique that does not present important drawbacks and it appears that the production function approach, with some refinement, is often a good starting point.

In an attempt to reconcile theoretical models with an intertemporal dimension and the empirical literature, Shioji (2001) examines the dynamic effects of public capital on output, highlighting the convergence implications in endogenous growth models. With an open economy model with a public capital augmented production function, the effects of public capital can be decomposed in direct growth effects and indirect effects working through the stimulating effect on private capital accumulation. The implied income convergence equation is in the spirit of Barro and Sala-i-Martin (2004) with the addition of public capital. This model is tested on Japanese and US data on infrastructure public capital, and the effect on growth is found to be positive and significant with a short-run elasticity of output to infrastructure of around 0.15. The main message is in favour of a growth-enhancing effect of productive government investment.

In a cross-country analysis, Easterly and Rebelo (1993) highlight the importance of distinguishing between different components of public expenditure, stressing the positive contribution to growth of investment in transport and communication using data for 28 countries between 1870 and 1988. Other variables are accounted for, showing how the government's budget situation is consistently and statistically significant in determining the sign of the effect of public capital on long-run growth, and the importance of the inequality levels of different countries, their size and income level.

Bleaney et al. (2001) test the endogenous growth model framework by incorporating revenue and expenditure public variables, and accounting for the government's budget constraint. With OECD data between 1970 and 1995, productive public expenditure, financed by a mix of non-productive expenditures and non-distortionary taxation, is shown to have the Barro (1990) predicted positive effects on growth, while distortionary taxes are growth-dampening.

Many economic and institutional variables, which vary significantly across countries, may shape the relationship between public investment and growth and recent empirical studies have added a set of controls to traditional growth regressions to account for these factors and differences across time and space. Vu Le and Suruga (2005) have examined the role of openness and FDI, finding that foreign, public and private investment foster economic growth, but excessive spending in public capital expenditure can hinder the beneficial effects of FDI.

Considering subsamples of developed and developing countries, several authors have found similarities and differences in the underlying mechanisms of the relationship between government expenditure and growth. With a panel of developing countries between 1970 and 1990 Bose et al. (2007) found a positive effect of public capital on growth only after controlling for the budget constraint and political instability and corruption issues. This last aspect is also analysed by Haque and Kneller (2008), which show that corruption increases public investment and reduces the returns to public investment, making it ineffective in promoting economic growth. Along the same line, looking at highly indebted low-income countries, Belloc and Vertova (2007) provide empirical support for the crowding-in hypothesis between private and public capital and a positive effect of public investment on output.

Considering OECD countries and using a new methodology for constructing comparable international public capital, Kamps (2005) reports positive and significant output effects. Concentrating on the EU, Afonso and Alegre (2008) highlight the role of public expenditure on education, health and social security on growth, while Arpaia and Turrini (2008) examine the relation between government expenditure and potential output, finding that the long-run elasticity decreased over the period considered (1970–2003) and is higher than unity in catching-up, fast-ageing and low-debt countries and in countries with weak budgetary constraints. By appropriately controlling for the cointegration relationship between public expenditure and growth, using the Pooled Mean Group Estimator (Pesaran et al., 1999), country heterogeneity is exploited and the shortcomings of previous empirical studies are eliminated.

1.3. Public and Private Capital Complementarity

When considering the growth impact of public investment and capital, a key concern is to account for issues of complementarity or substitutability with private sector's investment. Linkages between the public and private sector may be complicated, and the effect on private investment of an increase in public investment may be positive or negative (the so called *crowding-in* and *crowding-out* effects) ultimately determining the aggregate effect on the economy. In fact, one of the channels that may explain the pro-growth properties of public capital is related to increases in productivity of private capital and to a stimulating effect on investment.

The productivity link has been studied with industry and firm level data. As an example, Lynde and Richmond (1993) have shown how public capital has a significant effect on production costs in the manufacturing sector in the UK. Controlling for the non-stationarity issues in the data and exploiting the duality properties of cost and production functions, the authors show that in the 1970s the public capital–labour ratio accounted for approximately 17 per cent of overall manufacturing productivity growth. During the 1980s, however, the contribution of public capital seems rather scant, a result attributed to low levels of actual public infrastructure spending in those years. Some studies also report statistically insignificant or negative, crowding-out effects, of public capital on private capital productivity (Evans and Karras, 1994; Holtz-Eakin, 1994). A similar empirical strategy based on duality was proposed by Rovolis and Spence (2002) at a sub-national level, analysing the impact of public capital on manufacturing in Greek regions. They find that public productive investment is the main actor in fostering private sector productivity and in reducing costs, and stress the substitution relationship between public infrastructure and labour and intermediate inputs, while public and private capital behave as complements. Moving on to cross-country studies, Nourzad (2000) confirms the positive and significant effect of public capital on labour productivity in OECD and developing countries between 1975 and 1989. Demetriades and Theofanis (2000) show that, in OECD countries, public capital has positive effects on input demands, output supply and profits, a result related to previous findings of reduction in production costs.

The role of public sector accumulation on private sector performance has also been analysed in a dynamic dimension. Erenburg and Wohar (1995), using US data between 1954 and 1989, examine (within a Granger causality framework) the relation between private investment and public capital. By considering the public capital stock as a productive input, in the context of cash flow and Tobin's q models, they show that in the short run public investment exerts a financial crowding-out effect but, in the long run, public capital has a positive effect on private investment. The underlying idea is that private agents postpone their investment decisions in periods of high public investment, to fully reap the productivity benefits of public capital accumulation. They also show that the direction of causality runs both ways, and that increases in the private capital stock have a beneficial effect on public capital. The issue of complementarity between the two forms of capital has been addressed for a panel of 25 developing countries from 1980 to 2003 (Atukeren, 2005). The main results stem from long-term co-integration analyses and formal Granger causality tests: of the 25 countries examined, private investment crowds in public investment in 11 countries and displays a crowding-out effect in two. One possible explanation of the crowding-in effect is that an increase in the private sector investment in capital fosters the demand for infrastructure public capital.

Flores de Frutos and Pereira (1999) and Pereira (2001) apply a VAR framework to US data finding support for the crowding-in effect of public capital on private activity. Zou (2006) extends the dynamic analysis by considering the US and Japan, finding that while crowding-in effects and positive growth impact are present in both countries, public capital seems to have a more relevant role in the Japanese economy compared to the US. This differential effect provides grounding for studies focusing on subsamples of countries, mainly distinguishing according to the level of development. Agenor et al. (2007) examine the role of public infrastructure and private investment in Africa in a VAR framework. Their results point towards a crowding-in effect of public investment, conditional on the overall unfavourable environment for private investment in the considered countries. Along the same line, Erden and Holcombe (2005) examine a panel of developing countries and account for cointegration issues, finding evidence of a complementary relationship between public and private investment both in the short and long run.

This brief selection of applications has highlighted that public capital may indeed be complementary to private capital, by raising its marginal productivity in the production of output, but external market conditions must be taken into account, along with the composition of disaggregated public capital. Our focus in the next two sections will be on productive and infrastructure public capital and we will summarize results from the literature on the characteristics of this specific form of public capital stock.

1.4 Disaggregated Public Investment

The overall positive effect of public investment on growth seems to be now a rather accepted stylized fact, but it should be clear that it is mainly related to productive expenditure, aimed at the accumulation of capital stocks and assets, and that the issues of how it is financed are crucial. The next step is thus to examine the role of the composition of public expenditure, surveying empirical contributions that address this issue by considering disaggregated public expenditure categories. The greatest consensus has been reached with respect to public investment in education and infrastructure, justifying a more detailed analysis of the latter category, also in light of the issue of the optimal amount of public infrastructure capital in the economic system.

To introduce the review of selected contributions in this area, a meta-analysis (Nijkamp and Poot, 2004) may help in identifying the most growth-enhancing fiscal policy categories. By using a sample of 93 published papers, leading to 123 meta-observations due to the multi-policy issues in each contribution, the commonly held belief that education and infrastructure exert a positive growth effect is confirmed, though support for the enhancing effect of public expenditure and consumption in general is rather weak.

Analysing a selection of single studies, both for developed and developing countries, will strengthen the idea that the long-run effect on growth of fiscal variables is influenced by the level of disaggregation considered and that the importance of infrastructure capital, while generally supported, is linked to the issue of the optimal amount and provision of public capital in the economy.

Devarajan et al. (1996) consider the effect of the share of different components in total government on growth and account for a level effect by controlling for the size of total expenditure on GDP, and consider the possibility of non-linearities and differentiated effects between developing and industrialized countries. With data from 1970 to 1990 for a sample of 43 countries, it is shown that current expenditure has positive and significant growth effects while the capital component seems to exert a negative effect. However, when considering developed countries, the results are reversed, and the standard finding of a growth-enhancing effect of capital public expenditure is retained. This result might rest on the fact that developing countries present several distortions, with high levels of corruption and 'black market' issues, which could make additional expenditure on public capital unproductive. Overall, they conclude that public expenditures labelled as 'productive' may become unproductive due to general institutional and economic conditions, and in the case of excessive amounts.

This line of thought is also pursued by Gupta et al. (2005), who focus on a panel of low-income countries during the 1990s and add a set of economic, fiscal and institutional controls to the analysis. They consider fiscal adjustment achieved by cutting current and capital expenditures and show that focusing on the protection of capital expenditure seems more conducive to growth. Non-linearities are also considered, and this allows a further qualification: countries that have not achieved stable macroeconomic conditions are those that benefit most from fiscal consolidation through current spending cuts, while more stabilized economies may instead benefit from expansion of current spending categories.

Bose et al. (2007) consider the role of the government budget constraint in shaping the effects of disaggregated public spending in 30 developing countries between 1970 and 1990. They provide evidence of growth-enhancing effects of capital expenditure and show that public investment and expenditure in education exert the strongest effect once the budget constraint and omitted variables are accounted for. Agenor (2005) analyses the optimal expenditure structure in an endogenous growth model where government expenditure contributes to physical and human capital accumulation by means of infrastructure and education services. Modelling the positive impact of better infrastructure provision on individuals' education and skill acquisition, and allowing for congestion costs in education, the author derives the growth and welfare-maximizing allocations of government spending. The main result is that the optimal share of infrastructure spending depends on the quality of education services and on how much infrastructure affects the production of educated labour force.

Focusing on public infrastructure investment, an influential survey by Gramlich (1994) reports the initial empirical literature following Aschauer (1989). The author defines infrastructure as 'the tangible capital stock owned by the public sector' and highlights that different results may arise from the estimation of a production or cost function, and considers reverse causation between public capital and GDP. For a recent review with an explicit focus on infrastructure, see Romp and de Haan (2007). The rationale for focusing on infrastructure capital stems from the consideration of the crucial role of transportation, energy and telecommunication networks for production across sectors, as stressed in a World Bank Annual Report (1994). The positive externalities associated with public infrastructure have been modelled by introducing public capital in the production function of final output as a complement to private capital (Arrow and Kurz, 1970). Some of the channels through which the positive effect of a well developed infrastructure capital stock influences economic activity and growth are the reduction in transportation and transaction costs and the increased accessibility and attractiveness of countries and regions, allowing for a better distribution across space of production activities. Better telecommunication infrastructure facilitates business transactions, lowering production costs and fostering new links and synergies among economic actors. The quality of a country's infrastructure stock is important in an international context, with positive effects of a country's or region's attractiveness for FDI and openness to trade, through better accessibility to home and foreign markets. Investment in infrastructure may also have positive spillover effects on neighbouring areas and positively affect foreign producers and consumers (Bougheas et al., 2000), given the public good nature of this form of capital stock. The international dimension is considered also in terms of possible supranational co-funding (de Rus and Socorro, 2009).

Using dynamic panel data techniques and data for a panel of 15 developing countries between 1970 and 1987, Haque and Kim (2003), show that public investment in transportation and telecommunication has a positive dynamic effect on economic growth. Considering an endogenous growth model with differentiated public capital as an input in production, Rioja (2005), derives the rate of return to growth of education and transportation public expenditure. The theoretical findings, when the model is calibrated to Latin American data, suggest that public expenditure has positive growth effects for both categories of spending. When performing policy experiments, shifting resources from transport to education has positive effects, a result that is in part implied by the fact that the countries considered started from a relatively high share of GDP invested in transport and a low investment in public education. Estache et al. (2007) conclude that it is difficult to compare the contribution of different components of productive public capital across countries. By comparing expenditure on health, education and transport, they show that that low-income countries generally lag significantly behind higher-income countries, but show that efficiency has improved during the 1990s in energy and education but not as much in transport.

These results confirm the idea that the effect of reallocating public spending relies heavily on the initial country-specific macroeconomic conditions.

At the regional level, Mastromarco and Woitek (2006) show that the impact of core infrastructure investment on efficiency is always positive, while there is regional differentiation for non-core infrastructure capital. Del Bo and Florio (2008) examine the growth effects of disaggregated infrastructure stock components on regional growth, accounting for the presence of spatial issue in the data, and stress the importance of telecommunications and overall quality of transport infrastructure.

From a policy perspective, the World Bank has been conducting extensive empirical research on the subject. As an illustration of the interest in understanding the actual contribution to growth of public infrastructure, Agenor and Moreno-Dodson (2006) review the various channels through which this effect may take place, stressing the role played in decreasing adjustment costs and the promotion of health and education services. Sutherland et al. (2009) use Bayesian model averaging techniques to perform cross-country growth regressions and confirm that investment in public infrastructure, especially in the form of telecommunications and energy generation, have a strong and significant effect on economic growth. They also show that this effect is higher the lower the existing stock of a country's physical capital stock, a result in line with the analysis by Kamps (2005) for OECD countries.

1.5 Distributional Effects

While the previous sections have emphasized the role of public spending and capital on growth, the economic environment may be influenced through another channel as well, namely income and wealth distribution. Public spending in infrastructure or other productive capital may have an indirect growth effect by altering the economy's wealth distribution and inequality patterns.

Ferreira (1995) develops a general equilibrium model of wealth dynamics with public capital in the production function, acting as a complement to private capital. Public capital is produced by the government and provided at no cost to every firm. Private infrastructure capital is available at a cost. There are three sets of agents (subsistence workers, middle class and private infrastructure-owning entrepreneurs), and the main result is that there is a minimum level of public capital below which the middle class disappears, and reductions in the level of public investment lead to higher levels of inequality, since lower-income household-firms do not have the resources to access private infrastructure capital. It is also shown that productive public investment has a positive effect in reducing inequality, even if expenditures have no explicit redistributional content.

Monteiro and Turnovsky (2008) consider the two main categories of government investment thought to be the most conducive to growth (investment in infrastructure and education) simultaneously in a two-sector endogenous growth model. Public investment in human and physical capital accumulation are assumed to be productivity-enhancing. The welfare-maximizing tax rate is derived and is shown to be lower than the growth-maximizing counterpart, while productive expenditure exhibits the opposite behaviour in the sense that an increase in productive government investment is smaller than the growth-maximizing share. The equilibrium share of productive government spending depends on the parameters of both productive sectors of human and physical capital and the composition of public spending is independent of the size of total public expenditure.

Empirical studies have focused, with different econometric methods and looking at different time periods and countries, on assessing the effect of (mainly) public infrastructure on the distribution of income. The underlying prior is that infrastructure development may have a positive effect on the income of disadvantaged social groups above the average effect, therefore ameliorating overall inequality at the aggregate level. More and better infrastructure allows poorer areas and individuals a better connection to core economic activity (Estache, 2005), reduces transaction and transportation costs (Jacoby, 2000; van de Walle, 2002) and improves the welfare and wellbeing of individuals. Calderon and Chong (2004) consider data for most world countries between 1960 and 1995 and estimate static and dynamic panel models of income inequality as a function of infrastructure development (roads, railways, telecommunications and energy measures), considered in terms of physical stocks and taking quality of infrastructure components into account. Their findings show that higher quantity and quality of infrastructure reduces inequality, and that the strongest link, in developing countries, is through quality improvement. Quality is controlled for by considering the service provided by infrastructure. By explicitly controlling for the direction of causality, the authors stress that the negative link between infrastructure and inequality goes from the former to the latter. The main policy implication is that a higher quality (and, to a minor extent, quantity) of different components of infrastructure is associated with a statistically significant improvement of inequality. Calderon and Serven (2004) obtain similar for 100 countries between 1960 and 2000. The authors also provide simulations of positive impacts of infrastructure on inequality in Latin American countries. By simulating the closure of the existing infrastructure gap among Latin American countries, the authors estimate a decrease in the Gini coefficient between 0.02 and 0.10. By simulating a catching-up process to the East Asian median country, the decrease in inequality is even higher, ranging between 0.05 and 0.13 lower Gini indices. Simulations for sub-Saharan countries, based on similar regression specifications and a similar time period, show that infrastructure development has decreased inequality by approximately 3 basis points (Calderon and Serven, 2008).

Considering telecommunication infrastructure development, Lopez (2004) supports this finding, estimating a negative impact of public capital improvement on inequality, using dynamic panel techniques for 91 countries between 1960 and 2000.

This relatively new literature exploring the link between public capitals, especially in the form of physical measures of the stock of publicly provided infrastructure, and income distribution provides evidence in favour of a statistically significant contribution to the reduction of inequality. Higher levels and quality of infrastructure may affect income distribution both directly and indirectly, through positive growth effects. The

OECD (2006) has summarized these results by stating that 'infrastructure is important for pro-poor growth', thus recognizing the existence of both channels. Further research is needed to disentangle the direct and indirect effects and to assess the role of different components of public infrastructure capital, using different measures of income inequality and considering reverse causation issues explicitly, exploiting new advances in the analysis of cointegration in panel settings (for example Pesaran, 2007).

2. FISCAL POLICY AND GROWTH: THE INTERPLAY OF FISCAL ADJUSTMENTS AND PUBLIC INVESTMENT

In the previous sections we have analysed the growth and welfare contribution of public expenditure, focusing on public capital. We now want to look at the bigger picture, by assessing how and through which channels fiscal policy affects growth, taking into account government constraints and various forms of fiscal rules, adjustment and consolidation. This broader analysis is motivated by the increasing role of discretionary or mandatory rules on fiscal consolidation in determining national government revenue and expenditure policies. The SGP in Europe is a relevant example, while several national governments have put in place country-specific actions to enforce budget balance and debt controls.

In this section we want to review contributions analysing the following research questions:

1. What are the long-run effects of fiscal adjustments, with a distinction between the revenue and expenditure side?
2. What determines the different forms of fiscal adjustment strategies and what effect do they have on budgetary developments?
3. What is the link between government expenditure, public finance sustainability and growth?
4. Can we identify fiscal targets that take into account the intertemporal dimension of public sector solvency and the link between productive expenditure and growth?

2.1 Fiscal Adjustment Policies: Determinants and Effects

A fiscal rule is considered *successful* if it obtains its intended result in terms of a reduction of the debt to GDP ratio. On the other hand, a fiscal rule is said to be *expansionary*, if it leads to increases in the economy's growth rate.

Alesina and Perotti (1995) show that fiscal policies are more successful in reducing long-run deficits if they are based on current spending cuts more than on tax increases, providing support from the analysis of the fiscal policy experience of Denmark, Ireland and Italy. Many studies stress the fact that fiscal rules tend to succeed more if based on expenditure cuts (Alesina and Perotti, 1995; von Hagen et al., 2002) and if they are linked to the economy's general economic conditions (von Hagen et al., 2002). The EC (2007) and Guichard et al. (2007) consider the importance of fiscal governance, stressing how fiscal rules with explicit expenditure targets proved to be linked to larger and more permanent adjustments.

Tagkalakis (2009) examines the role of structural reforms in product and labour markets in determining the success or failure of a fiscal stabilization process, showing that in OECD countries between 1970 and 2000, reductions in the unemployment benefit system are highly beneficial, while traditional product market deregulation and relaxation of employment protection legislation have no significant effect.

Several economic conditions are considered key to successful fiscal adjustment and consolidation episodes, and relevant in reducing or cancelling negative effects on general economic activity and growth. Kumar et al. (2007) examine the determinants of fiscal adjustment policies implemented in OECD countries between 1990 and 2005. Their results support the view that fiscal consolidations achieved through cuts in public spending are generally more successful and have lower negative impacts on growth than cuts in productive investment, especially in the long run. The short-run contractionary effects are highest when the instrument used to reach the fiscal target is a cut in productive public investment. The role of strong and stable institutions is deemed key to fiscal adjustment, both in the cross-country analysis and in a case study perspective. This result is further analysed by Mulas-Granados et al. (2009) in the context of the EU NMS. By creating aggregate indices for budget institutions, the authors show that, between 1994 and 2004, institutional issues have strongly influenced and determined the success of fiscal consolidation policies, *ceteris paribus*. The institutional indices reflect the design of fiscal rules and the role of parliamentary approval. The analysis considers fiscal consolidation in terms of total budget balance and primary budget balance.

Ardagna (2004) empirically explores the determinants of successful and expansionary, or growth-enhancing, fiscal consolidations for 17 OECD countries from 1975 to 2002 in a simultaneous equation framework, allowing for non-linear effects of fiscal policies. The key results are that expansionary fiscal adjustments critically depend on the composition of the policy, with greater effects brought by expenditure curbing. Looking at the debt to GDP ratio, successful policies rely mainly on the size of the adjustment, regardless of composition issues. The author also controls for possible interactions with monetary policy, finding that the overall conclusions are unaffected. Muscatelli et al. (2004) show that countercyclical fiscal policy can be welfare-reducing if fiscal and monetary policy rules are not co-ordinated.

2.2 Fiscal Policies and Public Investment: Growth Implications

In a relevant contribution, Kneller et al. (1999) take endogenous models with public capital seriously, and test the growth effects of fiscal policy on growth for 22 OECD countries between 1970 and 1995. Their results support the Barro (1990) results of a positive growth effect of public expenditure, while distortionary taxation has the expected negative sign. Their main contribution is to properly account for the government budget constraint in their empirical analysis, by omitting a neutral (in growth terms) fiscal category and correctly interpreting parameter estimates of other relevant fiscal explanatory variables.

Arpaia and Turrini (2008) examine fiscal reaction functions and test the assumption that governments will decrease public investment in order to consolidate and ameliorate public debt. Results show that the share of GDP of government spending decreases as the ratio of debt to GDP falls, corroborating the view that expenditure curbing is a stance of fiscal consolidation.

A survey by Zagler and Durnecker (2003) highlights the long-run growth effects of government expenditure and revenues, with a positive contribution to economic activity of expenditure on education and infrastructure, and shows that tax rates alter the sectoral division of labour by influencing a key driver of growth, that is, the innovation rate. Their unifying analysis moves away from the short-run issues of fiscal policies and welfare considerations, but stresses the importance of the effects of fiscal policy on an economy's innovation structure.

This line of work is extremely promising, since it pushes the research agenda on fiscal policy issues from a purely short-run view to a more growth-rooted analysis within the framework of endogenous growth models. In this perspective, government expenditure, while causing short run budget deficits, may have a long-run positive effect on growth if the resulting increase in the tax base and revenue is strong enough as tested in a VAR setting for the Euro zone by Pereira and Pinho (2006).

The adoption of fiscal rules and concerns about public sector solvency, both at a national and supranational level, have given rise to contributions that aim at designing appropriate fiscal targets that go beyond the simple cash deficit criterion. Serven (2007) surveys recent contributions and provides a theoretical framework for proposing alternative fiscal rules that take into account the intertemporal dimension of public sector solvency and acknowledge the positive role of productive public investment on growth. Previously, Blanchard and Giavazzi (2004) advocated the use of a *golden rule* to assess fiscal solvency, preventing the government from running a deficit on current accounts but allowing borrowing in order to finance the creation of new public assets. Buiter and Graffe (2004) proposed another alternative, the *permanent balance rule*, based on the idea that fiscal variables should be valued in an intertemporal dimension and mimicking the permanent income hypothesis for households (Friedman, 1957). In the authors' words: 'Our Permanent Balance Rule for the share of taxes in GDP defines it as that constant value of the share of taxes in GDP whose present discounted value (over an infinite future time horizon) equals the outstanding stock of public debt plus the present discounted value of actual government spending minus government capital income, all taken as shares of GDP's (Buiter and Graffe, 2004, p. 76). This modified golden rule allows governments to borrow if present investment opportunities are greater than discounted future ones, and when current revenue is low.

Another possibility rests on the idea of the net worth of public capital, and devises a fiscal rule that has a target in terms of a desired net worth trajectory, to be reached by appropriate financing and expenditure decisions. This rule is extremely information-demanding, but is partly in use in public fiscal management in New Zealand (Janssen 2001).

Mintz and Smart (2006) have proposed yet another modified golden rule, which is based on the distinction between investments that will in time generate revenues for the government, implying that they will in the long run be self-sustainable, from those that finance services that will be offered at no charge. This modified rule recognizes that some public investment is productive in the long run, and may be a source of revenue, and should not be cut at the same level as the non-revenue-generating assets to achieve fiscal consolidation and solvency. This rule, however, limits the amount to be borrowed to a fraction of revenue-generating assets.

A theoretical analysis of the performance of different fiscal policy rules is provided in Agenor and Yilmaz (2006). In the framework of an endogenous growth model with public capital and debt, the simple primary surplus rule (according to which all non-interest spending must be financed by a fraction of total tax revenues) performs better than balanced budget rules (or of zero deficit) and standard and modified golden rules.

These modifications to the simple rule that looks at the evolution over time of budget deficits fully incorporate the intertemporal budget constraint and recognize that cutting public investment that may be profitable in the long run may be detrimental to growth. Serven (2007) provides evidence for Latin American and EU countries that indeed, in fiscal consolidation episodes, productive investment decline (especially in infrastructure) accounted for 40 per cent of fiscal adjustment in the former and characterized 25 out of 32 episodes in the latter. While a decline in infrastructure investment might be due to efficiency reasons, improved public procurement and public–private partnerships and in cases of an optimal existing capital stock, the figures provided above still seem implausibly high, especially considering the well documented infrastructure gap in Latin American countries (Calderon and Serven, 2004) and in the NMS.

A related issue regards monitoring and the derivation of adequate budgetary safety margins. Codogno and Nucci (2008) propose a methodology that takes into account heterogeneity in economies' volatility and cyclical fluctuations, by defining a Representative Output Gap based on a country specific and common component.

The previous discussion on the different fiscal rules available warrants a few words on the actual fiscal rules put in place in the EU countries in recent years. While the general Maastricht Treaty and SGP set overall targets, rules and monitoring procedures, national governments still show some heterogeneity in country-specific numerical rules. Ayuso-i-Casals et al. (2009) provide a comprehensive overview of what is happening to numerical fiscal rules in 25 EU countries between 1990 and 2005. The main data comes from an EU-wide survey conducted by the European Commission on issues of quality of public finances (Working Group on the Quality of Public Finances). Several results are worth mentioning. The first relates to the variety of numerical fiscal rules, which comprise budget balance rules (the most common), debt rules, expenditure rules and revenue rules. In terms of evolution over time, fiscal rules in the 1990s were applied mainly at a sub-national level, while in recent years the trend seems to be focusing on the general government sector. Looking at the determinants of different rules, the overall number is higher in countries with low deficits, and the introduction of fiscal targets does not seem to follow recession, crises or episodes of high deficits. Finally, looking at the effects exerted by numerical rules, it appears that the higher the share of public finances governed by rules the lower the budget deficits, and that the main characteristic driving a successful fiscal rule does not rest necessarily on the different targets used, but on the presence of a strong enforcement mechanism.

A detailed analysis of the fiscal condition of the EU NMS and the implications on the effects of the SGP is provided by Orban and Szapary (2004). They find evidence of relevant heterogeneity of initial fiscal conditions among the NMS and an overall need for reforms of the welfare state and infrastructure investment. Comparing these countries to Old Member States, it appears that, on average, they are facing lower debt and the potential of faster economic growth. These stylized facts led the authors to conclude that the SGP should be reformed on a country-by-country basis, and taking into account the role of net worth and future profitable assets. The homogeneity of fiscal rules amongst EU countries is also challenged by Afonso and Alves (2009), in light of the technological gap existing between more developed and developing Member States. They suggest a temporary differentiation of fiscal rules to allow innovation-driven and knowledge-creating public expenditures in small and less developed countries, allowing for temporary increases in public deficits.

3. CONCLUSIONS

This chapter has presented a selected overview of the main contributions, especially in the empirical literature, of the growth and, to a minor extent, welfare effects of fiscal policy, with a specific focus on public investment, fiscal consolidation rules and their interplay.

The first part has reviewed the traditional issue of whether government expenditure is conducive to growth and if some qualifications can be made. Given the existing literature, the answer appears to be overall positive, with a greater role for productive capital spending (for example in infrastructure and education) and attention to country-specific conditions, especially in terms of the optimal level of existing capital. A lesson to be learned from this literature is that there is no simple all-purpose recipe for growth-enhancing public investment rules, and that the expected positive effects may be reversed if institutional and economic elements are not appropriately factored into the analysis. In the case of infrastructure, for example, attention must be given to the existing level of the physical public capital stock and the positive spillovers additional investment could provide.

Shares of total government finances invested in different categories of spending should also be carefully assessed, given that there is no optimal, 'good for all', allocation of expenditure that automatically increases growth and well-being.

Welfare considerations are also crucial and this appears to be a relevant avenue for policy-oriented future research, given the rather few academic contributions in this area. Income distribution issues and inequality patterns may be significantly affected by public investment, along with the more traditional categories of current welfare public spending (such as unemployment benefits, transfers and pensions).

Interactions and complementarities, both in terms of growth and social welfare, between different categories of public spending may also be relevant at a sub-national level, calling for more analysis at the regional and provincial levels. There seems to be a recent strand of empirical analyses that examine these issues, given the increased data availability at the regional level on public finances, capital stocks and relevant economic variables. Welfare considerations should be included in these studies, especially in the EU with Structural Funds policies at the regional level in mind.

Obviously public spending, whatever the form and the final growth effect, must somehow be financed, which has led to the analysis of fiscal rules and policies aiming at consolidation and budget balances, which are particularly relevant in the EU, both at the national and supranational levels.

The second part of this chapter was devoted to the exploration of the main determinants and effects of different forms of numerical fiscal rules, and how they relate to public investment. The majority of the surveyed contributions considered indicated that fiscal consolidation based on productive investment curbing is generally detrimental to growth and has minor long-run effects on the budgetary balance. Other contributions have also stressed the different impacts of various designs of fiscal policies, and the importance of country-specific conditions and characteristics in determining the success and effectiveness of a fiscal rule. The general result is that fiscal rules have positive growth effects and are generally put in place by low deficit countries, and not necessarily following crises or 'bad times', but attention is given to the fact that productive, asset-building investment should not be sacrificed lightly to comply to budget rules *per se*.

Interesting extensions in this area of research include a thorough comparison of different fiscal rules with finely disaggregated categories of public spending. In the EU, more research is needed to understand the situation of NMS and accession countries, and the role of local public finance and its relation to the general government should also be taken into account, considering both the SGP and national fiscal rules.

To conclude, as the previous sections have hopefully highlighted, while our understanding of the role of public spending, investment and fiscal policy on growth has substantially increased in the past 20 years, there is still a need for more research in order to fine tune fiscal policies to accompany the path of world and European economies towards sustainable and equitable economic and welfare growth.

NOTES

* I wish to thank Massimo Florio for helpful comments and discussions. The usual disclaimer applies.

1. Government consumption may have important welfare and distributive effects (Turnovsky, 1996).

2. These figures were subsequently challenged, and a recent meta-analysis (Bom and Lighard 2008) found an average coefficient of 0.08.

REFERENCES

Afonso, A. and J. Alegre (2008), 'Economic Growth and Budgetary Components – A Panel Assessment for the EU', European Central Bank working paper series 848.

Afonso, O. and R.H. Alves (2009), 'Endogenous growth and European fiscal rules', *Applied Economics*, **41**(7), 849–58.

Agenor, Pierre-R. (2005), 'Infrastructure, public education and growth with congestion costs', University of Manchester Centre for Growth and Business Cycle Research discussion paper series 47.

Agenor, Pierre-R. and B. Moreno-Dodson (2006), 'Public infrastructure and growth: new channels and policy implications', World Bank policy research working paper 4064.

Agenor, P.R. and D. Yilmaz (2006), 'The Tyranny of Rules: Fiscal Discipline, Productive Spending, and Growth', The University of Manchester Centre for Growth and Business Cycle Research discussion paper series 73.

Agenor, Pierre-Richard, Mustapha Nabli and Tarik Yousef (2007), 'Public infrastructure and private investment in the Middle East and North Africa', in Mustapha K. Nabli (ed), *Breaking the Barriers for Higher Economic Growth*, Washington, DC: World Bank.

Alesina, A. and R. Perotti (1995), 'Fiscal expansions and adjustments in OECD countries', *Economic Policy*, **10**(21), 207–47.

Ardagna, S. (2004), 'Fiscal stabilizations: when do they work and why', *European Economic Review*, **48**(5), 1047–74.

Arpaia, A. and A. Turrini (2008), 'Government expenditure and economic growth in the EU: long-run tendencies and short-term adjustment', *European Economy Economic Papers*, 300.

Arrow, K. and M. Kurz (1970), 'Optimal growth with irreversible investment in a Ramsey model', *Econometrica*, **38**(2), 331–44.

Aschauer, D. (1989), 'Does public capital crowd out private capital?', *Journal of Monetary Economics*, **24**(2), 171–88.

Atukeren, E. (2005), 'Interactions between public and private investment: evidence from developing countries', *Kyklos*, **58**(3), 307–30.

Ayuso-i-Casals, J., D. Gonzalez, L. Moulin and A. Turrini (2009), 'Beyond the SGP: features and effects of EU national-level fiscal rules', in Joaquim Ayuso-i-Casals, Servaars Deroose, Elena Flores and Laurent Moulin (eds), *Policy Instruments for Sound Fiscal Policies*, City Palgrave Macmillan.

Barro, Robert J. and Xavier Sala-i-Martin (eds) (2004), *Economic Growth*, 2nd edn, McGraw-Hill, The MIT Press.

Barro, R. (1990), 'Government spending in a simple model of endogenous growth', *Journal of Political Economy*, **98**(5), S103–26.

Belloc, M. and P. Vertova (2006), 'Public investment and economic performance in highly indebted poor countries: an empirical assessment', *International Review of Applied Economics*, **20**(2), 151–70.

Blanchard, Olivier J. and F. Giavazzi (2004), 'Improving the SGP through a proper accounting of public investment', Centre for Economic Policy Research discussion papers 4220.

Bleaney, M., N. Gemmell and R. Kneller (2001), 'Testing the endogenous growth model: public expenditure, taxation, and growth over the long run', *The Canadian Journal of Economics*, **34**(1), 36–57.

Bloom, David E., D. Canning and J. Sevilla (2003), 'The effect of health on economic growth: a production function approach', *World Development*, **32**(1), 1–13.

Bom, Pedro R.D. and J. Lighard (2008), 'How productive is public capital? a meta-analysis', Center for Economic Studies Ifo Institute (CESifo) working paper series 2206.

Bose, N., M. Haque and D. Osborn (2007), 'Public expenditure and economic growth: a disaggregated analysis for developing countries', *Manchester School*, **75**(5), 533–56.

Bougheas, S., P. Demetriades and T. Mamuneas (2000), 'Infrastructure, specialization and economic growth', *Canadian Journal of Economics*, **33**(2), 506–22.

Buiter, Willem H. and C. Graffe (2004), 'Patching up the pact', *Economics of Transition*, **12**(1), 67–102.

Calderon, C. and A. Chong (2004), 'Volume and quality of infrastructure and the distribution of income: an empirical investigation', *Review of Income and Wealth*, **50**(1), 87–106.

Calderon, C. and L. Serven (2004), 'The effects of development on growth and income distribution', World Bank policy research working paper 3400.

Calderon, C. and L. Serven (2008), 'Infrastructure and economic development in sub-Saharan Africa', World Bank policy research working paper 4712.

Codogno, L. and F. Nucci (2008), 'Safety margins in EU budgetary surveillance: an assessment', in Banca d'Italia (AA.VV.) 'Fiscal Policy: Current Issues and Challenges', proceedings of the 9th Workshop at S.A.DI.BA

De Rus, G. and P. Socorro (2009), 'Infrastructure investment and incentives with supranational funding', University of Milan Department of Economics departmental working papers 2009-18.

Del Bo, C. and M. Florio (2008), 'Infrastructure and growth in the European Union: an empirical analysis at the regional level in a spatial framework', University of Milan Department of Economics departmental working papers 2008-37.

Delorme, Charles D., H.G. Thompson and R.S. Warren (1999), 'Public infrastructure and private productivity: a stochastic frontier approach', *Journal of Macroeconomics*, **21**(3), 563–76.

Demetriades, Panicos O. and M.P. Theofanis (2000), 'Intertemporal output and employment effects of public infrastructure capital: evidence from 12 OECD economies', *Economic Journal*, **110**(465), 687–712.

Devarajan, S., V. Swaroop and H. Zou (1996), 'The composition of public expenditures and economic performance', *Journal of Monetary Economics*, **37**(2), 313–44.

Easterly, W. and S. Rebelo (1993), 'Fiscal policy and economic growth: an empirical investigation', *Journal of Monetary Economics*, **32**(3), 417–58.

Erden, L. and R. Holcombe (2005), 'The effects of public investment on private investment in developing economies', *Public Finance Review*, **33**(5), 575–602.

Erenburg, S.J. and M.E. Wohar (1995), 'Public and private investment: are there causal linkages?', *Journal of Macroeconomics*, **17**(1), 1–30.

Estache, A. (2005), 'On Latin America's infrastructure experience: policy gaps and the poors', in John Nellis and Nancy Birdsall (eds), *Reality Check: the Distributional Impact of Privatization in Developing Countries*, Washington, DC: Center for Global Development, pp. 281–96.

Estache, A., M. Gonzalez and L. Trujillo (2007), 'Government expenditures on education, health, and infrastructure: a naive look at levels, outcomes, and efficiency', World Bank policy research working paper series 4219.

European Commission, 2007, *Public Finances in EMU*, Brussels: European Commission.

Evans, P. and G. Karras (1994), 'Are government activities productive? Evidence from a panel of US states', *The Review of Economics and Statistics*, **76**(1), 1–11.

Ferreira, F.G. (1995), 'Roads to Equality: Wealth Distribution Dynamics with Public-Private Capital Complementarity', London School of Economics STICERD theoretical economics paper series 286.

Flores de Frutos, R. and A.M. Pereira (1999), 'Public capital accumulation and private sector performance', *Journal of Urban Economics*, **85**(2), 3–34.

Friedman, Milton (ed.) (1957), *A Theory of the Consumption Function*, Princeton, NJ: Princeton University Press.

Glomm, G. and B. Ravikumar (1997), 'Productive government expenditures and long-run growth', *Journal of Economic Dynamics and Control*, **21**(1), 183–204.

Gramlich, E. (1994), 'Infrastructure investment: a review essay', *Journal of Economic Literature*, **32**(3), 1176–96.

Guichard, S., M. Kennedy, E. Wurzel and C. Andre (2007), 'What promotes fiscal consolidation: OECD country experiences', OECD Economics Department working papers 553.

Gupta, S., B. Clements, E. Baldacci and C. Mulas-Granados (2005), 'Fiscal policy, expenditure composition, and growth in low-income countries?', *Journal of International Money and Finance*, **24**(3), 441–63.

Haque, M. and D. Kim (2003), 'Public investment in transportation and communication and growth: a dynamic panel approach', University of Manchester School of Economics discussion paper series 0324.

Haque, M. and R. Kneller (2008), 'Public investment and growth: the role of corruption', University of Manchester Centre for Growth and Business Cycle Research discussion paper series 98.

Holtz-Eakin, D. (1994), 'Public-sector capital and the productivity puzzle', *Review of Economics and Statistics*, **76**(1), 12–21.

Irmen, A. and J. Kuehnel (2009), 'Productive government expenditure and economic growth', *Journal of Economic Surveys*, **23**(4), 692–733.

Jacoby, H. (2000), 'Access to rural markets and the benefits of rural roads', *The Economic Journal*, **110**(465), 713–37.

Janssen, J. (2001), 'New Zealand's fiscal policy framework: experience and evolution', New Zealand Treasury working papers 01/25, Wellington.

Kamps, C. (2005), 'The dynamic effects of public capital: VAR evidence for 22 OECD countries,' *International Tax and Public Finance*, **12**(4), 533–58.

Kneller, R., M.F. Bleaney and N. Gemmell (1999), 'Fiscal policy and growth: evidence from OECD countries', *Journal of Public Economics*, **74**(2), 171–90.

Kumar, Manmohan S., D. Leigh and A. Plekhanov (2007), 'Fiscal adjustments: determinants and macroeconomic consequences', *International Monetary Fund* working papers 07/178.

Lopez, H. (2004), 'Macroeconomics and Inequality', presentation to the World

Bank Research Workshop: Macroeconomic Challenges in Low Income Countries.
Lucas, R. (1988), 'On the mechanics of economic development', *Journal of Monetary Economics*, **22**(1), 3–42.
Lynde, C. and J. Richmond (1993), 'Public capital and total factor productivity', *International Economic Review*, **34**(2), 401–14.
Mastromarco, C. and U. Woitek (2006), 'Public infrastructure investment and efficiency in Italian regions', *Journal of Productivity Analysis*, **25**(1–2), 57–65.
Mintz, J. and M. Smart (2006), 'Incentives for public investment under fiscal rules', The World Bank policy research working paper series 3860.
Monteiro, G. and S.J. Turnovsky (2008), 'The composition of productive government expenditure: consequences for economic growth and welfare', *Indian Growth and Development Review*, **1**(1), 57–83.
Mulas-Granados, C., J. Onrubia and J. Salinas-Jiménez (2009), 'Do budget institutions matter? Fiscal consolidation in the EU Member States', *Eastern European Economy*, **47**(1), 60–91.
Munnell, A. (1990), 'Why has productivity growth declined? Productivity and public investment', *New England Economic Review*, **1**, 3–22.
Muscatelli, V., P. Tirelli and C. Trecroci (2004), 'Fiscal and monetary policy interactions: empirical evidence and optimal policy using a structural new-Keynesian model', *Journal of Macroeconomics*, **26**(2), 257–80.
Nijkamp, P. and J. Poot (2004), 'Meta-analysis of the effect of fiscal policies on long-run growth', *European Journal of Political Economy*, **20**(1), 91–124.
Nourzad, F. (2000), 'The productivity effect of government capital in developing and industrialized countries', *Applied Economics*, **32**(9), 1181–7.
Orban, G. and G. Szapary (2004), 'The Stability and Growth Pact from the perspective of the new member states', *Journal of Policy Modeling*, **26**(7), 839–64.
Organization for Economic Co-operation and Development (2006), *Promoting Pro-Poor Growth: Infrastructure*, Paris: OECD.
Pereira, A. (2001), 'On the effects of public capital formation and private investment: what crowds in what?', *Public Finance Review*, **29**(1), 3–25.
Pereira, Alfredo M. and M.D.F. Pinho (2006), 'Impact of public investment upon economic performance and budgetary consolidation efforts in the European Union', European Regional Science Association *conference papers ersa06p122*.
Pesaran, M. (2007), 'A simple panel unit root test in the presence of cross section dependence', *Journal of Applied Econometrics*, **22**(2), 265–312.
Pesaran, M., Y. Shin and R.P. Smith (1999), 'Pooled mean group estimation of dynamic heterogeneous panels', *Journal of the American Statistical Association*, **94**(446), 621–34.
Rioja, Felix K. (2005), 'Roads versus schooling: growth effects of government choices', *Topics in Macroeconomics*, **5**(1), article 7, 1084.
Romer, P. (1990), 'Endogenous technological change', *Journal of Political Economy*, **98**(5), S71–102.
Romp, W. and J. De Haan (2007), 'Public capital and economic growth: a critical survey', *Perspektiven der Wirtschaftspolitik*, **8**(1), 6–52.
Rovolis, A. and N. Spence (2002), 'Duality theory, and the cost function analysis in a regional context: the impact of public infrastructure capital in the Greek regions', *Annals of Regional Science*, **36**(1), 55–78.
Serven, L. (2007), 'Fiscal rules, public investment and growth', World Bank policy research working paper series 4382.

Shioji, E. (2001), 'Public capital and economic growth: a convergence approach', *Journal of Economic Growth*, **6**(3), 205–27.
Sturm, Jan-Egbert (ed.) (1998), *Public Capital Expenditure in OECD Countries: The Causes and the Impact of the Decline in Public Capital Spending*, Cheltenham, UK and Lyme, USA: Edward Elgar Publishing.
Sutherland, D., S.Araujo, B. Égert and T. Kozluk (2009), 'Infrastructure investment: links to growth and the role of public policies', OECD Economics Department working paper 686.
Tagkalakis, A. (2009), 'Fiscal adjustments: do labor and product market institutions matter?', *Public Choice*, **139**(3), 389–411.
Turnovsky, S. (1996), 'Fiscal policy, growth, and macroeconomic performance in a small open economy', *Journal of International Economics*, **40**(1–2), 41–66.
van de Walle, D. (2002), 'Choosing rural road investments to help reduce poverty', *World Development*, **30**(4), 575–89.
von Hagen, J., A.H. Hallett and R. Strauch (2002), 'Budgetary consolidations in EMU', *European Economy – Economic Papers*, 148.
Vu Le, M. and T. Suruga (2005), 'Foreign direct investment, public expenditure and economic growth: the empirical evidence for the period 1970–2001', *Applied Economics Letters*, **12**(1), 45–9.
Zagler, M. and G. Durnecker (2003), 'Fiscal policy and economic growth', *Journal of Economic Surveys*, **17**(3), 397–418.
Zou, Y. (2006), 'Empirical studies on the relationship between public and private investment and GDP growth', *Applied Economics*, **38**(11), 1259–70.

3. Public investment under disequilibrium: a post Keynesian viewpoint

Massimo Cingolani*

1. INTRODUCTION

If the neoclassical optimum is used as a reference concept for economic equilibrium, it should be recognized as a very specific ideal case. Real life policy choices would then have to be assessed in a disequilibrium context, with specific analytical tools. The chapter discusses the evaluation of economic policies in the field of public investment in a disequilibrium context, where underemployment of the labour force and a suboptimal utilization of the resources and productive capacity prevail. It is argued that the model of the monetary circuit as developed more particularly by Parguez and Graziani (Halevi and Taouil, 2002), put into the more general perspective of post Keynesian analysis (Eichner and Kregel, 1975), is useful to illustrate policy choices under disequilibrium.

In the canonical version of the neoclassical model, given convex technology and preferences, equilibrium coincides with the optimum and can be reached through the decentralized decisions of atomistic producers and consumers that take prices as given parameters, in a barter economy with no State. This optimum is a reference for normative analysis. In a context where the State is present it leads naturally to a presumption that any economic policy will be harmful, as it will cause a departure from some conditions for optimality. Usually 'out of equilibrium' positions are ignored because of their transient nature, despite the fact that in general it is not possible to demonstrate the stability of the neoclassical equilibrium under sufficiently general conditions, which would be a prerequisite for its application to the description and diagnosis of real world problems.

Therefore, rather than being unstable and deprived of practical interest, the situations where not all optimality conditions are fulfilled are of interest because they better describe the economic reality and are relevant for policy design. Moreover, if one generalizes the neoclassical model by introducing money, the neoclassical equilibrium remains a particular 'limit' solution and can therefore be kept as an indirect reference for normative analysis when technology is fixed, as it obviously keeps all its optimality features.[1]

Monetary equilibria correspond in general to neoclassical disequilibria. They can explain why situations of insufficient effective demand tend to become permanent, why investment causes savings and why the whole is not the sum of the parts, justifying the claim for macro foundations of microeconomics. As emphasized by Seccareccia (1995), monetary equilibria call for a macroeconomic demand management that should be oriented towards the long term, as originally proposed by Keynes.[2]

In this context public expenditure in general and public investment in particular have completely different effects than in the 'canonical' version of the neoclassical model. In particular, when new money creation is a possible means of financing public investment, the model of the circuit shows that if the State budget is restricted to previously accumulated savings for financing its expenditures, it deprives itself of an important instrument for planning long-term budgetary policies that could stabilize the economy by anchoring the diverging expectations of the private sector. This type of 'expectational' externality should be quantified in cost–benefit analyses that look at the comparison of alternative ways of financing public investment policies. It also gives support to the idea of coordinating European fiscal policy at the continental level through the collective management of investment and other public expenditure.

After having reviewed the use of the concepts of equilibrium and disequilibrium in the neoclassical model in section 2, section 3 proposes a more general definition of these concepts arguing that post Keynesian analysis *lato sensu* provides a generalization of neoclassical equilibrium and that it is suitable to address these 'out of equilibrium' situations that are in fact the more relevant for real life economic policy choices. Uses of the equilibrium concept in the economic literature and the related causality structures are reviewed in section 4. The argument is further developed in section 5, which examines the causal role of distributive variables in non-monetary post Keynesian models in the tradition of Sraffa and Kalecki, and in section 6, which looks at the related model of the monetary circuit. In section 7, the assumption of constant technology is dropped. Section 8 discusses in more detail some implications of the analysis for European public investment policies with particular reference to the countries having integrated more recently into the EU or in the process of doing so. Some implications of the analysis for European fiscal policy coordination are sketched out and could be developed later.

2. EQUILIBRIUM AND DISEQUILIBRIUM IN THE NEOCLASSICAL MODEL

The neoclassical synthesis focuses on a very specific and detailed form of static equilibrium, but the main authors that developed it just before and after the Second World War also gave a fair treatment to the case of disequilibrium, mainly in connection with the extension of their analysis to dynamics.[3] For instance in *Value and Capital* Hicks (1939, pp. 130–40), includes a Chapter X, entitled 'Equilibrium and disequilibrium', while in chapters II and XI of the *Foundations*, entitled respectively 'Equilibrium systems and comparative statics' and 'The stability of equilibrium: comparative statics and dynamics', Samuelson (1947, pp. 7–20 and 257–83) addresses (and avoids) the problem through the use of the concept of 'comparative statics', which states that it is legitimate to restrict attention to static equilibrium positions only, as long as the conditions for dynamic stability are assumed to hold. It is noteworthy that the classic texts that gave an organic systematization to the concepts of neoclassical equilibrium and disequilibrium in the 1930s and 1940s were also key contributions in the field of welfare economics. In this respect, it is probably Allais ([1943] 1994) who developed more thoroughly the link between the definitions of equilibrium and disequilibrium and welfare analysis. Indeed, a substantial portion of his *Traité d'économie pure*, is made of two large sections on the 'Dynamique du déséquilibre' (Allais, 1943, Chapter III, pp. 272–513) and the 'Dynamique de l'équilibre' (Chapter IV, pp. 514–686).[4] His whole book can actually be seen as an attempt to build the treatment of equilibrium and its use in welfare comparisons on the basis of what one can assume happens out of equilibrium. In particular Allais uses the neoclassical equilibrium as a reference point to compare two states of the economy, both out of equilibrium, from the welfare point of view. For that purpose he derives a function (called '*la perte*' or 'the loss'), which measures the relative distance of both points from the neoclassical equilibrium. This function is derived from the concept of '*surplus distribuable*'. Later, Allais offered a better algebraic derivation of these concepts and presented them as the basis for the generalization of the neoclassical model in his *Théorie Générale des Surplus* ([1981] 1989). A relatively simple development of Allais' points on these two concepts can be found in a small model annexed to the *Introduction* of the 1994 edition of his 1943 book, which will be briefly described in the two paragraphs below.[5]

The model has two goods, two factors, two agents, two producers and no money. In line with the neoclassical approach, it assumes fixed resources, technology and preferences. Equilibrium is defined as a situation where, given relative prices between the two goods and the two factors of production, consumers maximize their utility under constraint of revenue and producers maximize revenue (or profit) under a technology constraint. Allais derives the usual first and second order conditions for the optimum showing that they are necessarily fulfilled on the frontier of maximum efficiency in the space of satisfactions, or on the frontier of maximum efficiency in the space of productions. He also defines a curve of minimal production costs given output and derives that the neoclassical equilibrium of 'maximum efficiency' corresponds to the point of tangency between the line of maximum efficiency and the curve of minimal production costs in the space of productions. Any point below the line of maximum efficiency is sub-optimal and therefore allows for a 'surplus' to be distributed if the economy moves closer to the line of maximum efficiency.[6]

Whereas the developments above are standard, Allais derives an explicit expression for this surplus (*surplus distribuable*). This is defined as the amount of one of the two goods that, starting from any point below the curve of maximum efficiency, could be distributed in moving to another point, which could also be suboptimal, while keeping the level of utility constant. Given the starting point, the surplus depends only on the target point and can be expressed in terms of its parameters. By maximizing the surplus with respect to the parameters of the target point and solving the resulting system of equations, Allais finds an expression for the 'loss' associated with any suboptimal point. This is the maximum of the surplus that can be liberated starting from this point and respecting all the constraints of the model. By studying the first and second differential of the surplus and of the loss, Allais further shows that in any situation of maximum efficiency the surplus that can be distributed is null and its derivative is negative or null, which implies that the *surplus distribuable* is minimized on the maximum efficiency line. He also shows that in the neighbourhood of equilibrium, the first differential of the loss is null and the second one is negative or null, which also implies that the loss is minimized at maximal efficiency.[7] A remarkable implication of this way of setting the problem is that in moving between two suboptimal points A and B, the change in the loss between these two points can be approximated by the change in consumption, which sets the basis for the cost–benefit analysis. However, it is only when the starting point is sufficiently close to equilibrium that it is legitimate to value this change in consumption at the starting (market) prices.

The concept of surplus and loss can be interpreted as providing the basis for the dynamic of a market economy out of equilibrium. Allais ([1981] 1989) argued in particular that the existence of a *surplus distribuable* out of equilibrium is the root of the instability of suboptimal positions, as in any of these situations it would be possible to obtain the same satisfaction at a lesser cost, or, alternatively, that at that cost the agents that form part of the economy can attain a higher level of satisfaction. Therefore Allais's conception of disequilibrium dynamics consists of the frictionless search of new combinations of factors of production to obtain similar or higher levels of satisfaction that will stop when all possibilities for improvement are exhausted, that is when the economy is on the frontier of maximum efficiency, illustrating the fact that only the points that pertain to the frontier of maximum efficiency can be equilibria of the model. Despite assertions to the contrary, the process through which equilibrium is reached is not explicitly described in the model of Allais, implying that the 'instability' of non-equilibrium positions is an assumption that is imposed from outside,[8] as in the case of the restrictions imposed by stability conditions for comparative statics in Samuelson's analysis. It therefore falls under the same criticism.

One can observe that this 'out of equilibrium' dynamics develops on a path where 'real profits' vanish progressively and indeed it stops at a point where real and nominal profits are zero, as required by the conditions for maximum efficiency and as results from the definition of static equilibrium with perfect competition. One can also observe that on the frontier of maximum efficiency factors of production are fully employed, otherwise there would also be a waste and therefore a *surplus distribuable*. Therefore one can retain four main properties of the neoclassical equilibrium of maximum efficiency:

1. there exists a system of prices that clears all markets,[9] present and future, implying notably the equality between investment and savings;
2. marginal distribution relations hold (the remuneration of different production factors is equal between them and proportional to their marginal productivities);
3. profits vanish, at least in the long term when technology is fixed;[10]
4. production factors are fully employed.

Conversely, any situation where marginal distribution relations do not hold, profits are different from zero and there is unemployment and underutilization of productive capacity, are 'disequilibrium situations' from the neoclassical viewpoint. In these situations it is presumed that savings is a causal factor of investment (see sections 4.4 and 4.5). Therefore, the practical question is whether or not equilibrium is something that is normally reached in reality. The results of the *tâtonnement* and related stability literature are quite negative, Franklin Fisher (1983, 2003) concludes that in order to have stability one must assume the absence of 'favorable surprises', which by and large excludes dynamics (see below section. 3.3).

Guerrien (1992) provides an introductory review of the consequences of the so-called Sonnenschein–Mantel–Debreu theorem for the stability of the neoclassical equilibrium. He notes that: 'le cas où il y a instabilité est bien plus "probable" que celui où il y a stabilité . . . cela signifie que, en règle générale, le tâtonnement ne mène pas à un équilibre walrasien'. Therefore it would be rational to assume that most of the time a real economy will be out of equilibrium,[11] with disequilibrium positions that are not necessarily unstable but could be seen instead as rest points of unspecified processes that end up in situations where real and nominal profits have not vanished.

3. POST KEYNESIAN ANALYSIS AS A DYNAMIC GENERALIZATION OF THE NEOCLASSICAL EQUILIBRIUM

Although it may sound unduly restrictive to qualify post Keynesian economics as an analysis of what happens 'out of neoclassical equilibrium', some of the economists more clearly associated with what Pasinetti (2007) called a 'revolution to be accomplished', such as Nicholas Kaldor (1972, p. 1240), have clearly espoused 'anti-equilibrium' viewpoints:

> equilibrium theory has reached the stage where the pure theorist has successfully (though perhaps inadvertently) demonstrated that the main implications of his theory cannot possibly hold in reality, but has not yet managed to pass his message down the line to the textbook writer and to the classroom.

Other closely related authors, such as the structuralist Lance Taylor (2004), reject the relevance of the notion of equilibrium altogether.

Post Keynesian authors such as Barrère (1952), Robinson (1962, p. 26), Pasinetti (1964–65, pp. 243–5), or Eichner (1991, pp. 18–29) have argued that a fundamental difference between neoclassical and post Keynesian analysis is that the latter admits a causal structure, whereas the former does not.[12] Indeed, with reference to the discussion in paragraph 2 above, Allais ([1943] 1994, pp. 542–43) noted that simultaneity is a property of equilibrium, whereas causality is a property of disequilibrium.[13]

Robinson (1956, 1962 and 1974) developed in particular the relations between causality and time, introducing the difference between logical and historical (or dynamic) time. She stressed in particular that neoclassical theory is associated with equilibrium and logical time, whereas post Keynesian theory is typically associated with historical time and path dependency (Dutt, 2005).

Post Keynesian analysis can thus be seen as providing a generalization of neoclassical equilibrium under conditions that admits a causality in historical time, that is a framework of analysis more relevant for economic policy. This argument is further developed below based on the definition of equilibrium as a point of rest of a system (section 3.1), where there are endogenous and exogenous variables that are linked by causal relations (3.2), which involve a time element (3.3).

3.1 Definition of Equilibrium

As seen above, the neoclassical characterization of equilibrium assumes given resources, as well as tastes and technology. Quantities demanded and supplied result from a process of optimization under the constraints imposed by the predetermined parameters, which include also prices, assumed to be the equilibrium ones. The rigorous mathematical conditions and properties of this type of equilibrium have been made explicit in the classical works of Arrow and Hahn (1971), Debreu (1959), McKenzie (2002) and others that, while confirming the main results obtained by early writers, also detailed how particular and strong were the conditions required for the neoclassical equilibrium to hold.

Machlup (1978) used instead a more general definition of equilibrium, which can be better applied in characterizing different economic theories:

> The equilibrium concept in economics is primarily a tool for the explanation of movement: we explain a movement by pointing to 'causes' that are responsible for the departure from one position and an approach to another one. These two positions are idealized as positions of rest, an initial equilibrium and a 'new' equilibrium. The movement is thus 'understood' as an adjustment to a 'disequilibrating' change. We need the assumed 'balance of forces' in this initial position in order to isolate the 'disequilibrating change', that is in order to make sure that nothing else has occurred and that the movement exhibited by the operation of the model can be attributed without any doubt to the specified disturbance. We need the assumed 'balance of forces' in the new position in order to make sure that the adjustment is complete and all the effects of the disequilibrating change have been fully recorded. (Machlup 1978, pp. 77–8, footnote)

In this definition, equilibrium is defined as a balance between some variables, which are 'caused', and other variables, which are 'causing'. Caused variables are sometimes called 'endogenous', and are determined within a particular theory, whereas causal variables are called exogenous, or predetermined, and are treated as given parameters not explained by the theory, although the meanings of those terms do not always coincide (see. below, section 3.2). According to Machlup's definition, equilibrium is thus defined as the rest point of the endogenous variables, once the exogenous ones have exerted all their effects. There is no requirement that the equilibrium value of the endogenous variables be the result of an optimization process, nor any specific indication of which variables should be endogenous and which should be exogenous.

3.2 Endogeneity, Exogeneity, Causality and Simultaneity

Before looking at equilibrium and causality in a temporal context in the next section, it is useful to elaborate on the differences between the related concepts of simultaneity, causality and exogeneity.

When there is simultaneity, two variables are determined together, whereas as emphasized by Simon (1953), causality is typically associated with an asymmetric relation: if variable A causes variable B, the converse is not true. Causality does not however always coincide with exogeneity, as it is clear from linear analysis where a distinction is made between systems that are undetermined, where the number of variables, *a priori* all unknown, exceeds the number of equations, and systems that are exactly determined, that is where the number of equations of the final form[14] is equal to the number of unknowns.

If a linear system that it is undetermined is solved by, say, the method of Gauss, some variables, that can be labelled endogenous, can be expressed as a function of some others, which can be labelled exogenous. Endogenous variables are thus those that are determined by the system itself (are on the left of the equal sign of one of the equations of the final form of the system), whereas exogenous variables are determined outside the system and are thus on the right of the equal sign of its final form. Exogeneity implies causality, as usually quantified by the *multiplier*, that is the response of an endogenous variable to a unit change in an exogenous variable.[15]

Causality can, however, also be found in non-homogeneous systems that are exactly determined, where there are no exogenous variables, if the associated matrix can be made triangular or block triangular. In the extreme case of a completely recursive system, there is only one endogenous variable that, once set at a certain constant level, determines the whole system. In a fully determined linear post Keynesian model, one variable would set the second, which in turn could determine the next one and so on for the whole system, whereas in a fully determined linear neoclassical model all variables would simultaneously impact on all the others and no causality could be identified (given technology, resources and preferences), in particular for the variables under the influence of economic policy (interest rate, budget deficit).

3.3 Causality and Historical Time

The reference to linear algebra above clarified that to have causality one must have either an undetermined system or an exactly determined one that can be reduced to a triangular structure.[16] In both cases, following Machlup, equilibrium can be defined as the point of rest of a process originated by an external cause,[17] that is the terminal point of a chain of causes and effects. However, exogeneity strictly applies only to the first case, when the model 'explains' only some of its variables (partial equilibrium), whereas in the second case the model can explain all of its variables (general equilibrium). If the causal system is time dated, it describes the motion in time of the endogenous variables based on the value set previously for the exogenous ones. Samuelson (1947, p. 315) distinguished six different ways of modelling interactions between endogenous (Y_t) and exogenous variables (X_t) in time (t):

1. Static and stationary models:

$$Y = f(X) \quad \text{or} \quad y = f(x) \quad \text{with} \quad y = \frac{dY}{Y} \qquad x = \frac{dX}{X}$$

2. Static and historical models:

$$Y_t = f(X_t, t) \quad \text{or} \quad y_t = f(x_t, t) \quad \text{with} \quad y_t = \frac{dY_t}{dt}\frac{1}{Y_t} \quad x_t = \frac{dX_t}{dt}\frac{1}{X_t}$$

3. Dynamic and causal models (non-historical):

$$Y_t = f(t - t_0, Y_0, X_0) \quad \text{or} \quad y_t = f(t - t_0, y_0, x)$$
$$\text{with} \quad Y_0, X_0, y_0, x_0 \quad \text{as initial conditions}$$

4. Dynamic and historical models:

$$Y_t = f(t, t_0, X_t, Y_0, X_0) \quad \text{or} \quad y_t = f(t, t_0, x_t, y_0, x)$$
$$\text{with} \quad Y_0, X_0, y_0, x_0 \quad \text{as initial conditions}$$

5. Stochastical and non-historical models:

$$Y_{t+1} = f(Y_t, X_t) + \{h_t\}$$

6. Stochastical and historical models:

$$Y_{t+1} = f(t, Y_t, X_t) + \{m_t\}$$

The first category covers purely static or stationary systems where the endogenous variable is either constant in level or in its rate of change and for which time is irrelevant. The second category covers a static model where exogenous variables are allowed to move, and thus the endogenous variable depends on time. In the third category the behaviour of the system depends only upon the initial conditions and the time that has elapsed since the establishment of these conditions, which defines completely causally determinate models. In the fourth category, calendar time enters in the solution through the initial conditions. In the fifth category, the random variable $\{h_t\}$ is drawn from an unchanging (stationary) universe, whereas in the latter category the random variable $\{m_t\}$ is drawn from a universe changing at each instant of time.[18]

One can characterize the first, third and fifth categories as 'closed models' not depending on exogenous time, whereas the second, fourth and sixth categories could be seen as 'open models' with respect to exogenous time. This can also be related to Robinson's distinction between logical and historical time, where historical time affects the solution of the model that could therefore be considered as dynamic.[19]

One could thus conclude that the post Keynesian model differs from the neoclassical one in that it is essentially an open dynamic model, as noted by Robinson (1962, pp. 22–34), Parguez (1996, p. 159) and Chick (2004). In this sense it provides the elements for a dynamic generalization of the neoclassical model as discussed notably by Arena (1987) and Henry (1982a).

4. EXAMPLES OF THE USE OF EQUILIBRIUM AND RELATED CONCEPTS IN THE LITERATURE

The discussion in sections 2 and 3 above has shown that equilibrium has a different meaning according to the economic theory considered and the way in which this theory defines the relations between endogenous and exogenous variables. Although generally neglected by the influential literature of public choice and rarely brought out in policy discussions at official level, post Keynesian analysis offers equilibrium concepts that generalize the neoclassical one:

1. they refer to situations that in the neoclassical approach are qualified as disequilibria, where for instance underutilization of capacity and unemployment prevail or distribution does not comply with marginal rules;
2. they assume the pricing decision is taken in historical time. They thus reject the simultaneous determination of prices and quantities, which are determined in sequence in different periods of time and not simultaneously at the equilibrium.

3. they integrate the fact that profits are different from zero and they must therefore enter in the pricing decision;
4. they open the way for a causal analysis, which is of interest for economic policy.

Below, a brief literature review illustrates these aspects, in particular: the link between different theoretical regimes and equilibrium in rationing models (4.1): the choice of endogenous and exogenous variables in post Keynesian and neoclassical closed models (4.2); the use of historical and logical time (4.3); and the resulting causality between investment and savings (4.4) as well as its implications for economic policy and for public investment.

4.1 Rationing Equilibria

Leijonhufvud noted that only a limited number of problems in economics would have the same answer independently from the equilibrium assumption retained, a statement he applied in particular to the assessment of the social cost and benefits of public investment (Leijonhufvud 1973, p. 19, footnote 5).

Drèze, Marchand, Johansson and others have elegantly illustrated this point in the context of the different 'regimes' of a 'fix-price' model in the tradition of Malinvaud (1977) and Benassy (1982). This literature, which is in the tradition of 'quantity rationing' equilibria, examines the cases where, given a 'short-term' neoclassical static framework where all resources are fixed, not all the markets 'clear' (or balance) through price adjustments due to some 'exogenous' price rigidity. As a result, some market participants are rationed in the quantities they supply or demand (for instance unemployed customers rationed in their labour supply or firms rationed in their output due to lack of demand). The rationing in one market produces spillover effects on other markets, providing a microeconomic base for the macroeconomic multiplier, in the tradition of Clower (1965).

Typical 'regimes' are distinguished, depending on who is rationed on which market. The welfare analysis of a small change in economic conditions in each of these 'regimes', such as the one brought by a small project, confirms that the effects of the change depend on the type of equilibrium prevailing in the initial situation.[20]

This literature confirms that the impact of an investment should be assessed taking into consideration the type of equilibrium prevailing in the economy.[21] Closed form expressions have been derived for each of the possible economic regimes (typically classical unemployment, Keynesian unemployment and repressed inflation) showing how the shadow prices at which inputs should be valued out of the traditional Walrasian equilibrium depend also on the usual macroeconomic multipliers, particularly in the Keynesian unemployment case, which is the most relevant empirically.[22] In particular Drèze (1984) has developed the dependence of the shadow prices on the traditional 'Keynesian' multiplier.

The literature on rationing attempted to provide a more solid foundation for economic policy than that offered by the hypothesis of wage rigidity in the IS-LM model, but has not succeeded in becoming as popular. Kahn (1977) and Taylor (2004) have criticized it from a post Keynesian viewpoint, the first because its treatment of the Keynesian regime is not consistent with Keynesian analysis, notably because of the equalization of investment demand and savings supply by the interest rate, whereas the second noted the practical difficulty that when more than the three markets are considered, the number of possible regimes increases so much as to make the mathematical treatment of the model impossible. Parguez (1975 and 1977) demonstrated the shortcomings in the analysis of Clower (1965).

4.2 Endogenous and Exogenous Variables in Post Keynesian Models

Rationing equilibria are based on the same grouping of variables between endogenous and exogenous as in the neoclassical model: prices are parametrically taken as given by optimizing agents in the determination of quantities demanded or supplied, but they are not the market clearing ones.

Post Keynesians writers have defined other types of equilibria characterized by a different grouping of endogenous and exogenous variables that do not necessarily require an optimization process for the determination of the endogenous variables. Petri (1989, p. 291) looked for instance at a price/quantity model in the tradition of Walras. He argued that in the 'classical' approach,[23] for what concerns the determination of the rate of profit,[24] the pre-determined variables are:

(a) the quantity produced;
(b) the real wage rate (or, alternatively, the rate of profit, if the wage is endogenous, see below section 5.1);
(c) the technology.

whereas in the neoclassical model what are assumed as given instead of (a) and (b) are the quantities of available factors of production and preferences. The neoclassical model looks at the equilibrium where all prices, including wages and the rate of interest, are determined simultaneously together with the associated quantities. On the contrary, by construction, the classical equilibrium, although simultaneous, admits a separation between the determination of some prices relating to distribution (either the wage or the rate of interest) and some quantities (demand).

Similarly, Marglin (1984), looking at a growth model studied in the long run and characterized by a simple linear technology showed that depending on the choice of essentially the same variables and their grouping between endogenous and exogenous, three different models can be derived, one which is illustrative of the neoclassical approach, a second which is closer to the Keynesian approach and a third which is typical of Marxian analysis, each economic theory relying on its own characterization of equilibrium.

The examples above show that even within a model that describes the same set of variables, a different identification of the exogenous variables determines equilibrium in a different way and thus shapes the questions that can be answered with the associated theory.

Equilibrium and the associated theory can also differ if, having the same endogenous variables, the models used to represent them differ in the number of exogenous and predetermined variables. In the *carré des éventualités*, Robert Leroy (1983, p. 264) illustrated nicely the idea of the neoclassical equilibrium as a limit case of a model with a more general set of predetermined variables and a larger set of possible outcomes with reference to the functioning of the labour market.

4.3 Logical versus Historical Time

In the neoclassical model time is purely logical: not only it does not have any relation with calendar time, but in general it can be neglected from the analysis, either because the focus is put on a stationary state (where endogenous variables are constant) or on a steady state (where the endogenous variables grow at a constant rate)[25] or because adjustments to equilibrium are assumed to be instantaneous. This static dimension results notably from the assumption of given resources. A typical illustration is provided by the model of Walras, where prices and quantities adjust instantaneously to equate supplies and demands in different markets and where the analysis remains static even after the introduction of capital goods (Graziani, 1965). In logical time, equilibrium can either be *intertemporal*, in the sense that the present and the future are collapsed into a single unit of time where it is admitted that a system of prices exists and can be found that clears all present and future market supply–demand balances, or *temporary*. In this case equilibrium involves only the clearing of current demand and supplies. Temporary equilibrium will coincide with the neoclassical one when it can be assumed that the given resources of capital available for optimization are the equilibrium ones (Schefold, 1997, p. 440, see also Petri, 1999, 2003 and 2004 and Garegnani, 2003). In general this assumption is implicitly retained in the temporary equilibrium literature, making time irrelevant. Another variant is that expectations, introduced for agents to be able to make their choice on the future, must be rational in order to reach the neoclassical equilibrium (see section 4.5).

Post Keynesian analysis refers to the 'classical' notion of 'production' or 'natural' prices. These are the prices that allow the economic system to reproduce itself either identically in each period or on an expanding path from one period to another. The equilibrium concept associated with 'production prices' is sometimes defined as a 'long-term' one and it is based on the uniformity between the rates of profit in different sectors: prices stop changing when all sectors in the economy generate the same rate of profit, in whatever way this common rate of profit is determined (Kurz and Salvadori, 1995, pp. 15–20). Apart from natural resources, there are no fixed 'factors of production' as all commodities can be produced and reproduced provided that the price system allows generating the surplus necessary to that effect (Gram and Walsh, 1980). Despite being sometimes developed in purely logical or static time, such as in Sraffa (1960),[26] the analysis is intrinsically dynamic: the existence of a positive surplus is the condition for the system to be viable and grow (Sylos Labini, 2004). In these models, the fact that either interest rates or real wages are exogenous implies a causality that goes from distribution to allocation, contrary to the neoclassical model where in equilibrium both are determined simultaneously. This is also true whether or not logical time is retained in the analysis. However, when production is viewed as taking place in sequential time, causality between distribution and allocation also implies causality between investment and savings.

4.4 Deterministic Causality between Investment and Savings

Following Robinson (1962), the idea that in the post Keynesian model time is 'historical' or dynamic was developed notably by Henry (1982a, 1991) who applied it to the field of international trade theory. Looking at the dynamic interaction between prices and quantities, starting from a model similar to the original one of Walras, Henry argued that in the post Keynesian model prices and quantities are set separately in time, with the causality running from quantities to prices,[27] or, what is the same, from investment to savings (Henry, 1982b).

For neoclassic analysis, out of equilibrium this causality goes instead from savings to investment: in order to achieve a higher level of economic activity, first savings should increase and then higher investment would follow. This mechanism applies also to the public sector and it underlies the fiscal policy arguments in favour of budget surpluses that have dominated EU policy since the beginning of the 1980s.[28] However, the argument is not entirely consistent as it tends to confuse equilibrium – when investment and savings are equalized by the interest rate, the resource constraint is binding and thus crowding out can in principle prevail but there is no causality possible due to simultaneity, and thus no *a priori* presumption that increased savings will lead anywhere – with disequilibrium – where exogenous households' tastes or government decisions can change and impact on savings independently from investment, but where the rationale for the causal link between savings and investment cannot be supported by neoclassical arguments. In both cases post Keynesian authors have demonstrated the neoclassical analysis runs into major logical contradictions (see for instance Graziani, 1994; Petri, 2003 and 2004). Moreover, a body of empirical analysis found that causality runs the other way round, from investment to savings (see for instance Gordon, 1995).[29]

In the post Keynesian literature in the tradition of Kaldor (1955–56) and Pasinetti (1962), the assumption of full utilization of capacity and full employment are retained. In this deterministic framework, 'the adjustment of saving to investment is envisaged to be effected via price changing relative to money wages and thus a redistribution of income between wages and profits or classes of income recipients' (Kurz and Salvadori, 2008, p. 1). The Keynesian causality of investment on savings under a steady state of full employment takes the form of a causality from the rate of growth of economic activity, which coincides with that of investment, to the rate of profit (corporate savings), the rate of growth being exogenously determined by technological progress and labour supply growth, like in Harrod (1948) (see also Steindl, 1985).

However, as noted by Panico (1997), the rate of profit could be influenced not only by the rate of growth, but also by the rate of interest, which in the endogenous money approaches is exogenously set by the monetary authority, in line with Sraffa's (1960) view that it is indeterminate.[30] From this point of view, Sraffa's model of production prices can be interpreted as a block of a larger model determining distribution for a given level of expected output. When this block is inserted in historical time, results similar to those of the monetary circuit obtain (see below section 6), where authorities can influence the path of growth of an economy through both interest rates, which impact distribution and inflation, and public expenditure, which affects mainly effective demand.[31]

4.5 Uncertainty and Causality between Investment and Savings

In a more general stochastic framework, causality from investment to savings becomes a causality between exogenous output expectations of producers and effective demand as determined by households' decisions on savings. If the model is 'non-ergodic' (category 6 in the typology of Samuelson presented above), expectations must necessarily be exogenous, since there is no way to render them meaningfully endogenous (Davidson, 1982–83). This implies that when the parameters of the model are not stationary, rational expectations (Muth, 1960) are impossible. Since rational expectations are a necessary condition for a temporary neoclassical equilibrium and are implicit in the definition of logical time used in the intertemporal version of the neoclassical model developed by Arrow–Debreu, this implies that in a fully dynamic setup there can be no neoclassical equilibrium with endogenous expectations but, on the contrary, expectations must be assumed to be exogenous and concur in the determination of equilibrium.[32] This is an important point to the extent that authors working along the lines of Lucas (1980), and other macro-monetarists associated with the Chicago School, claim that the wider generality of the neoclassical model rests on the fact that, thanks to the hypothesis of rational expectations, it can integrate as endogenous the formation of expectations,[33] whereas in fact in the more general dynamic models, that apply for instance in the case where there is technical progress and demand behaviour changes (see section 7.1), the absence of ergodicity is both the cause and the effect of having expectations exogenous. Since in an uncertain environment expectation must be exogenous, they are an explanation for the causality of investment on savings. The latter implies also that public investment creates the savings necessary to finance it (see section 6.1).[34]

More generally, if expectations cannot be rational, they must entail systematic errors on average and there is thus an intrinsic market failure associated with the impossibility of having a neoclassical equilibrium in a fully dynamic model, which also offers an *a priori* argument in favour of policy intervention. This is an example of what Guesnerie (2001, 2005) calls the 'expectational market failure' that it is the role of the government to correct, an idea that he traces back to Massé (1965) and that is also one of the main features of Parguez's (2008) model of the circuit (see section 6.4.2). The post Keynesian literature argues that, because of this expectational failure, effective demand cannot generally be expected to be the full-employment one. In such a disequilibrium setting, public investment can play a stabilizing role, independently from the way it is financed, if it contributes to the managing of Keynes's two-thirds of total investment necessary to keep market economies on a stable long-term growth path (Seccareccia, 1995).

5. INVESTMENT-SAVINGS CAUSALITY IN POST KEYNESIAN MODELS WITHOUT MONEY

This section presents two reference post Keynesian models in which distribution affects allocation through prices, with the latter being based on a variant of the full cost principle,[35] rather than on profit maximization. In this case, which corresponds to a disequilibrium in the neoclassical model, distribution impacts on allocation and therefore it is not possible to separate the two, contrary to what happens in the neoclassical model where distribution is studied assuming that optimal allocation has already been reached. Money is absent and technology is fixed. The models are steady state models.

5.1 The Model of Production Prices

Kurz and Salvadori (2003) present a model inspired from Sraffa (1960) with two commodities 'corn' *c* and 'iron' *i* which are both 'basic', meaning that they enter directly into the production of each other.[36] In this model the rate of profit is exogenous, but, as noted by the authors (p. 241), the model is also compatible with the post Keynesian analysis of distribution developed by Kaldor, Robinson and Pasinetti, that assumes that it is the rate of growth of investment demand that determines the rate of profit based on animal spirits. The technical features of the production processes are summarized in the table below, which presents the technical coefficients of production of a two-sector economy:

	Material Inputs		Labour		Outputs	
	Corn	Iron			Corn	Iron
Corn process	a_{cc}	a_{ci}	l_c	→	1	–
Iron process	a_{ic}	a_{ii}	l_i	→	–	1

where a_{cc} (a_{ci}) is the quantity of corn and l_c (l_i) the amount of labour necessary to produce a unit of corn (iron) and the arrows represent the production process. Let p_i be the price of one unit of iron in terms of corn (the price of corn in term of corn is 1). If the rate of profit is uniform and the wage is set to 0, the following equations define the unitary value balances of the production process:

$$(1 + R)a_{cc} + (1 + R)a_{ci}p_i = 1$$
$$(1 + R)a_{ic} + (1 + R)a_{ii}p_i = p_i$$

where R is the maximum rate of profits,[37] $p_i > 0$ and $R \geq 0$. It can be shown that the system above has a solution only if the economy is viable, that is if the economy is able to reproduce itself, which, defining Y_c and Y_i as the activity levels of the two processes, requires:

$$Y_c \geq Y_c a_{cc} + Y_i a_{ic}$$
$$Y_i \geq Y_c a_{ci} + Y_i a_{ii}$$
$$Y_c \geq 0, \quad Y_i \geq 0, \quad Y_c + Y_i > 0$$

It can also be shown that $R > 0$ if and only if the economy is able to produce a surplus and $R = 0$ if the economy is just viable. When the economy is viable and the rate of profit is less than the maximum rate R, it will set at a lower value $r \leq R$ corresponding to positive wages. The pricing equations become:

$$(1 + r)a_{cc} + (1 + r)a_{ci}p_i + wl_c = 1$$
$$(1 + r)a_{ic} + (1 + r)a_{ii}p_i + wl_i = p_i$$

where the wage rate w and the price of iron p_i are measured in terms of corn. For each given profit rate r below the maximum rate R (such that $0 \leq r \leq R$) the two equations above represent a linear system in p_i and w, which can be solved, bringing as solution for w and p_i an expression which is function of the technical coefficients and of the rate of profit r:

$$w = \frac{1 - (a_{ii} + a_{cc})(1 + r) + (a_{ii}a_{cc} - a_{ci}a_{ic})(1 + r)^2}{(1 + r)a_{ci}l_c + [1 - (1 + r)a_{ii}]l_c}$$

$$p_i = \frac{[1 - (1 + r)a_{cc}]l_i + (1 + r)a_{ic}l_c}{(1 + r)a_{ci}l_c + [1 - (1 + r)a_{ii}]l_c}$$

the first equation being known as the wage–profit or w–r relationship. It can be shown that:

1. if the rate of profit is comprised between −1 and the maximum rate R ($-1 \leq r \leq R$), wages w and prices p_i will be positive. If the rate of profit sets at its maximal value $r = R$, prices p_i are positive and wages nil ($w = 0$);
2. if the rate of profit is below its maximum value R and above −1 ($-1 < r < R$), there is a decreasing relation between wages and profits, the w–r relationship, which defines the trade-off between wages and profits once expected output is determined.

This model shows that, for given quantities, prices and wages depend on the rate of profit, which is set exogenously. This result, which can be extended to economies in which not all goods are basic, means that exogenous profits do not correspond necessarily to the marginal pricing rules, which would imply $r = 0$, and thus distribution between capital and labour can set market prices away from neoclassical equilibrium, and thus impact in the same way on allocation.[38] As noted previously, Henry (1991) showed how, in a model where quantities are not given, this notably implies that causality goes from quantity to prices and from investment to savings.

5.2 Kaleckian Models[39]

The simple Keynes–Kalecki macroeconomic model presented in this paragraph illustrates the causality between investment and savings in a non-monetary post Keynesian framework. It serves also to introduce the Kalecki identity of section 7.2. Consider a simplified Keynesian model completed with Kalecki's saving identity and price equation as the one presented below.

$$X = C + I \tag{1}$$

$$C = cX \tag{2}$$

$$I = \bar{I} \tag{3}$$

$$N = \frac{X}{\pi} \tag{4}$$

$$p = \frac{w}{\pi}(1 + q) \tag{5}$$

$$\frac{I}{X} = \frac{q}{1 + q} \tag{6}$$

$$W = wN \tag{7}$$

$$P = pX - W \tag{8}$$

$$U = L - E \tag{9}$$

The exogenous variables of the model are: $\bar{I}$, the quantity of investment I; c, the propensity to consume; π, the average labour productivity, w, the wage rate and L, the labour force. The model determines eight endogenous variables: consumption C; output X; employment N; price of output p; the mark-up q; the wage bill W, total profits P and unemployment U.

The Keynesian relations (1)–(3) allow obtaining the familiar expression of the traditional multiplier:

$$\begin{cases} X = C + 1 \\ C = cX \\ I = \bar{I} \end{cases} \rightarrow X = \frac{1}{1-c}\bar{I} \tag{a}$$

For the sector of enterprises as an aggregate costs are equal to the wage bill, because payments between firms cancel out. Average cost is obtained by dividing the wage bill by output, expressed by the simple linear production function (4). Average costs are thus equal to the ratio of wages to productivity.

$$Average\ cost = \frac{wN}{\pi N} = \frac{w}{\pi} \tag{b}$$

Relation (5) represents the price mark-up equation, where q is the mark-up in percentage over average costs w/π and reflects the assumption that out-of-equilibrium enterprises can realize positive profits, which they integrate in their pricing.[40] It implies that the wage share in national income is:

$$\frac{W}{pX} = \frac{wN}{p\pi N} = \frac{w}{p\pi} = \frac{1}{1+q} \tag{c}$$

From which the share of profits is:

$$\frac{P}{pX} = 1 - \frac{1}{1+q} = \frac{q}{1+q} \tag{d}$$

Relation (6) expresses Kalecki's identity in a model that assumes that investments are financed out of profits only, hence capitalists own fully the capital goods they use.[41] It expresses that, having decided to invest an amount $\bar{I}$, firms also fix the mark-up in order to create enough profits to finance investment. From (c) and (d) one gets:

$$W = wN = \frac{pX}{1+q} = \frac{P^*}{q} \tag{e}$$

Relation (e) links the wage bill to profits, which, in the post Keynesian equilibrium, will have to be set to a value P^* that covers investment. It shows the role of the inverse of the mark-up, which is Parguez's (2008, 2009) version of the multiplier of profits on employment given the wage rate. This is seen more clearly when (e) is solved for employment:

$$N = \frac{W}{w} = \frac{P^*}{wq} \tag{f}$$

which shows that by deciding the breakdown of total output between consumption and investment and thus targeting the necessary level of profits, producers also define the level of employment that, given exogenous wages and a target rate of return, cannot be expected to be the full-employment level $N = L$, generally being below and generating an unemployment of U given by (9).[42]

A numerical illustration can help in fixing ideas. Assume an economy where the active population is 250 people. Technology is such that four people are needed to produce one unit of output. Wage is at its exogenous subsistence level of 0.4. The share of output consumed (propensity to consume) is 0.80. In this economy if producers target a level of nominal investment of 20, equal to profits, they must set the mark-up in real terms at 25 per cent. For this level of investment, output is at 50, GDP at 100 and the level of employment at 200, leaving 50 people (20 per cent of the labour force) unemployed. By increasing investment progressively to 12, unemployment can be reduced to 4 per cent. This 'comparative dynamics' result, which emerges from the comparison of two steady states, shows that where the causality from private investment to corporate profits prevails, as it is the case in the Kaleckian variant of the post Keynesian model (and thus out of the neoclassical equilibrium), more investment would generate more employment. This cannot happen in the neoclassical model, which assumes full employment from the start and where therefore more investment means less consumption and thus less employment. In this context, the starting unemployment rate of 20 per cent would be considered as the 'natural' one and, by definition, an economic profitability calculation based on market prices would result in no further investment, failing to take into account the welfare gain associated with a decrease of the unemployment rate from 20 per cent to 4 per cent. The latter corresponds to an increase in employment from 200 to 240, the welfare value of which, valued at the starting wage rate of 0.4, is 16, that is, four times the necessary increase in investment. If an external actor such as the State would intervene to realize this increase in investment of 4, this could be paid entirely out of a tax on profits, with the latter still increasing by a net amount of 12.

The model above illustrates Kalecki's identity in its simplest form, where investment is equal to profits and it is entirely realized by the private sector.[43] As noted by Robinson (1977), in this form the identity makes clear that profits are determined by savings. The identity can be generalized to situations where both the State and the external sectors exist (section 7.2).

6. MONETARY EQUILIBRIA IN THE APPROACH OF THE CIRCUIT

In the post Keynesian model examined in real terms, section 5 has shown that when technology is given, out of the neoclassical equilibrium causality goes from investment to savings. Keeping technology fixed, this section shows that the introduction of endogenous money and banks in a sequential model allows for a simple explanation of this investment to savings causality, symmetrical to the causality of loans on deposits. As shown in section 6.3, by making the relation between banks and the rest of the private sector explicit, the monetary circuit illustrates the monetary causes of unemployment. It will be seen in section 7.1 that, once structural change is also taken into account in a multi-sectoral model,[44] it is very unlikely that full employment will prevail, even without money.

6.1 Macroeconomic Aspect of Money in a Sequential Model

Frank Hahn noted the inconsistencies in the microeconomic treatment of money in a book he edited in 1965, which also contained the famous article by Clower quoted above. Grandmont (1983) discussed several shortcomings of the neoclassical model when money is introduced from a 'rationing' perspective. But it was Parguez (1969, 1975, 1977)[45] who developed thoroughly the argument that the introduction of money necessarily breaks down the neoclassical equilibrium, in which, when it exists, money is a veil spread out on a barter equilibrium. True monetary equilibria correspond to what in neoclassical analysis is a disequilibrium, and are thus of a more general nature.

The theory of the monetary circuit integrates in sequential time[46] the theory of distribution of Kalecki (1942), which gives an important role to the mark-up in the pricing decision, with the monetary analysis developed by Keynes in the *Treatise* (1930) and, given some different assumptions, also in the *General Theory* (1936). As such it can be seen as illustrating a monetary variant of post Keynesian analysis that retains the essential aspect of money endogeneity underlined by Kaldor and Trevithick (1992). The links between the circuit and post Keynesian theory are developed in Lavoie (1992, ch. 4), Deleplace and Nell (1996) and Rochon (1999).

In the circuit money is a flow and not a stock, as it is in the monetarist and in most of the neo-Keynesian approaches. It is defined as a liability created by the banking system in favour of a borrower in exchange for his promise to repay back a loan. The liability issued by a third party is more liquid and generally accepted by the public than the original promise to pay back the loan by the borrower himself, which does not circulate and is not accepted by parties external to the original transaction as a mean of payment.

The macroeconomic aspect of money derives from its definition as a liability issued by a third party (the banking sector), which implies the rejection of the neoclassical individualism.[47] The explicit recognition of the banking sector as a producer of money is an original feature of the monetary circuit, which allows for a full integration of banks in macro-policy analyses. Money is one of the reasons for a *fallacy of composition*:[48] its presence breaks one or several of the conditions necessary for the aggregation of microeconomic neoclassical equilibria (see Malinvaud, 1956). It is possibly in view of this aspect that Hahn (2003) came to suggest that there could be 'macroeconomic foundations for micro-economics', paradoxically taking a position not far from a circuitist like Cencini (2006). Indeed, as Parguez came to assert more recently, money is the instrument that, by transferring liquidity and purchasing power from one period to another, allows disequilibria to be sustainable as long as producers' expectations are validated by the banking sector. It is thus an essential macroeconomic condition for economic agents to realize their expectations.

The analysis of the circuit focuses on how money is created and destroyed. Given the rejection of micro-based approaches, the conditions of its creation and its destruction are analysed at the level of macro-sectors.[49] Not all sectors have equal access to money newly created: there is a hierarchy amongst them, which, in a closed economy with a separate central bank, is as follows:

1. the Central Bank, creates 'external money', it can provide any amount of it that is requested by the Central State or by the private banking sector by extending them advances;
2. the commercial banking sector is the supplier of 'internal money'. It gets whatever amounts of 'external money' it needs from the Central Bank and can thus supply any quantity of money requested by the non-financial producers' sector (corporate sector or 'firms') once it accepts to validate their bets on the future;
3. non-financial enterprises establish their production and employment plans as a function of their perception of the future and, given the banking sector's readiness to share this vision, they fix consequently their demand for credit money, which creates the deposits used to pay revenues (salaries and profits);
4. households supply labour and receive revenues, which they consume or save.

Whereas the State and commercial banks' capacity to issue new money is in principle unrestricted (at least at the level of the consolidated banking system, see Graziani, 1990), the possibility for enterprises to create money is subordinated to the validation by banks of their production plans, whereas households' revenues are limited by the decisions of banks and firms. To the extent that households keep part of their savings in cash, firms cannot recover all revenues they have put into circulation and in general cannot repay in full the loan they have taken from banks, which must thus provide them with new credits. There is an infinity of possible equilibria corresponding to the various conditions at which banks accept to revalidate the enterprises' bets, the most simple being that where enterprises' debt is constant, either in absolute terms or in a proportion of their revenues.

6.2 The Phases of the Circuit in Sequential Time

The triangular definition of money requires considering at least three macro-sectors: producers, consumers and the banking sector, a framework corresponding to the so-called *pure credit economy* of Wicksell, where there is no State and the banking sector is consolidated in a single bank which, to simplify further, is assumed to make no profits. This simplified framework will be used below to illustrate the functioning of the circuit, where flow money is created and destroyed in sequential time, in parallel with the needs of production.

6.2.1 Initial finance

The balance sheets of the three sectors of this economy (Enterprises, Households and Banks) show their assets, liabilities and net worth at a given moment in historical time. The circuit starts at the time $t = 0$ when enterprises ask the banks for a loan L_0 to finance the purchase of fixed and circulating capital necessary to start production. To underline the role of money in production, it is assumed that before that, at time -1, all sectors had zero balance sheets, as shown in Table 3.1, Panel BS 1, (BS = Balance Sheet). The consolidated banking sector[50] finances the loan by issuing deposits D_0 in an amount that matches the credit granted. Obviously, as a counterpart, Enterprises have deposits D_0 in their assets that are matched by a liability L_0 towards the banking sector.[51]

Initially the transaction is purely financial. Money is created by banks at the request of firms to start production ('endogenously') but no production has started yet and no real wealth has been created.

Table 3.1 Changes in assets and liabilities

Sequential Time	Panel BS-1					
	Enterprises		Banks		Households	
	Assets	Liabilities & NW	Assets	Liabilities & NW	Assets	Liabilities & NW
−(1)	0	0	0	0	0	0
(0)	+ D_0 Deposit	+ L_0 Bank Debt	+ L_0 Loan to E	+ D_0 Deposit to E	0	0
Sequential Time	**Panel T-1**					
	Enterprises		Banks		Households	
	Δ assets	Δ Liabilities & NW	Δ assets	Δ Liabilities & NW	Δ assets	Δ Liabilities & NW
(0–1)	− W_1 deposits + ΔWK_{1e} due from H − INV_1 deposits + ΔWIP_{1e} due from E + INV_1 deposits	+ ΔWIP_{1e} due to E		− W_1 Deposit of E + W_1 deposit of H	+ W_1 deposit	+ ΔRL_{1h} due to E

Source: own elaboration.

6.2.2 Revenue formation

Real value creation takes place in a second step of the circuit, when revenues (salaries and profits) are created for the payment of the services of labour and capital. In the jargon of the circuit it is at this time that money acquires value as it was previously a pure number in the balance sheet of the banking sector. By assumption, the payment of revenues takes place at the beginning of the production period, when enterprises also decide on the distribution of the new money between wages and profits through their pricing decision, which fixes the level of the mark-up.

6.2.2.1 Salaries Graziani (1994) noted that in the classical tradition, in which money is absent, the payment of salaries in kind takes place at the beginning of the production period and is financed out of previously accumulated real savings. This explains the classical causality between savings and investment (in fixed and circulating capital). On the contrary, in the neoclassical model salaries are paid at the end of the production period (except in the variant of Wicksell), because only at that time is it possible to determine the marginal productivity of labour, to which they must be brought equal. Hence in the neoclassical model there is no explanation for the causality from savings to investment, which in general is presumed to hold out of equilibrium. By retaining the classical hypothesis that salaries are paid at the beginning of the production period, but introducing the finance motive as a determinant of money demand by enterprises, the circuit offers an explanation of the Keynesian causality from investment to savings that is exactly symmetrical to the causality from loans to deposits retained by the Banking School.[52]

6.2.2.2 Profits If enterprises do not spend on salaries the entire amount of money that they have borrowed (D_0), a part of this liquidity will remain in their accounts as an anticipated financing of investment and profits. In connection in particular with the payment of interest (Segura, 1995), there has been a debate in the circuit literature on whether profits give rise to a monetary creation, are realized in money at a later stage of the circuit or represent an accumulation of real assets. If newly created money finances only salaries, profits can potentially never be transformed into money and the monetary circuit can provide support to a labour theory of value. In particular Bellofiore (1989) argued that this reading of the circuit can solve the problem of transformation of value into prices, and thus provide an explanation for exploitation, an unresolved issue in Marxian economic theory. Parguez (2004) has considered sympathetically the argument of Lavoie (1987) against the monetization of profits, but finally took position against what he calls the 'wage postulate'. His position will be followed here that profits are financed, at least partially, from new money creation.[53]

6.2.2.3 Changes in assets and liabilities Revenue formation can be described by looking at the variation of assets and liabilities between instant 0 and instant 1, a period of time noted '0–1' on the left of Table 3.1, Panel T-1.[54] The payment of salaries (W_1) decreases liquid holdings of enterprises and increases those of the households. This is matched by a real liability of households for the working time to be provided in the course of the period (ΔRL_{1h}), which corresponds to a real working capital claim in the assets for enterprises (ΔWK_{1e}). For the same reason and to be consistent with the anticipated payment of profits, some enterprises accumulate a work in progress capital asset (ΔWIP_{1e}) paid for an amount $INV1$, whereas others receive this payment and have as a real liability the obligation to deliver this asset.

As shown in Table 3.2, Panel BS-2, after the payment of revenues, enterprises keep a net liquid holding of D_{e1}, which corresponds to money initially created less that paid for salaries ($D_0 - W_1$), whereas some enterprises have a work in progress claim and others a corresponding liability.

The payment of salaries does not change the quantity of money in circulation, that is the liquid liabilities of the banking sector (D_0), for which only payments between sectors are shown. It only moves part of it (W_1) from the account of enterprises to that of households. For households deposits of W_1 are compensated by a real liability towards enterprises (R_{L1h}).

6.2.3 Production and consumption

In the next stage of the circuit production takes place. As shown in Table 3.2, Panel T-2, which covers the period between instants 1 and 2, for investing enterprises the Work In Progress claim ΔWIP_{2e} disappears and becomes a real capital accumulation ΔFA_2, which corresponds to the amount of investment I realized in the period. At the same time, for capital goods suppliers, the real obligation to deliver capital goods leaves room for the realization of a profit in the form of an increase in net worth ΔNW_{e2}.

The claim on households for working hours due (WK_{1e}) is replaced by the accumulation of a stock of finished consumption goods (WK_{e2}). These are sold to households for a money amount D_{h2}. This payment is the only movement in the account of the banking sector and it is compensated in the accounts of household by the reduction of their real liabilities towards enterprises ΔRL_{2h}.

Table 3.2 Production and consumption

Sequential Time	Panel BS-2					
	Enterprises		Banks		Households	
	Assets	Liabilities & NW	Assets	Liabilities & NW	Assets	Liabilities & NW
(1)	WK_{1e} $(=\Delta WK_{1e})$ WIP_{1e} $(=\Delta WIP_{1e})$ D_{e1} deposits $(=D_0 - W_1)$	L_0 Bank Debt WIP_{1e} $(=\Delta WIP_{1e})$	$+ L_0$ loan to E	D_{e1} deposits to E $(=D_{e0} - W_1)$ D_{h1} deposits to H $(= W_1)$ $\Sigma = D_0$ deposits	$+ W_1$ deposit	RL_{1h} $(=\Delta RL_{1h})$

Sequential Time	Panel T-2					
	Enterprises		Banks		Households	
	Δ assets	Δ Liabilities & NW	Δ assets	Δ Liabilities & NW	Δ assets	Δ Liabilities & NW
(1–2)	$-\Delta WIP_{2e}$ $+\Delta FA_2$ $(=I)$ $-\Delta Wk_{e1}$ $+\Delta Wk_{e2}$ $-\Delta WK_{e2}$ $+\Delta D_{h2}$ deposit	$-\Delta WIP_{2e}$ $+\Delta NW_{e2}$		$-\Delta D_{h2}$ deposit to H $+\Delta D_{h2}$ deposit to E	$-\Delta D_{h2}$ deposit	$-\Delta RL_{2h}$

Source: own elaboration.

At the end of the production and consumption stage, the resulting balance sheets are shown in Table 3.3, Panel BS-3. Enterprises have liquid assets in an amount D_{e2}, which have increased by the amount of sales of consumption goods to households ΔD_{h2} compared to Table 3.2, Panel BS-2. They have also accumulated real capital goods assets for an amount I, which corresponds to their net worth, and they keep all their debt to the banking sector. Households have paid ΔD_{h2} deposits for buying the consumption goods and retain an amount of deposits D_{h2}, which is equal to the part of their wages they have not used for consumption ($= W_1 - \Delta D_{h2}$), and thus corresponds to savings, supposed initially to be kept in liquid form. The amount of money in circulation is still the same (D_0), as shown by the liability side of the banking sector balance sheet, but it has now come back in majority in the assets of enterprises.

However, due to the savings kept in liquid form by households, enterprises have not recovered all the money they have initially borrowed from banks and put into circulation: there is thus a leakage from the circuit corresponding to the savings of households.

6.2.4 Final finance

As shown in Table 3.3, Panel T-3, in the third and final phase of the circuit enterprises attempt to recover households' savings by issuing bonds for an amount B_e, which they sell to households against an amount D_{h3} of deposits. All money recovered by enterprises through sales (D_{e2}) or through the capital market (D_{h3}) is used to repay the loan back to the banks, which destroys an equal amount of money ($D_{e2} + D_{h3}$). To the extent that households do not spend all their savings in the acquisition of the bond issued by enterprises, they keep a part of these in liquid form.

As shown by the final balance sheet position of the three sectors in Table 3.3, Panel BS-4, at the end of the circuit, enterprises have increased their real assets of I. They remain indebted towards banks for an amount L_3 ($=L_0 - D_{e2} - D_{h3}$), while they also have a debt towards households of B_e. To the extent that the value of their assets exceeds these cumulated debts, they have accumulated profits, which have in the end created a net worth NW_e. Households remain with liquid holdings of D_{h4} and financial assets of B_e, corresponding to the net worth created. The liability side of the banking sector balance sheet shows that the amount of money in circulation is now reduced to the cash holdings of households D_{h4}, which banks are supposed to immediately lend again to enterprises (L_3) and that is transferred to the following period.

Kalecki's identity[55] is fulfilled: the accumulation of fixed assets I is balanced by enterprises' profits, NWE, and households savings (final finance), which are in part held as securities (B_e) and in part as deposits

Table 3.3 *Final finance*

Sequential Time	Panel BS-3					
	Enterprises		Banks		Households	
	Assets	Liabilities & NW	Assets	Liabilities & NW	Assets	Liabilities & NW
(2)	D_{e2} deposits (=$D_{e1} + \Delta D_{h2}$) I fixed Assets	NW_{e2} (=ΔNW_{e2}) L_0 Bank Debt	+ L_0 loan to E	D_{e2} deposits to E D_{h2} to H $\Sigma = D_0$ deposits	D_{h2} deposits (=$W_1 - \Delta D_{h2}$)	S_2 savings

Sequential Time	Panel T-3					
	Enterprises		Banks		Households	
	Δ assets	Δ Liabilities & NW	Δ assets	Δ Liabilities & NW	Δ assets	Δ Liabilities & NW
(2–3)	$-D_{e2}$ deposits	$-D_{e2}$ Bank Debt	$-D_{e2} - D_{h3}$ Loan	$-D_{h3}$ deposits to H	$-D_{h3}$ deposits	
	+ D_{h3} deposits	+ B_e bond to H		+ D_{h3} deposits to E	+ B_e Bond from E	
	$-D_{h3}$ deposits	$-D_{h3}$ Bank debt		$-D_{e2} - D_{h3}$ deposits		

Sequential Time	Panel BS-4					
	Enterprises		Banks		Households	
	Assets	Liabilities & NW	Assets	Liabilities & NW	Assets	Liabilities & NW
(3)	I Fixed assets	L_3 Debt to B (= $L_0 - D_{e2} - D_{h3}$) B_e Bond to H NWE Net worth	L_3 loan to E (=$L_0 - D_{e2} - D_{h3}$)	D_{h4} deposits to H (=$D_0 - D_{e2} - D_{h3}$) (Stock of money transferred to next period)	D_{h4} deposits (=$W_1 - D_{h2} - D_{h3}$) B_e Bond	NW_{h3} Net Worth of H ($D_{h4} + B_e$)

Source: own elaboration.

(D_{h4}). The latter corresponds to a debt of enterprises towards banks which is transferred to the next period.

6.3 A Formalization of the Financial and Labour Market Equilibria

The model of the circuit presented in this section, taken from Graziani (2003, ch. 6), points at the financial equilibrium between firms and banks as a possible cause for unemployment and formalizes the basic properties of monetary equilibria illustrated in the previous section.[56] The notations are:

Z = total monetary base
Z_B = legal tender held by banks
Z_P = legal tender held by the public
D = deposits
r = reserve ratio of commercial banks
β = ratio of legal tender to deposits
L = loans
S = households' savings
M^o = liquid balance from previous period
W = money wage rate
c, s = propensities to consume and save
N = employment
i_D = interest on bank deposits
i_L = interest on bank loans
i_B = interest rate on securities
B^d = demand for securities
b^d, b^s = fraction of savings placed in securities
B^o = securities held at the beginning of the period

Households have the choice between investing their financial savings in banks' deposits D or in firms' securities B. In the money market banks pay an interest i_D to households for their deposits. In the financial market firms pay interest i_b on securities to savers and in the loan market firms pay interest i_L to banks. Assume that at the beginning of the period producers as a whole request loans $L_{(1)}$ only to finance wages and their residual debt M^0, which corresponds to the pre-existing money stock. Then:[57]

$$L_{(1)} = M^0 + wN_{(1)} \tag{g}$$

The balance sheet identity of the banking sector requires that new loans refinance old ones plus the new liquidity needs arising from production:

$$Z_{P(1)} + D_{(1)} = \frac{1+\beta}{r} Z_{B(1)} = M^0 + wN_{(1)} \quad \text{(h)}$$

after some substitutions it results that the liquidity in existence immediately after the wage bill has been paid and before households take their expenditure and saving decisions depends strictly on the wage bill and therefore on the decisions of producers on the level of output[58]

$$Z_{B(1)} = \frac{r}{1+\beta}(M^0 + wN_{(1)}) \quad \text{(i)}$$

In an economy without a State, as the one considered here, money in existence cannot be a debt of the State to the Central Bank, as money is usually defined in neoclassical and neo-Keynesian monetary approaches, but only a debt of firms to the banking system. However, the existence of this debt implies that enterprises can spend more than what they earn, something which in a strict neoclassical framework would be indicative of a disequilibrium. At the same time, once debt is allowed, there is no obvious equilibrium amount of it. Even in a stationary economy, constancy of firm debt is not necessarily a requirement for equilibrium since for instance in the case of an increase in liquidity preference of the public β the money stock and debts of firms towards banks must increase. The equilibrium thus depends on the banks' willingness to provide firms with the required lending and on the possible reaction of firms to an increase in interest to be paid on loans.

Banks and firms compete in attracting the savings of households through interest rates they pay respectively on deposits and firms' securities. Once they have taken the consumption decision, households divide their savings between an increase in liquid holdings dM^d and an increase in holding of securities issued by firms dB^d. It is assumed that the purchase of new securities is a fraction b^d of total savings that is an increasing function of the interest paid on securities and a decreasing function of the interest paid on deposits. Then:

$$S = (1 - c)wN = dM^d + dB^d f \quad \text{(j)}$$

$$dM^d = (1 + b^d)(1 - c)wN \quad \text{(k)}$$

$$b^d = b^d(i_B/i_D) \quad \text{(l)}$$

The demand for securities at the end of the period (indicated by the subscript (2)), which includes the amount of securities B^0 held at the beginning of the period, can thus be defined as:

$$B^d_{(2)} = B^0 + b^d(i_B/i_D)(1 - c)wN \tag{m}$$

On the other hand, the supply of securities at the end of the period will be a fraction b^s of total savings that is a decreasing function of the interest paid on securities i_B and an increasing function of the interest paid on bank loans i_L:

$$B^s_{(2)} = B^0 + b^s(i_L/i_B)(1 - c)wN \tag{n}$$

The equilibrium value of the fraction of savings placed in securities will be determined by the condition:

$$b^d(i_B/i_D) = b^s(i_L/i_B) \tag{o}$$

Since there are three unknowns the equilibrium condition can only determine one of the three as a function of the two others. The bank debt of producers outstanding at the end of the period will equal the debt at the beginning of the period minus the amount of new securities issued by producers and sold to savers:

$$L_{(2)} = M^0 + wN - b(1 - c)wN = M^0 + [1 - b(1 - c)]wN \tag{p}$$

If producers considers themselves in equilibrium only once their debt is constant, this means that the money stock is also constant. In this case, enterprises capture all savings through bonds and:

$$b^d(i_B/i_D) = b^s(i_L/i_B) = 1 \tag{q}$$

If, for example it is assumed that the rate on deposits i_D is known (say = 0), then the ratio i_L/i_B determines the constancy of the money stock. As shown by the graphical example developed by Graziani (2003, p. 127) the model illustrates that there can be a financial equilibrium between bank and firms that is not an equilibrium in the labour market. In other terms:

> for full equilibrium to be attained, two different conditions must be satisfied. The first is the usual Keynesian condition that the interest rate and the corresponding level of investment be such as to generate a full-employment level of activity. The second is that a financial equilibrium between banks and firms prevail. The second condition is often neglected in macroeconomic analysis since, as already remarked, in most macroeconomic models, banks and firms are merged in one single sector. (Graziani, 2003, p. 128)

6.4 Remarks

6.4.1 Causality between investment and savings

The money that is not destroyed by loan repayment after consumptions and bond issuance by producers remains in the system and 'creates' the savings necessary to complete the final financing of investment in fixed capital (accumulation of real assets). The various steps of the circuit thus provide a monetary explanation for the post Keynesian causality of investment on savings or, as Eichner and Kregel (1975, p. 1301) have put it, between discretionary expenditures and discretionary income: 'it is the discretionary income (savings) that will necessarily have to adjust to the level of discretionary expenditures (investment) and not *vice versa*.'

6.4.2 Dynamic effects of diverging private sector expectations

To the extent that enterprises failed to anticipate the amount of actual households' savings, they will sell less than expected and will thus revise downwards their sales' expectations for the following periods. This will in turn reduce effective demand in the next round of the circuit, when employment will be possibly reduced as well, causing increased unemployment and therefore increased risk aversion of households. The latter will increase their savings accordingly and particularly their demand for liquidity, which in the end increases the savings leakage from the circuit. In these circumstances only an external intervention, in the form of increased expenditures from the State or the foreign sector, could stop this contraction spiral and reestablish a positive business climate.

6.4.3 Monetary and barter economy equilibria

Any configuration of private (or public) sector expectations, reflected in the amount of money requested for financing private (or public) investment, is causal and thus exogenous in determining the resulting level of economic activity and of employment in the monetary circuit as long as it is validated by the banking sector through new loans. As discussed with reference to a formal model of the circuit in section 6.3, there is no obvious way to define monetary equilibria in the circuit. Since there are no profit maximization, zero profit conditions, marginal distribution relations and so on, this monetary equilibrium is different from the neoclassical one that would prevail in a barter economy and thus corresponds to what neoclassical analysis would call a disequilibrium. Moreover, there is no reason to presume that the monetary equilibrium obtained should be a full employment one.

6.4.4 Integration of the public sector

The illustration of the monetary circuit based on the pure credit economy given above can be easily adapted to an economy where the State is present.[59] If enterprises are replaced by the State and the consolidated banking sector by the Central Bank, the same argument can be developed: money is created at the request of the State by the Central Bank, represents the liquidity necessary to finance public expenditure and it is destroyed when taxes are paid. The idea was already clearly expressed in the following passage of Kalecki ([1935] 1990):

> Let us assume that the Government issues treasury bills and sells them to banks. The Government spends the money, e.g. on the construction of railways. As in the cases described above, employment in investment goods industries increases, and subsequently, as a result of the higher purchasing power of workers, in consumer goods as well. The amounts spent by the Government flow as profits directly or through spending of the workers into the pockets of capitalists, and return to the banks as their deposits. On the side of bank assets, the government debt accrues in the form of discounted bills; on the side of liabilities, there is an increase in deposits equal to the additional profits. Thus the Government becomes indebted, via banks, to the private capitalists by an amount equal to the investment effected. . . . It should be emphasized that the pattern of public investment taken up is not essential for the effect of government intervention; what matters is that investment should be financed by additional purchasing power.

An empirical confirmation of the causality between public expenditure and growth can be found in Giovannoni (2006) and Giovannoni and Parguez (2007) who investigated econometrically the macroeconomic identities of the national accounts for the US and concluded that government expenditures are strongly exogenous, that is, they are the drivers of the American business cycle.

6.4.5 Nominal or real wealth creation (good or bad credits)

When the banks confirm that the value of the asset created has sufficient profitability, they validate the solvability of the borrower with a new loan that will be repaid back in the future. The good credit is thus the one that creates liquidity having as a counterpart the creation of real wealth (in the form of present or future consumption). The bad credit is the one that creates liquidity without having a balancing real asset as a counterpart and that thus creates a net liability that one day the banking system will be no longer able to refinance. This implies that, to be successful, Keynesian policies should be oriented towards real wealth creation and not extra profit or rent financing (Renaud, 2000).

7. POST KEYNESIAN AND MONETARY EQUILIBRIA WITH STRUCTURAL CHANGE

In sections 2 to 6, the models presented assumed constant technology. In this section two post Keynesian models are presented that apply to situations with technical change.

7.1 The Post Keynesian Dynamic Condition for Full-Employment

Pasinetti (2007, p. 278) argued that there is a common 'foundational framework' for the works of the Cambridge UK post Keynesian economists (Richard Kahn, Joan Robinson, Nicholas Kaldor and Piero Sraffa). It can be illustrated in its simplest form in the framework of a pure labour economy, that is an economy where production requires only labour. In the simplified scheme,[60] the economy is portrayed by a linear technology of the input–output type. There are m sectors.[61] Sectoral consumption per capita, labour demand and total population are exogenous and grow at constant exponential rates ρ_i, r_i, different in each sector, and g. These exogenous rates drive the structural dynamics of the model:

Exogenous factors

Labour coefficients	$l_i(t) = l_i(0)e^{-\rho_i t}$	$i = 1, \ldots, m$
Per capita consumption	$c_i(t) = c_i(0)e^{-r_i t}$	$i = 1, \ldots, m$
Population	$N(t) = N(0)e^{-gt}$	
Structural dynamics	$\rho_i \neq \rho_j, \quad r_i \neq r_j, \quad r_i \neq \rho_j, \quad \left.\begin{matrix}\rho_i \\ r_i \\ g\end{matrix}\right\} \begin{matrix}\geq \\ <\end{matrix} 0$	

The physical quantity system is given in matrix form by:

$$\begin{bmatrix} 1 & 0 & \cdots & 0 & \cdots & 0 & -c_1(t) \\ 0 & 1 & \cdots & 0 & \cdots & 0 & -c_2(t) \\ \vdots & \vdots & \ddots & \vdots & \ddots & \vdots & \vdots \\ 0 & 0 & \cdots & 1 & \cdots & 0 & -c_i(t) \\ \vdots & \vdots & & \vdots & & \vdots & \vdots \\ 0 & 0 & \cdots & 0 & \cdots & 1 & -c_m(t) \\ -l_1(t) & -l_2(t) & \cdots & -l_3(t) & \cdots & -l_m(t) & \mu(t)\nu(t) \end{bmatrix} \begin{bmatrix} Q_1(t) \\ Q_2(t) \\ \vdots \\ Q_i(t) \\ \vdots \\ Q_m(t) \\ N(t) \end{bmatrix} = \begin{bmatrix} 0 \\ 0 \\ \vdots \\ 0 \\ \vdots \\ 0 \\ 0 \end{bmatrix}$$

Where:

$N(t)$ = total population
$l_i(t)$ = labour coefficients
$c_i(t)$ = per capita consumption
m = number of production sectors
n = $m + 1$
t = time
g = rate of growth of population
ρ = rate of growth of labour productivity in sector i
r_i = rate of change of per capita consumption of commodity i

The commodity price system is given by:

$$\begin{bmatrix} 1 & 0 & \cdots & 0 & \cdots & 0 & -l_1(t) \\ 0 & 1 & \cdots & 0 & \cdots & 0 & -l_2(t) \\ \vdots & \vdots & \ddots & \vdots & \ddots & \vdots & \vdots \\ 0 & 0 & \cdots & 1 & \cdots & 0 & -l_i(t) \\ \vdots & \vdots & & \vdots & & \vdots & \vdots \\ 0 & 0 & \cdots & 0 & \cdots & 1 & -l_m(t) \\ -c_1(t) & -c_2(t) & \cdots & -c_3(t) & \cdots & -c_m(t) & \mu(t)\nu(t) \end{bmatrix} \begin{bmatrix} p_1(t) \\ p_2(t) \\ \vdots \\ p_i(t) \\ \vdots \\ p_m(t) \\ w(t) \end{bmatrix} = \begin{bmatrix} 0 \\ 0 \\ \vdots \\ 0 \\ \vdots \\ 0 \\ 0 \end{bmatrix}$$

Where:

$Q_i(t)$ = physical quantities of produced commodities
$Q_n(t) = \mu(t)\ \nu(t)\ N(t)$ = total quantity of labour to be employed
m = number of production sectors
μ = proportion of active to total population
ν = proportion of working time to total time
$p_i(t)$ = natural commodity prices
$w(t)$ = wage rate.

When the exogenous factors are set, the quantity and price closed Leontief models determine the evolution of quantities produced and prices over time. The two systems of equations being linear and homogeneous, a condition for their solution is that the determinant of the relevant matrix is zero. This condition is given by:

$$\frac{1}{\mu(t)\nu(t)}\sum_{i=1}^{m} c_i(t)\ell_i(t) - 1 = \frac{1}{\mu(t)\nu(t)}\sum_{i=1}^{m} c_0\ell_0 e^{(r_i-\rho_i)t} - 1 = 0 \qquad \text{(r)}$$

which is also the aggregate condition for full employment and for the full use of expenditure. Each addendum in the condition above, $(c_i\ell_i 1/\mu\nu)$ expresses at the same time the proportion of total employment in sector i and the proportion of total demand for the outputs of sector i. The sum of all these proportions must be unity to ensure full employment. Condition (r) thus expresses the idea that the totality of national income must be spent as required by Keynes's principle of effective demand in order to reach full employment. It can be noted that in a pure labour model such as the one retained in this simplified presentation, total income (wages) must be spent on consumption goods and there are no aggregate savings.

As noted by Roncaglia (2009, pp. 146–7), Pasinetti's approach provides a normative condition. Condition (r) makes clear that nothing ensures that the overall availability of labour and the sum of sectoral employment demands will be kept equal to each other in an actual economy. For any sector two opposite forces are at work in any point of time: technology, which modifies l_i, and effective demand, which changes c_i. In general the two do not match, hence there is constantly a change in the sectoral rate of employment ε_i:

$$\varepsilon_i = g + r_i - \rho_i \gtreqless 0 \qquad \text{(s)}$$

implying expulsions or absorptions of labour in the sector depending on the sign of ε_i. These sectoral employment balances do not necessarily compensate at the macroeconomic level, even taking into account possible changes in the number of sectors. When the system is out of full employment the first m conditions expressed by the price and quantity system continue to hold, thus in the end quantity produced is less than at full employment and total expenditure is less than full employment, which is likely to be the most frequent situation most of the time, unless corrective policy action is taken.[62]

7.2 Kalecki's Identity

The model in section 5.2 presented Kalecki's saving identity in its most simple variant, which asserts that investment is equal to producer profits (or savings). The identity is central as it defines the balances that are used by the macroeconomic sectors in the acquisition and disposal of financial assets.[63] It is valid independently of any assumption on technology and applies both to a monetary and a non-monetary economy. In a more general case, five institutional sectors can be distinguished: households h, domestic producers p, the State g, banks b and the foreign sector f. Therefore taking S as net financial savings and P as net profits, the identity can be written as:

$$P_p = D_g - S_h - S_b - S_f \qquad \text{(t)}$$

where:

P_p = Net profit of domestic producers (accumulation of financial surplus)
D_g = State deficit (increase in net State financial liabilities)
S_h = Net acquisition (sale) of financial assets by households (opposite of the net increase in households financial liabilities)
S_b = Net interest revenue (profit) of banks (accumulation of financial surplus)
S_f = Net saving of the foreign sector (balance of payments current account deficit on goods and services with negative sign)

Alternative presentations and more detailed discussions of Kalecki's identity can be found in Minsky ([1980] 1982), Steindl (1982), Parguez (2008, 2009) or Cingolani (2008a, 2008b) and the consequences for full employment are discussed also in Bliek and Parguez (2006 and 2007). Relation (t) is both an *ex post* accounting identity applying at any time in actual monetary economies as a result of a certain pattern of distribution and market prices, and an equilibrium condition based on the production prices that would ensure equality between the sectoral rates of profits.[64] Being fully consistent with the analysis of the circuit, it has consequences that run against what is generally considered as received policy wisdom, particularly the fact that, *ceteris paribus* (in comparative statics terms):

1. the state deficit increases domestic producers' profits. Therefore, as developed in Steindl (1979), a policy of permanent deficit reductions can generate long-term stagnation;
2. banks compete with domestic producers in attracting the available savings, and therefore the profits they accumulate are subtracted from the profits of private producers;
3. assuming that households are in financial balance and abstracting from net interest to banks, if the State generates a surplus, producers can be profitable only if the current account of the balance of payments is in deficit in excess of the State surplus (plus net interest to banks in case the latter are included);
4. if investment of domestic enterprises increases other sectors must increase their debts for enterprises to continue accumulating savings (that is generating profits) and keeping positive views on the future. In a context of reduced foreign direct investment and limited room for increasing households' debts, as is the case in most of EU12 (New Member States) as well as in Candidate and Pre-Accession countries after the crisis, this leaves only increased State debt as a possible way to fight against a reduced growth contribution of external demand.

8. CONCLUSIONS AND POLICY IMPLICATIONS

In the last three decades faith in the markets has been strong and the view was held widely that the main task of economic policy was to create the conditions for private economies to reach an optimum of allocation, considering issues of distribution and redistribution as a separate problem. This was translated into monetary policies geared towards the control of inflation and fiscal policies oriented towards achieving fiscal balances, which were assumed to reduce inflationary expectations and provide incentives to savings (Blanchard et al., 2010). These 'new consensus' macroeconomic policies (Arestis and Sawyer, 2004) and the related *Efficient Market Theory* (Davidson, 2007, pp. 190–95) were accompanied by a movement of financial deregulation. During this period, long-term interest rates exceeded GDP growth (Cingolani, 2008b), while salaries tended to grow less than productivity in real terms (for the US see Florio, 2010). At the same time, economic policy neglected the role of effective demand and abandoned the objective of full employment (Mitchell and Muysken, 2008). Whereas this trend was a worldwide one, it was particularly evident in Europe, where the fiscal aspects of this policy mix were codified and inserted into several treaties.

Paradoxically, these policies developed at a time when several mainstream and non-mainstream economists were pointing to the limits of validity of the core neoclassical propositions resting behind the 'new consensus' views, calling implicitly or explicitly for alternative approaches at the theoretical and applied policy levels. Indeed, whereas all policy conditions were fulfilled to stimulate private profits and real investments, these policies unexpectedly contributed to generate the crisis of 2008–09, in a manner that has not yet received a fully satisfactory explanation.

The case of public investment is emblematic of this paradox. There is no doubt that, notably in the New Member States of the European Union (now called EU12), public investment was one of the components of public expenditure that was sacrificed to the objective of achieving fiscal consolidation. The Maastricht requirement to keep the budget deficit below 3 per cent of GDP implies an equal upper bound on the amount of public investment that can be financed by debt, as any transfer from the banking sector to the sector of general government is accounted 'below the line' as part of the public deficit. This upper bound falls to zero in the medium term if one retains the stability pact requirement that the public budget should be balanced on average during the cycle. This upper limit cannot, however, be reached due to the need to finance other expenditures classified as current, while continuing to service existing public debt. An illustration can be given by breaking down public debt into a component of previously accumulated debt, a component of public investment, a component of interest payments and a balance, which represents the current surplus before interest payments.

$$\frac{DEBT_t}{GDP_t} = \frac{DEBT_0}{GDP_t} + \sum_{i=1}^{t} \frac{\overline{DCAP}}{GDP_t} + \sum_{i=1}^{t} \frac{INT}{GDP_t} + \sum_{i=1}^{t} \frac{\overline{DCURP}}{GDP_t} \quad \text{(u)}$$

In the formula (u) above, the left-hand side represents the current public debt to GDP ratio, whereas on the right-hand side the first term represents the ratio of initial debt to current GDP, the second represents capital expenditure realized in the period, the third interest paid on existing debt and the last net current expenditure before interest (Cingolani, 2006). Figure 3.1 presents this decomposition for the period 1999–2005.[65]

The figure shows that on average public investment has been close to the 3 per cent limit in the New Member States (17 per cent of GDP in six years). Some countries with a relatively low initial debt have accumulated debt fast through increases of public investment, whereas in others public investment has been lower, being constrained by debt inherited from the past. On average in EU25 the surplus before interest and investment (column with squares in the negative quadrant) covered interest payments (dashed bar).

If public investment (white bar) was estimated correctly, it could be identified with that part of public debt that is 'good debt', because it would correspond to the accumulation of a productive asset that generate in principle economic and/or financial benefits and revenues. However, as argued notably by Eisner (1995, pp. 89–119), a large part of current public expenditures are expenditures on human capital and other intangibles such as education and research and development. Therefore also part of the squared bar could in principle be adding to 'good debt'. As shown in the figure, however, the balance of net current expenditures before interest is negative, which means that this part of 'good debt' is decreasing, that is net public current expenditures before interest have been reduced to realize a current surplus before interest. At the same time, since it is socially difficult to reduce current expenditure, public investment in tangibles and intangibles has been constrained as well, reaching barely 3 per cent on average in countries in need of fast catching up.

The financial constraints put on public investment appear an inevitable necessity in a neoclassical perspective, as the theory foresees that in equilibrium investment and savings are equalized instantaneously by the interest rate, whereas it is generally assumed that out of equilibrium savings determines investment. Therefore, if any, the role of the government budget is to accumulate savings in order to finance the required public investment, as necessary to reach the country's growth objectives.

Out of the restrictive hypotheses of the pure neoclassical equilibrium,

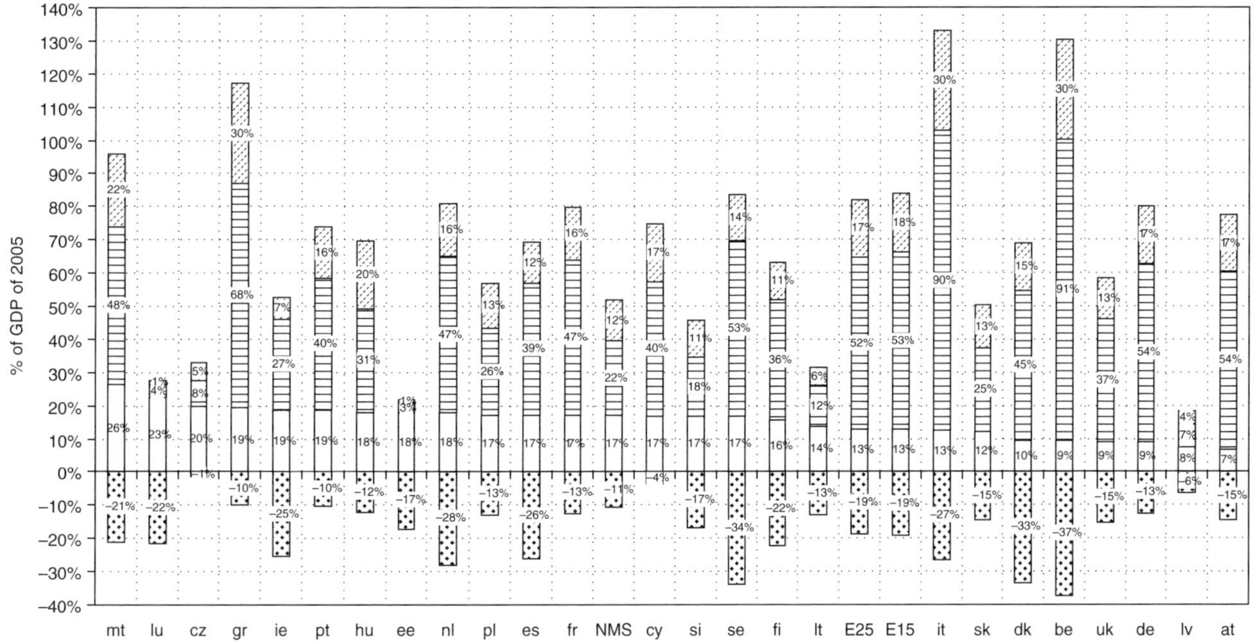

Source: EDP data from Eurostat and calculations □ Public investment (cumulated) ▤ Initial debt ▨ Interest paid (cumulated) ⊡ Surplus before interest and investment (balance).

Figure 3.1 Decomposition of Public Debt 1999–2005 (ranked by decreasing share of cumulated public investment in 2005 GDP)

which apply to closed, static and simultaneous models, disequilibrium prevails, implying notably a causality between distribution and allocation that, considered in historical time, provides an explanation for the causal effect of investment on savings highlighted by Kalecki and retained in most of the post Keynesian literature. Indeed, Kalecki's identity (5) makes clear that any reduction in the government deficit decreases profits of the private producing sector immediately. This negative impulse perpetuates itself and becomes more permanent once, in a second round, it has reached taxes, which are reduced through the fall in economic activity. At that time, the initial stimulus requires a higher current fiscal surplus to be corrected. Out of neoclassical equilibrium public investment can thus provide a policy weapon against perverse circles of reduced expectations of the private producers, which are generally followed by periods of increased risk aversion of consumers, feeding in turn negative producer's expectations and so on, in a spiral of economic contraction that keeps the economy on a low growth path.

In the model of the monetary circuit, it is because access to liquidity creation removes the scarcity constraint for producers that a wider range of equilibria than the pure neoclassical one can be generated. Defined as a financial liability issued by the banking sector, money is essentially an endogenous macroeconomic phenomenon. It explains why, in sequential time, expectations of the government and the entrepreneurs, embedded in their investment decisions, must be exogenous and thus causal with respect to savings. In this context, there is no reason to expect that, left to itself, a market economy will converge towards a balanced equilibrium characterized by the neoclassical conditions for optimality, including full employment, not only in the short term, but also in the long run. Public investment can then become a strong tool to fight against the permanent underemployment tendency of a monetary production economy with endogenous money (Seccareccia, 1995; Gnos, 2005).

In particular, in a context of constant technology, it is not possible to measure capital independently from distribution when out of the neoclassical equilibrium. This also implies that factor demands for labour and capital cannot be equalized to factor supplies through wage and the interest rate adjustments (Roncaglia, pp. 103–9). In reality the most likely case is thus that of involuntary unemployment and suboptimal utilization of the productive capacity. If the assumption of constant technology is removed, this result is reinforced as, unless one assumes rational expectations, which is not possible in fully dynamic (non-ergodic) environments (Davidson, 1982–83) and/or an extremely favourable combination of circumstances that allows abiding by the dynamic condition (r), the economy will not be on the full-employment path.

The causality relations prevailing out of neoclassical equilibrium thus confirm that economic policy can have a positive influence on economic activity and employment, notably through the action of macroeconomic instruments such as reduced interest rates or increased public expenditure, including investment. In particular, in the model of the monetary circuit, public investment can become a powerful macroeconomic tool, because, when it is economically justified, the possibility always exists to finance it out of new State money creation if needed. The possible favourable effects of using the public investment policy instrument to attain the full-employment objective should be taken into account in *ex ante* policy design, since it remains true today as in the 1930s that: 'all forms of the "diversion argument" break down at a time when unemployment prevails' (Kahn, 1935, p. 1). This macroeconomic effect is not always captured by conventional cost–benefit analysis, at least in the way as it is usually practiced in EU countries.

Some post Keynesians such as Parguez have linked the emergence of the present crisis to the long-term lack of effective demand generated by the policy mix referred to above and particularly the insufficient level of public debt.[66] This raises the question of how to arrive at a change in the direction of European economic policies to avoid repeating past errors. This change requires changing the way economic knowledge is interpreted and used so that it is understood that the economy needs to be constantly brought back on the full employment path, as confirmed by the recent crisis. Healthy economic growth requires that, in order to succeed, these efforts should be part of a concerted policy change at the international level, which would also help to stabilize international trade and exchange rate imbalances (Parguez, 2009).

There is no space here to examine in full the implications that the ideas presented in this chapter have for European economic policies and particularly for the financing of public investment in a regional context and for the related issue of the coordination of economic policies in a monetary union, some of which can be guessed from Kalecki's identity (5), from the effect of distribution on allocation out of equilibrium and from the associated fallacy of composition. They give support to the idea of coordinating European fiscal policy at a continental level through the collective management of investment and other public expenditure and could be developed as a possible future extension of the present analysis.

NOTES

* The views expressed are personal. The author is grateful for comments received on previous versions from Michel Deleau, Massimo Florio, Yves Mersch, Alain Parguez,

Malcolm Sawyer, Mateu Turró Augusto Graziani, Mare Lavoie and Christian Zellner. The intermediary steps of the reflections that produced this version of the chapter benefited from comments from Jean-Paul Guichard, as well as participants in the workshops "Vth Conference on Applied Infrastructure Research", Berlin 6–7 October, 2006 and "Highways: cost and regulation in Europe", Bergamo 26–27 November, 2004, who are also warmly thanked. These reflections developed substantially during research financed by the STAREBEI programme of the European Investment Bank on the application of the monetary circuit to the EU12, made together with Jean-Paul Guichard and Matthieu Llorca, who are also thanked. The author is also grateful to the Centre d'Etudes en Macroéconomie et Finance Internationale (CEMAFI) of the University of Nice and the Centre d'Etudes Monétaires et Financières (CEMF) of the University of Bourgogne for several discussions. The usual disclaimer applies.

1. By indirect it is meant here that the neoclassical equilibrium can still be a reference for comparing two alternative real life suboptimal positions, as opposed to comparing directly the pure neoclassical equilibrium to a given suboptimal real life situation. This corresponds to the distinction between *feasible* and *potential* welfare, made respectively in chapters V and IV of Graaff, de V. (1957). See also the discussion of Allais' model in section 2.
2. 'The modern neoclassical economist, trained in the tradition of Friedman and Lucas, would be surprised to discover that, together with his support of the "euthanasia of the rentier", Keynes's argument in favour of the "socialisation of investment" constitutes the only explicit long-term policy proposal to be found in the General Theory' (Seccareccia, 1995, p. 47). 'Keynes envisaged that in his proposed system as much as "two-thirds or three-quarters of total investment" would be directly influenced by public and semi-public bodies whose activities would be guided by the traditional "motive of private exchange" as well as by the "technically social" motives that have normally justified investment in social infrastructure' (Seccareccia, 1995, p. 48).
3. Later texts such as Arrow and Hahn (1971, pp. 263–81) or Mas-Colell et al. (1995, p. 625) were more laconic on the subject.
4. The part of this book devoted to welfare analysis (*Rendement social*, pp. 588–664) is included in the section on the dynamics of equilibrium.
5. Allais ([1943] 1994, Annex IV pp. 139–51). The author is grateful to Annabelle Assemat and Alessandro Fortunelli for help in going through the mathematical developments of this Annex.
6. Massé (1953, p. 87) noted that points on the frontier of maximum efficiency in the space of satisfactions are the domain of neoclassical analysis, whereas points below the possibility frontier, where maximum efficiency is not attained, are relevant for Keynesian analysis.
7. Allais ([1981] 1989, pp. 301–4) notes that concepts similar to his *perte* have been used by his pupils Boiteux (1951), and Debreu (1951 and 1954), but he comments that Boiteux's *perte*, which is based on revenue and thus on prices, depends on the initial situation (and is in fact only relevant starting from a situation of maximum efficiency), whereas Debreu's *coefficient of resource utilisation*, defined for a composite commodity and based on the convexity of the consumption and production sets, is not suitable for the analysis out of equilibrium. According to Allais, the definitions of Boiteux and Debreu, like those of Dupuit, Pareto, Barone and Hotelling that preceded them, do not respect all the 12 desirable properties of a proper indicator of inefficiency such as the loss should be (pp. 159–295). From these properties it results that such an indicator must be maximal and null in a situation of maximal efficiency (pp. 328–9). It can thus be interpreted as a measure of the distance from equilibrium, which clearly puts his approach of welfare, already fully developed in the *Traité* of 1943, in the disequilibrium perspective of comparing two suboptimal positions and thus on firmer grounds than the second best analysis developed by Boiteux and others.
8. There is probably an implicit argument of the type developed in the theory of the core, see Hildenbrand and Kirman (1976), but it is not made explicit.

9. A market is 'cleared' by prices when at that price supply equals demand.
10. See McKenzie (2002 p. 192, condition II) or Guerrien (undated). With reference also to the discussion in sections 3 and 4, the term profit actually means different things in classical and neoclassical approaches, at least if one compares the 'natural price' of Smith and Ricardo, which corresponds to the 'price of production' of Marx and Torrens, to the 'long-period normal price' of Marshall. As noted by Kurz and Salvadori (1995, p. 29), the 'profit' for Marshall is the 'extra profit' of classical economists, whereas what classical economists called profit is what Marshall calls interest. In this sense a uniform rate of profit in the classical sense is compatible with the fact that 'extra profits' vanish in the long term as long as the there is a single rate of interest in the economy.
11. Since out of the neoclassical equilibrium, the 'law of present value' does not hold: it is by definition not true that 'A l'équilibre, la valeur d'un bien durable à un instant donné est égale à la somme des valeurs actuelles à cet instant de ses revenus futurs' (Allais, [1943] 1994, p. 337). More generally one can observe with Davidson (2009, *Postscript on The Great Financial Crisis of 2008–2009*, pp. 190–91) that one of the causes of the recent crisis is that the financial deregulation that started in the 1970s and that progressively eliminated the regulatory framework established after the Great Depression was based on efficient market theory, which essentially translates real neoclassical equilibrium theory in financial jargon and notably assumes that asset prices are always the equilibrium ones.
12. See Arena and Maricic (1988) for other references in the French Keynesian literature. Causality has been a much debated concept in economics, see, for instance: Simon (1953), Strotz and Wold (1960), Demaria (1974).
13. 'La notion d'interdépendance fonctionnelle ne s'applique rigoureusement que dans la Dynamique de l'équilibre et elle ne saurait être généralisée sans précaution à la Dynamique du déséquilibre. En fait, dans cette Dynamique, les phénomènes se succèdent dans un ordre bien déterminé, qui fait intervenir sans aucune contestation possible des liens de causalité. En réalité, causalité et interdépendance ne sont nullement contradictoires, mais ces notions s'appliquent à des ordres de phénomènes différents: la première est relative au déséquilibre, la seconde à l'équilibre. La notion d'interdépendance ne peut s'appliquer à la Dynamique du déséquilibre que dans la mesure même où cette dynamique peut être représentée en première approximation par une dynamique de l'équilibre' (Allais, [1943] 1994, pp. 542–3).
14. The final form corresponds to a 'complete solution' of the system, where only endogenous variables are on the left-hand side.
15. For a mathematical derivation and the associated definition of the multiplier as a measure of the causal relation between an exogenous shock and the endogenous response of the system, see Artus et al. (1986, pp. 123–30). See also Klein et al. (1999, pp. 286–97).
16. To the extent that any nonlinear system can be locally approximated by a linear one, this definition can be considered sufficiently general.
17. This definition of equilibrium is also retained as a possible one by Vercelli (1994).
18. This corresponds to the 'non-ergodic' case. See discussion on rational expectations in section 3.5. For most of the arguments developed in this section, a rigorous treatment at a more advanced level can be found in Artus et al. (1996, chapter 6).
19. Robinson (1977, p. 12) ironically defined the term post Keynesian as relating to 'an economic theory or method of analysis which takes into account of the difference between the future and the past'. As discussed in section 7, category 5 is not truly dynamic, in the sense that it assumes the parameters of the model, such as for instance technology, to be constant.
20. See Johansson (1982), Marchand et al. (1985) and Drèze (1984). The case corresponding to the more traditional IS-LM interpretation of Keynes is treated in Hill (1999).
21. As noted by Florio (1991), this idea is already implicitly present in the formula for shadow wages proposed by Little and Mirrlees for use in projects appraisal in

developing countries, which contains a term corresponding to the usual macroeconomic multiplier.

22. See Sneessens and Drèze (1986) or Lambert (1988). One can also note that studies on the long run properties of large macro-econometric models conclude that the long term is non-Walrasian. These studies look at the internal dynamics of models taken as representative of actual economies, at least at the level of the interrelationships existing between observable variables: 'It is clear that the long run of macroeconometric models is not walrasian: it would be advantageous for firms to produce more and for consumers to work more at equilibrium prices; this is blocked by the monopolistic behavior of the agents' (Deleau et al., 1991).
23. Classical is used here in the sense of 'pre-neoclassical', that is the type of analysis that dominated economics before marginalism: going from Petty to the Physiocrats, Smith, Ricardo and ending with Marx.
24. Which in this context is equivalent to the rate of interest of the neoclassical model.
25. In both cases the value of the endogenous variables does not depend on time.
26. Roncaglia (2009, pp. 50–51) notes that Sraffa's production prices model 'abstracts from technological change, from movements in the level of activity' and so on, thus giving a 'photograph' or 'snapshot' of the economic system.
27. Prices are set based on a Sraffian model, whereas quantities follow a Keynesian model and both intervene at different point in historical time, which shows how both models can be integrated in a dynamic approach.
28. Parguez (2000), in commenting on the causes of the Asian crisis, noted that this trend was a worldwide one.
29. Gordon (1995, p. 98) notes: 'It is reasonable to argue, in short, that neoclassical policy analysts are wrong on two out of two counts. First, promoting saving by itself is unlikely to stimulate investment. Second, public policies promoting productivity growth, with the corollary objective of stimulating investment, can work and should be pursued much more aggressively. The case for tighter austerity regimes rests on remarkably weak foundations. By contrast, the case for a progressive alternative appears substantially more persuasive.'
30. Roncaglia (2009, p. 134) reminds of Sraffa (1960, p. 33) assertion that 'The rate of profit is [. . .] susceptible of being determined from outside the system of production, in particular by the level of the monetary rates of interest'. Panico (1997, p. 83) develops a post Keynesian model that integrates the Government sector in the spirit of Kaldor (1966) which attempts to 'characterise monetary and fiscal policies by assuming: (1) an endogenous money supply; (2) a government expenditure varying to maintain steady-growth conditions in the economy. . . . by assuming that both g and R_b (respectively the growth rate and the rate of interest, NdA) are exogenous variables' his model is 'able to support a theory of income distribution where the rate of profit can be influenced both by the rate of growth of the economy (as underlined by Kaldor, Pasinetti and a large part of post-Keynesian literature) and by the money interest rate, as suggested by Sraffa (1960, p. 33), and by the subsequent elaboration of a monetary theory of distribution.' For recent empirical evidence that the US FED controls the yield curve by setting short-run interest rates, see Galbraith et al. (2007).
31. As discussed in section 6.1, the sequence of the circuit in historical time is: (1) determination of expected output by enterprises; (2) pricing decision by enterprises; (3) start of the production process by payment of salaries to households; (4) determination of savings by households; (5) realization of effective demand on the market.
32. Davidson (2009, p. 184) quoted Samuelson (1969, p. 184) in saying that 'the "ergodic hypothesis [axiom]" is a necessary foundation of economic theory if economics is to be a hard science'. Davidson also notes that Hicks wrote him in 1983, after having read his piece on rational expectations that: 'I missed a chance of labelling my own point of view as non-ergodic' (p. 186). Similarly, Robert Solow wrote to Davidson in 1985: 'I have always admired that article of yours on non-ergodic processes and thought it was right on the button' (Devidson, 2009, p. 186). Douglas North also agreed on the importance

of non-ergodic processes in his book *Understanding the Process of Economic Change* (North, 2005, p. 19). To the extent that one agrees that economics cannot be a hard science, non-ergodicity explains why and there is no contradiction in the position of these authors.

33. With endogenous and rational expectations, 'Ricardian equivalence' arguments hold: if the government increases debt, households will immediately anticipate higher taxes and will reduce consumption accordingly, that is the government deficit will crowd out private expenditure completely.
34. This causality is not present in Dynamic Stochastic General Equilibrium (DSGE) models (Wickens, 2008), which imply either causality from savings to investment or equality between the two. In their New Keynesian variant (Woodford, 2003) DGSE models allow for a departure from the neoclassical optimum due to price stickiness. They could thus be seen as dynamic-stochastic extension variants of the IS-LM model and its static developments in the rationing literature. Being micro-economically based, they do not allow for the emergence of money as a macroeconomic phenomenon (see section 6) and indeed they do not retain a separate treatment for the banking sector. In their Real Business Cycle variant (Kydland and Prescott, 1992) DGSE models assume full price flexibility and thus continuous realization of the neoclassical optimum.
35. Empirical investigations on the price-setting behaviour of firms based on the principle of the 'full cost' developed in the 1930s (Hall and Hitch, 1939). They found that enterprises do not equate price to marginal cost but fix cost with a margin above their average costs, generating an extra profit that under pure competitive conditions would not exist. This tradition has been fully integrated in post Keynesian analysis (see Weintraub, 1959; Eichner, 1973 and 1976; Sylos Labini, 1967), and forms part of the price block of most macroeconomic models (Eckstein and Fromm, 1968; Artus et al. 1986, pp. 91–5).
36. Their 1995 book generalizes the results obtained in this simple example in several directions. The interpretation of Sraffa's contribution is still source of many discussions. A very clear and authoritative introduction is provided by Roncaglia (2009).
37. In these models, linked also to von Neumann (1945), the maximum rate of profit is equal to the maximum rate of growth and they are both determined by the conditions of production. When production is viable as defined in the text, the largest eigenvalue λ of the matrix of production coefficients is not larger than 1 and the maximum rate of profit is $R = (1 - \lambda)/\lambda$, see for instance Kurz and Salvadori (1995, p. 98).
38. In models that also integrate fixed capital, a corollary of the above result is that it is impossible to measure the value of the capital stock independently from its price, which breaks down the traditional neoclassical argument for the determination of the rate of interest in terms of marginal productivity of capital. In general, in post Keynesian models (that is, out of the neoclassical equilibrium), there is no unique inverse relationship between the quantity of capital, whatever measured, and the rate of interest, nor between the quantity of labour and the wage rate. This absence of negatively sloped factor demand functions prevents determining factor prices according to neoclassical rules.
39. Kalecki followed the work of Hall and Hitch (1939) of the Institute of Statistics of Oxford University when he was in Cambridge, where he participated with Keynes, Kahn, Sraffa and others in a connected research on Prime Costs, Proceeds and Output (see López and Assous, 2010, p. 6). This gave him an opportunity to be hired by Hall (Kalecki, 1991, p. 522). Kalecki's ([1939–40], 1991) own theory of prices was indeed close and influenced by the research carried out by Hall and others. Basile and Salvadori (1984/85) show the continuity in Kalecki's thinking on pricing theory and the related degree of monopoly and distribution theories. On Kalecki's theory of pricing see also Steindl (1987). The model presented in this section is mainly inspired from Graziani (1993 pp. 692–9) and Graziani (2001, pp. 116–19), but also combines ideas from Graziani (2003, pp. 100–105), Parguez (2008, p. 56, relation 11) and Parguez (2009, p. 13, relation 8).

40. Profit maximization under constraint of given technology (or cost minimization under constraint of given output) loses its relevance for determining the level of output and factor demand in a context where the average cost function is constant and coincides with the marginal cost curve, as was assumed by Kalecki (1938), and retained in this model, as in the one in the previous section. See also Sylos Labini (1988, pp. 269–71).
41. The identity must be read here in gross terms, that is before investment (see section 7.2). In this context, where households do not save, it is correct to say that producers earn what they spend while workers spend what they earn, a sentence attributed to Kalecki but that Kaldor argued Kalecki never wrote as such, although his analysis clearly implies it (see Robinson, 1977, p. 12).
42. Relation (f) illustrates the analogy between the multiplier and the process of distribution already noted by Kaldor (1955–56): 'The principle of the Multiplier . . . could alternatively be applied to a determination of the relation between prices and wages, if the level of output and employment is taken as given, or to the determination of the level of employment, if distribution (i.e. the relation between prices and wages is taken as given).'
43. Sector is used here in the sense of 'institutional sector' retained by national accounting, for which what is usually called 'sector' in ordinary language (like the agricultural sector) is called a branch.
44. To be consistent with the National Accounting (NA) jargon used before, the term 'multi-branch' should be used instead of multi-sectoral, as what in input–output analysis is called a sector is called a branch in NA. For NA a branch is an aggregation of statistical units that are homogeneous in terms of activity, a sector being an aggregation of enterprises that could be involved in activities covering several branches (see note 49).
45. In his rather difficult 1975 book, Parguez showed notably why Clower (1965) was wrong, which he then stated much more clearly in Parguez (1977). Clower later recognized in a private exchange that Parguez's criticism was well grounded (oral communication by Prof. Parguez).
46. In a monetary production economy, fundamental uncertainty prevails (see section 4.5). Contrary to risk, this uncertainty cannot be addressed by probability calculus. In this context, money is the unit of account that allows making bets on the future: 'La monnaie se définit sans aucune ambiguïté en dehors de tout calcul subjectif des agents: c'est l'ensemble des signes des dettes émises pour anticiper les surplus de l'avenir' (Parguez, 1984, p. 98). In such a monetary production economy, time is sequential and is the support of agents' bets on the future. These bets become a causality factor for the variables endogenous to the model, both present and future. For Parguez (1980, pp. 436–7), this sequential or historical time could also be a logical time, that is, different from calendar time: 'Le *temps de la monnaie* (période du flux monétaire), le *temps du revenu* (période revenu) et le *temps des prix* (période prix) sont donc *identiques* (*temps du circuit*). La période du circuit est donc parfaitement définie dans l'ordre des temps logiques.' Later Parguez (1984, p. 94) noted also that in the circuit 'Le temps n'est ni vide ni neutre', whereas in non-monetary economies everything happens 'dans un éternel Présent. *Le temps est neutre quand la monnaie est inutile* dans les deux variantes du monde classique, le modèle Hayekien et le modèle de l'accumulation classico-marxiste' (pp. 88–9).
47. On the circuit definition of money as a third part liability, see Parguez and Seccareccia (2000). Graziani notes that: 'any theory based on the individualistic approach is necessarily confined to microeconomics and is unable to build a true macroeconomic analysis. . . . In the perspective of the circuit theory, a simple aggregation of the individual behaviour functions doesn't turn a microeconomic model into a true macroeconomic theory' (Graziani, 2003, pp. 18–19). Guerrien (1992) elaborates on the limits of methodological individualism from a microeconomic perspective.
48. This fallacy of composition has been underlined in particular by post Keynesian writers: 'The Cambridge School proposed an analysis in which the macroeconomic

dimension always came first with respect to the microeconomic dimension' (Pasinetti, 2005, p. 843).

49. Used in the sense of institutional sectors. The European ESA system distinguishes the following institutional sectors: Non-financial Corporations (S11); Financial Corporations (S12), of which the sub-sector S121 is the Central Bank; General Government (S13); Households (S14) and Non-profit Institutions Serving Households (S15); Rest of the World (S2). See: http://circa.europa.eu/irc/dsis/nfaccount/info/data/esa95/en/een00069.htm.
50. There is no issue of primary versus secondary money emission since there is no separate central bank. Also, since there is no competition between different private banks, there is no limit to the capacity of the banking sector as a whole to create all the money requested, see Graziani (1990).
51. The recording of this transaction illustrates the 'quadruple entry' principle of national accounting (without matrices).
52. The Banking School's claim that loans create deposits was endorsed by Schumpeter, see Graziani (2003, pp. 82–8). In nineteenth-century England, the *Banking School* opposed the *Currency School*, of which the quantity theory of money is the modern successor. For an exhaustive historical review of the debate of the period 1900–1940, see Realfonzo (1996). On the link between Keynes and the banking school see Mondello (1985). Kaldor and Trevithick (1981, p. 8) claim that Adam Smith can be regarded as a follower of the Banking School: 'He cited the example of numerous towns in which after the opening of a bank, or a local branch of a bank, was quickly followed by increased production and employment in the activity'.
53. The position of Graziani is that at the macroeconomic level payments internal to the enterprise sector cancel out, thus *de facto* in net terms new credit money is created only for salaries. However, given that in reality enterprises self-finance the majority of their investments (or in any model where households do not save), this precludes the initial monetary financing of real capital accumulation, which Graziani accepts (2003, p. 69). Graziani's position is in agreement with that of Schmitt (1966, 1984) and is also supported by Gnos (2003). Rochon (2005, 2009) and Renaud (2000) conclude broadly in line with Parguez (2004).
54. The recordings shown in Table 3.1, Panel T-1 are consistent with the principle of quadruple entry. The latter was integrated in the last revision of the national accounts (SNA 1993) and foresees that for each monetary transaction four entries are booked (two for each party in the transaction), see Gorter and Shrestha (2004). The format of this table is inspired from the 'T accounts' used by accountants, hence the 'T' in the title of the table, but here each sector is aggregated into a single 'net worth account' and real flows are also reported to underline the production aspect behind the monetary flow. In accounting practice T accounts are closer to the presentation of the Journal in terms of debits and credits and there is a different T account for each position of the balance sheet. The conventions followed here are thus closer to those of the 'fundamental accounting equation', which is: Assets = Liabilities + Net Worth, see Pratt (2003, pp. 114–16).
55. Relation (t) of section 7.2 presents Kalecki's identity in terms of net financial balances after investment, whereas above the identity is expressed in gross terms, like in relation (d) in section 5.1, which corresponds, however, to the case where households do not save.
56. The model reflects the assumptions of Graziani that interest is paid in kind (Graziani, 2003, p. 118), in line also with the assumptions retained by Bossone (2001). As discussed in section 6.2.2.2, this position differs from that of Parguez (2004) and Rochon (2005), but it does not have major consequences for the policy conclusions of the model. For a more general presentation of the monetary approach of Graziani, see Graziani (2001, ch. 7) and Graziani (1987) for a discussion of efficiency in a monetary economy.
57. M^0 represents households' liquid balances coming from previous periods and is also equal to the debt of the producers at the beginning of the new period. It is not the monetary base M_0. With reference to paragraph 6.2, relation (g) corresponds to the case

where, starting from Table 3.3, Panel BS-4 with some debt to banks in the balance sheet of enterprises, in the following round of the circuit a new loan is extended by banks to refinance the previous one and pay salaries corresponding to the new production period (at the exclusion of profits, see footnote 56 above). Apart from pre-existing debt, the situation corresponds to Table 3.1, Panel BS-1 in the previous section.

58. Apart from pre-existing debt, and the explicit introduction of a Central Bank, the situation corresponds to Table 3.2, Panel BS-2 in the previous section.
59. The introduction of public finance in the circuit is addressed by Graziani (1985), Parguez (2002) and Bougrine and Seccareccia (2002). These contributions can be viewed as building blocks of a unified post Keynesian theory of public finance which, to the knowledge of the author, remains to be completed. This could be one of the reasons why this approach is ignored by the Public Choice literature. Other relevant post Keynesian contributions in this field are Panico (1997), Bougrine (2000), and Mitchell and Muysken (2008, pp. 209–11).
60. Pasinetti (1962, 1964–65, 1981) has enlarged this scheme to economies where material goods are also used as means of production. See in particular Pasinetti (1981) for the general scheme where capital is also present. Pasinetti (1980) derives the matrix of vertically integrated sectors.
61. In the sense of branches.
62. Bhaduri (2006) presents an explicit formalization of the dynamic process that would normally be brought a long-term underemployment equilibrium in a model inspired from classical analysis, where investment causes savings and growth is endogenous. In this model the dynamics are driven by the distributive conflict, in particular the model shows that unless salaries grow in line with productivity, effective demand will become insufficient to guarantee full employment.
63. Here sector refers again to institutional sectors.
64. Kalecki's identity can be tracked empirically, as it is the equivalent of the balancing of the 'net lending' and 'net borrowing' positions (S9) of the various institutional sectors in the UN SNA93 national accounts, the basis for the EU ESA95 accounts, where net lending is defined as representing the net amount a unit or a sector has available to finance, directly or indirectly, other units or other sectors after investment.
65. Countries are ranked in decreasing order of cumulated public investment share over GDP. The height of the column on the positive quadrant is the sum of the first three terms of the right-hand side of (u), corresponding respectively to public investment, initial debt and the interest payment components, all expressed in percentage of current GDP, whereas the column in the negative quadrant represents the current surplus before interest payments, also as a share of current GDP (the last term in (u)).
66. Parguez recently formulated a 'Harrodian' principle of debt stability requiring that public debt must grow at the same rate as private debt in order to avoid financial crises (personal exchange).

REFERENCES

Allais, Maurice (ed.) ([1943] 1994), *A la Recherche d'une Discipline Économique,* published under the title *Traité d'Économie Pure*, Paris: Clément Juglar.

Allais Maurice. ([1981] 1989), *La Théorie Générale des Surplus*, Paris and Grenoble: ISMEA and Presses Universitaires de Grenoble, originally published in *Economies et Sociétés*, Cahiers de l'ISMEA, **1**(5).

Arena, R. (1987), 'La dynamique économique: nouveaux débats, nouvelles perspectives', *L'Actualité Économique*, **63**(1), 77–117.

Arena, R. and A. Maricic (1988), 'Les réactions françaises à la théorie générale (1936–1951)', *Cahiers d'Économie Politique*, **14–15**, 15–41.

Arestis, Philip and Malcolm Sawyer (eds) (2004), *Re-examining Monetary and Fiscal Policy for the 21st Century*, Cheltenham, UK and Northampton, MA, USA: Edward Elgar Publishing.
Arrow, Kenneth and Frank Hahn (eds) (1971), *General Competitive Analysis*, Amsterdam: North-Holland.
Artus, Patrick, Michel Deleau and Pierre Malgrange (eds) (1986), *Modélisation Macroéconomique*, Paris: Economica.
Barrère, Alain (ed.) (1952), *Théorie Économique et Impulsion Keynesienne*, Paris: Dalloz.
Basile, L. and N. Salvadori (1984/85), 'Kalecki's pricing theory', *Journal of Post Keynesian Economics*, **7**(2), 249–62.
Bellofiore, R. (1989), 'A monetary labour theory of value', *Review of Radical Political Economics*, **21**(1–2), 1–25.
Bhaduri, Amit (2006), 'The role of income distribution in long run endogenous growth', in Neri Salvadori (ed.), *Economic Growth and Distribution*, Cheltenham, UK and Northampton, MA, USA: Edward Elgar Publishing, pp. 40–57.
Blanchard, O., G. Dell'Arriccia and P. Mauro (2010), 'Rethinking macroeconomic policies', International Monitory Fund staff position note SPN/10/03.
Bliek, Jean-Gabriel and Alain Parguez (eds) (2006), *Le Plein Emploi ou le Chaos*, Paris: Economica.
Bliek, Jean-Gabriel and Alain Parguez (2007), 'Full employment: can it be a key policy objective for Europe?', *International Journal of Political Economy*, **36**(3), 26–46.
Boiteux, M. (1951), 'Le revenu distribuable et les pertes économiques', *Econometrica*, **19**(2), 112–33.
Bossone, B. (2001), 'Circuit theory of banking and finance', *Journal of Banking and Finance*, **25**(5), 857–90.
Bougrine, Hassan (2000), 'Fiscal policy and the current crisis: are budget deficits a cause, a consequence or a remedy?', in Hassan Bougrine (ed.), *The Economics of Public Spending. Debts Deficits and Economic Performance*, Cheltenham, UK and Northampton, MA, USA: Edward Elgar Publishing, pp. 6–29.
Bougrine, H. and M. Seccareccia (2002), 'Money, taxes, public spending, and the state within a circuitist perspective', *International Journal of Political Economy*, **32**(3), 58–79.
Cencini, Alavaro (ed.) (2006), *Macroeconomic Foundations of Macroeconomics*, New York: Routledge.
Chick, V. (2004), 'On open systems', *Brazilian Journal of Political Economy*, **24**(1),1–16.
Cingolani, Massimo (2006), 'Public investment and government budgetary ceilings', unpublished background study prepared on the occasion of the presentation of a road project for EIB loan approval.
Cingolani, M. (2008a), 'Full employment as a possible objective for EU policy – I. a perspective from the point of view of the monetary circuit', *Panoeconomicus*, **1**, 89–114.
Cingolani, M. (2008b), 'Full employment as a possible objective for EU policy – II. review of some empirical aspects', *Panoeconomicus*, **2**, 167–84.
Clower, Robert W. (1965), 'The Keynesian counter-revolution: a theoretical appraisal', in Frank Hahn and F. Brechling (eds), *The Theory of Interest Rates*, London: Macmillan.
Davidson, Paul (1982–83), 'Rational expectations: a fallacious foundation

for studying crucial decision-making processes', *Journal of Post Keynesian Economics*, **5**(2), 182–98.
Davidson, Paul (ed) (2007), *John Maynard Keynes*, paperback edn with new postscript on the crisis published 2009, New York: Palgrave Macmillan.
Debreu, Gerard (1951), 'The coefficient of resource utilisation', *Econometrica*, **19**(3), 273–92.
Debreu, Gérard (1954), 'A classical tax-subsidy problem', *Econometrica*, **22**(1), 14–22.
Debreu, Gérard (ed.) (1959), *Theory of Value. An Axiomatic Analysis of Economic Equilibrium*, New Haven, CT, and London: Yale University Press.
Deleau, M., C. Le Van and P. Malgrange (1991), 'The long run of macroeconometric models', in Paul Champsaur et al. (eds), *Essays in Honor of Edmond Malinvaud, Vol.2*, Cambridge, MA: The MIT Press, pp. 205–25.
Deleplace, Ghislain and Edward J. Nell (eds) (1996), *Money in Motion. The Post Keynesian and Circulation Approaches*, London: Palgrave Macmillan and The Jerome Levy Economics Institute Series.
Demaria, Giovanni (ed.) (1974), *Trattato di Logica Economica, Vol. III: L'Esogeneità*, Padova, Italy: CEDAM.
Drèze, Jacques (1984), 'Second-best analysis with markets in disequilibrium: public sector pricing in a Keynesian regime', in Maurice Marchand, Pierre Pestieau and Henry Tulkens (eds), *The Performance of Public Enterprises: Concepts and Measurement*, New York: North-Holland, Elsevier Science Ltd.
Dutt, Amitava K. (2005), 'Robinson, history and equilibrium', in Bill Gibson (ed.), *Joan Robinson's Economics: A Centennial Celebration*, Cheltenham, UK and Northampton, MA, USA: Edward Elgar Publishing, pp. 123–72.
Eckstein, O. and G. Fromm (1968), 'The price equation', *The American Economic Review*, **58**(5), 1159–83.
Eichner, Alfred S. (1973), 'A theory of the determination of the mark-up under oligopoly', *The Economic Journal*, **83**(332), 1184–200.
Eichner, Alfred S. (ed.) (1976), *The Megacorp & Oligopoly. Microfoundations of Macro Dynamics*, Cambridge: Cambridge University Press.
Eichner, Alfred S. (ed.) (1991), *The Macrodynamics of Advanced Market Economies*, New York: Sharpe.
Eichner, Alfred S. and J. Kregel (1975), 'An essay on post keynesian theory: a new paradigm in economics', *Journal of Economic Literature*, **13**(4), 1293–314.
Eisner, Robert (ed.) (1995), *The Misunderstood Economy: What Counts and How to Count It*, Boston, MA: Harvard University Business School Press.
Fisher, Franklin M. (ed.) (1983), *Disequilibrium Foundations of Equilibrium Economics*, Econometric Society monographs in pure theory no. 6, Cambridge: Cambridge University Press.
Fisher, Franklin M. (2003), 'Disequilibrium and stability', in Petri Fabio and Hahn Frank (eds), *General Equilibrium, Problems and Prospects*, New York: Routledge, pp. 74–94.
Florio, Massimo (ed.) (1991), *Economia del benessere in regime di disequilibrio generale*, Milan Italy Franco Angeli.
Florio, M. (2010), 'The real roots of the financial crisis: income distribution and investment decisions', manuscript presented at OpsA's Thursdays, EIB conference, 18 March.
Galbraith, James K., O. Giovannoni and Ann J. Russo (2007), 'The Fed's *real* reaction function monetary policy, inflation, unemployment, inequality and presidential politics', The Levy Economics Institute working papers 511.

Garegnani, Pierangelo (2003), 'Savings, investment and capital in a system of general intertemporal equiibrium', in Frank Hahn and Fabio Petri (eds), *General Equilibrium Problems and Prospects*, London: Routledge, pp. 439–67.

Giovannoni, O. (2006), 'Croissance, répartition et politique économique. Théorie et application au cas des Etats-Unis', thesis for obtaining a doctorate in Science Economics at Université de Nice-Sophia Antipolis et CEMAFI.

Giovannoni, O. and A. Parguez (2007), 'What drives profits? An income spending model', in Eckhard Hein and Achim Truger (eds), *Money, Distribution and Economic Policy*, Cheltenham, UK and Northamptom, MA, USA: Edward Elgar Publishing, pp. 97–118.

Gnos, Claude (2003), 'Circuit theory as an explanation of a complex real world', in Louis-Philippe Rochon and Sergio Rossi (eds), *Modern Theories of Money: The Nature and Role of Money in Capitalists Economies*, Cheltenham, UK and Northamptom, MA, USA: Edward Elgar Publishing, pp. 322–38.

Gnos, Claude (2005), 'Circuit theory and the employment issue', in Giuseppe Fontana and Riccardo Realfonzo (eds), *The Monetary Theory of Production. Tradition and Perspectives*, New York: Palgrave Macmillan, pp. 173–83.

Gordon, David M. (1995), 'Putting the horse (back) before the cart: disentangling the macro relationship between investment and saving', in Gerard A. Epstein and Herbert M. Gintis (eds), *Macroeconomic Policy After the Conservative Era*, Cambridge: Cambridge University Press.

Gorter, C. and M. Shrestha (2004), 'Bookkeeping conventions and the micro–macro link', *Review of Income and Wealth*, **50**(2), 181–201.

Graaff, de V., J. (ed.) (1957), *Theoretical Welfare Economics*, London: Cambridge University Press.

Gram, Harvey and Vivian Walsh (eds) (1980), *Classical and Neoclassical Theories of General Equilibrium, Historical Origins and Mathematical Structure*, New York: Oxford University Press.

Grandmont, Jean-Michel (ed.) (1983), *Money and Value: A Reconsideration of Classical and Neoclassical Monetary Economics*, Econometric Society monographs in pure theory no 5, Paris and Cambridge: Cambridge University Press.

Graziani, Augusto (ed.) (1965), *Equilibrio generale ed equilibrio macroeconomico*, Naples, Italy: Edizioni Scientifiche Italiane.

Graziani, A. (1985), 'Monnaie, intérêt et dépenses publiques', *Economies et Sociétés*, **2**, series MP.

Graziani, A. (1987), 'Efficiency criteria at the micro and macro level', *Rivista Internazionale di Scienze Economiche e Commerciali*, **34**(10), 957–69.

Graziani, A. (1990), 'La théorie du circuit et la théorie macroéconomique de la banque', *Economies et Sociétés*, **24**(2), 51–62.

Graziani, Augusto (ed.) (1993), *Teoria economica: prezzi e distribuzione*, Naples, Italy: Edizioni Scientifiche Italiane.

Graziani, A. (1994), 'Real wages and the loans–deposits controversy', *Economie Appliquée*, **47**(1), 31–46.

Graziani, Augusto (ed.) (2001), *Teoria economica: macroeconomia*, Naples, Italy: Edizioni Scientifiche Italiane.

Graziani, Augusto (ed.) (2003), *The Monetary Theory of Production*, Cambridge: Cambridge University Press.

Guerrien, B. (1992), 'Où en est le programme de recherche néo-classique?', *L'Actualité économique*, **68**(4), 564–86.

Guerrien, B. (undated), 'Concurrence et profit nul', accessed at www.bernardguerrien.com/concurrence-et-profit-nul.pdf.
Guesnerie, Roger (ed.) (2001), *Assessing Rational Expectations. Sunspot Multiplicity and Economic Fluctuations*, Cambridge, MA: The MIT Press.
Guesnerie, Roger (ed.) (2005), *Assessing Rational Expectations. Eductive Stability in Economics*, Cambridge, MA: The MIT Press.
Hahn, F. (1965), 'On some problems in proving the existence of equilibrium in a monetary economy', in Frank Hahn and F. Brechling (eds), *The Theory of Interest Rates*, London: Macmillan, pp. 126–35.
Hahn, F.(2003), 'Macro foundations of micro-economics', *Economic Theory*, **21**(2–3), 227–32.
Halevi, J. and R. Taouil (2002), 'On a post-Keynesian stream from France and Italy: the circuit approach', in Philip Arestis, Meghnad Desai and Sheila Dow (eds), *Money, Macroeconomics and Keynes: Essays in Honour of Victoria Chick, Volume One*, New York: Routledge, pp. 91–102.
Hall, R.L. and C.J. Hitch (1939), 'Price theory and business behaviour', *Oxford Economic Papers*, **2**(2), 12–33.
Harrod, Roy (ed.) (1948), *Towards a Dynamic Economics*, London: Macmillan.
Henry, Jacques (1982a), 'Les méthodes post-Keynesiennes et l'approche post-classique', *L'Actualité économique*, **58**(1–2), 17–60.
Henry, Jacques (1982b), 'La veritable nature de l'épargne', *Economie Appliquée*, **35**(3), 339–60.
Henry, Jacques (ed.) (1991), *Le commerce extérieur dans le temps historique*, Paris: P.U.F.
Hicks, John R. (ed.) (1939), *Value and Capital. An Enquiry Into Some Fundamental Principles of Economic Theory*, Oxford: Clarendon Press.
Hildenbrand, Werner and A.P. Kirman (eds) (1976), *Introduction to Equilibrium Analysis*, Amsterdam: North-Holland.
Hill, G. (1999), 'Project appraisal for the Keynesian investment planner', *Economics of Planning*, **32**(2), 153–64.
Johansson, Per-O. (1982), 'Cost benefit rules in general disequilibrium', *Journal of Public Economics*, **18**(1), 121–37.
Kahn, R. (1935), 'Some notes on ideal output', *The Economic Journal*, **45**(177), 1–35.
Kahn, R. (1977), 'Malinvaud on Keynes', *Cambridge Journal of Economics*, **1**(4), 375–88.
Kaldor, N. (1955–56), 'Alternative theories of distribution', *Review of Economic Studies*, **23**(2), 83–100.
Kaldor, N. (1966), 'Marginal productivity and the macroeconomic theories of distribution: comment on Samuelson and Modigliani', *Review of Economic Studies*, **33**(4) (October), 309–19.
Kaldor, N. (1972), 'The irrelevance of equilibrium economics', *Economic Journal*, **82**(328), 1237–55.
Kaldor, N. and J. Trevithick (1992), 'A Keynesian perspective on money', *Lloyds Bank Review*, pp. 1–19.
Kalecki, M. (1938), 'The determinants of distribution of the national income', *Econometrica*, **6**(2), 97–112, reprinted in Jerzy Osiatynisky (ed.) (1990), *Collected Works of Michal Kalecki Vol II*, Oxford: Oxford University Press, pp. 3–20.
Kalecki, M (1939–40), 'The supply surve of an industry under imperfect competition', *Review of Economic Studies*, **7**(2), 91–122, reprinted in Jerzy Osiatynisky

(ed.) (1990), *Collected Works of Michal Kalecki Vol II*, Oxford: Oxford University Press, pp. 51–78.
Kalecki, M. (1942), 'A theory of profits', *Economic Journal*, **52**(206/207), 258–67. reprinted in Jerzy Osiatynisky (ed.) (1990), *Collected Works of Michal Kalecki Vol II*, Oxford: Oxford University Press, pp. 151–61.
Kalecki, M. ([1935] 1990), 'The essence of the business upswing [*Istota poprawy koniunkturalnej*]', in Jerzy Osiatynisky (ed.), *Collected Works of Michal Kalecki Vol. I*, Oxford: Oxford University Press, pp. 188–94, originally published in *Polska Gospedarcza*, **16**(22), 701–3.
Keynes, John M. (ed.) (1930), *A Treatise on Money*, London: Macmillan.
Keynes, John M. (ed.) (1936), *A General Theory of Employment, Interest and Money*, London: Macmillan.
Klein, Lawrence R., Aleksander Welfe and Wladyslaw Welfe (eds) (1999), *Principles of Macroeconometric Modelling*, Amsterdam: North-Holland.
Kurz, Heinz D. and Neri Salvadori (eds) (1995), *Theory of Production: a Long Period Analysis*, Cambridge, New York and Melbourne: Cambridge University Press.
Kurz, Heinz D. and N. Salvadori (2008), 'The post-Keynesian theories of growth and distribution: a survey', accessed at: www-dse.ec.unipi.it/persone/docenti/Salvadori/pdf/PostKeynesian.pdf.
Kydland, F.E. and E.C. Prescott (1982), 'Time to build and aggregate fluctuations', *Econometrica*, **50**, 1345–70.
Lambert, Jean-Paul (ed.) (1988), *Disequilibrium Macroeconomic Models, Theory and Estimation of Rationing Models Using Business Survey Data*, Cambridge: Cambridge University Press.
Lavoie, Marc (ed.) (1992), *Foundations of Post-Keynesian Economic Analysis*, Aldershot, UK and Brookfield, US: Edward Elgar Publishing.
Leijonhufvud, Axel (1973), 'Effective demand failures', *The Swedish Journal of Economics*, **75**(1), 27–48, reprinted in Axel Leijonhufvud (ed.) (1981), *Information and Coordination. Essays in Macroeconomic Theory*, New York: Oxford University Press.
Leroy, Robert (ed.) (1983), *Un Scénario Égalitaire. La Distribution des Revenus en Perspective*, Louvain-la-Neuve, Belgium: CIACO éditeur.
López, Julio G. and Michaël Assous (eds) (forthcoming), *Michal Kalecki*, New York: Palgrave Macmillan.
Lucas, Robert E. (1980), 'Methods and problems in business cycle theory', *Journal of Credit Banking and Money*, **12**(4), 696–715.
Machlup, Fritz (ed.) (1978), *Methodology of Economics and Other Social Sciences*, New York: Academic Press.
Malinvaud, E. (1956), 'L'Agrégation dans les modèles économiques', *Cahiers du Séminaire d'Économétrie*, **4**, 69–146.
Marchand, M., J. Mintz and P. Pestieau (1985), 'Public production and shadow pricing in a model of disequilibrium in labour and capital markets', *Journal of Economic Theory*, **36**(2), 237–56.
Marglin, Stephen A. (ed.) (1984), *Growth Distribution and Prices*, Cambridge, MA: Harvard University Press.
Mas-Colell, Andreu, Michael Whinston and Jerry Green (eds) (1995), *Microeconomic Theory*, Oxford: Oxford University Press.
Massé, Pierre (1954), 'Aperçus économiques sur l'efficience, le risque et l'investissement', *Revue de statistique appliquée*, **1**(2), 85–94.

Massé, Pierre (ed.) (1965), *Le Plan ou l'anti-hasard*, 1991 edn, Paris: Hermann, editeurs.
McKenzie, Lionel (ed.) (2002), *Classical General Equilibrium Theory*, Cambridge MA: The MIT Press.
Minsky Hyman P. ([1980] 1982), 'Finance and profits: the changing nature of American business cycles', in *Joint Economic Committee, Congress of the United States, The Business Cycle and Public Policy, 1929–1980*, Washington, DC: US Government Printing Office, reprinted 1982 as Chapter 2 in H.P. Minsky (ed.), *Can 'It' Happen Again ? Essays on Instability and Finance*, New York: Sharpeß.
Mitchell, William and Joan Muysken (eds) (2008), *Full Employment Abandoned. Shifting Sands and Policy Failures*, Cheltenham, UK and Northampton, MA, USA: Edward Elgar Publishing.
Mondello, G. (1985), 'Etude de la liaison monnaie-revenu. Demande effective: les théories de Thomas Tooke et J. M. Keynes', *Revue économique*, **36**(3), 509–54.
Muth, J.F. (1960), 'Rational expectations and the theory of price movements', *Econometrica*, **29**(3), 315–35.
North, Douglas (ed.) (2005), *Understanding the Process of Economic Change*, Princeton, NJ: Princeton University Press.
Panico, C. (1997), 'Government deficits in post Keynesian theories of growth and distribution', *Contributions to Political Economy*, **16**(1), 61–86.
Parguez, Alain (1969), 'L'intégration des variables financières dans le modèle de Don Patinkin', *Economies et Sociétés*, **15**, séries P.
Parguez, Alain (1975). *Monnaie et macroéconomie. Théorie de la monnaie en déséquilibre*, Paris: Economica.
Parguez, Alain (1977), 'Monnaie et demande effective en déséquilibre', in Christian Boissieu, Alain Parguez and Paul Zagamé (eds), *Economie du déséquilibre*, Paris: Economica, pp. 97–131.
Parguez, Alain (1980), 'Profit, épargne, investissement: elements pour une théorie monétaire du profit', *Economie appliquée*, **33**(2), 425–55.
Parguez, Alain (1984), 'La dynamique de la monnaie', *Economie et Sociétés*, **18**(4), ISMEA series Monnaie et Production, MP, no. 1.
Parguez, Alain (1996), 'Beyond scarcity: a reappraisal of the theory of the monetary circuit', in Ghislain Deleplace and Edward J. Nell (eds), *Money in Motion. The Post-Keynesian and Circulation Approaches*, London: Macmillan, pp. 155–99.
Parguez, Alain (2000), 'The long-run fiscal deflation: a real interpretation of the late twentieth-century world crisis', in Hassan Bougrine (ed.), *The Economics of Public Spending. Debts Deficits and Economic Performance*, Cheltenham, UK and Northampton, MA, USA: Edward Elgar Publishing.
Parguez, Alain (2002), 'Monetary Theory of Public Finance', *International Journal of Political Economy*, **32**(3), 80–97.
Parguez, Alain (2004), 'The solution of the paradox of profits', in R. Arena and N. Salvadori (eds), *Money, Credit and the Role of the State. Essays in Honour of Augusto Graziani*, Aldershot: Ashgate, pp. 257–70.
Parguez, Alain (2008), 'Money creation, employment and economic stability: the monetary theory of unemployment and inflation', *Panoeconomicus*, **55**(1), 39–67.
Parguez Alain (2009), unpublished manuscript on the opening of the circuit to external trade.
Parguez, Alain and Mario Seccareccia (2000), 'The credit theory of money: the

monetary circuit approach' in John Smithin (ed.), *What is Money?*, New York: Routledge, pp. 101–23.
Pasinetti, Luigi L. (1962), 'Rate of profit and income distribution in relation to the rate of economic growth', *Review of Economic Studies*, **29**(4), 267–79.
Pasinetti, Luigi L. (1964–65), *Causalità e Interdipendenza nell'analisi econometrica e nella teoria economica*, Milan, Italy: Annuario dell'Università Cattolica del Sacro Cuore, Vita e Pensiero, pp. 233–50.
Pasinetti, Luigi L. (1980), 'The notion of vertical integration', in Luigi L. Pasinetti (ed.), *Economic Analysis, in Essays on the Theory of Joint Production*, New York: Columbia University Press.
Pasinetti, Luigi L. (ed.) (1981), *Structural Change and Economic Growth: A Theoretical Essay on the Dynamics of the Wealth of Nations*, Cambridge: Cambridge University Press.
Pasinetti, Luigi L. (2005), 'The Cambridge School of Keynesian economics', *Cambridge Journal of Economics*, **29**(6), 837–48.
Pasinetti, Luigi L. (ed.) (2007), *Keynes and the Cambridge Keynesians. A Revolution in Economics to be Accomplished*, Cambridge: Cambridge University Press.
Petri, Fabio (ed.) (1989), *Teorie del valore e della distribuzione. Un confronto fra classici e neoclassici*, Roma: La Nuova Italia Scientifica.
Petri, Fabio (1999), 'Professor Hahn on the 'neo-Ricardian' criticism of neoclassical economics', in Gary Mongiovi and Fabio Petri (eds), *Value, Distribution and Capital. Essays in Honour of Pierangelo Garegnani*, London: Routledge, pp. 19–68.
Petri, Fabio (2003), 'A 'Sraffian' critique of general equilibrium theory, and the classical Keynesian alternative', in Frank Hahn and Fabio Petri (eds), *General Equilibrium, Problems and Prospects*, New York: Routledge, pp. 387–421.
Petri, Fabio (ed.) (2004), *General Equilibrium, Capital and Macroeconomics. A Key to Recent Controversies in Economic Theories*, Cheltenham, UK and Northampton, MA, USA: Edward Elgar Publishing.
Pratt, Jamie (ed.) (2003), *Financial Accounting in an Economic Context*, John Wiley & Sons, Inc.
Renaud, Jean F. (2000), 'The Problem of the monetary realization of profits in a post Keynesian sequential financing model: two solutions of the Kaleckian option', *Review of Political Economy*, **12**(3), 285–302.
Robinson, Joan (ed.) (1956), *The Accumulation of Capital*, London: Macmillan.
Robinson, Joan (ed.) (1962), *Essays in the Theory of Economic Growth*, London: Macmillan, St. Martin's Press.
Robinson, J. (1974), *History versus Equilibrium*, Thames papers in political economy, Thames Polytechnic, London.
Robinson, J. (1977), 'Michal Kalecki on the economics of capitalism', *Oxford Bulletin of Economics & Statistics*, **39**(1), 7–17.
Rochon, Jean-Philippe (ed.) (1999), *Credit Money and Production. An Alternative Post-Keynesian Approach*, Cheltenham, UK and Northampton, MA, USA: Edward Elgar Publishing.
Rochon, Jean-Philippe (2005), 'The existence of monetary profits within the monetary circuit', in Giuseppe Fontana and Riccardo Realfonzo (eds), *The Monetary Theory of Production. Tradition and Perspectives*, New York: Palgrave Macmillan, pp. 125–38.
Rochon, Louis-Philippe (2009), 'The existence of profits within the monetary circuit: some unanswered questions revisited', in Jean-Francois Ponsot and

Sergio Rossi (eds), *The Political Economy of Monetary Circuits Tradition and Change in Post-Keynesian Economics*, Basingstoke: Palgrave Macmillan.
Roncaglia, Alesandro (ed.) (2009), *Piero Sraffa*, New York: Palgrave Macmillan.
Samuelson, Paul A. (ed.) (1947), *Foundations of Economic Analysis*, Cambridge, MA: Harvard University Press.
Samuelson, Paul A. (1969), 'Classical and neoclassical theory', in Robert W. Clower (ed.), *Monetary Theory: Selected Readings*, Harmondsworth: Penguin.
Schefold, B. (1997), 'Classical theory and intertemporal equilibrium', in Bertrand Schefold (ed.), *Normal Prices, Technical Change and Accumulation*, London: Macmillan, pp. 425–501.
Schmitt, Bernard (ed.) (1966), *Monnaie Salaires et Profits*, Paris: Presses Universitaires de France.
Schmitt, Bernard (ed.) (1984), *Inflation, Chômage et Malformations du Capital*, Albeuve, Switzerland: Castella, and Paris: Economica.
Seccareccia, M. (1995), 'Keynesianism and public investment: a left-Keynesian perspective on the role of government expenditures and debt', *Studies in Political Economy*, **46**, 43–78.
Segura, A. (1995), 'Le profit et l'intérêt dans le circuit', *L'Actualité Économique*, **71**(1), 53–70.
Simon, H.A. (1953), 'Causal order and identifiability', in William C. Hood and Tjalling C. Koopmans (eds), *Studies in the Econometric Method*, New York: John Wiley & Sons, Inc..
Sneessens, H. and J.H. Drèze (1986), 'A discussion of Belgian unemployment combining traditional concepts and disequilibrium econometrics', *Economica*, **53**(210), S89–S119.
Sraffa, Piero (ed.) (1960), *Produzione di merci a mezzo di merci: premesse a una critica della teoria economica*, Turin, Italy: Einaudi.
Steindl, J. (1979), 'Stagnation theory and stagnation policy', *Cambridge Journal of Economics*, **3**(1), 1–14.
Steindl, Joseph (1982), 'The role of household savings in the modern economy', *Banca Nazionale del Lavoro Quarterly Review*, 140, reprinted in Joseph Steindl (ed.) (1990), *Economic Papers 1941–1988*, London: Macmillan, pp. 183–207.
Steindl, Joseph (1985), 'Distribution and growth, political economy', *Studies in the Surplus Approach*, **1**(1), republished 1990 in *Joseph Steindl Economic Papers 1941–1988*, London: The Macmillan Press, pp. 149–65.
Steindl, Joseph (1987), 'Kalecki's theory of pricing: notes on the margin', in G. Kink, G. Pöll and M. Riese (eds), *Economic Theory, Political Power and Social Justice*, *Festschrift Kazimierz Laski*, Vienna and New York, Springer Verlag, reprinted in Joseph Steindl (ed.) (1990), *Economic Papers 1941–1988*, London: Macmillan, pp. 303–16.
Steindl, Joseph (ed.) (1990), *Economic Papers 1941–1988*, London: Macmillan, pp. 149–65.
Strotz, Robert H. and H.O.A. Wold (1960), 'Recursive versus nonrecursive systems: an attempt at synthesis (part I of a triptych on causal chain systems)', *Econometrica*, **28**(2), 417–27.
Sylos Labini, Paolo (1967), 'Prices and wages: a theoretical and statistical interpretation of Italian experience', *Journal of Industrial Economics*, **15**, (2) (April), 109–28.
Sylos Labini, Paolo (1988), 'The great debates on the laws of returns and the value

of capital: when will economists finally accept their own logic?', *Banca Nazionale del Lavoro Quarterly Review*, **41**(166), 263–9.

Sylos Labini, Paolo (ed.) (2004), *Torniamo ai classici. Produttività del lavoro, progresso tecnico e sviluppo economico*, Roma: Laterza.

Taylor, Lance (ed.) (2004), *Reconstructing Macroeconomics. Structuralitst Proposals and Critiques of the Mainstream*, Cambridge, MA: Harvard University Press.

United Nations (1993), System of National Accounts (SNA), accessed at http://unstats.un.org/unsd/sna1993/toctop.asp.

Vercelli, Alessandro (1994), 'Equilibrio, squilibrio e teoria economica', in Giovanni Caravale (ed.), *Equilibrio e Teoria Economica*, Bologna, Italy: Il Mulino.

von Neumann, J. (1945), 'A model of general economic equilibrium', *Review of Economic Studies*, **13**(1), 1–9.

Weintraub, Sydney (ed.) (1959), *A General Theory of the Price Level, Output, Income Distribution and Economic Growth*, Philadelphia, PA: Chilton Co. Book Division.

Wickens, Michael (ed.) (2008), *Macroeconomic Theory*, Princeton, NJ: Princeton University Press.

Woodford, Michael (ed.) (2003), *Interest and Prices. Foundations of a Theory of Monetary Policy*, Princeton, NJ: Princeton University Press.

PART II

Public investment and fiscal conditions in the EU New Member States

4. Patterns and trends of public investment in the New Member States of the European Union

Ángel Catalina Rubianes

INTRODUCTION

Due to a number of reasons, public expenditure is lower in New Member States (NMS) than in the EU-15 countries. Lower social protection in NMS is a key source of the difference. Nevertheless, despite restrictions on total expenditure, public investment is on average higher in NMS in terms of GDP. This higher investment can be linked to a significant extent to the support from the EU Cohesion Policy, which accounts in NMS for 75 per cent of environmental protection and 10 per cent of economic affairs and human capital investment. Following the economic crisis, public investment is under pressure and declining in NMS, underlining the importance of continued efforts under the European cohesion policy.

Article 174 of the new Treaty of Lisbon empowers the European Community to promote its harmonious development through actions which strengthen economic, social and territorial cohesion and, thus, reduce disparities between the levels of development of the various regions. Article 175 also involves Member States in this role by asking them to conduct their economic policies in such a way as to attain the objectives set out in Article 174.

Public spending is one of the most typical actions of the public sector to promote development and to tackle disparities across regions. Spending policies can be carried out in the context of a specific regional policy or, on the contrary, through spatially-blind decisions which do not aim specifically at addressing regional disparities. Regardless of their specific policy objectives virtually all public spending policies, either spatially oriented or nor, have a territorial and personal impact in terms of disparities. This chapter is aimed at appraising the composition of public expenditure[1] and public investment[2] in the EU, with a particular focus in those areas related to regional development and to the scope of the European cohesion policy.

The first part of this chapter focuses on the differences in the total levels of public expenditure between Member States of the EU and the weight of public investment within this total public expenditure. It also looks at the trends observed in the last decade and assesses to what extent public investment is co-related with the 'catching-up' process in GDP per head.

The second part pays attention to the composition of public expenditure in the EU. It draws the main patterns of public expenditure and the trends observed in its composition over time. The chapter aims to find out in which areas lay the differences observed across countries in terms of total public expenditure. The contribution of the European cohesion policy to public expenditure in the different areas is also analysed. Finally, the third part aims to depict the impact of the crisis on public spending and public investment and sketches out some possible trends looking at the public deficit and public debt positions of Member States.

1. PUBLIC EXPENDITURE AND PUBLIC INVESTMENT IN THE NEW MEMBER STATES OF THE EU

1.1 The Size of the Public Sector is Higher in the EU-15 Member States . . .

The size of the public sector varies markedly across the different Member States of the EU. It means that the availability of financial resources to achieve the functions attributed to the public sector differ substantially across the Union, including the allocation of non-market public goods and services. Public expenditure accounted on average for 46.8 per cent of GDP in the EU in 2008 with, nevertheless, significant differences across countries which may attain almost 20 percentages points (between more than 53 per cent in Sweden to less than 35 per cent in the Slovak Republic).

Figure 4.1[3] shows the different levels of public expenditure in Member States and the functional composition of this expenditure according to the standardised Classification of Functions of Government (COFOG[4]). It also compares the total public expenditure in NMS and EU-15 countries.

Public spending tends to be higher in countries with higher levels of GDP per head. It is even above 50 per cent of GDP in three Member States (Sweden, France and Denmark). The different traditions in the preferences of the society also explain to some extent the differences in the levels of public expenditure. The Nordic, French and German traditions advocate in general for more powerful public sectors than in the Mediterranean and Central and Eastern European countries. Public expenditure was

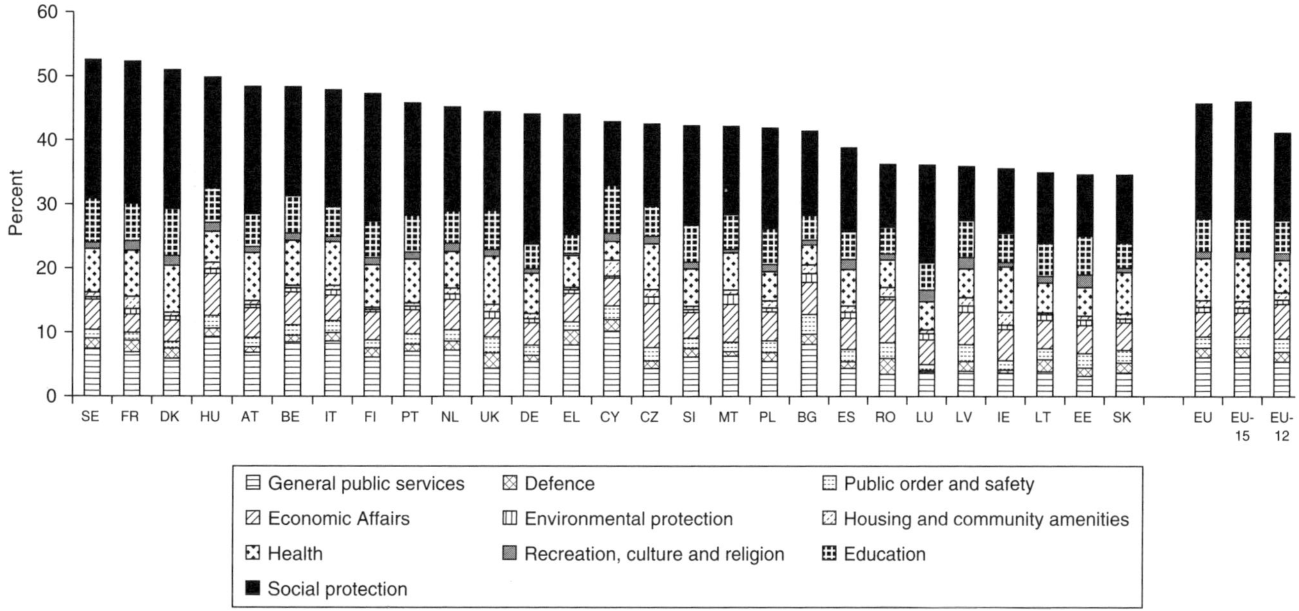

Source: Eurostat

Figure 4.1 Total public expenditure as a percentage of GDP (2007)

on average about 5 percentage points higher in terms of GDP in the old EU-15 (47.2 per cent) that in NMS (42 per cent) in 2008.

The gap soared in the last decade as a result of some reductions in total public expenditure observed in most NMS over the period 1999–2008. On average, the share in terms of GDP declined from 43.5 per cent in 1999 to 41.2 per cent in 2007 while it was very stable in the EU-15 countries. In 2008 total public expenditure increased slightly until 42 per cent of GDP as a result of the first impact of the economic downturn and the consequent effects of the automatic stabilisers.

Only one NMS (Hungary) is above the EU average in terms of total public expenditure. Also Italy is slightly above the EU average as the main exception among Southern European countries. Nevertheless, the interest payments to be paid every year as a result of the high public debt (7 per cent of the total public expenditure) explain this 'exception' to some extent.

Most of the public expenditure in the EU is overwhelmingly devoted to current expenditure (91.3 per cent) while just a relatively small part of it is devoted to public investment (8.7 per cent). The border between both kinds of expenditure is, however, not always easy to draw. In general, those types of expenditures that are consumed within the current year are called current expenditure. Conversely, capital expenditure is not just consumed in the same year but the assets are used repeatedly in production processes for more than one year. This is what in general is called investment. Thus, some kinds of expenditure are classified as current expenditure while it may be advocated that they are producing returns over several years. The most typical cases are education, training and, in general, public expenditure aimed at upgrading human capital. Also expenditures in research and development and software are recorded under current expenditure although they have a clear impact on the productive process over several years.

1.2 . . . But Public Investment is Higher in New Member States (and also the Total Investment in the Economy) . . .

Figure 4.2 shows the levels of public investment undertaken by the General Government in the periods 1999–2003 and 2004–2008.[5] Despite their lower levels of total public spending, public investment has consistently been substantially higher in NMS in terms of GDP. This favourable gap has oscillated between 1.2 and 2.4 points of GDP. The peak was hit in 2002. In 2008 public investment accounted for 5.5 per cent of GDP in NMS while it was just 4 per cent in the EU-15 countries. In principle, this gap should widen in the forthcoming years as a result of the significant allocations granted to NMS by the European Cohesion Policy.[6]

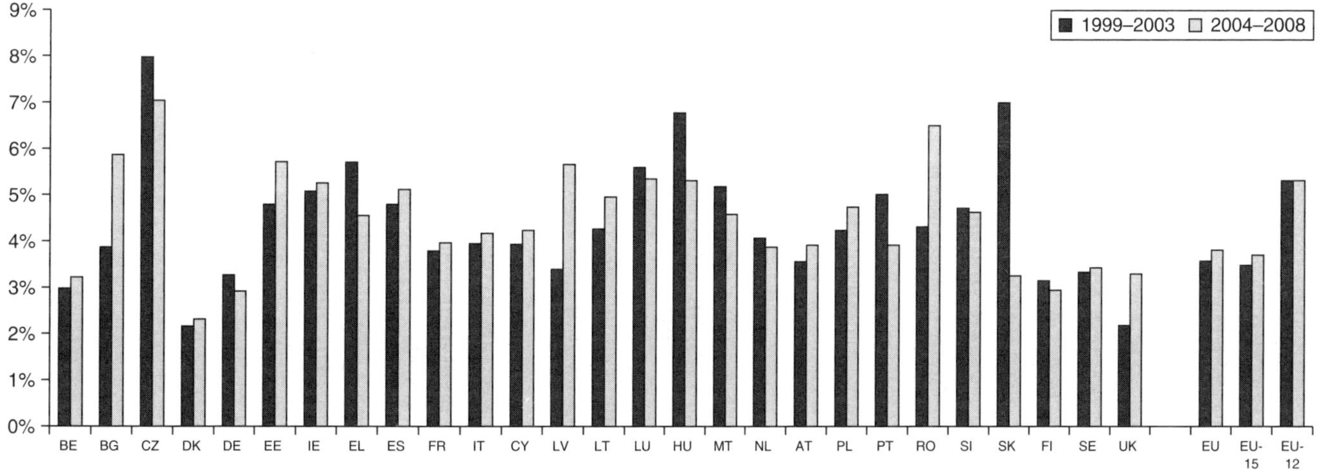

Source: Eurostat

Figure 4.2 Public investment as a percentage of GDP

In the period 2004-2008 the five first countries in the top list in terms of public investment were NMS (Czech Republic, Romania, Latvia, Estonia and Hungary) while four of the five last were from the EU-15 (Denmark, Germany, Finland and Belgium) with the exception of the Slovak Republic. In the first group public investment was on average over 5 per cent of the national GDP in all cases (more than 6 per cent in Romania and 7 per cent in the Czech Republic) and below 3.5 per cent of GDP in the latter (even below 3 per cent in Finland, Germany and Denmark). This divide also reflects the differences observed in the rates of total investment (public and private) in the economy. Over the same period, total investment was 3 points of GDP higher in NMS (23.3 per cent) than in the EU-15 (20.4 per cent). The public sector accounts for a higher share of the total investment in NMS (23.2 per cent against 17.7 per cent) explaining therefore some part of their higher rates of total investment.

There are few exceptions to the sharp divide between NMS and old EU-15 Member States in their relative levels of public investment. The Slovak Republic is the only NMS in which public investment is on average below 4 per cent of GDP in the period 2004–2008. However, its rate of private investment was higher than in its neighbour countries (Poland, Austria, Hungary or the Czech Republic) over the same period suggesting a more dynamic private sector though far from the rates of the Baltic States and Romania and Bulgaria. This is probably one of the reasons why the public sector was not playing so significant a role in terms of investment. In addition, the endowment of capital stock of the Slovak Republic in terms of GDP (5.6 per cent of its GDP) is similar, even slightly higher, to some mature economies such as France, Italy and Germany.

Among EU-15 countries, Luxembourg, Ireland and Spain stand out with levels of public investment higher than 5 per cent of GDP over the same reference period. The two latter are also those with the most dynamic private sectors in terms of investment as a share of the national GDP.

This divide reveals also that public investment (and probably more surprisingly also private investment) in the EU tends to be smaller in terms of GDP in those countries with the highest levels of total public expenditure. The most likely reason is that countries with high levels of expenditure are rather mature economies with relatively high endowments of physical capital. Additional investments in physical capital provide fewer returns and may also entail a higher opportunity cost.

1.3 . . . Though it was Decreasing Over Time in Some of Them

When looking at the trends over the two reference periods taken, the picture is more mixed. Public investment decreased in 11 Member States.

Five of them are NMS (Slovak Republic, Hungary, Czech Republic, Malta and Slovenia). The sharpest decline in the EU occurred indeed in the Slovak Republic (−3.7) and Hungary (−1.5). Some reductions happened, however, in a context of very high initial levels of public investment such as the case of the Czech Republic (from 8 per cent to 7 per cent) which remains the country with the highest levels of public investment in the EU even after this decline. However, it is important to point out that total investment (public and private) soared to 3 points of GDP in the Slovak Republic and 0.6 in Slovenia over the two periods, which reveal dynamic private sectors that play an increasing role as engines of the economy. Conversely, total investment declined too in the other three mentioned NMS. They are the only NMS in which total investment was downward.

In contrast, five out of the six countries in which public investment increased the most across the two reference periods are NMS (the United Kingdom is the only exception). Latvia, Bulgaria and Romania are the three first countries in the top list with increases higher than 2 percentage points of GDP in all of them. They are the three Member States in the EU scoring the highest increases in total investment in the economy (at least 6 points of GDP, even over 9 points in Bulgaria).

In consequence, although it was slightly more volatile than in the EU-15, public investment in NMS was on average maintained over the period 1999–2008 in a context of some budgetary restrictions. Total investment showed a very similar pace with some few exceptions such as the mentioned cases of the Slovak Republic and, to a lesser extent, Slovenia.

1.4 Some NMS were Able to Combine Reductions of Public Expenditure with Increases of Public Investment . . .

Figure 4.3 shows the combined patterns of public expenditure and public investment in the EU over the period 1999–2008. Average data for the periods 1999–2003 and 2004–2008 are compared.

Total public expenditure decreased in 11 Member States. Eight of them are NMS which confirms that most of these countries have been facing some budgetary restrictions in the last decade. The highest decline is by far observed in the Slovak Republic (−9.1 percentage points of GDP). However, public investment just ebbed in three of them (Slovak Republic, Czech Republic and Slovenia). This feature confirms that, in general, the reductions of public expenditure in these countries were not made at the expense of public investment.

The fourth quadrant of the figure (bottom right) shows those countries which have been able to combine cuts in total spending with increases in public investment. Bulgaria and Romania stand out. Along with Latvia,

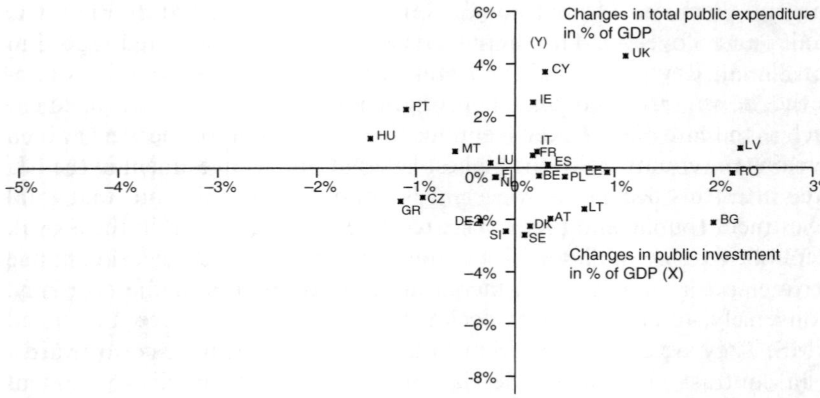

Source: Eurostat

Figure 4.3 Changes in public investment compared to changes in total public expenditure, (1999–2003 and 2004–2008)

they are the Member States that scored the highest increases in public investment in the EU despite reductions in total public spending. Other cases such as Estonia, Lithuania or Poland are also worth underlining. In Latvia, the increase in public investment was much higher than the increase in public expenditure.

Conversely, Malta and Hungary along with Portugal showed reductions in public investment in a context of budgetary expansion. They are exceptional cases among NMS. Nonetheless, public investment was still well above the EU average in both countries.

In the EU-15 the most typical case is a slight reduction both in total public expenditure and public expenditure. The main exceptions are Ireland and the United Kingdom. In the latter, public spending soared more than 4 percentage points of GDP compared to the period 1999–2003. A bit more than 1 percentage point of this increase was devoted to public investment.

1.5 . . . And it seems it was a Good Policy Choice for 'Catching-Up' with the EU GDP per Head Average

In general, a parallel trend is found in levels of public investment in terms of GDP in the last decade (1999–2008) and the trends in their levels of GDP per head expressed in Purchase Power Standards (PPS) in the same reference period. The five Member States which enjoyed the best levels of 'catching-up' (Luxembourg, the three Baltic States and Ireland) present levels of public investment significantly higher than the EU average. The same finding applies to the total levels of investment except in the case of Luxembourg.

In contrast, only one of the ten countries with the lowest levels of public investment improved its score in terms of GDP per head in PPS compared to the EU average. This is the case of the United Kingdom, where public investment was on a rise over time. The other nine countries, which are from the EU-15, scored negative levels compared to the EU average. In other words, there seems to be a significant co-relation at the national level between the levels of public investment and the increases in GDP per head over time.

Nonetheless, the reader should be cautious in establishing a direct co-relation between both variables because GDP per head in PPS is influenced by a high number of factors of very different natures. In any event, it is unquestionable that investment is a significant component of the aggregated demand and that its total level was on average about 3 points of GDP higher in NMS that in the other countries of the EU.

In conclusion, most NMS were facing budgetary restrictions while increasing their levels of public investment in the last decade. Their total levels of public spending were lowered on average by more 1 percentage point of GDP. As a result, public expenditure was in these countries on average 5 percentage points lower than the total public expenditure in the EU-15 countries in 2008. Yet, the weight of public investment is still 1.5 percentage points of GDP higher in the NMS which means that the reduction of the total expenditure was not made at the expense of 'productive expenditure'. Public investment accounted for more than 12.5 per cent of the total public expenditure in NMS in 2008 while it was barely 8 per cent in the EU-15 countries. This choice of economic policy seems to explain to some extent the good performance of these countries in terms of 'catching-up' with the GDP per head average of the EU.

2. THE COMPOSITION OF PUBLIC EXPENDITURE AND PUBLIC INVESTMENT IN THE NEW MEMBER STATES OF THE EU

The provision of non-market public goods and services is one of the traditional functions of the public sector (allocative function). Public goods and services enhance development opportunities of people living in a territory by improving the endowment of physical and human capital.

For the purposes of this chapter, the analysis of public spending by function will be focused on four COFOG Divisions[7] either because they are especially relevant in terms of total public spending (social protection) or they are 'investment intensive' and the most relevant under the scope of the European cohesion policy (Economic Affairs, Environmental Protection and Education).

The differences observed in the previous section in terms of total public expenditure may arise either from the 'productive expenditure' aimed at increasing physical and human capital or, conversely, from current expenditure aimed principally at providing social transfers to individuals and modifying the initial distribution of income.

The European cohesion policy[8] plays a prominent role in supporting public spending in 'Economic Affairs', 'Environmental Protection' and 'Education'. These three categories together account for a significant part of the eligible areas under the EU cohesion policy. The total amount captured is about €262 billion for the period 2007–2013 which represents about 75 per cent of the policy. The main category which is left out is 'Business Support' (some €70 billion for the whole period) and 'Governance' (some €10 billion).

Most of the capital expenditure of the General Government, especially GFCF, is concentrated in a small number of COFOG divisions. More than one-third of the total GFCF made by the public sector in the EU happens in the area of economic affairs (mostly in the area of transport). The two other significant areas are Education and Housing and community amenities (both slightly above 10 per cent) but nevertheless far from the former. GFCF of the public sector attained more than €314 billion in 2007 in the EU.

Social protection is by far the main division in terms of public spending. Four out of ten euros are spent under this area even though significant differences across Member States can be observed as outlined in the previous section. The other three areas which are analysed in this chapter account altogether for about 21 per cent of the total public expenditure in the EU.

2.1 New Member States Stand Out in terms of Public Expenditure in Physical Infrastructure . . .

The division 'Economic Affairs' includes a rather heterogeneous array of domains which include *inter alia* agriculture and forestry, fuel and energy, transport, communication and the related research and development in these areas.

Economic affairs accounts for more than 33 per cent of the total GFCF in the EU. It is therefore a 'capital-intensive' field. Figure 4.4 shows that NMS stand out in public expenditure in this category. It accounts for almost 7 per cent of the national GDP in the Czech Republic and Romania

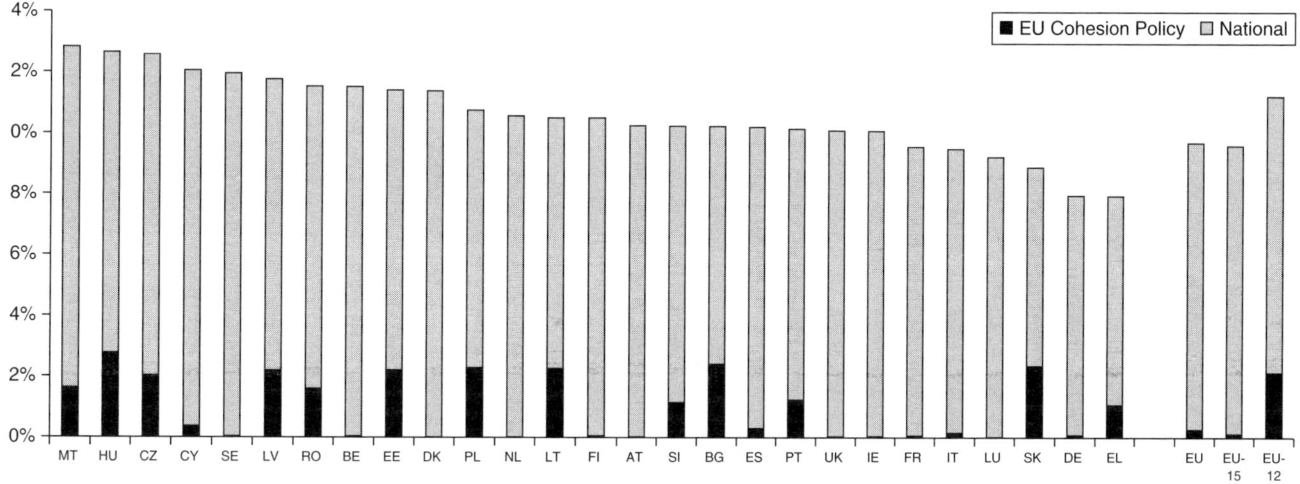

Figure 4.4 Total public expenditure in economic affairs, environment and human capital as a percentage of GDP

and largely exceeds 6 per cent in Hungary. In other words, NMS devote higher levels of public spending to these areas while their levels of public spending are on average lower than in the EU-15. While the investments in this division account on average just for 4.4 per cent of GDP in the old EU-15, this proportion amounted to 5.8 per cent of GDP in NMS in 2007. Given that this category is 'capital-intensive' this finding is consistent with the conclusions of the previous section.

In all Member States, the main group under this category is expenditure in transport. In the countries for which expenditure data on transport are available,[9] it varies between 56 per cent and 67 per cent of the total. This proportion is less than 50 per cent in most of the old EU-15 countries for which data are available.[10] Therefore, NMS tend not only to present higher levels of public investment (in terms of GDP) in those areas which are more 'physical capital-intensive' but also give a prominent place to transport-related investments compared to the other EU Member States.

The European cohesion policy[11] explains to a very significant extent the favourable gap of the NMS in the area of economic affairs. The Structural Funds and the Cohesion Fund account for more than 25 per cent of the total investment in this area in three NMS (Poland, Slovakia and Lithuania) and is, in any case, above 14 per cent in all the others except in Romania (11 per cent), Malta (11 per cent) and Cyprus (2 per cent). While Romania, the Czech Republic, Hungary and Malta are still nevertheless in the first four positions if we do not take account of the EU cohesion policy allocations, the gap considerably narrows. Moreover, there are some NMS which rank much lower (Bulgaria, Poland) in the list by removing the EU cohesion policy. For example, one out of three Euros invested in economic affairs in Poland is paid by the Structural Funds and the Cohesion Fund. In consequence, this policy is crucial in most of the NMS to keep the public investment effort to increase their endowments of physical capital.

2.2 . . . and Devote similar Sums than EU-15 Countries to Environmental Protection . . .

In the past few years, protection of the environment has gradually come to the forefront of the policy agenda and is now among the top priorities to be addressed in the challenges with which Europe is confronted in the coming decades (for example climate change, energy efficiency). Sustainable development is not only about tackling pollution but also about ensuring growth and employment over the medium and long term.

While not perfect, COFOG Division 5 ('Environmental Protection') is an indicator of the public investment effort in ensuring sustainable development. This division is based upon the Classification of Environmental Protection Activities (CEPA) as elaborated in the European System of Collection of Economic Information of the Environment (SERIEE) of Eurostat. It mostly includes all the direct investment aimed at protecting the environment and excludes those areas with an indirect impact which are recorded under other categories of expenditure (for example energy efficiency investment).

European governments are devoting on average about 0.78 per cent of GDP to the items of expenditure recorded under this category. There are not significant differences between NMS (0.72 per cent) and the old EU-15 (0.79 per cent). Malta and Bulgaria are, however, at the top of the list. Only these Member States spend more than 1 per cent of their GDP on direct investments to preserve the environment.

Yet, when matching the Structural Funds and the Cohesion Fund[12] with the total investment, the main finding is that the environmental policy in NMS is overwhelmingly led by the European cohesion policy. It accounts on average for 75 per cent of the total direct investments in this area in NMS (2.9 per cent in the old EU-15) and is above 40 per cent in all of them.[13] In consequence, the European cohesion policy is critical for sustainable development policies in NMS and also in some EU-15 countries such as Portugal or Greece.

2.3 . . . and also to Upgrade Human Capital

Human capital is the other factor of production which is behind GDP performance. It refers to the skills and knowledge that individuals accumulate over time. While statistics on capital expenditure do not capture public spending aimed at upgrading human capital, this category is included in this chapter in order to secure a comprehensive picture of public policies aimed at enhancing the development opportunities of people and competitiveness of the economy over the medium and long term. Endowments of human capital increasingly explain gains of productivity. Given that the total number of hours worked is rather stable in the current social legal framework, a significant part of future increases in GDP will be mostly obtained by enhancing the productivity of labour.

Productivity of labour is increased by improving the qualifications of the labour force and adapting it to the needs of the economy. The total expenditure in education which a country incurs, albeit not perfect, is a good indicator of public investment in upgrading human capital. Moreover, education is a very strong channel for social mobility and, therefore, social cohesion and regional convergence. By investing in education, public authorities may pursue efficiency (through a best use of factors of production) and equity (this is what is called 'transfers in kind') objectives simultaneously.

Expenditures recorded under COFOG Division 9 ('Education') include government outlays on services provided to individual pupils and students and expenditures on education services provided on a collective basis.

From the outset it was underlined that total public expenditure in most of the EU-15 Member States was significantly higher than in some NMS in terms of GDP. This gap was even over 20 percentage points in some cases. When assessing public expenditure in physical capital we found that it does not account for these differences, even the opposite.

The picture of public expenditure in human capital is slightly different. While there seems to be some positive co-relation with levels of total public expenditure, this co-relation is not too high. Many NMS score fairly well. Seven of them are among the top half with higher levels of expenditure in this area. On average, the total public expenditure in human capital is the same in the old EU-15 and NMS (5.1 per cent of GDP).

The European cohesion policy explains a much lower proportion of the differences across Member States in the area of human capital.[14] The main reason is that this is an area which entails a relatively high public expenditure compared to the others and, especially, that only a small part is eligible for the co-financing by the Structural Funds. Primary and secondary education expenses, which are the main groups under this Division, are barely eligible to be funded by the Structural Funds. Nevertheless, Structural Funds interventions in the area of human capital represent more than 10 per cent of the total expenditure in five Member States and also in Greece and Portugal.

2.4 But Public Expenditure in Social Protection in New Member States is much Lower and Explains Almost Completely the Differences in Total Public Expenditure

Social protection is by far the major COFOG Division in terms of public expenditure (18 per cent of GDP, about 40 per cent of the total public expenditure in the EU). Expenditure under this division relates mostly to services and transfers provided to individual persons and households. It does not include health care which is recorded under COFOG Division 7. It means that medical goods and services provided to persons who receive cash benefits and benefits in kind related to health are not recorded under social protection. This category includes, for instance, sickness and disability, old age (for example pensions), survivors (for example widows or children's pensions), family and children's allocations, unemployment benefits and housing aids.

Social protection is without doubt the area which presents the highest co-relation with total expenditure. The first three Member States in terms of social protection (as a percentage of GDP) are those with higher levels of total public expenditure (Figure 4.5). In addition, there is also a clear divide between the old EU-15 Member States (18.3 per cent of GDP on average) and NMS (13.6 per cent of GDP on average) in this division. Indeed, the first nine countries are old EU-15. Hungary, which is the fourth Member State in total expenditure, ranks just tenth in public expenditure on social protection. On the other side of the picture, the last eight countries are NMS with the exception of Ireland which is, by the way, one of the Member States with the lowest levels of public expenditure in terms of GDP.

In summary, the significant differences between Member States in the size of their public sectors are due almost completely to their different levels of expenditure on social protection. Conversely, they have not had any influence in determining investments in physical capital (for example transport or communication), human capital and those aimed at upgrading the quality of the environment.

2.5 NMS have Substantially Lowered their Public Expenditure in Social Protection in the Last Five Years while Increasing Spending in Infrastructure

The analysis of the dynamics in public expenditure is restricted to this period because 2002 is the earliest year in which complete and reliable data on public spending by area are available for all Member States.

The trends in public spending show (Table 4.1) that there was a significant reduction in public spending in social protection in NMS. This cut amounts to about 13 per cent of total expenditure in this area (about 2 percentage points of GDP). This is by far the area in which public expenditure most varied. It is important to underline that total public expenditure in the same period ebbed from 44 per cent to 41.2 per cent of GDP in NMS. It means in fact that most of the cuts in public spending were made at the expense of spending in social protection. Some reductions are also observed in the EU-15 though its extent is much smaller (just slightly over 3 per cent of the total original expenditure in social protection or 0.66 percentage points of GDP).

Education is the other area which suffered from cuts in public spending in NMS. Yet, this reduction was less than 3 per cent of the total original expenditure (0.2 percentage points of GDP). The slump observed is slightly higher than the average of the whole EU where total spending in education was also downward.

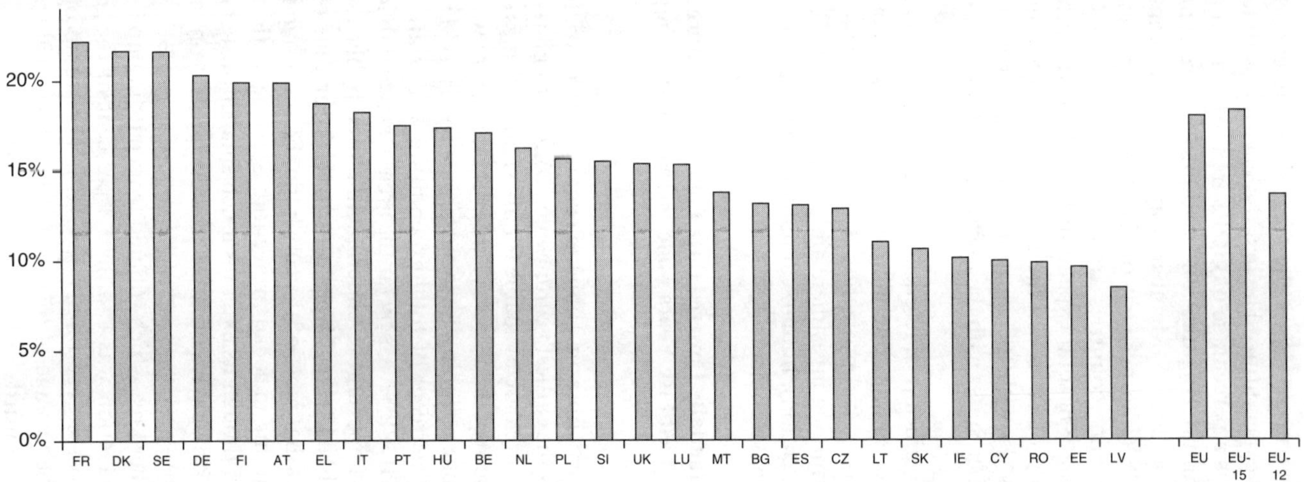

Source: Eurostat

Figure 4.5 Total public expenditure in social protection as a percentage of GDP (2007)

Table 4.1 Public expenditure 2002–2007 (as a percentage of GDP)

	2002	2007
Economic affairs		
EU	3.9	3.8
EU-15	3.8	3.7
EU-12	5.2	5.4
Environmental protection		
EU	0.7	0.8
EU-15	0.7	0.8
EU-12	0.6	0.7
Education		
EU	5.3	5.1
EU-15	5.2	5.1
EU-12	5.5	5.1
Social protection		
EU	18.6	18.0
EU-15	18.7	18.3
EU-12	15.6	13.6

Source: Eurostat.

Economic affairs is the only area in this analysis in which public spending was rising in NMS while it dropped in the EU-15 countries. The increase in NMS was about 3 per cent (0.2 percentage points of GDP) of the original expenditure in 2002 which confirms the prominent place of investments in physical capital in public spending decisions in NMS.

In consequence, the figures show that governments of NMS privileged investments in physical capital at the expense of spending in social protection and human capital in a general context of budgetary restrictions. The picture differs in EU-15 countries in which both the changes in total public spending and across the different categories of expenditure were not so significant.

3. THE EFFECTS OF THE ECONOMIC CRISIS ON PUBLIC INVESTMENT

In autumn 2008 the collapse of the banking system in the United States triggered the worst economic global crisis since the end of the Second World War. The crisis spread throughout the planet. As a result, most

European economies entered into recession and unemployment started to rise. All the national economies in the EU except Poland underwent negative growth rates in 2009. On average, GDP declined by 4.2 percentage points in the EU. While the impact was on average similar in NMS and the EU-15, the impact was rather heterogeneous in both groups of countries. For instance, the three Baltic States scored 2-digit rates of negative economic growth. Furthermore, the unemployment rate of the European Union jumped from 7.6 per cent at the end of 2008 to 9.8 per cent at the end of 2009 with very significant peaks in some Member States (for example more than 22 per cent in Latvia and close to 20 per cent in Spain).

3.1 Public Investment is Decreasing in most NMS During the Economic Crisis . . .

Public finances are not immune to the effects of the crisis. The public deficit rose to −2.3 per cent of the EU-27 in 2008. Moreover, this deterioration has just started and is likely to further deepen in 2009 (−6 per cent) and 2010 (−7.3 per cent) with very significant differences across Member States. These high levels of public deficits will result in a dramatic increase of the public debts ratios in a very short time frame. In the EU, this ratio is expected to rise from 58.7 per cent of GDP in 2007 to almost 80 per cent in 2010.

Figure 4.6 shows the first reactions of public expenditure and public investment[15] to the effects of the economic downturn. It compares nominal data of the first three quarters of 2008 with nominal data for the same period in 2009 which were released recently by Eurostat.[16]

The results are significantly different in NMS and the EU-15 countries. The latter were in general running countercyclical policies which consist of expanding both public spending and public investment during the worst months of recession. Moreover, public investment in the EU-15 (+11.4 per cent) was increasing faster than public expenditure (+5.5 per cent) which suggests that many national governments were focusing on public investment recovery measures. Public investment was upward in all EU-15 Member States except Ireland and Portugal compared to the first half of 2008. The picture is much more varied within NMS. Public investment declined in six NMS (more than 30 per cent in Malta and more than 20 per cent in Latvia and Lithuania) but Bulgaria and Cyprus were the Member States which witnessed the highest increases of public investment in the EU. This increase was also significant in the Czech Republic and Poland.

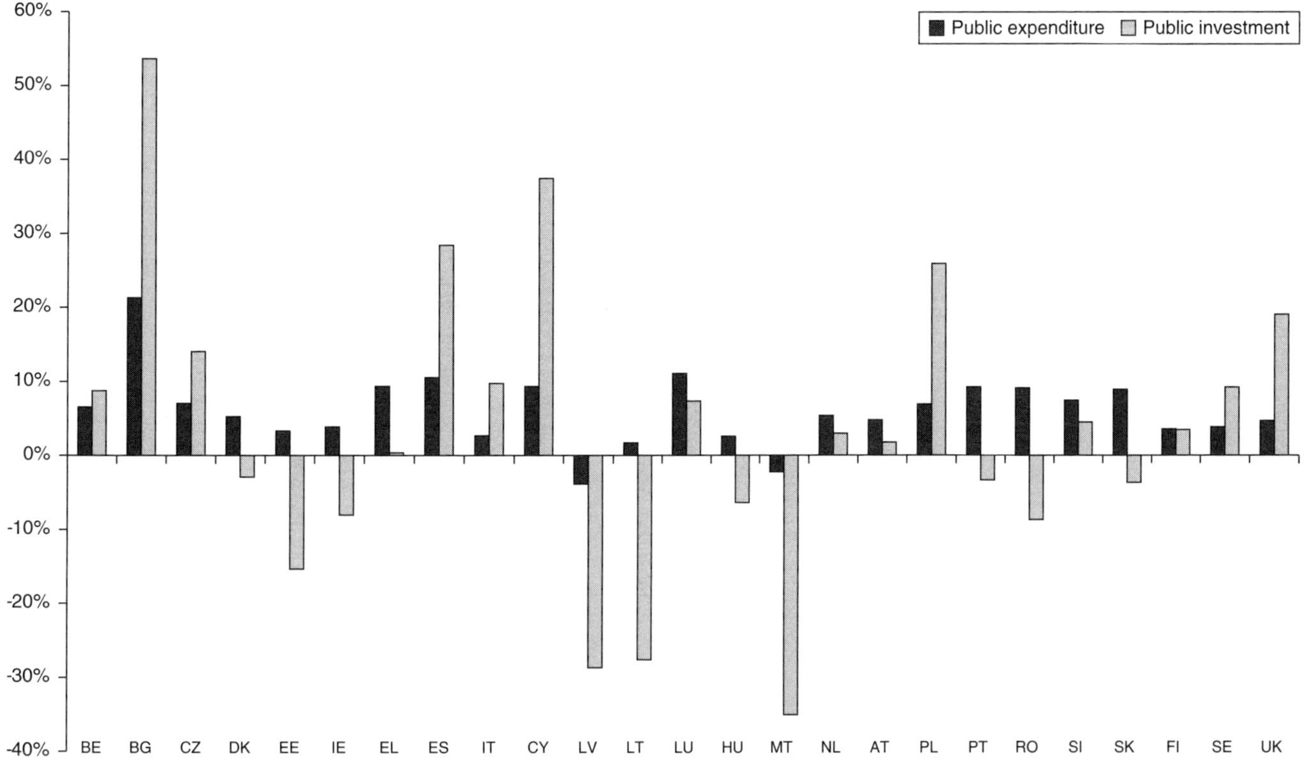

Figure 4.6 Impact of the crisis on public expenditure and public investment

Table 4.2 The impact of the crisis on public investment in New Member States

	Increasing total public investment in the first half of 2009	Decreasing public investment in the first half of 2009
Rate of public investment in 2008 higher than the EU-12 average	BG, CZ, PL	EE, LV, RO, LT
Rate of public investment in 2008 lower than the EU-12 average	CY, SI	HU, MT, SK

3.2 . . . Even in Some Countries with Relatively Low Rates of Public Investment

Table 4.2 classifies NMS according to their initial level of public investment in 2008 and the trends observed during the first half of 2009 compared to the same period in 2008. It shows that there are very different cases within this group and also that differences in terms of public investment are likely to widen across NMS. The most concerning cases are the Slovak Republic and Malta in which public investment decreased in 2009 while their rates were already well below the EU-12 average and even the total EU average. For instance, public investment in the Czech Republic was more than double compared to Malta and the Slovak Republic and the gap is still widening in 2008. On the other side of the picture, Bulgaria is the most prominent case. Public investment in this country in 2008 accounted for 6 per cent of GDP and was increased by 92 per cent in 2009.

3.3 The Sharp Deterioration of Public Finances may Lead to Low Rates of Public Investment in some NMS

The sharp increases of public deficits and public debt which result from the crisis will put enormous pressure on public finances in many Member States. It may compromise their ability to provide *inter alia* resources for public investment without jeopardising the sustainability of their financial position or the stability of the economy. This is an issue of concern in those countries with relatively high levels of public debt in which rates of public investment are relatively modest.

Malta and Hungary are the NMS in which public debt was over 60 per cent in 2010 while they are amongst those with relatively low levels of public investment. In the event the necessary adjustment of public finances is made at the expense of public investment; it could even fall below the current levels and compromise competitiveness and gains of productivity in the medium term in these countries. Another case of concern is Latvia. Public debt in this country will leap from less than 10 per cent of GDP in 2006 to more than 50 per cent in 2010 while the first data show that it has undertaken some cuts in public investment. In the case that public debt is still increasing at the current pace, it is very likely to affect public investment which could drop quickly below the trend line which shows the average area of public investment in the EU-12 (5.3 per cent).

In summary, public investment is declining (in nominal terms) in some NMS as a result of the impact of the crisis on public finances. This scenario is likely to narrow their overall favourable gap in terms of public investment which was observed in previous sections of this report. While some reduction happened in countries with relatively high levels of public investment (Romania, Lithuania), there are some cases of concern due not only to their relatively low initial rates of public investment but also to the pressure that public finances may exert on their budgetary decisions in the coming years (Hungary, Malta). In contrast, increases in public investment were significant in Bulgaria, Cyprus, the Czech Republic and Poland, showing that the impact of the crisis and the reaction of national governments in the short term varied markedly across NMS.

4. CONCLUSIONS

- The New Member States (NMS) of the European Union have been confronted in the last decade with some restrictions in public financial resources compared to the other countries of the European Union. Public expenditure decreased about 1.5 percentage points of GDP in NMS over the period 1999–2008 while it remained on average stable in the EU-15 (around 47 per cent of GDP).
- Partly as a result of these budgetary restrictions, total public expenditure in the NMS was about 5 percentage points lower than in the old EU-15 countries in the period 2004–2008.
- Budgetary restrictions did not affect the levels of public investment in NMS. Overall it remained stable at slightly more than 5 per cent of GDP on average and significantly higher than in EU-15 countries in which it was around 3.5 per cent of GDP.
- New Member States stand out on public expenditure on physical infrastructure compared to the EU-15 countries while the

expenditure on sustainable development and human capital is virtually the same in relative terms in both groups of countries.

- The European cohesion policy supports a very significant part of the investments made in NMS in these fields. In the area of Environmental Protection, it accounts on average for about 75 per cent of the total investments. In the areas of Economic Affairs and Human Capital it accounts for about 10 per cent of the total public expenditure.
- Public expenditure on social protection explains almost completely the differences in the levels of total public expenditure between both groups of countries.
- The trends of public expenditure observed in the last five years confirm that NMS privilege public expenditure on physical infrastructure at the expense of social protection. The gaps observed in these areas with the EU-15 widened further over this period.

NOTES

1. The notion of public expenditure in this chapter comprises all the spending decisions of the General Government (Central and sub-central levels) excluding the public corporations.
2. Public investment is the sum of Gross Fixed Capital Formation (P51) and Capital Transfers consolidated (D9_CO). 'Consolidated' means that capital transfers between the different levels of government are removed in order to take just account of capital transfers to individuals and firms. The codes in brackets are provided according to the nomenclature used in the European System of Accounts (ESA95). Unless specified otherwise, capital expenditure and public investment will be used as synonyms throughout this chapter.
3. The figure refers to 2007 as there are not yet complete data available for 2008 on the composition of public expenditure in Member States.
4. The classification of the functions of government (COFOG) is a standardised international classification used to identify the socio-economic objectives of current transactions, capital outlays and acquisition of financial assets by the general government and its sub-sectors.
5. The analysis is made on a multi-annual basis in order to avoid the distorting effects of peaks of public investment observed in some countries in a given year.
6. The principle of additionality enshrined in Article 15 of the General Regulation No. 1083/2006 which lays down the provisions of the Structural Funds and the Cohesion Fund sets that 'contributions from the Structural Funds shall not replace public or equivalent structural expenditure by a Member State'.
7. COFOG breaks down public expenditure into 10 Divisions, 69 groups and several hundreds of classes. Complete data across countries are only available at the Division level. The four categories assessed in this chapter are 'Economic Affairs' (Division 4), 'Environmental Protection' (Division 5), 'Education' (Division 9) and 'Social Protection' (Division 10).
8. The allocations of the EU cohesion policy to each country were obtained from the total commitments in the period 2007–2013. The allocations per year are the result of dividing the total commitments per MS by seven.

9. Bulgaria, Czech Republic, Estonia, Cyprus, Latvia, Lithuania, Hungary, Malta and Poland.
10. Germany, Greece, Spain, Italy, Austria, Portugal, Finland, Sweden and the United Kingdom.
11. The codes taken into account for the comparison are the following: 10-15 (Information Society), 16-32 (Transport) 33-43 (Energy) according to the spending categories of Annex IV of the EC Regulation No. 1083/2006.
12. Codes 44–54 according to the spending categories 2007–2013 of Annex IV of the EC Regulation No. 1083/2006.
13. In the cases of Hungary and Romania, the total expenditure recorded under this COFOG Division is lower than the total commitment 2007–2013 of the Structural Funds and the Cohesion Fund in the relevant codes divided by seven.
14. Codes 65–79 according to the spending categories of Annex IV of the EC Regulation No. 1083/2006.
15. In this case, public investment is limited to Gross Fixed Capital Formation. Quarterly data on capital transfers are not consolidated.
16. *Quarterly Summary Government Finance Statistics.* There are no data available for France and Germany.

5. EU New Member States: public sector accounts and convergence criteria

Giuseppe Bognetti and Giorgio Ragazzi

INTRODUCTION

In this chapter we analyse the recent economic performance of six New Member States (NMS), with particular regard to the convergence criteria required in order to join the Euro area. The first sections are dedicated to a review of the definitions and consistency of the public finance targets set by the Maastricht rules, which may help to understand and evaluate the performance of NMS.

1. THE MAASTRICHT FISCAL TARGETS

The Maastricht rules set two targets for members' public finances: net indebtedness (deficit) must not exceed 3 per cent of GNP and public debt should converge towards 60 per cent or less of GNP. The first target presumably aims at limiting the negative effects that expansionary policies of one member might have on others, the second target at reducing the risk that an excessive debt might lead to the insolvency of a Member State.

Both targets were set at 'arbitrary' levels. The debt target simply reflected the average debt/GNP ratio of the largest Member States at the time; the literature on state insolvency indicates that many more factors in addition to the debt/GNP ratio contribute to the risk of insolvency, while a 60 per cent debt ratio does not appear to have any particular relevance. The 3 per cent deficit target represents the historic average ratio of public investment to GNP in most European countries: an implicit reference to the 'golden rule'.

Whatever the opinion may be regarding the level of the targets, they appear to be logically incoherent and prone to induce procyclical fiscal policies (Forte 1997 and Ragazzi 2007).

The debt/GNP ratio changes over time as follows:

$$d_1 = d_0\,(1/1 + y) + s_1 + \varepsilon$$

where d is debt/GNP, y is the rate of change of nominal GNP, s is the ratio deficit/GNP and ε is the stock-flow discrepancy (in per cent of GDP).

Forgetting for the moment the term ε (that is assuming the debt to increase by the same amount of the deficit) the debt/GNP ratio tends to increase over time whenever:

$$\mathrm{s}_1\,(1 + \mathrm{y/y}) > d_0 \qquad (1)$$

for any given deficit (s) the debt ratio (d) tends to converge over time towards an equilibrium level that depends upon the nominal growth rate of GNP (y). If y and s were equal in all Member States, countries with an initially high debt ratio would progressively reduce it towards the equilibrium level and vice versa: *ceteris paribus* the Maastricht targets tend to make the debt ratios of all countries converge towards a common level. However, this 'equilibrium' level depends, for any level of deficit, upon the growth rate of nominal GNP. For instance, from (1) we obtain that if the deficit remains at 3 per cent (average over the cycle) the debt ratio tends to converge towards 60 per cent but only if nominal GNP grows at 5.2 per cent; if y is lower the equilibrium level of the debt ratio is higher and vice versa. For s = 3 per cent and y = 3 per cent d tends over time to 103 per cent.

In periods when the growth rate of nominal GNP is 'low' (less than 5 per cent) to keep the debt ratio at 60 per cent Member States should limit the deficit well below the 3 per cent level, that is they should adopt restrictive fiscal policies more the lower is the nominal growth of GNP (and vice versa).

There may be room for countercyclical fiscal policies even respecting the 3 per cent deficit limit if countries aim at keeping the budget in balance over the cycle. This seems to be a policy recommended by the Commission (communication dated 21 November 2002) and by the European Council. However, such a policy would lead over time to a progressive reduction of the debt ratio well below the 60 per cent target, the faster and the higher is the growth of nominal GNP, which appears unjustified and even undesirable (Brunetta and Tria, 2003; Buiter 2003).

Maintaining a debt ratio stable around 60 per cent is compatible with deficits higher than 3 per cent if nominal GNP increases by more than 5 per cent. Therefore, if the main concern is the debt ratio, countries which experience a fast rate of growth might be allowed to run larger deficits, especially if their initial debt ratio is relatively low, the more so in periods when growth in the rest of the community is relatively weak and larger deficits of some members may have positive rather than negative effects on other Member States. At such times it would be desirable to allow larger deficits by countries with relatively low debt ratios.

As a matter of fact, the Commission has focused almost exclusively on the deficit ratio while very little attention has been given to the debt ratio apart from the request that highly indebted countries like Italy and Greece should aim at reducing their debt ratio. The 3 per cent GDP deficit limit, arbitrary as it may be, has, however, become an indicator of the financial markets easily understood also by the general public. Thus it has certainly been effective in discouraging Member States from adopting expansionary fiscal policies even at times of low demand, not for fear of Community penalties but for the negative effects on the domestic electorate (Donnelly 2005).

In March 2005[1] it was agreed to allow Ecofin and the Commission a greater discretion in evaluating Member States' fiscal policies; GDP targets have thus become somewhat less stringent (Calmfors 2005).

2. THE MEASURE OF THE DEFICIT

Defining and measuring fiscal deficits is a complex exercise, with several alternatives available (Blejer and Cheasty 1991). For the Maastricht target, the deficit is measured with reference to the national account statistics, that is on an accrual basis, and it should in principle reflect the change in the net indebtedness of the public sector (consolidated account).

Planning and controlling this deficit (net indebtedness) is not easy for governments, for two main reasons. First, budgets approved by parliaments are generally based on cash accounts and may include revenues and expenditures of a 'financial' nature, which are excluded from net indebtedness. Thus, estimating the impact of the central government budget on net indebtedness may not be easy and it may leave room for sizeable uncertainties. Governments must control net indebtedness but they face also targets and constraints related to budgetary rules and cash accounts. Second, net indebtedness includes operations of many public entities which may not be directly controlled by the central government. A large share of public expenditure and investment is carried on by local governments which may be financially independent (to some degree). At times, local governments may actually try to counterbalance restrictive policies imposed by the central government. Imposing strict discipline on all public entities may not be easy and it may be in contrast with a desirable degree of fiscal autonomy and responsibility.

Net indebtedness is not approved *ex ante* by governments or parliaments; it is only estimated *ex post* by statistical institutes, with time delays and presumably with a sizeable degree of discretionality. The most important aspect of uncertainty in the measure of net indebtedness is the discrepancy between cash and accrual accounts for tax revenues and payments to suppliers. According to Eurostat rules, taxes are recorded as revenues 'above the line' when they are assessed, even if they have not been collected, and payments to suppliers are recorded as expenditure when the goods or services are delivered, even if they were not paid. In some countries differences between tax assessments and collections are large, and often only a small portion of these differences may actually be collected, with long time delays due to legal controversies or taxpayers' failures. Estimating the proportion which is likely to be collected (and recorded above the line) implies a substantial degree of discretionality by the statistical institutes.

Tax revenues tend to be overestimated and States' credit towards taxpayers accumulates over time (although the amount of such credit is not shown in Eurostat statistics). Periodically such credit may be abated, in recognition of the fact that part of it is definitely 'lost', but the loss is then computed as a capital loss, 'below the line'.

Calculating payments due to suppliers with reference to the moment the goods are delivered or the service is rendered is also difficult even for statistical institutes, as budgetary accounting rules generally follow different criteria. Expenditure, as defined by Eurostat rules, tends therefore to be underestimated. In some countries the national health service accumulates large arrears towards suppliers which are not properly accounted for. In Italy, for instance, arrears to suppliers by the public sector are estimated to be equivalent to 2 per cent of public debt. Discrepancy between cash and accrual accounts are one of the reasons why net indebtedness may not be reflected in equivalent changes in 'Maastricht debt', which does not include arrears to suppliers nor governments' credits towards taxpayers.

In the case of investments, expenditures are recorded above the line if it is a 'material' asset, and below the line if it is a 'financial' asset. The distinction is not always clear-cut: the expenditure for purchasing a building is above the line; that for purchasing the shares of a company which owns the building is recorded below the line. Net indebtedness may be artificially reduced if a public institution sells its office building (the income is recorded as a revenue, above the line) and leases it back.

This is just an example of the difficulty, common to any budgetary process, of accounting for commitments extending over several years. Public investments may be financed by private capital in project financing, against commitments by the State to pay annuities to the private company over many years. If the private company bears some risk, the expenditure is excluded from net indebtedness and future State commitments are not counted among debts, even if payments over time by the State would be equivalent to those of a public investment financed by public debt.

Amounts involved in such operations may be quite relevant. For instance, it has been estimated (Sawyer 2005) that UK public debt would be higher by some 20 per cent of NP if commitments under PPI were included.

In order to reduce net indebtedness (in the Eurostat definition), many countries have resorted to 'financial engineering' or 'creative accounting' operations with negative effects on the transparency of public accounts (Milesi-Ferretti 2004; Ragazzi 1997, 2002, 2003). Such operations are mostly based upon: (1) sale of assets; (2) exclusion from public sector consolidated accounts; (3) subsidies recorded below the line as credits or capital subscriptions; (4) differences between accrual and cash accounts. An OECD working paper by Koen and van den Noord (2005) estimated that, thanks to such operations, over the years 1997–2003 Greece, Portugal and Italy were able to reduce net indebtedness respectively by 18.7, 5.3 and 4.7 of GNP.

3. THE MEASURE OF PUBLIC DEBT

There may be sizeable differences between net indebtedness and the change in 'Maastricht debt', for many reasons such as:

- changes in deposits with the central bank;
- changes in debts to suppliers or in the volume of taxes assessed but not recovered;
- changes in liabilities other than those included in the definition of public debt;
- exchange gains/losses on the portion of debt denominated in foreign currencies;
- acquisitions/sales of financial assets.

In the Maastricht definition, debt is measured at the nominal value, not at market value. If a zero coupon bond is issued, the Maastricht debt is increased by the face (final) value of the bond, not by the initial issue price. There is thus a tendency to overestimate 'real' debt.

If inflation and interest rates increase, the face value of the debt remains unchanged even if its market value declines. This opens the opportunity for governments to reduce the Maastricht debt by repurchasing old debts at a discount and issuing new bonds at higher interest. In Italy, the Maastricht debt was reduced by some 2 per cent of GNP by swapping with the Bank of Italy a debt with low interest rates with a new one with higher interest (Ragazzi 2003), even if interest payments due by the government over the years remained unchanged. Similar results can be obtained through swaps of debt denominated in foreign currency. There would be no incentive for such 'financial engineering' operations if debt was measured at market prices.

Debt is defined gross, that is without offsetting it against financial assets, not even those fully liquid like governments' deposits with the central bank. These deposits may vary from year to year by considerable amounts; this should be taken into account in evaluating annual changes of debt.

Guarantees and several other kinds of liabilities are excluded from the definition of Maastricht debt (Bardozzetti and Momigliano 2006).

To reduce the debt ratio, countries have sold assets and privatized state owned enterprises, often even beyond what would have been justified for the purpose of greater efficiency. Highway concessionaires in France and Italy, for instance, were privatized exclusively in order to raise cash and reduce public debt, even if at the cost of loss of future revenues for the government and higher costs for the users. In some cases the sale of assets reflects only 'financial engineering', for example the sale of ENI and ENEL shares to a 'privatized' Cassa Depositi e Prestiti in Italy, still fully controlled by the State. Another case is the sale and lease back of public office buildings, which reduces debt but tends to increase operating costs in following years.

The incentive for such operations would be eliminated if the debt target was replaced with a target based on the public sector net financial worth (PSNFW), that is considering all financial assets and liabilities of the public sector (for a critical view on this point see Robinson 1996). This would make clear, even to the electorate, if a reduction in the debt ratio reflects a real improvement in the government's financial position or merely the sale of assets. Reducing debt through the sale of financial assets does not improve the government's financial solidity (Easterly 1999).

Over the last year several EU governments have financed large amounts of bank shares or bonds against increases of their public debt. But these financial assets may generate over time enough cash inflows to repay the additional debt and perhaps even generate a profit for the public sector. Such an increase of public debt is clearly much less worrisome than an increase of debt to finance deficit spending, and this should be somehow reflected in GDP targets, even if they are not restated in terms of public sector net worth.

Five out of six NMS considered here not only have a low public debt (in per cent of GNP) but have actually a sizeable positive financial net worth (see section 6), which might well justify greater leeway for countercyclical expansionary fiscal policies.

The PSNFW/GNP ratio is more relevant than the debt/GNP ratio as an indicator of the insolvency risk. However, the insolvency risk perceived by the market also reflects other factors such as long-term payment commitments other than debt repayments (for example prospective deficits of public pension schemes), the growth potential of the economy, the level of foreign exchange debts of the private sector, the balance of payments and the country's political resolve to reduce deficits over time by increasing taxes or reducing expenditures.

4. THE NMS CONVERGENCE CRITERIA

Until now, 16 EU states have adopted the euro and another eight states[2] (NMS) are committed by the Treaty to adopt the euro, which implies that they must strive to fulfil all the convergence criteria. Only two countries, the UK and Denmark chose to opt-out of the Treaty.

Two kinds of conditions have to be met by NMS before adopting the euro: first, compatibility of national legislation with the *acquis* (existing EU legislation) as regards the national central bank, notably its independence, its objectives and its integration into the European System of Central Banks. Second, each country must meet five convergence criteria in order to go to the third stage:

- price stability: the rate of inflation may not exceed the average rates of inflation of the three Member States with the lowest inflation by more than 1.5 per cent;
- financial stability: long-term interest rates may not vary by more than 2 per cent in relation to the average interest rates of the three Member States with the lowest inflation;
- deficits: national budget deficits must be below 3 per cent of GDP;
- public debt: this may not exceed 60 per cent of GDP;
- exchange rate stability: exchange rates must have remained within the authorised margin of fluctuation for the previous two years.

5. NMS RECENT ECONOMIC PERFORMANCE

During the period 2003–2008 all six NMS considered here have experienced a high and steady rate of growth, except for Hungary where the

Table 5.1 Growth rate of real GNP (%), growth rate of nominal GNP (%), consumer price index (% change)

Country	2003	2004	2005	2006	2007	2008	Avg. 03–08
Growth rate of real GNP (%)	Source Eurostat						
Poland	3.9	5.3	3.6	6.2	6.6	5	5.1
Hungary	4.2	4.8	4.0	4.1	1.1	0.5	3.1
Romania	5.2	8.5	4.2	7.9	6.2	7.1	6.5
Bulgaria	5.0	6.6	6.2	6.3	6.2	6.0	5.1
Czech Rep.	3.6	4.5	6.3	6.8	6.0	3.2	5.1
Lithuania	10.2	7.4	7.8	7.8	8.9	3.0	7.5
Growth rate of nominal GNP (%)	Source Eurostat						
Poland	9.1	9.6	6.3	7.8	10.9	17.3	7.1
Hungary	7.2	9.4	6.3	8.1	6.9	3.9	7.0
Romania	9.1	24.7	12.3	16.7	16.9	19.6	17.4
Bulgaria	4.8	12.1	10.2	15.3	14.5	15.8	12.0
Czech Rep.	10.2	9.2	6.0	7.8	9.8	15.5	9.7
Lithuania	11.6	9.5	14.9	14.9	18.5	14.3	11.1
Consumer price index (% change)	Source AMECO						
Poland	1.0	4.0	2.0	1.0	3.0	4.0	3.0
Hungary	5.0	7.0	3.0	4.0	8.0	6.0	6.0
Romania	15.0	12.0	9.0	7.0	5.0	8.0	9.0
Bulgaria	2.0	6.0	6.0	7.0	8.0	12.0	7.0
Czech Rep.	0.0	3.0	2.0	2.0	3.0	6.0	3.0
Lithuania	−1.0	1.0	3.0	4.0	6.0	11.0	4.0

Sources: Eurostat, AMECO.

economy stagnated after 2006 (Table 5.1, top panel). Their growth rate was substantially higher than that of EU-15 countries, thus confirming the tendency of real per capita income to converge as in previous years (Kočenda et al. 2006). This fast real growth was accompanied by a relatively high rate of inflation, above the convergence criterion for price stability, especially in Romania, Bulgaria and also in Hungary, while Poland and the Czech Republic succeeded to restrain price inflation. However, inflation accelerated everywhere after 2006 (Table 5.1, bottom panel). The fast increase of nominal GNP (Table 5.1, middle panel) was a main

Table 5.2 Long-term nominal interest rate and national budget deficits (% of GNP)

Country	2003	2004	2005	2006	2007	2008	Avg. 03–08
Long-term nominal interest rate Source: AMECO							
Poland	5.8	6.9	5.2	5.3	5.5	6.9	5.8
Hungary	6.8	8.2	6.6	7.1	6.7	8.2	7.3
Romania	–	–	–	7.2	7.1	7.7	7.3
Bulgaria	6.4	5.2	3.8	4.0	4.4	5.8	4.9
Czech Republic	4.1	4.8	3.5	3.8	4.3	4.6	4.2
Lithuania	5.3	4.5	3.7	4.1	4.6	5.6	4.6
EU 15	4.2	4.3	3.6	3.9	4.4	4.3	4.2
National budget deficits (% GNP) Source: Eurostat (GFS)							
Poland	−6.3	−5.7	−4.3	−3.8	−2.0	−3.9	−4.3
Hungary	−7.2	−6.4	−7.8	−9.3	−5.0	−3.4	−6.5
Romania	−1.5	−1.2	−1.2	−2.2	−2.6	−5.4	−2.3
Bulgaria	−0.3	1.6	1.9	3.0	0.1	1.5	1.3
Czech Republic	−6.6	−3.0	−3.6	−2.6	−1.0	−1.5	−3.0
Lithuania	−1.3	−1.5	−0.5	−0.4	−1.2	−3.2	−1.3
EU 15	−3.0	−2.9	−2.5	−1.3	−0.6	–	–

Sources: AMECO, Eurostat 'Government Finance Statistics' (2008).

factor which contributed to reduce the public debt/GNP ratio (Section 6). Long-term interest rates (Table 5.2, top panel) have remained surprisingly low within the convergence criterion, but for Hungary and Romania. In these two countries, and in Bulgaria, long-term interest rates were negative in real terms, and this certainly contributed to fuel domestic demand. Instead, one can say that fiscal policy was prudent; actually, these countries had low deficits even long before joining the EU (Kočenda et al. 2008). Over the six years 2003–2008 national budget deficits were generally low and below the 3 per cent target (Table 5.2, bottom panel). Only Hungary ran large deficits, showing some restraint only after 2006, and approaching the 3 per cent target only in 2008.

6. NMS PUBLIC DEBT

The public debt of NMS is generally very low relative to GNP, and well below the EU-15 average, with the only exception of Hungary (Table 5.3). Hungary is also the only country among the six considered here which increased the debt ratio over the four years 2003 to 2007.

Over this period, fiscal policies were not restrictive, judging from the fact that all countries run primary deficits, with the only notable exception of Bulgaria (Table 5.3). A sizeable factor contributing to the reduction of the debt ratio was the stock-flow adjustment: public debt (as defined according to Eurostat rules) increased by less than the deficit, mainly because of (net) sales of financial assets and/or increases in liabilities excluded from the definition of public debt.

However, the major factor in reducing the debt ratio was the 'snowball effect'[3]: the rate of growth of nominal GNP was substantially higher than the rate of interest (average interest cost on public debt), with the only notable exception of Hungary. The case of Italy illustrates an opposite story: fiscal policy was relatively restrictive, with a primary surplus of 6.3 per cent of GNP (cumulative, over the four years), but this was almost entirely offset by a low rate of increase of nominal GNP, lower that the average interest cost on public debt. To be more specific, the average over the period 2003–2007 of the percentage interest cost of debt and the

Table 5.3 Changes in the public debt/GNP ratio and their causes (2003–2007)

	D/Y%			Primary deficit	Stock-flow adjustment	Snowball effect
	2003	2007	2007−2003 due to	(Σ 2004–7)	(Σ 2004–7)	(Σ 2004–7)
	1	2	3	4	5	6
Poland	47.1	44.9	−2.16	5.09	−3.0	−4.25
Hungary	61.1	68.8	7.75	11.94	−3.32	−0.87
Romania	21.4	12.9	−8.44	3.12	−4.4	−7.16
Bulgaria	45.9	18.2	−27.70	−12.50	−5.88	−9.32
Czech Rep.	30.1	28.9	−1.16	5.64	−2.31	−4.49
Lithuania	21.0	17.0	−3.95	0.53	1.82	−6.30
Italy	104.3	104.1	−0.23	−6.33	1.46	4.64
Spain	48.7	36.2	−12.58	−11.94	4.89	−5.53

Source: own elaboration from Eurostat 'Government Finance Statistics' (2008).

Table 5.4 Public debt and financial net worth

	Debt/ GNP%	Financial net worth/GNP%	Debt/GNP % (2007 − 2004)	Financial net worth/GNP % (2007 − 2004)
	1	2	3	4
Poland	44.9	−20.9	−0.8	0.0
Hungary	68.8	−52.7	6.4	−11.0
Romania	12.9	16.4	−5.9	−8.1
Bulgaria	18.2	13.0	−19.7	5.2
Czech Republic	28.9	13.9	−1.5	4.5
Lithuania	17.0	11.6	−2.4	−0.4
Italy	104.1	−87.8	0.3	4.6
EU 15	66.3	−43.1	−3.3	8.6

Source: Eurostat 'Government Finance Statistics' (2008).

percentage growth of nominal GNP were 6.2 and 8.7 in Poland, 7.3 and 7.7 in Hungary, 7.2 and 16.4 in Romania and 4.7 and 3.6 in Italy. The recession which started in mid-2008 and is expected to be long and severe is bound to reverse the trend of the 2004–2007 period and lead to sharp increases in the debt ratios, both because of higher primary deficits and of slower growth (or even decline) of nominal GNP which will reverse the sign of the 'snowball effect'.

It is worth noticing, however, that the NMS here considered not only had (2007 data) low debt ratios but they had also a positive net financial position, that is they had financial assets worth more than public debt and other liabilities (Table 5.4), again with the only notable exception of Hungary. Over the three years 2004–2007, in Hungary the net financial position worsened by more than the increase of debt, underlining the difficult position of this country. Romania reduced public debt but its net financial position worsened; Bulgaria improved its net financial worth but by less than suggested by the reduction of public debt. Liabilities other than public debt generally tend to increase relative to GNP, causing the financial net worth to worsen by more than the increase of debt (or to improve by less than its decline), with the only exception of the Czech Republic.

7. NMS PUBLIC INVESTMENT

Public investments as a share of GNP were very high relative to the EU average, in all six NMS, during the four years 2004 to 2007. Hungary, while running a large primary deficit, invested less than the average of the other countries. Bulgaria had a relatively high investment ratio even with a large primary surplus. There seems to be no correlation between the primary balance and the investment ratio. Looking at average figures for 2004–2007, public investment, measured as gross fixed capital formation in per cent of GNP, was 3.67 in Poland, 3.87 in Hungary, 5.30 in Romania, 4.02 in Bulgaria, 4.87 in the Czech Republic, 4.06 in Lithuania, 2.37 in Italy and 2.49 in the EU15.[4]

8. NMS EXTERNAL POSITION

In different degrees the countries we examined show an important exposure to the international cycle, the most critical situations being those of Hungary, Bulgaria and Lithuania. In order to consider briefly the external position of these countries we examine three indexes: foreign trade (current account, degree of openness), external debt and foreign direct investments. As a general remark we can say that they show a remarkable degree of openness. Hungary and the Czech Republic have a degree of openness over 130 per cent (Table 5.5).

All countries have deficits in the current account (Table 5.5); three countries show very strong imbalances: the deficits of Romania, Bulgaria

Table 5.5 BOP current account (% of GNP) and degree of openness of the economy: exports + imports (% of GNP)

	BoP (% GNP)							Openness (%GNP)
	2002	2003	2004	2005	2006	2007	Σ − 2002	2007
Poland	−2.5	−2.1	−4.2	−1.6	−3.2	−4.4	−18.07	71.7
Hungar	−7.1	−8.0	−8.4	−6.9	−5.5	−4.9	−40.62	134.7
Romania	−3.3	−5.6	−8.4	−8.7	−10.5	−13.7	−43.49	62.3
Bulgaria	−2.0	−5.1	−6.8	−11.9	−15.8	−22.0	−63.63	119.2
Czech Rep	−5.7	−6.3	−5.2	−1.6	−3.2	−1.9	−23.88	141.2
Lithuania	−5.1	−6.9	−7.6	−7.0	−10.8	−14.6	−37.98	103.4

Source: International Financial Statistics IMF.

Table 5.6 Debt denominated in foreign currencies (% of GNP)

% GNP	2003	2007
Poland		
Total external debt	41.5	42.0
Government external debt	17.7	16.7
Short-term external debt	4.5	5.7
Hungary		
Total external debt	52.2	95.1
Government external debt	18.6	29.8
Short-term external debt	6.6	10.5
Bulgaria		
Total external debt		72.1
Government external debt		
Short-term external debt		22.1
Czech Republic		
Total external debt	29.6	33.2
Government external debt	2.0	7.0
Short-term external debt	8.5	8.6
Lithuania		
Total external debt		53.1
Government external debt		10.0
Short-term external debt		14.4

Source: Joint External Debt Hub (JEDH).

and Lithuania are greater than 10 per cent of GNP, with a clear worsening in recent years. Hungary started with a large deficit at the beginning of the century but its position has improved in the last years, even if the imbalance is still significant. Only the Czech Republic and Poland, although in deficit, present a more balanced situation. The current account is expected to improve, but mainly due to the downturn of domestic demand.

The size of the external debt (Table 5.6) is significant for sustainability (especially considering the effects that would result from a devaluation of the domestic currency and for the risk of a foreign capital flight during a general financial crisis), and is certainly a problem for at least three countries: Hungary, with an external debt of 95 per cent of GNP, Bulgaria with 72 per cent and Lithuania with 53 per cent. For Hungary and Lithuania the situation has been critical enough to require an intervention by the IMF. For Poland and the Czech Republic the degree of indebtedness has

Table 5.7 Foreign direct investment

	FDI flows as percentage of gross fixed capital formation				FDI stocks as a percentage of gross domestic product			
	1990–2000 (annual average)	2005	2006	2007	1990	2000	2006	2007
Czech Republic								
Inward	14.2	37.4	17.1	21.6	–	38.2	55.8	57.7
Outward	–	−0.1	4.2	3.2	–	1.3	3.5	4.0
Bulgaria								
Inward	18.1	59.7	91.4	71.6	0.5	21.5	72.2	92.3
Outward	–	4.7	2.1	2.3	0.6	0.5	0.9	1.5
Hungary								
Inward	28.3	30.7	27.7	19.3	1.5	4.7	72.3	70.5
Outward	–	8.8	14.8	14.2	0.4	2.7	10.8	13.2
Lithuania								
Inward	11.9	17.6	25.0	19.0	–	20.4	37.0	38.3
Outward	–	5.8	3.9	5.9	–	0.3	3.5	4.1
Poland								
Inward	11.7	18.7	28.5	18.7	0.2	20.0	36.4	33.8
Outward	–	6.1	13.2	3.6	0.1	0.6	4.8	4.7
Romania								
Inward	9.4	28.5	40.1	25.5	–	18.8	37.4	36.7
Outward	–	−0.1	1.5	−0.2	0.2	0.4	0.7	0.6
European Union								
Inward	11.9	18.2	18.6	22.6	10.6	25.9	39.0	40.9
Outward	16.0	22.2	21.2	32.1	11.3	36.1	44.9	48.1

Source: UNCTAD.

not worsened in recent years and is not as critical. The increase in external debt was mainly caused by bank loans to the private sector while the external government debt is limited (with the possible exception of Hungary) and does not constitute a problem.

The dynamic of foreign direct investment, starting from the beginning of the new century, has been remarkable; this has been a general trend in the international economy but it has been more sustained in the countries examined than in the European Union as a whole.

Table 5.7 shows that foreign direct investment was a relevant quota of

Table 5.8 Asset share of foreign-owned banks (% of banking sector)

	2002	2007
Poland	70.7	75.5
Hungary	85.0	64.2
Romania	52.9	87.3
Bulgaria	75.2	82.3
Czech Rep	85.8	84.8
Lithuania	96.1	91.7

Source: EBRD (2008) quoted in Connolly (2009).

the gross fixed capital formation, around 20–25 per cent. This is actually not much higher than the average inward investment in the European Union, but from these countries there are practically no outward flows (but for Hungary), thus the net inflow is large for its impact on the balance of payments. Bulgaria is an exceptional case: the stock of foreign direct investment amounts to 90 per cent of GNP and inwards flows have reached up to 90 per cent of gross fixed capital formation. Other countries where foreign direct investments play a major role are Hungary and the Czech Republic.

The dependence on foreign direct investment makes these countries vulnerable to changing external conditions. According to estimates made by the Institute of International Finance, private capital flows to the emerging European economies will decrease from $254bn in 2008 to $30bn in 2009 (Connolly 2009). The situation is even more critical given the weight of foreign banks (mainly European) in their financial system (Table 5.8).

The sizeable, and increasing, current account deficits were more than offset by the large inflow of foreign capital, both for direct investment as well as in the form of bank loans to the private sector. Consequently, overall these countries succeeded in keeping their foreign exchange rate stable or even in appreciating it *vis-à-vis* the euro (Table 5.9, top panel). Bulgaria and Lithuania have kept a fixed exchange rate *vis-à-vis* the euro, the Czech and Polish currencies appreciated markedly up to 2007, that of Hungary fluctuated widely but overall has not depreciated (at least until the end of 2008). In real effective terms their currencies shared to appreciation of the euro which, together with their inflationary process made their effective real exchange rate appreciate substantially in the period (Table 5.9, bottom panel).

Table 5.9 Exchange rates (local currency per euro, year end) and real effective exchange rate (period average) – year 2000 = 100

	2002	2003	2004	2005	2006	2007	2008
Exchange rates							
Poland	4.02	4.7	4.1	3.76	3.82	3.6	4.15
Hungary	2.35	2.63	2.46	2.5	2.53	2.53	2.68
Romania				3.6	3.14	3.6	4.0
Bulgaria	1.95	1.96	1.96	1.96	1.96	1.96	1.96
Czech Rep.	31.8	32.4	30.4	28.8	27.8	26.3	28.1
Lithuania	3.45	3.45	3.45	3.45	3.45	3.45	3.45
Effective Exchange Rate							
Hungary	118.9	121.6	130.0	132.6	127.0	142.5	143.0
Romania	102.3	99.09	101.61	119.84	128.9	140.53	133.09
Bulgaria	109.63	113.97	119.6	120.23	125.38	133.87	144.39
Czech Rep	118.7	116.78	118.35	125.26	132.29	136.78	154.71

Source: AMECO and IMF.

9. EFFECTS OF THE ONGOING RECESSION

The recession that started in the second half of 2008 is bound to have heavy repercussions on NMS. According to EU forecasts (April 2009), real GNP will fall in all NMS as indicated in Table 5.10. Lithuania and Hungary, that is, those who relied more heavily on borrowings from abroad, will be the hardest hit. Public sector deficits are expected to increase well above the 3 per cent level, like in the rest of the EU, with the notable exception of Bulgaria; Hungary has been required by the IMF to introduce restrictive measures to limit its deficit, which will contribute to the decline of GNP. Public debt is going to increase everywhere, except in Bulgaria, but it will still remain well below the average of EU Member States. Only Hungary's debt level may be considered worrisome.

Whether these countries will be able to defend their currencies from the risk of sharp depreciations remains an open question.

Table 5.10 EU forecasts for the NMCs (April 2009)

	GNP (% change)	Deficit (% of GNP)	Public Debt (% of GNP)	
	2009	2009	2007	2010
Poland	−1.4	−6.6	44.9	50.7
Hungary	−6.3	−3.4	68.8	82.3
Romania	−4.0	−5.1	12.9	22.7
Bulgaria	−1.9	−0.3	18.2	17.3
Czech Republic	−2.7	−4.3	28.9	37.9
Lithuania	−11.0	−5.4	17.0	31.9

Source: Eurostat.

10. CONCLUSIONS

We discuss first some general problems concerning the definition and measurement of deficits and public debt, suggesting that the relevant figures should be evaluated with great care, having regard to the specific situation and institutional framework of each country. The rationality of the two Maastricht targets for public finance is also critically analysed.

As to the six NMS considered here, our findings may be summarized as follows. During the six years 2003–2008 all of them experienced a high and steady rate of growth, with only the exception of Hungary where the economy stagnated after 2006. This fast real growth was accompanied by a relatively high rate of inflation, above the convergence criterion for price stability, especially in Romania and Bulgaria. After 2006 price inflation accelerated at worrisome rates in all countries.

Long-term interest rates have remained surprisingly low within the convergence criterion, with the exception of Hungary and Romania. In these two countries, and in Bulgaria, long-term interest rates were negative in real terms, and this certainly contributed to fuel domestic demand. Instead, one can say that fiscal policy was prudent: in spite of a high investment ratio by the public sector, national budget deficits were generally low and below the 3 per cent target. Only Hungary ran large deficits, showing some restraint only after 2006, and approaching the 3 per cent target only in 2008.

Thanks also to the rapid expansion of nominal GNP, the public sector debt ratio declined in all countries, even by large amounts, with only the exception of Hungary. Moreover all countries have a positive net financial position, except Hungary (and Poland, for a smaller amount). We may thus conclude that these countries (except Hungary) have met the convergence criteria for public sector accounts and have followed prudent fiscal policies: the causes for large current account deficits and excessive inflation are to be found in lax monetary policies (with some exceptions like the Czech Republic) and in the large inflow of foreign capital, primarily for direct investment but also on account of bank lending to the private sector. Their dependence on external demand and foreign capital inflow is a weak point and threatens the stability of the exchange rate.

NOTES

1. Council Resolutions 1055 and 1056/2005, and Ecofin Report 7423/2005.
2. The Czech Republic, Estonia, Hungary, Latvia, Lithuania, Poland, Romania and Bulgaria
3. The 'snowball effect' reflects the impact on the debt ratio of the difference between the rate of interest (average interest cost of the public debt) and the rate of change of nominal GNP. Given the public debt (D), nominal GNP (Y), interest payments on public debt (I), primary deficit (PD), stock-flow adjustment (SFA), rate of interest (i), rate of growth of nominal GNP (g), we have:

$$D_1 = D_0 + I + PD + SFA$$
$$D_1 = D_0 (1 + i) + PD + SFA$$
$$D_1/Y_1 = D_0(1 + i)/Y_0 (1 + g) + PD/Y_1 + SFA/Y_1$$
$$D_1/ Y_1 - D_0/ Y_0 = D_0/Y_0 * (1 + i)/(1 + g) - D_0/Y_0 + PD/ Y_1 + SFA/Y_1$$
$$D_1/Y_1 - D_0/Y_0 = D_0/Y_0 * [(1 + i)/(1 + g) - 1] + PD/ Y_1 + SFA/Y_1.$$

   The first term is the 'snowball effect'.
4. Source: Eurostat 'Government Finance Statistics' (2008).

REFERENCES

Bardozzetti, A. and S. Momigliano (2006), 'Le finanze pubbliche dei nuovi stati membri dell'Unione Europea', *Economia Pubblica*, **5–6**, 1–30.
Blejer, M. and A. Cheasty (1991), 'The measurement of fiscal deficits: analytical and methodological issue', *Journal of Economic Literature*, **29**(4), 1644–78.
Brunetta, R. and G. Tria (2003), 'Il patto di stabilità e crescita: regole fiscali da cambiare', *Rivista di Economia Italiana*, **2**, 303–50.
Buiter, W. (2003), 'Ten commandments for a fiscal rule in the E(M)U', *Oxford Review of Economic Policy*, **19**(1), 84–99.
Calmfors, L. (2005), 'What remains of the Stability Pact and what next?', Swedish Institute for Economic Policy Studies report 8, Stockholm.
Connolly, R. (2009), 'Financial vulnerabilities in emerging Europe: an overview', *BOTIF on line*, **3**, 3–29.
Donnelly, S. (2005), 'Explaining EMU reform', *Journal of Common Market Studies*, **43**(5), 947–68.

Easterly, W. (1999), 'When is fiscal adjustment an illusion?', *Economic Policy*, **14**(28), 57–84.
Forte, Francesco (1997), 'The inadequacies of Maastricht excessive deficit rules', International Monetary Fund working paper.
Forte, F. (1997), 'I bilanci pubblici italiani alla luce della costituzione fiscale di Maastricht', *Economia Pubblica*, **4**, 5–56.
Kočenda, E., A.M. Kutan and T.M. Yigit (2006), 'Pilgrims to the Eurozone: how far, how fast?', *Economic Systems*, **30**(4), 311–27.
Kočenda, E., A.M. Kutan and T.M. Yigit (2008), 'Fiscal convergence in the European Union', *North American Journal of Economics and Finance*, **19**(3), 319–30.
Koen, V. and P. Van den Noord (2005), 'Fiscal gimmickry in Europe: one-off measures and creative accounting', Organisation for Economic Co-operation and Development working paper, 417.
Milesi-Ferretti, Gian M. (2004), 'Good, bad or ugly? On the effects of fiscal rules with creative accounting', *Journal of Public Economics*, **88**(1–2), 377–94.
Ragazzi, G. (1997), 'Conti pubblici: finalità e trasparenza', in Giorgio Ragazzi (ed.), *Trasparenza dei conti pubblici e controllo della spesa*', Milan, Italy: Franco Angeli, pp. 38–62.
Ragazzi, G. (2002), 'Sulla riforma dei conti pubblici', *Economia Pubblica*, **3**, 5–26.
Ragazzi, G. (2003), 'Quali indicatori sintetici per la finanza pubblica?', *Economia Pubblica*, **4**, 5–31.
Ragazzi, Giorgio (2007), 'Maastricht, politiche fiscali e trasparenza dei conti pubblici', in Brosio, G. (ed.) (2008), *Criteri per le scelte pubbliche – saggi in onore di Francesco Forte*, Milano: Giuffrè, pp. 349–60.
Robinson, M. (1996), 'Public sector net worth: is it worth measuring?', Department of Parliamentary Library research paper, **36**.
Sawyer, M. (2005), 'The private finance initiative: the UK experience', in Giorgio Ragazzi and Werner Rothengatter (eds), *Procurement and Financing of Motorways in Europe*, Elsevier, pp. 231–45.

6. Public investment and growth in the EU New Member States: an overview

Jan Hanousek and Evžen Kočenda*

INTRODUCTION

This overview provides a thorough description of the major macroeconomic developments in the New Member States (NMS) that joined the European Union (EU) in 2004 and 2007.[1] A particular focus is the NMS' public investment developments and trends, including the implications of the global financial crisis. As a complement to this overview a disaggregated structural database has been completed, which is useful for a detailed analysis and cross-country comparison. The overview also contains new member country profile pages with template indicators, an analysis and a database appendix for quick reference.

Regarding post-accession performance, most of the new EU Member States exhibited accelerated growth after joining the EU, which resulted in a very fast convergence, far exceeding expectations (Rosenberg, 2008). Increased access to foreign capital and financial deepening are seen to be among the major driving forces (Figure 6.1). This post-accession boom exposed the region to new vulnerabilities such as large current account deficits, cross-border contagion risks and currency mismatches. These vulnerabilities have limited the effectiveness of the region as large corporations had vast opportunities to borrow directly from abroad.

Even though the overall macroeconomic environment in the region was fairly good during the early 2000s, a lack of fiscal adjustments remained one of the major concerns (Kočenda et al., 2006). For instance, public debt ratios were not declining and exceeded the maximum prudent level for key new EU Member States as indicated in Figure 6.2.

With the global financial crisis that commenced in late 2008, both macroeconomic and public finance conditions have changed drastically. The European Union economy has been hit particularly hard as most of its Member States have a strong dependence on exports, extensive

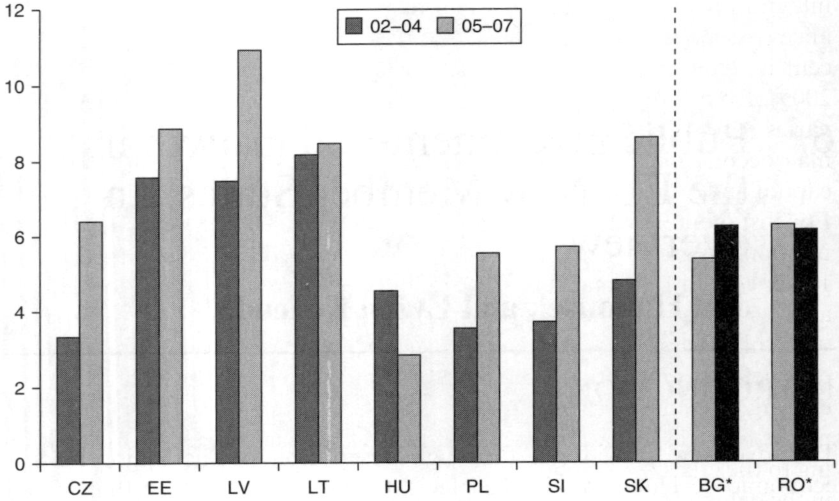

Source: Eurostat (2008).

Figure 6.1 Average GDP growth of new EU members

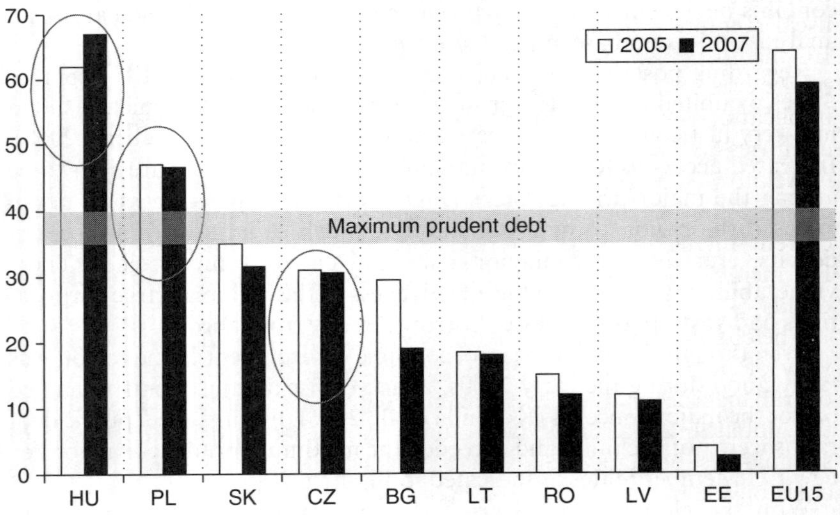

Source: European Commission Forecast (2007).

Figure 6.2 Public debt in new EU members, percentage of GDP

integration with global capital markets and large macroeconomic imbalances. As a consequence, the EU's real GDP was projected to fall by 4 per cent in 2009 and stabilize at around −0.1 per cent growth in 2010 (EC, 2009). Even though the crisis has hit all of the Member States, the impact varies across the countries due to the heterogeneity in the magnitude of macroeconomic imbalances, different degrees of integration in trade, capital and labour markets and differences in overall pre-crisis conditions. For instance, Baltic countries are expected to suffer the most severe contraction. In the first quarter of 2009, the reduction in GDP ranged from 18 per cent in Latvia and 16 per cent in Estonia to 3.5 per cent in Bulgaria and 3.4 per cent in the Czech Republic (IMF, 2009c).

In this recessionary period public finances play a more crucial role than ever before as monetary policy instruments have been less effective in leveraging the economic stability. Given the depth and scope of the recession, public finances in the EU are shouldering a particular burden in responding to the crisis through meeting three objectives: (i) addressing the decline in the demand through fiscal stimulus and automatic stabilizers, (ii) restoring the financial sector's health and support the intermediation function of financial markets and (iii) contributing to long-term growth prospects by ensuring sustainable budgetary developments (EC, 2009).

The European Economic Recovery Programme (EERP) adopted by the European Council in December 2008 envisages combining active fiscal stimulus with structural reforms. Public investment plans for the EU members have been amended and reconsidered in view of the pressure of the crisis situation reflecting cross-country peculiarity. The budgetary implications of the crisis and its vast heterogeneity among the EU member countries are reflected in Figure 6.3.

Acknowledging the importance of public finances and the drastic changes that occurred during the post-EU-accession period and the current financial crisis, this overview presents an analysis of the new EU members' economic situation, emphasizing NMS' public investment trends.

The chapter is organized as follows: Section 1 provides a general overview of public finance in the EU and the NMS. Section 2 reviews the overall macroeconomic developments, the trends in public investment and the global financial crisis implications for each country. The conclusion summarizes the main findings and provides the general implications of the crisis on the macroeconomic situation in the new EU members and their public expenditure prospects.

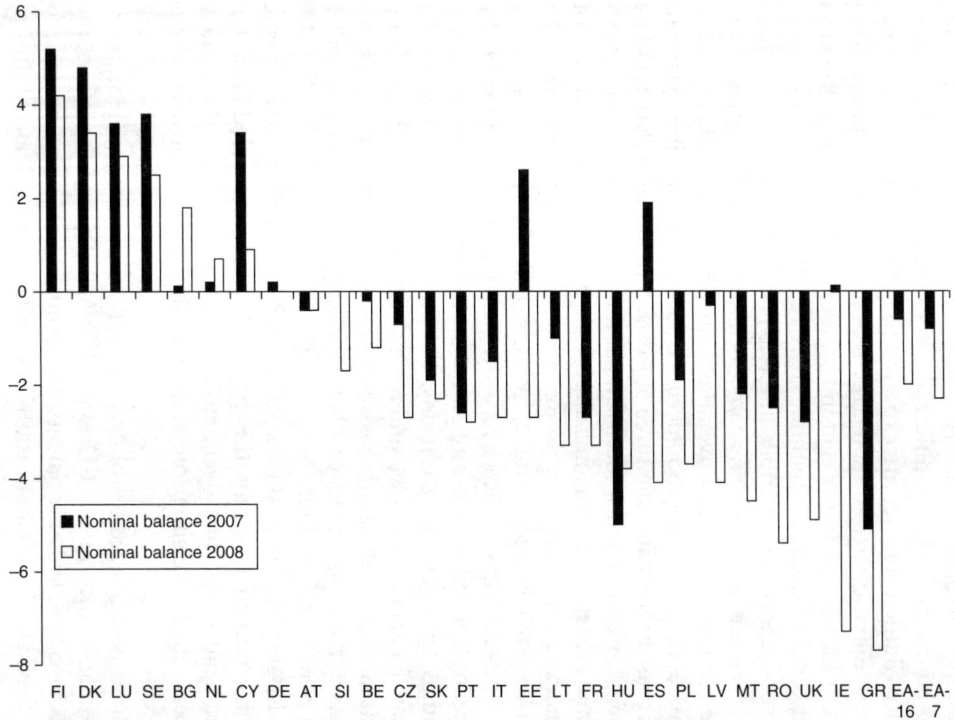

Source: European Commission (2009).

Figure 6.3 Government balances of EU members in 2007 and 2008, percentage of GDP

1. PUBLIC FINANCE IN EU AND NEW EU MEMBERS: DEVELOPMENT AND PROSPECTS

The economic development of the new EU members varies from state to state and can be traced through the key macroeconomic indicators presented in Table 6.1. Fiscal policy within the European Union is governed by the Growth and Stability Pact. It applies to all Member States, however for euro area members a specific rule is applied – the deficit must not exceed 3 per cent of GDP and public debt must not exceed 60 per cent of GDP. In reality, many larger EU members have consistently run deficits far exceeding the 3 per cent limit and the euro area as a whole has a debt percentage exceeding 60 per cent (EC, 2009).

Despite the fact that new EU members are not yet bound by the Stability and Growth Pact formally as they are not part of the euro area, they should aim to converge towards it through the fiscal Maastricht criteria. However, such a convergence posed considerable challenges as quantitatively evidenced by Kočenda et al. (2008). Table 6.1 shows that Hungary had problems with both measures of fiscal stability. The rest of the countries were relatively fine with the exception of Cyprus and Malta in terms of the public debt measure.

The state of public finances in all European Union members before the global crisis of 2008 was characterized by sharp contrasts between fiscal stance, budget revenues and expenditures (EC, 2008a). The fiscal position of the euro area and the whole EU in 2007 was the best it had been for several decades. Cross-country differences in EU members remained large, yet the general government deficit in 2007 in both the euro area and the EU as a whole fell below 1 per cent of GDP, to 0.6 per cent and 0.9 per cent, respectively (EC, 2008a, p. 11). In most of the EU countries the notified outcome for 2007 was somewhat better than the targets defined in the stability and convergence programmes accepted in 2006. The overall progress also reflected the fiscal corrections put in place by countries that were in excessive deficit (Uctum et al., 2006).

With the commencement of global recession in autumn 2008 there was significant deterioration in most of the macroeconomic indicators for new EU members (Table 6.1). The whole European Union and the euro area faced a dramatic increase of government debt-to-GDP ratios in 2008, reaching 61.5 per cent and 69.25 per cent, respectively, which is far in excess of the limits of the Stability and Growth Pact (EC, 2009, p. 42). The debt ratios are expected to rise even further in 2009–2011, particularly for Latvia, Ireland, Spain and the United Kingdom, breaching the 60 per cent threshold. Deteriorating debt ratios along with projected negative real GDP growth (see Table 6.2) and lower inflation mirror the negative

Table 6.1 Macroeconomic indicators for New EU Members

Member State	GDP (PPP) millions, euro (2008)	GDP (PPS) per capita, euro (2008)	Public Debt as % of GDP (2008)	Deficit (−)/ Surplus (+) % of GDP (2008)	Inflation % Annual (2009)	Unemployment % (09 2009)
European Union	12506778.5	25100	61.5	−2.0	1.0	9.1
Bulgaria	78799.9	10400	14.1	1.8	2.5	6.8
Czech Republic	210158.4	20200	30.0	−2.1	0.6	7.5
Estonia	22649.9	16900	4.6	−2.7	0.2	14.6
Hungary	162038.8	16100	72.9	−3.8	4.0	10.6
Latvia	32554.1	14400	19.5	−4.1	3.3	19.4
Lithuania	52115.7	15500	15.6	−3.2	4.2	13.8
Poland	539271.9	14100	47.2	−3.6	4.0	8.2
Romania	259022.3	10300	13.6	−5.5	5.6	6.8
Slovenia	46090.4	22800	22.5	−1.8	0.9	6.3
Slovakia	97917.2	18100	27.7	−2.3	0.9	13.1
Cyprus	19061.0	24000	48.4	0.9	0.2	5.4
Malta	7890.2	19100	63.8	−4.7	1.8	7.1

Source: Eurostat.

Table 6.2 Budgetary developments according to the 2008–2009 Stability and Convergence Programme updates

	Real GDP growth			Government balance			Structural balance			Government gross debt		
	2009	2010	2011	2008	2009	2010	2008	2009	2010	2008	2009	2010
EU27	−4.1	0.7	1.6	−1.6	−3.4	−3.3	−2.0	−2.7	−2.4	67.8	71.4	73.1
EU16*	−4.0	0.7	1.5	−2.0	−3.8	−3.5	−2.3	−3.1	−2.7	61.4	65.4	67.2
Bulgaria	−5.9	−1.1	3.1	3.0	3.0	3.0	2.6	3.2	3.6	15.4	15.4	15.3
Czech Republic	−4.8	0.8	2.3	−1.2	−1.6	−1.5	−1.9	−1.7	−1.3	28.8	27.9	26.8
Estonia	−13.7	−0.1	4.2	−1.9	−1.7	−1.0	−2.4	−0.1	0.4	3.7	3.7	3.5
Hungary	−6.5	−0.5	3.1	−3.4	−2.6	−2.5	−3.5	−1.8	−1.6	71.1	72.5	72.2
Latvia	−18.0	−4.0	2.0	−3.5	−5.3	−4.9	−5.1	−4.9	−3.3	19.4	32.4	45.4
Lithuania	−15.0	−3.9	2.5	−2.9	−2.1	−1.0	−4.9	−1.8	0.1	15.3	16.9	18.1
Poland	1.2	1.8	3.2	−2.7	−2.5	−2.3	−3.1	−2.5	−1.9	45.9	45.8	45.5
Slovenia	−7.4	1.3	2.0	−0.9	−5.1	−3.9	−2.9	−4.1	−2.3	22.8	30.5	34.1
Slovakia	−5.8	1.9	2.6	−2.2	−3.0	−2.9	−3.8	−4.4	−3.5	27.6	31.4	32.7
Cyprus	−0.7	0.1	1.3	1.0	−0.8	−1.4	0.7	−0.8	−1.2	49.3	46.8	45.4
Malta	−2.2	0.7	1.6	−3.3	−1.5	−0.3	−3.7	−1.7	−0.2	62.8	61.9	59.8

Note: (*) Includes Denmark.

Source: European Commission (2009).

consequences of the crisis and worsening budgetary positions. According to European Commission estimates, the debt ratio should hit 84 per cent and 79 per cent in 2010 in the euro area and the European Union, respectively (EC, 2009).

1.1 Taxation

Analysing the fiscal stance of the EU members it is noticeable that the decreasing of tax ratios that started in 1999 in most of the Member States stopped by 2005. As such, weighted tax-to-GDP ratios in the EU27[2] were slowly increasing from 39.3 per cent in 2005 to 39.9 per cent in 2006 (Eurostat News Release, 2008). In 2006, the overall tax ratio in the euro area (EU15)[3] was 40.5 per cent, up from 39.8 per cent in 2005.

Despite the observed trends, the tax levels in the EU remain generally high in comparison with the rest of the world. For instance EU27 tax ratios exceed those of the USA and Japan by some 12 percentage points. At the same time, the tax burden varies significantly from state to state, ranging in 2006 from less than 30 per cent in Romania (28.6 per cent), Slovakia (29.3 per cent) and Lithuania (29.7 per cent), to almost 50 per cent in Denmark (49.1 per cent) and Sweden (48.9 per cent) (Eurostat News Release, 2008, p. 3). In the past decade the largest fall was recorded in Slovakia, where the overall tax burden dropped from 39.4 per cent in 1996 to 29.3 per cent in 2006 and Estonia, where it dropped from 35.1 per cent to 31.0 per cent.

Analysing the pre-crisis conditions of the new EU members, it is clear that the observed improvement in budgetary positions in 2007 was chiefly the result of a lower expenditure-to-GDP ratio. The decline in the ratio was due to lower social transfers and other in-kind expenditures. On the revenue side, a major positive contribution came from taxes on income and wealth, which increased by 0.4 per cent of GDP in the euro area and by 0.2 per cent in the whole EU in 2007. During 2005–2007 most of the EU members managed to narrow the budgetary gap, thus ensuring the sustainability of public financing including the budgetary costs of ageing (Rahman, 2008).

Addressing the severe impact of the current economic downturn, the European Council endorsed the EERP in December 2008, which outlines the general rescue plan for European Union Member States. The EERP is based on building an effective combination of active fiscal stimulus and structural reforms. Thus, the degree of fiscal discipline required from the EU Member States is strengthened further, also calling for a more coordinated response among the member countries. Amidst the economic downturn a coordinated response is of particular importance and it is expected that members with sufficiently large fiscal space can fill in the short-term demand gaps. According to the European Commission all EU members have committed to fiscal stimulus totalling 1.1 per cent of GDP in 2009 and 0.7 per cent of GDP in 2010 of which 1 per cent of GDP is on the revenue side and 0.8 per cent of GDP is on the expenditure side (EC, 2009, p. 1). The estimated contribution of this fiscal stimulus is around 0.75 per cent of real GDP growth in 2009 and around 0.33 per cent of real GDP growth in 2010. There are also vast cross-country differences in the scale of the fiscal stimulus. Countries that have undertaken significantly large fiscal stimuli are Spain (2.3 per cent of GDP), Austria (1.8 per cent of GDP) and Malta (1.6 per cent of GDP). There are however several new EU Member States (that is Slovakia, Bulgaria, Estonia, Hungary, Lithuania, Latvia and Romania) that could not effectively contribute to the EERP due to their limited space for fiscal measures (EC, 2009, pp. 14–15). Acknowledging the strong pressure on their public finances as well as large external/internal imbalances, these new EU members requested balance-of-payment support from the International Monetary Fund (IMF) and other international institutions.

1.2 General Trends in New EU Member Public Investment

As for other macroeconomic indicators there are sharp differences in trends in the public investment of the new EU members before and during the current economic recession. In particular, in 2007 public investment as a percentage of GDP in the new EU members was higher than the EU15 average level of public investment, which was 2.4 per cent of GDP. The only exception was Slovakia with a 1.9 per cent investment-to-GDP ratio.

Public investment per inhabitant, however, remained lower than the average level of old EU Member States. By this indicator, the closest countries to the EU15 were Slovenia and Estonia, while the lowest level of public investment per inhabitant in 2007 was registered in Slovakia and Bulgaria.

During 2002–2007 the major sectors to receive government investment in the new members were economic affairs, general public services, housing and community amenities and education by COFOG[4] classification. In Malta the most important part of public investment has been attributed to the health sector. The largest share of economic investment by the government aimed at developing the transport sectors (see the tables on public investment for each new EU member, found in the separate country pages).

By 2006 the total public expenditure increased in all of the new members, while in 2007 there was a decline in Slovakia and Hungary. The largest increase in public investment in 2007 was registered in the Baltic countries and Romania, with an increase of 59 per cent in Latvia. Public investment has been growing at a higher pace in the new members of the EU in comparison with EU15 economies. For instance, public investment in France increased only by 6 per cent in 2007.

Based on the data on public investment from Eurostat, public investment in economic affairs had increased on average by about 20 per cent in the new members in 2007. This investment decreased only in Hungary (Table 6.8). The major sector that benefited from growth in public investment for economic needs was the transport sector. Public expenditure in education has been growing steadily in all of the NMS. However public investment in education in 2007 remained at the same level as in 2006 in the Czech Republic and decreased in Hungary and Slovakia (Tables 6.6, 6.8 and 6.15). The education sector in Latvia benefited from a doubling in investment expenditure by the government for the same year (Table 6.9). The public investment for environmental protection needs increased significantly on average for all new EU members. The largest increase in 2007 was registered in Estonia (Table 6.7). In 2007 the largest growth of public investment in general public services and defence was registered in Lithuania, followed by Cyprus (Tables 6.10 and 6.16). In the same year the most important increase in public expenditure in the health sector was in Romania, while Latvia benefited from the largest increase in public investment in the recreation sector and Estonia in social protection (Tables 6.7, 6.9 and 6.12).

It is evident that while the EU15 economies have remained on top of the list when assessing public investment level per capita, governments in the new EU members have been rapidly increasing their investment expenditure since accession to the European Union (Figure 6.4).

Since 2008 there has been a significant ongoing deterioration in public finances of all the members of the European Union. The average nominal budget deficit increased in 2008 to 1.9 per cent of GDP (a 1.3 percentage point increase) in the euro area and to 2.3 per cent of GDP (a 1.5 percentage point increase) in the whole European Union (EC, 2009, p. 39). Even though the majority of the EU members recorded an aggravation of government balances in 2008 there were some exceptions. For instance Bulgaria, the Netherlands, Hungary and, to a lesser extent, Austria and Germany recorded improvements in the budgetary position that was better than targeted.

An analysis of the recessionary period that commenced in autumn 2008 shows that the public finances of all EU members have come under excessive stress as the crisis-exit strategies envisage a strong reliance

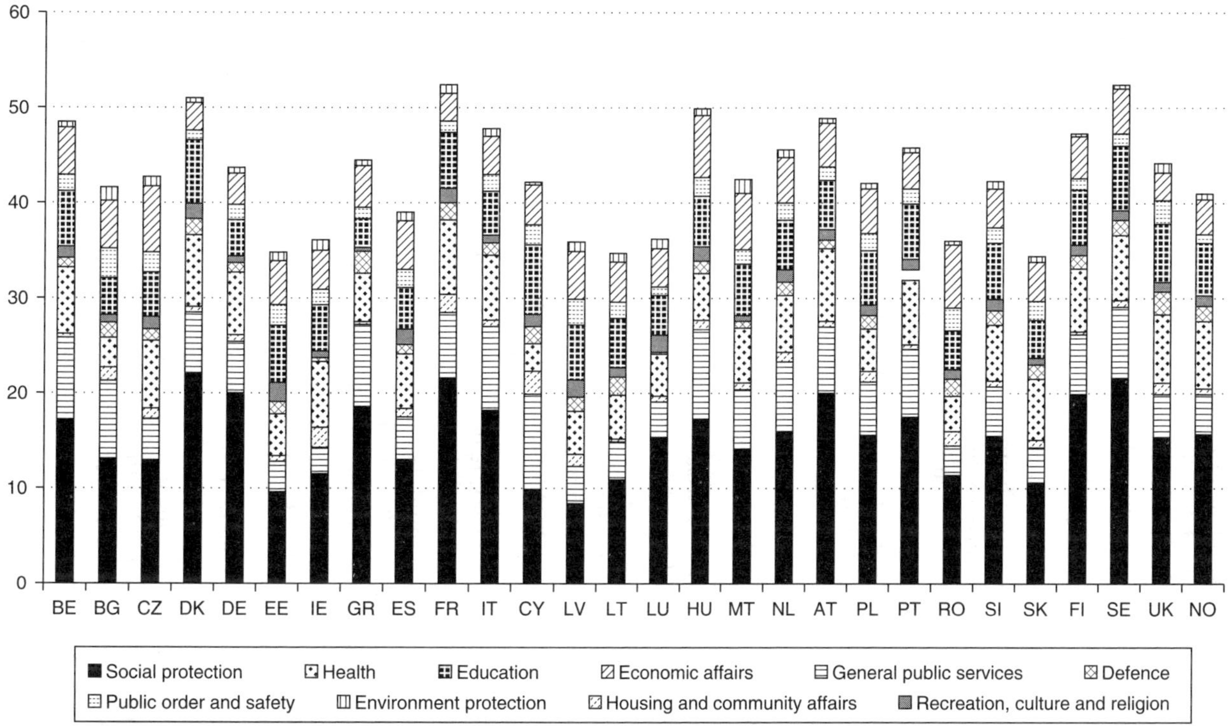

Source: Eurostat, European Commission.

Figure 6.4 Structure of government expenditure by EU countries in 2007

on two pillars: fiscal stimulus and structural reforms. As such, public finance should take the burden of the crisis by meeting three objectives: (i) address the decline in demand through fiscal stimulus and automatic stabilizers, (ii) restore the financial sector's health and support the intermediation function of financial markets and (iii) contribute to long-term growth prospects ensuring sustainable budgetary developments (EC, 2009).

Along with tightened fiscal discipline there are greater requirements to enhance the quality of public finance in EU members. Increased requirements envisage effective use of scarce public resources aiming to create immediate fiscal space, although it is more important to ensure sufficient provision for long-term growth and economic sustainability (EC, 2009, p. 6). For instance a number of EU Member States initiated 'greener' investment, regional policies, more efficient targeting of resources and other provisions.

1.3 Projections

Even prior to the economic crisis of late 2008, the projections of public finances for the new EU members were not optimistic and most of the members were expecting a slowdown of economic activity (Table 6.3).

The recent global financial crisis has negatively affected the economies of the new EU members and has caused a slowdown in implementing the policies aimed at the faster economic convergence of the new members (EC, 2008a). Most of the EU members have had to revise short- and long-term projections and strategies. As such, the economic situation and outlook remains uncertain and difficult to predict. The European Commission still tries to simulate future scenarios and forecasts −4.0 per cent real GDP growth in 2009 for both the EU and the euro area. The economic downturn is sharply visible on the labour market and in the unemployment rate, which was recorded at 8.3 per cent in March 2009 and was expected to reach an EU average of 10 per cent by 2010 (EC, 2009, p. 13).

The impact of the crisis and hence projections vary from country to country, reflecting different levels of integration with global markets and structural imbalances. Implications of the economic downturn for each Member State are presented in the relevant country profile page. A more detailed description of the developments related to the financial turmoil for whole new EU member region is provided in the concluding section.

Table 6.3 Budget balances in new EU members, percentage of GDP

	Budget Balance				Structural Balance				Structural Primary Balance			
	2007	2008	2009	2010	2007	2008	2009	2010	2007	2008	2009	2010
Bulgaria	−1.6	−1.4	−1.1	−0.3	3.1	−1.9	−1.5	1.6	−1.2	−0.8	−0.4	2.4
Czech Republic	2.8	0.4	−0.7	−4.9	1.3	0.4	0.6	−3.7	1.4	0.5	0.8	−2.5
Estonia	−5.5	−4.0	−3.6	−3.9	−4.7	−3.7	−3.3	−1.9	−0.6	0.5	0.8	−1.4
Hungary	0.0	−1.1	−2.1	−3.9	−1.4	−1.3	−1.1	−2.0	−0.8	−0.8	−0.6	2.9
Latvia	−2.0	−2.5	−2.6	−13.6	−2.5	−2.7	−2.3	−11.5	0.1	0.0	0.3	−9.2
Lithuania	−1.2	−1.7	−1.5	−8.0	−1.4	−2.0	−1.3	−5.5	−0.6	−1.3	−0.6	−3.9
Poland	−2.5	−2.9	−3.7	−7.3	−3.4	−3.7	−4.1	−5.6	−2.7	−2.9	−3.2	−2.7
Romania	−0.1	−0.6	−0.6	−5.6	−0.7	−1.1	−0.7	−4.7	0.6	0.1	0.4	−3.1
Slovenia	−2.2	−2.0	−2.3	−6.5	−2.6	−2.8	−3.1	−5.2	−1.2	−1.5	−1.7	−3.4
Slovakia	−3.3	−1.7	−1.8	−5.4	3.5	1.9	2.0	−4.7	6.7	4.8	4.8	−3.3
Cyprus	−1.8	−1.6	−1.0	−2.6	−2.4	−1.7	−1.0	−2.1	0.9	1.5	2.1	0.1

Source: European Commission (2009).

2. MEMBER STATES DEVELOPMENTS

2.1 Bulgaria

Bulgaria became a member of the European Union in 2007 and is classified as an 'upper–middle-income economy' (World Bank, 2008a). Since its accession to EU, the country made substantial progress towards long-term macroeconomic stability: growth was re-established, per capita income improved, inflation remained low and poverty decreased while the external debt-to-GDP ratio declined. By 2007 the share of the private sector in the economy had been increasing, major regulatory reforms were underway, the banking sector was on a more solid footing and energy reforms achieved more efficiency while the fiscal burden was decreasing (IMF, 2007a). Despite rapid economic growth and rising standards of living, the country is still ranked as the second-poorest EU Member State (CIA, 2008).

Amidst the current financial crisis, Bulgaria is one of six Central and Eastern European countries whose economies revealed marginal growth in 2009 (EC, 2009). Bulgaria's currency board is seen to help mitigate the economic turbulence as it was stable enough to deal with the shocks. However, due to the failure to proceed with fiscal reform right after the stabilization of the currency board, for now alternatives like currency devaluation or euro adoption are not seen as the best solutions (Bivol, 2009).

Analysing the pre-crisis condition of Bulgaria, the European Commission recommended further improvement of public expenditure efficiency, which is a prerequisite of the EU Convergence Programme (EC, 2008a). The Convergence Programme envisages fiscal and macroeconomic policy and presented 2007–2009 medium-term plans for the macroeconomic stability of the country. The medium-term state of the Bulgarian budget was stable and the country has been maintaining its fiscal stance, in particular aiming to increase its budget surplus from 0.08 per cent to 0.2 per cent in 2007 (EC, 2007).

Undertaking key structural reforms has proven difficult for Bulgaria, due to fragile politics and the deep-rooted interests of separate groups (Dimova, 2003). The country's potential for sustainable convergence is highly dependent on productivity increase of its human and real resources. The development rate of structural reforms in Bulgaria is in line with its peers in areas where EU legislation tends to enforce regulatory homogeneity: price liberalization, trade and the foreign exchange system. However, where EU accession has provided only a weak reform anchor, progress has been slow due to the following reasons: (1) the public sector's efficiency has been low, as reflected in indicators for corruption, red tape, quality of the judiciary and education standards; (2) businesses face costly administrative burdens and (3) rigidities in the labour market hinder the reallocation of labour and there is a question whether the labour market could deliver the degree of wage flexibility needed to support the currency board under adverse shock scenarios.

The fiscal policy stance of Bulgaria has been broadly neutral over the 1990s as shown by Polackova et al. (2000). Since 2004, fiscal policy revealed larger surpluses generated by revenue windfalls and an absorption boom. The budgeted fiscal surplus of 0.75 per cent of GDP for 2007 was based on highly conservative revenue projections. In 2007 pensions were raised by an additional 10 per cent and the social contribution rate was cut by 3 percentage points (IMF, 2007a). Bulgaria's general government balance was strong during 2005–2007, reflecting the prudent fiscal policy stance of the country. However, in 2008 the government surplus reached only 1.5 per cent of GDP against the official target of 3 per cent, which was determined in the December 2007 update of the Convergence Programme (EC, 2009, p. 200). The reasons behind such underperformance are lower revenues due to the global crisis and a lack of strict expenditure control.

Due to lack of fiscal space and large external/internal imbalances it was not expected that Bulgaria would undertake any fiscal stimulus in 2009 as envisaged by the EERP. The prospects for 2009 and 2010 were modest. The European Commission forecasts a general government deficit of 0.3 per cent of GDP in 2010, which is far below the projected 1.5 per cent surplus (EC, 2009, p. 200).

Summarizing the pre-crisis public investment for Bulgaria, its share in GDP was increasing gradually from 3.7 per cent in 2000 to 4.8 per cent in 2007, representing a 29 per cent growth rate. Private investment increased from 12.1 per cent to 25 per cent of GDP, thus revealing huge growth. For the same period, Gross Capital Formation increased from 4894 to 20 798 million Bulgarian levs, which is equal to a 3.2 times increase during 2000–2007 (Table 6.4).

The Gross Fixed Capital Formation (GFCF) is an important indicator of the public investment trend. According to the European Bank for Reconstruction and Development (EBRD) Economic Statistics and Forecasts, the GFCF in Bulgaria increased from 15.4 per cent to 21.7 per cent in real terms for the period 2000–2007. In comparison with the National Statistics, the GFCF increased from 4206 to 16 832 million Bulgarian levs, which represents a 3 per cent increase for the whole period of 2000–2007.

One of the representative indicators of public investment is the Acquisition of Tangible Fixed Assets (TFA). The total expenditure on

Table 6.4 *Public investment by category in Bulgaria*

Variable	2000	2001	2002	2003	2004	2005	2006	2007	2008
Public investment, % of GDP	3.7	3.5	2.8	2.7	2.9	4.1	4.2	4.9	
Private investment, % of GDP	12.1	14.7	15.4	16.6	17.6	20.0	21.8	25.0	27.7
Gross fixed capital formation, percentage change in real terms (source: EBRD – Economic Statistics and Forecasts):									
Gross capital formation	15.4	23.3	8.5	13.9	13.5	23.3	14.7	21.7	
Gross capital formation (in millions of national currency):									
Gross fixed capital formation	4206	5415	5909	6694	7969	10347	12805	16832	
Changes in inventories	688	726	497	816	1006	1624	2862	3965	
Total	4894	6141	6405	7511	8976	11971	15667	20798	
Public expenditure on acquisition of tangible fixed assets by economic activity groups (in thousands of national currency):									
Agriculture, hunting and forestry	108822	145931	203517	265536	373124	438857	463635	638208	
Fishing	1983	375	1268	1955	3231	1263	3329	3906	
Mining and quarrying	115619	103202	115119	119742	157178	295384	350753	472495	
Manufacturing	1290594	1549317	1921066	2004112	2086358	2705800	3648165	4769227	
Electricity, gas and water supply	573359	527693	503255	1024336	1053722	1213337	1709015	2297576	

Construction	343 113	419 245	409 892	490 746	762 644	1 106 864	1 755 812	3 631 362
Trade, repair of motor vehicles and personal and household goods	778 355	880 388	1 151 134	1 322 928	1 485 599	1 888 363	2 588 146	3 774 781
Hotels and restaurants	232 480	336 957	439 005	508 781	703 892	797 224	772 486	895 073
Transport, storage and communication	1 231 564	1 740 139	1 378 906	1 467 796	1 759 361	2 187 883	2 269 423	3 139 847
Financial intermediation	124 019	159 456	129 848	138 466	174 081	271 772	325 177	662 680
Real estate, renting and business activities	223 609	367 798	450 680	522 757	716 503	1 423 892	2 583 465	5 269 987
Public administration, compulsory social security	207 874	166 017	128 759	177 969	233 850	278 027	435 165	512 680
Education	31 719	44 374	62 541	64 113	68 604	125 817	150 289	255 680
Health and social work	54 762	108 559	104 320	136 427	136 538	206 904	167 936	222 925
Other community, social and personal service activities	91 571	144 840	221 216	257 394	234 869	321 130	520 067	900 135
Total	5 409 443	6 694 291	7 220 526	8 503 058	9 949 554	13 262 517	17 742 863	27 446 562

Source: National Institute of Bulgaria, Eurostat.

TFA increased from 5409443 to 27446562 thousand Bulgarian levs during 2000–2007. In percentage terms this translates to an increase of 4.1 per cent. The largest part of the expenditure was attributed to manufacturing- and transportation-related items. The share of manufacturing in the total expenditure decreased from 23.8 per cent to 17.3 per cent during 2000–2007, while transportation increased from 0.4 per cent to 3.7 per cent (Table 6.4).

In response to the global economic crisis of 2008, revised budgetary measures were taken by Bulgaria in 2009. On the revenue side the measures include a reduction in the pension social contribution rate by 4 per cent (−0.9 per cent of GDP), an increase in the minimum insured income (0.7 per cent of GDP) and an increase in excise rates for fuel, administrative needs and property valuations (0.6 per cent of GDP). The measures on the expenditure side include a limitation on the disbursement of non-interest expenditures (−2.3 per cent of GDP), higher capital spending (0.1 per cent of GDP) and an increase in pensions (1 per cent of GDP) and salaries (0.3 per cent of GDP) (EC, 2007; 2009, pp. 200–201). These measures are expected to generate a government deficit of 0.3 per cent of GDP in 2010 against the officially projected 1.5 per cent of GDP surplus.

2.2 The Czech Republic

The Czech Republic joined the European Union in 2004 and since then has been part of its single market. The country has fully implemented the Schengen Agreement and on 21 December, 2007 completely opened its borders with all its neighbours: Germany, Austria, Poland and Slovakia. The country has a rapidly developing, high-income economy with a GDP per capita of 82 per cent of the European Union average (Bruha et al., 2007). Despite the political turbulences following the 2006 election and the deepening structural deficit of public finances, in 2007 the Czech economy performed outstandingly, with GDP growth reaching 6.6 per cent (CERGE-EI, 2008). This growth was maintained by exports to the European Union, the largest portion to Germany.

During three consecutive years, from 2005 to 2007, the Czech Republic had exceptionally rapid expansion. However, the economic downturn that commenced with the global financial crisis is expected to continue. Growth in 2008 was only 4 per cent of GDP and was supported largely by domestic demand and private consumption. High oil and food prices and an increase in the value-added tax eroded growth in household incomes. Tight labour market policies and the strong exchange rate of the Czech koruna in 2008 prevented the outflow of fixed investment. The growth of the Czech economy started to slow significantly in the last quarter of 2008, driven by deepening recession in the advanced economies and the country's significant trade openness. Forward-looking indicators of domestic demand suggest that the downturn continued to deepen in 2009 and 2010 (IMF, 2009f).

During the first decade of transition the share of output produced by privately-owned firms in the Czech Republic rose dramatically from only 13 per cent of GDP in 1990 to more than 77 per cent in 1999 (Czech Statistical Office, 2001). However, public expenditure remained at a relatively constant share of GDP during the period 1993–1999. In 2000, public expenditures rose to 48.4 per cent of GDP (Nam and Parsche, 2001) and nowadays are above the Organisation for Economic Co-operation and Development (OECD) average and higher than in Hungary and Poland. However, government revenues have grown less quickly and, as a result, the general government deficit has increased substantially. Moreover, the current imbalance is largely structural in nature and could threaten economic stability over the medium term.

Similar to the rest of Europe, the pension system and ageing are acute issues for public sector reforms in the Czech Republic. Following current demographic projections, the pension system of the Czech Republic will go into deficit in about 2020, at which point the deficit would accelerate very quickly. By 2050, the annual deficit will amount to about 4 per cent of GDP while cumulative debt would gradually approach 43 per cent of GDP (CERGE-EI, 2008, section VI.2).

A reform of the health care system was publicly introduced in November 2006 and approved by the Czech Parliament on 21 August 2007. It is aimed at addressing the current deficiencies of the system. Even though total health care expenditures reached only 7.2 per cent of GDP in 2005, which is 2.8 per cent below the OECD average, the government estimates that 20 per cent of these expenditures were allocated inefficiently. Kovacs (2003) also addressed this issue and contrasted political transformations in the welfare reforms of several Central and Eastern European (CEE) countries with advanced EU Member States.

Recent developments in the global economy have corrected the projections for the government balance in 2009. The target for the general government balance in the Czech Republic in 2009 is −4.5 per cent of GDP, compared to a target of −1.6 per cent in the latest November 2008 convergence programme. Two packages were adopted by the Czech government to stimulate economic activity. The first package mainly focuses on cutting social security contributions paid by employees as well as additional spending on infrastructure investment. The second package is aimed at supporting mainly small- and medium-sized enterprises during the downturn. Government debt is projected to increase to about 34 per cent of

Table 6.5 *Structure of general government tax revenue in the Czech Republic (in % GDP)*

	2004	2005	2006	2007	2008	2009
Tax revenue and social contributions	37.3	36.8	36.5	36.9	36.0	34.3
individual income tax	4.8	4.6	4.2	4.3	3.9	3.7
corporate income tax	4.7	4.5	4.8	5.0	4.7	3.9
VAT	7.2	7.1	6.5	6.4	7.0	6.6
excise taxes	3.5	3.7	3.8	4.0	3.4	3.8
social contributions	16.1	16.2	16.3	16.3	16.2	15.5
other taxes and contributions	1.0	0.9	0.8	0.8	0.8	0.8

Source: Ministry of Finance of the Czech Republic (2009).

GDP in 2009 and 38 per cent of GDP in 2010 due to the impact of worsening cyclical factors (EC, 2009).

In January 2008 the Czech Republic became the thirteenth country in the CEE region with a flat tax rate on personal income. Beyond replacing the progressive marginal tax rates ranging from 12 per cent to 32 per cent by a single 15 per cent rate, the personal income tax itself was redesigned (Table 6.5). The corporate income tax rate was reduced to 22 per cent and further reduced to 20 per cent in 2009 and 19 per cent in 2010. Several exemptions and deductions were eliminated in personal as well as corporate income tax.

In terms of the deficit-to-GDP ratio the Czech Republic has been trying to improve on its early poor performance, as shown in Kočenda et al. (2008). However, according to IMF recommendations, fiscal consolidation needs to be sustained beyond 2008 to meet the challenges posed by the ageing population and to ensure smooth euro entry (IMF, 2008a). Public debt, which has been low and stable in recent years owing to strong growth and the use of privatization revenues for financing, is projected to rise faster than it will for regional peers. An annual consolidation of at least 0.5 per cent of GDP would help stabilize debt over the medium term, provide a safety margin in respecting the Stability and Growth Pact limit of 3 per cent of GDP under more adverse cyclical conditions and help create fiscal space for accommodating age-related spending. However, despite having one of the most rapidly ageing populations in the European Union, the Czech Republic remains one of the few countries that has yet to start reforming its pension system. Correspondingly, the fiscal gap that needs to be filled in order to ensure long-term sustainable public finances is one of the largest in the EU. In order to prepare for the inevitable spending pressures associated with this demographic transition, a multi-pronged strategy is urgently required (CERGE-EI, 2008, p. 85).

Public investment in the Czech Republic reveals different patterns before and after accession to the EU. During 1999–2004 public investment was growing steadily from 3.3 per cent to 4.8 per cent of GDP, while after accession to the EU, the growth pattern has slowed down and has maintained around 4.9 per cent on average during 2004–2007 (Table 6.6). The share of private investment in the Czech Republic is significantly larger than public investment. Private investment increased from 23.8 per cent to 21.1 per cent of GDP during 1999–2004 and also slowed down after accession reaching 20 per cent on average for four years.

The largest part of the public investment in the country is attributed to economic affairs (Table 6.6). The share of this category in total public investment increased from 49.4 per cent in 2004 to 53.5 per cent in 2007, as can be seen from Table 6.6. The second largest category in public investment is education, constituting 13.4 per cent of total investment in 2007, while it increased by 0.6 per cent during 2004–2007.

The Total Gross Fixed Capital Formation (GFCF) by main asset types in the Czech Republic increased from 727 182 to 857 726 Czech korunas after accession, thus representing 17.9 per cent growth. Construction is the largest area for both public and private investment: its share in total GFCF increased from 49.2 per cent in 2004 to 53.3 per cent in 2007. The second most important is metallurgy and machinery, although its investment pattern decreased by 0.89 per cent after the accession of the Czech Republic to the EU and it reached only 2.8 per cent of the total GFCF. One of the rapidly growing sectors is recreation, culture and religion, according to the COFOG classification. The volume of government investment in fixed capital has increased 1.4 times thus revealing a 35.5 per cent growth rate during 2004–2007. Such a trend is in line with the tourism and recreation specialization for which the Czech Republic is famous.

2.3 Estonia

Until 2006, the Estonian economy was one of the fastest-growing in the world with growth rates exceeding 10 per cent annually (IMF, 2008b). Energy resources are a vital source for the Estonian economy. The country is nearly energy independent, supplying over 90 per cent of its electricity needs with locally mined oil shale. In addition to oil energy, telecommunications, textiles, chemical products, banking, services, food and fishing, timber, shipbuilding, electronics and transportation are key sectors of the economy. Estonia today is mainly influenced by the development of its three main trade partners: Germany, Finland and Sweden. At the same

Table 6.6 Public investment by categories and asset type in the Czech Republic

Variable	COFOG code/ Measure	1999	2000	2001	2002	2003	2004	2005	2006	2007	2008
Public Investment	% of GDP	3.2	3.5	3.6	3.9	4.4	4.7	4.9	5.0	4.6	
Private Investment	% of GDP	23.8	24.4	24.5	23.6	22.1	21.0	20.0	19.7	20.5	19.0
Public investment by categories (COFOG classification):											
General public services	GF01	861.0	931.0	668.0	1 192.0	1 147.0	2 698.0	874.0	−1 757.0	−1 198.0	
Defence	GF02	1 621.0	1 830.0	1 726.0	1 709.0	5 515.0	2 062.0	4 095.0	6 357.0	6 357.0	
Public order and safety	GF03	2 514	2 865	2 835	3 605	2 672	4 969	5 653	5 760	5 760	
Economic affairs	GF04	33 932	40 018	40 622	30 815	39 265	67 447	80 488	89 932	89 932	
Environment protection	GF05	7 193	8 477	9 785	10 174	14 428	14 175	15 684	15 994	15 994	
Housing and community amenities	GF06	4 424	5 220	6 051	6 914	14 871	10 073	3 956	1 678	7 630	
Health	GF07	1 585	1 585	1 551	2 369	2 134	2 592	2 170	2 237	2 237	
Recreation, culture and religion	GF08	4 710	5 548	6 393	8 486	8 872	9 809	10 188	13 296	13 296	
Education	GF09	8 522	9 895	10 704	20 034	20 485	17 526	18 665	22 602	22 602	

Social protection	GF10	2306	2702	3041	9913	7789	5076	4735	5384	5384	
Total:		67668	79071	83376	95211	117178	136427	146508	161483	167994	
Public investment by main asset types (public and private):											
Products of agriculture, forestry, fisheries and aquaculture		2542	4763	5355	4941	4729	5283	4600	4453	4419	4173
Metal products and machinery		209964	234503	239159	232737	211668	227869	215988	227632	259504	245290
Transport equipment		53487	68472	88531	100206	101294	100186	106088	118175	137280	134727
Construction work: housing		68740	73544	73088	75260	76872	86918	88351	95823	135665	131178
Construction work: other constructions		205202	204358	223280	232192	261330	271364	293352	313957	312277	322865
Other products		22325	26829	29875	32451	31575	35562	33515	36273	41106	44943
Total:		562260	612469	659288	677787	687468	727182	741894	796313	890251	883176

Source: National Statistical Office, Eurostat.

time, Ireland was sometimes seen as a model for the Estonian economic future, as discussed by Maiväli and Lubenets (2007).

The growth recovery of Estonia's economy will depend to large extent on the competitiveness of the economy. Consumption is likely to remain restrained because households are saving to build financial buffers in light of increased economic uncertainties and global financial contractions. Therefore, a revival of exports or investment will be needed for a quick recovery. At the same time, Granlund (2008) claims that for investment growth to resume and exporters to be competitive in relatively sluggish global markets, wage growth should be consistent with productivity gains, not higher, as in the recent years of 2006–2007.

The general government surplus in Estonia was 2.8 per cent of GDP in 2007 and turned into a deficit of 3 per cent in 2008 after six years of subsequent positive government balance. The outcome in 2008 was worse than the projected 1.3 per cent surplus due to a considerable decline in economic activity. Total expenditure increased by close to 20 per cent compared to 2007, worsening the structural balance and implying a significantly countercyclical fiscal stance. The debt-to-GDP ratio increased from 3.5 per cent of GDP in 2007 to 4.8 per cent in 2008, mainly on account of new borrowing by local governments, since the deficit of the central government was extensively financed by the accumulated surpluses of previous years. Further projections of the debt-to-GDP ratio follow the same tendency: 6.8 per cent in 2009 and 7.8 per cent in 2010 (EC, 2009, p. 209).

The November 2007 update of the Convergence Programme set a headline surplus target of 1.0 per cent of GDP for 2009, slightly declining subsequently towards the end of the programme period in 2011 (EC, 2008a, p. 237). Meanwhile the general government debt-to-GDP ratio was expected to stabilize at around 3.5 per cent in 2008 and 2009, somewhat higher than the 2–2.25 per cent projected in the 2007 Convergence Programme update. The difference largely reflects the impact of a statistical reclassification. In addition, the worsened outlook for public finances is likely to result in local governments financing deficits by new debt issuance, whereas any central government deficit is likely to result in recourse to existing gross financial assets.

Estonia has been aiming at improving its deficit-to-GDP ratio lately but its budget performance was not improving much, as evidenced in Kočenda et al. (2008). In 2007, the government had for the first time presented a surplus budget to parliament, setting an important precedent and sending a helpful signal of fiscal restraint. The strong fiscal outcomes during 2005–2007 masked large increases in current expenditures (40 per cent over the years 2006–2007) that were covered by exceptionally high revenues related to the economic boom. Further increases in 2008 resulted in an expansionary budget and with the economic slowdown the fiscal outcome converged to a negative balance (IMF, 2008b). The approved 2008 supplementary budget introduced adjustments that should have reduced the projected deficit while leaving a positive fiscal surplus. In early 2008 the Estonian authorities have indicated that they will take further steps to balance the budget, as documented in consultations with the IMF (2008b).

With the commencement of the crisis in late 2008 the situation has changed drastically. The general government deficit was 3.0 per cent of GDP in 2008 after six years of budgetary surpluses (EC, 2009, p. 209). Such a record was significantly worse than the projection of 1.3 per cent according to the November 2007 Convergence Programme. In mid-2008 the Government of Estonia adopted a restrictive supplementary budget. However, total expenditures continued increasing up to 20 per cent compared to 2007, which deteriorated the structural balance.

In 2008 the debt-to-GDP ratio increased from 3.5 per cent of GDP at the end of 2007 to 4.8 per cent. The rise was mainly attributed to new borrowing by local governments since the deficit of the central government was largely financed by running down the accumulated surpluses of previous years.

Since its accession to the EU, the public investment in Estonia increased from 3.8 per cent of GDP in 2004 to 5.4 per cent in 2007, while private investment reached 27 per cent of GDP at the end of this period. For the same period, the volume of total public investment increased by 126 per cent, thus revealing the high importance of and priority given to this sector (Table 6.7).

The largest part of total public investment was attributed to economic affairs and education, following the COFOG classification, where their shares reached 30.2 per cent and 21.3 per cent in 2007, respectively. The growth in economic affairs during the post-accession period was 109 per cent while in education it was 138 per cent (Table 6.7).

The public finance trends in Estonia have changed during 2008–2009, addressing the consequences of the economic crisis. As a result, a new set of budgetary measures for 2009 were adopted. On the revenue side they included an increase in social tax contributions (+0.5 per cent of GDP), a suspension of the mandatory pension scheme (+0.6 per cent of GDP) and an increase in unemployment insurance (+0.3 per cent of GDP). On the expenditure side the measures included the advancement of the enforcement of the new labour law (+0.2 per cent of GDP) and an increase in pensions (+0.6 per cent of GDP).[5] Assuming that no further policy changes occur, these budgetary measures are projected to yield a deficit of 3.9 per cent of GDP (EC, 2009, p. 209).

Table 6.7 Public investment by categories and asset type in Estonia

Variable	COFOG code/ Measure	1999	2000	2001	2002	2003	2004	2005	2006	2007	2008
Public Investment	% of GDP	4.2	3.8	4.1	5.3	4.4	3.8	4.0	4.8	5.2	5.5
Private investment	% of GDP	20.4	22.0	22.3	24.4	27.2	27.1	28.1	30.2	29.3	24.0
Public investment by categories (COFOG classification):											
General public services	GF01	308.8	268.2	332.9	936.4	649.9	159.7	322.2	860.2	1176.6	−137.1
Defence	GF02	419.3	366.8	429.4	603.2	625.7	655.8	514.6	534.4	487.2	812.9
Public order and safety	GF03	252.3	223.1	260.6	370.3	382.3	165.8	510.5	579.8	808.5	1713.0
Economic affairs	GF04	666.7	684.0	853.5	1120.9	1058.4	2097.3	2616.2	3654.6	3851.8	4079.3
Environment protection	GF05	120.3	147.2	192.1	234.1	201.8	172.5	207.3	80.8	422.4	418.2
Housing and community amenities	GF06	170.1	222.8	302.1	358.8	294.7	45.0	−268.8	−235.4	651.6	426.9
Health	GF07	277.5	244.4	277.4	497.3	501.9	213.9	428.0	912.3	1366.9	1730.3
Recreation, culture and religion	GF08	333.5	358.0	477.9	571.3	596.6	735.0	1125.5	1171.7	1011.0	1373.1
Education	GF09	937.6	993.1	1231.9	1629.3	1524.8	1289.7	1394.4	2298.5	2731.0	2696.7

Social protection	GF10	72.2	81.7	104.2	131.8	118.4	207.7	74.4	−48.5	228.4	266.8
Total:		3558.3	3589.2	4461.9	6453.4	5954.5	5742.2	6924.3	9808.4	12735.4	13380.2
Public investment by main asset types (public and private):											
Products of agriculture, forestry, fisheries and aquaculture		65.0	137.5	186.6	180.2	145.7	162.7	185.4	236.0	250.7	241.3
Metal products and machinery		6983.6	8567.9	9357.4	11169.7	12290.9	13250.3	15396.7	18568.8	19574.3	19606.8
Transport equipment		2406.8	3379.2	4435.7	6018.0	9766.0	7916.1	6406.7	9617.9	11232.8	10037.5
Construction work: housing		1786.4	1940.4	2246.1	3094.2	4296.1	5781.2	8562.7	12801.6	14481.0	10169.1
Construction work: other constructions		9175.8	10523.8	12237.8	15212.4	16157.8	19053.7	24761.8	29563.6	37334.9	32452.0
Other products		215.0	215.6	361.0	433.6	401.4	616.8	801.5	1537.2	1511.5	1222.8
Total:		20632.6	24764.3	28824.5	36108.0	43057.9	46780.8	56114.8	72325.1	84385.2	73729.4

Source: National Statistical Office, Eurostat.

2.4 Hungary

The Hungarian economy is medium-sized, structurally, politically and institutionally open and part of the European Union single market. In 2006 Prime Minister Ferenc Gyurcsány was re-elected promising economic 'reform without austerity' (Campos and Jolliffe, 2007). However, after the elections in April 2006, the Socialist coalition unveiled a package of austerity measures that were designed to reduce the budget deficit to 3 per cent of GDP by 2008. Because of the austerity programme, the economy of Hungary slowed down in 2007 (OECD, 2007).

The macroeconomic policies of the Hungarian economy have produced important results between accession and the 2008 crisis. The fiscal consolidation that began two years ago has narrowed the general government deficit from 9.25 per cent of GDP in 2006 (IMF, 2008c). Reflecting fiscal consolidation, the current account deficit narrowed to 6.25 per cent of GDP in 2008. Measures focused on achieving a 3 per cent inflation target and the removal of the exchange rate band in early 2008 has overcome a potential conflict between monetary policy objectives. Inflation fell from 9 per cent in early 2007 to 5.75 per cent in September 2008 despite significant commodity price shocks and was projected to fall further in 2009, although the recent depreciation of the Hungarian forint may slow the decline (IMF, 2008c).

The global financial turmoil adversely and immediately affected the Hungarian economy. On 10 October, 2008 the Hungarian forint dropped by 10 per cent, which adversely affected the economic balance as a majority of international loans are made in euros and Swiss Francs in Hungary. On 27 October 2008 Hungary reached an agreement with the IMF and EU for a rescue package worth USD 20 billion (IMF, 2008c). During that shaky period, financial stress in Hungary increased sharply, mainly due to external factors. Investors' extreme risk aversion and constraints in global financial markets has negatively affected the foreign exchange, government securities and equity markets in Hungary. The effect in Hungary may have been more pronounced than elsewhere in the region because underlying stock vulnerabilities (public and external debt) are still high and financial markets are developed and deeply integrated with EU markets.

By the end of 2008 the budget deficit was 3.4 per cent of GDP, sharply lower than 9.2 per cent in 2006 and 4.9 per cent in 2007 (EC, 2009). Significant reductions in the deficit by 0.6 per cent of GDP was achieved mainly due to better than expected revenues that came from two sources: (a) the effect of tax evasion policies that resulted in a 0.2 per cent of GDP increase in personal income tax and (b) revenue inflows of budgetary institutions of over 0.5 per cent of GDP in 2008 (EC, 2009, p. 234).

The overall fiscal performance of the country continues to strengthen, which is in line with the determined fiscal objectives. The monthly path of the primary balance in 2008 shows a substantial improvement with respect to 2007 and 2006. Although there is some weakness in VAT collection, overall revenue has been resilient, reflecting continued progress in tax compliance and a temporary lag in the impact of the economic downturn on the labour market (IMF, 2009a). Specific legal requirements represent a domestic anchor for fiscal policy and introduce numerical and procedural rules for the preparation of annual budgets, including the obligation to achieve a decline in public debt in real terms, the prohibition of primary deficits, compliance with medium-term expenditure ceilings and a requirement to offset the impact of legislative initiatives on the budget balance (IMF, 2009a).

Amidst the financial crisis, the government of Hungary has implemented a range of EU-funded measures to mitigate the economic downturn (IMF, 2008d). However, given the macroeconomic imbalances the Government of Hungary did not adopt fiscal stimulus measures unlike many other new members of the EU. This is yet fully in line with the EERP. The response to the financial crisis was thus comprised of budget-neutral measures such as the strengthening of labour market policies and the support of a package for small and medium-sized enterprises (SMEs). These actions are aimed at alleviating financing stress for SMEs through investment subsidies, credit guarantees and refinancing facilities for commercial bank lending. Infrastructure-related measures – including railroad and school refurbishment – are designed to boost demand.

Similar to the public investment patterns in other EU NMS, economic affairs is the largest category with a 47.8 per cent share in the total volume of public investment in 2007, which was also evidenced by Cekota et al. (2002). The share grew from 37 per cent in 2004 and increased 1.6 times in volume during 2004–2007. The largest share in this category is invested in construction, both housing and other types: this share constituted 54.6 per cent of all public investment on economic needs in 2007 (Table 6.8).

In contrast to other EU NMS, among other important categories in public investment are general public services and environment protection, following the COFOG classification. The share of general public services in total public investment volume actually decreased from 20.6 per cent in 2004 to 11.3 per cent in 2007, despite the fact that it is one of the most important categories. The volume of public investment into environmental protection increased 1.5 times and its share in total public investment reached 11.1 per cent in 2007. Growth rates in social protection and recreation categories revealed a negative growth rate during 2004–2007: −10 per cent and −48 per cent, respectively. For the same period, public

Table 6.8 Public investment by categories and asset type in Hungary

Variable	COFOG code/ Measure	2001	2002	2003	2004	2005	2006	2007	2008
Public investment	% of GDP	3.7	4.9	3.5	3.5	4.0	4.4	3.6	
Private investment	% of GDP	19.3	18.2	18.8	19.0	19.1	17.3	17.6	18.1
Public investment by categories (COFOG classification):									
General public services	GF01	157 100.9	240 371.1	151 363.5	151 516.5	193 627.6	116 620.0	101 913.8	
Defence	GF02	22 261.0	58 416.8	35 071.9	34 772.5	37 708.7	28 064.2	29 182.4	
Public order and safety	GF03	22 102.3	46 973.0	33 182.3	29 279.3	30 187.2	33 863.8	35 935.3	
Economic affairs	GF04	181 681.6	165 731.9	193 276.8	271 904.5	344 716.4	498 551.8	432 680.5	
Environment protection	GF05	70 371.1	87 156.3	59 329.2	68 955.7	84 771.9	119 117.7	100 424.0	
Housing and community amenities	GF06	−4 753.0	19 547.2	13 010.3	28 878.2	34 573.4	65 585.6	60 087.9	
Health	GF07	29 494.1	53 705.8	53 037.4	42 960.1	47 013.0	69 037.9	47 729.2	
Recreation, culture and religion	GF08	34 534.1	68 719.3	47 674.4	45 685.8	33 068.5	31 603.1	23 978.9	
Education	GF09	42 714.3	90 681.7	54 393.9	44 443.9	58 643.0	70 224.0	58 503.5	

Social protection	GF10	11 972.8	15 907.9	17 825.2	14 974.6	12 987.3	16 677.7	13 479.5	
Total:		567 479.3	847 211.0	658 165.0	733 371.0	877 297.0	1 049 346.0	903 914.8	
Public investment by main asset types (public and private):									
Products of agriculture, forestry, fisheries and aquaculture		55 726	61 232	54 943	41 316	41 035	37 657	39 600	45 474
Metal products and machinery		1 215 550	1 227 149	1 306 062	1 472 116	1 482 327	1 553 450	1 684 235	1 701 941
Transport equipment		284 670	334 464	425 426	434 971	484 859	508 412	508 975	529 281
Construction work: housing		668 748	831 089	942 016	1 107 411	1 009 686	902 021	1 022 974	1 139 930
Construction work: other constructions		1 118 756	1 327 593	1 264 490	1 470 164	1 816 598	1 977 322	1 913 031	1 911 894
Other products		174 834	193 830	197 099	151 806	231 368	182 415	211 728	230 568
Total:		3 518 284	3 975 357	4 190 036	4 677 784	5 065 873	5 161 277	5 380 543	5 559 088

Source: National Statistical Office, Eurostat.

investment in education increased by 31.6 per cent and increased 1.3 times by 2007.

The key challenges ahead in improving the infrastructure and structural policies include the following: (a) measures to reduce public expenditures; (b) investment into the diversification of energy supply, reductions of energy intensity and meeting environmental targets; (c) improving transport and environmental infrastructure with the assistance of EU Structural and Cohesion Funds, private-sector involvement and commercial co-financing from local sources and (d) financial institutions benefiting from the introduction of new products, increased efficiency of the pension fund system, and diversification of their investment portfolios (EBRD, 2008c).

2.5 Latvia

Latvia was the fastest growing economy in Europe until the middle of 2008 experiencing high GDP growth since 2000. In particular, GDP growth was 7.5 per cent and inflation was 2.9 per cent in 2003. Unemployment was 8.8 per cent in 2003 and almost unchanged compared to the previous two years (MoF of Latvia, 2005). Privatization is mostly complete, except for some of the large state-owned utilities.

On 1 May 2004, Latvia joined the European Union and like other recent EU entrants, has benefited from an accession-related boost to income convergence. Closer integration with the rest of Europe in goods, financial markets and labour markets, as well as access to substantial EU grants, have helped Latvia to create favourable investment opportunities and attract large inflows of foreign financing (World Bank, 2002). Consequently, capital and technology stocks and consumption and living standards have risen. As a result, the country has enjoyed very rapid convergence in income levels over the past decade (IMF, 2007b).

The current global financial crisis has brought a number of vulnerabilities for Latvia. Years of unsustainably high growth and large current account deficits have merged into a financial and balance of payments crisis for the country. Since the end of August 2008, private sector deposits have fallen by 10 per cent, led by a run on Parex Bank,[6] which encountered severe liquidity problems after it lost more than a quarter of its deposits. During August–November 2008, official reserves fell by almost 20 per cent to EUR 3.4 billion, one third of short-term external debt and just over 100 per cent of the base money (from 127 per cent in September 2008), as the central bank sold foreign currency to defend the peg (IMF, 2009b). Despite this substantial intervention since early October 2008 the exchange rate has remained at its depreciated band. Concerns over the financial system and external debt sustainability increased and the exchange rate peg came under threat, according to IMF evaluations (IMF, 2009b).

As of April 2009 the actual government deficit in Latvia was 4.0 per cent of GDP (EC, 2009, p. 228). This is a weaker indicator compared with the 0.7 per cent of GDP target set in the 2008 budget and weaker than the 3.5 per cent of GDP deficit projected in the convergence programme. Such a performance reflects a significantly worsened economic environment, a sharp contraction of tax revenues and unexpectedly high budget expenditures. As a result the debt-to-GDP ratio increased from 9.0 per cent (2007) to 19.5 per cent (2008), that is, within just one year (EC, 2009). A dramatic increase in public debt was mainly due to the bail-out financing of Parex Bank, Latvia's largest domestic bank.

In early 2009 Latvia implemented measures to increase VAT and address the economic downturn. However, increases in VAT have failed to bring the expected revenues and as a consequences public expenditures in the first quarter of 2009 were far above the corresponding 2008 levels. For 2009–2010 public finances are expected to deteriorate further due to the weak macroeconomic environment and exceptionally high discretionary expenditures (EC, 2009, p. 228). The European Commission projects the general government deficit to exceed 11 per cent of GDP in 2009–2010.

Latvia joined the EU in May 2004 and since then the country's public investment increased dramatically from 3.1 per cent to 5.6 per cent as a share of GDP, which was also predicted by Friedrich et al. (2003). Meanwhile private investment increased slightly from 25.6 per cent to 26.9 per cent during 2004–2007, thus revealing a 5 per cent growth rate. The total volume of public investment in Latvia increased 3.6 times during the post-accession period and as much as 13 times during 1999–2007, shown in Table 6.9.

Economic affairs is the largest category: its share in total amount of public investment increased from 22.6 per cent in 2004 and reached 35 per cent in 2007, thus revealing a growth rate of 455 per cent (Table 6.9). Education is the second-largest category and its share in total public investment has slightly decreased from 14 per cent in 2004 to 13.7 per cent in 2007. Despite this, capital formation in this category increased 3.5 times during 2004–2007, thus representing 252 per cent growth rate. At the same time, these abnormal growth rates are in line with the overheating Latvian economy which was discussed in more detail above. The amount of public investment for environment and social protection almost tripled in Latvia during the post-accession period, though these two categories represent the smallest portion in overall public investment: 2.4 per cent and 1.7 per cent, respectively, at the end of 2007. The Gross Fixed Capital Formation (GFCF) was the largest in construction and metal production/machinery.

Table 6.9 Public investment by categories and asset type in Latvia

Variable	COFOG code/ Measure	1999	2000	2001	2002	2003	2004	2005	2006	2007	2008
Public investment	% of GDP	1.4	1.4	1.2	1.4	2.7	3.5	3.3	5.1	6.3	
Private investment	% of GDP	23.8	22.5	22.0	24.4	27.5	28.0	28.0	24.6	23.8	22.5
Public investment by categories (COFOG classification):											
General public services	GF01	17.4	19.4	18.4	21.0	50.1	70.4	39.3	65.2	87.6	
Defence	GF02	1.0	1.4	1.3	2.8	10.8	17.7	9.6	40.4	45.1	
Public order and safety	GF03	3.2	2.8	2.4	3.3	9.0	14.6	15.5	50.2	67.6	
Economic affairs	GF04	18.6	14.6	11.3	15.3	33.2	52.4	82.5	158.3	266.0	
Environment protection	GF05	2.9	3.2	3.2	1.9	2.4	8.7	13.1	22.9	30.7	
Housing and community amenities	GF06	4.2	6.5	4.8	7.7	8.0	11.7	34.7	50.6	86.2	
Health	GF07	1.4	1.8	1.3	2.4	7.3	12.2	37.5	52.8	73.4	
Recreation, culture and religion	GF08	3.5	3.2	2.4	3.7	45	6.5	7.6	14.6	57.1	
Education	GF09	8.4	9.1	11.5	13.4	22.6	32.2	33.3	50.3	109.4	

Social protection	GF10	1.3	1.6	1.1	1.4	3.8	4.8	6.6	10.1	13.3	
Total:		62.0	63.4	57.7	72.9	151.7	231.0	279.7	515.4	836.5	
Public investment by main asset types (public and private):											
Products of agriculture, forestry, fisheries and aquaculture		4.4	5.2	5.5	6.3	8.6	6.7	10.9	14.3	7.2	2.1
Metal products and machinery		389.8	457.0	429.0	491.8	522.7	590.3	929.4	1078.4	1465.4	1486.5
Transport equipment		119.4	142.1	247.4	187.8	191.6	297.3	458.9	681.3	667.3	520.5
Construction work: housing		102.4	107.2	118.7	110.5	122.9	211.1	228.5	354.9	608.7	834.8
Construction work: other constructions		330.1	410.8	464.2	509.3	665.7	861.9	1076.7	1424.1	2138.0	1849.4
Other products		33.9	29.1	32.8	64.9	48.2	74.6	69.4	91.1	88.5	83.9
Total:		980.0	1151.5	1297.5	1370.6	1559.8	2041.8	2773.8	3644.1	4975.1	4777.3

Source: National Statistical Office, Eurostat.

Both public and private investment increased 2.78 times in both asset types during 2004–2007.

2.6 Lithuania

The Lithuanian economy has revealed high growth rates in the last decade since joining the European Union together with other Baltic states. The government pursues a flat tax policy and the unemployment rate is fairly low in comparison to neighbouring countries. This along with other policies has led to the notion of a 'Baltic Tiger'. The country has been in transition from a communist planned economy as a part of the Soviet Union, when it also conducted most of its trade with Russia (Iinskas et al., 1995). However, it faced its own economic and financial crisis in 1999 partly due to the 1998 Russian financial crisis and reoriented itself towards the European Union. In 2005 the GDP grew by 7.5 per cent and the inflation rate was 3 per cent.

Economic growth continued to be robust in 2007 and reached 8.9 per cent growth of real GDP. The recent financial crisis, however, has had a major negative effect on the economic situation in the country. The real GDP growth was only 3 per cent in 2008 and was predicted to decline to −10 per cent in 2009 and still be negative in 2010 (IMF, 2009c). The financial sector of Lithuania as in the two other Baltic economies had significant exposure to toxic financial assets and faced financial constraints with the crisis. Inflation in 2007 was 5.8 per cent and reached 11.1 per cent in 2008. Consumer prices, however, declined to 5.1 per cent in 2009 and were projected to decline 0.6 per cent in 2010 (IMF, 2009c).

The recent rapid GDP growth in Lithuania has reached or exceeded its fiscal targets (Kočenda et al., 2008). The budget remained in deficit and budgetary improvement has been mainly due to revenue surprises rather than expenditure restraint. Government expenditure has increased at a similar pace as GDP: after peaking in 1997 at around 50 per cent following the Russian financial crisis, the ratio to GDP of government expenditure decreased gradually and stood at around 33 per cent over the period 2003–2006 (EC, 2008a, p. 236). However, it started to increase again in 2007 as a consequence of strong increases in social transfers and public investment. With a spending ratio of below 40 per cent of GDP over the period 2000–2007 as a whole, Lithuania is considered to have a relatively small government sector. Despite this relatively small size, the share of productive spending represented by investment and education has been relatively high in Lithuania.

In 2008, the general government deficit was 3.2 per cent of GDP mainly due to an expansionary fiscal policy. This exceeds the target due to weak revenue growth and slowing GDP growth. In particular, VAT collection was significantly lower than planned. Moreover, the sharp rise in the government deficit mostly reflects a considerable upward revision of expenditure, without the adoption of a supplementary budget. The budget for 2009 was approved with a deficit of 2.1 per cent of GDP. The main measures on the revenue side include a cut in the personal income tax rate, an increase in the VAT rate, substantial increases in excise duties on tobacco, fuel and alcohol and the abolition of most existing tax exemptions. On the expenditure side, the budget foresees significant cuts in current expenditure but also reflects higher social transfers and wage increases for certain categories of public sector employees.

The fiscal stance of Lithuania was in common with other Baltic states during the transition period (Tang et al., 2000). Recent policy changes, however, deserve special attention. The fiscal contraction envisaged for 2008 was helpful but more is needed amidst the global financial crisis. The cyclically-adjusted fiscal deficit was projected to narrow by 1 per cent of GDP, which helps to relieve demand pressures (IMF, 2008e). However, with increasing spending of EU funds, the overall withdrawal of demand is only 0.5 per cent of GDP. The larger fiscal contraction called for by the IMF is claimed to not only have a direct impact on aggregate demand but also provide a credible signal of the government's commitment to macroeconomic stability, helping to boost investor confidence and to focus expectations on the need for slower growth. Potential ways to achieve fiscal contraction are to postpone restitution payments and accelerating planned increases in excise taxes (IMF, 2008f).

Similar to neighbouring Latvia, the amount of public investment increased significantly after joining the European Union. Public investment increased from 3.4 per cent of GDP in 2004 to 5.2 per cent in 2007 while private investment also increased from 18.9 per cent to 22.8 per cent during the same period. The total volume of public investment increased 2.4 times during 2004–2007 and as much as five times during 2000–2007 (Table 6.10). Economic affairs constitutes the largest category, following the COFOG classification. Its share in total public investment actually decreased from 51.9 per cent in 2004 to 34.7 per cent in 2007 though the growth rate remained high, 58.2 per cent. Among other important categories is defence, with a 13.4 per cent share in total public investment in 2007 and a seven-times increase during the 2004–2007 period, as can be seen from Table 6.10.

In 2008, the general government deficit was 3.2 per cent of GDP mainly due to an expansionary fiscal policy compared with a target deficit of 0.5 per cent of GDP set in the 2007 update of Lithuania's Convergence Programme. The revenue growth in 2008 was somewhat weaker than

Table 6.10 Public investment by categories and asset type in Lithuania (in millions of national currency)

Variable	COFOG code/ Measure	2000	2001	2002	2003	2004	2005	2006	2007	2008
Public investment	% of GDP	2.4	2.2	3.0	3.0	3.5	3.5	4.2	5.2	
Private investment	% of GDP	17.4	18.1	18.8	19.3	21.0	23.1	20.2	17.4	18.1
Public investment by categories (COFOG classification):										
General public services	GF01	12.0	16.4	98.6	137.3	221.2	245.0	315.6	552.4	
Defence	GF02	32.1	43.7	107.1	111.0	97.6	150.2	368.7	685.9	
Public order and safety	GF03	25.9	39.6	55.7	62.1	104.9	120.9	156.7	234.8	
Economic affairs	GF04	828.4	767.5	894.2	1 005.9	1 122.4	1 071.8	1 280.9	1 776.3	
Environment protection	GF05	1.4	1.1	0.5	1.1	74.0	196.5	338.7	548.2	
Housing and community amenities	GF06	34.5	33.3	68.4	41.6	48.7	53.9	59.6	67.7	
Health	GF07	61.0	65.6	88.6	109.0	164.4	203.9	292.8	426.2	
Recreation, culture and religion	GF08	10.6	12.8	35.1	65.5	94.5	124.6	160.0	222.9	
Education	GF09	12.5	40.4	121.2	130.0	177.7	241.0	350.2	464.6	

Social protection	GF10	68.0	61.7	25.3	32.8	55.1	77.9	103.5	136.3	
Total:		1086.3	1082.2	1494.7	1696.3	2160.5	2485.7	3426.7	5115.1	
Public investment by main asset types (public and private):										
Products of agriculture, forestry, fisheries and aquaculture		20.1	163.8	147.6	126.8	89.6	199.5	365.8	387.0	239.7
Metal products and machinery		2574.1	3116.2	3362.5	3526.3	4087.0	4703.7	5402.9	5976.5	5170.3
Transport equipment		775.3	997.6	953.0	962.4	1414.4	1491.2	1801.0	3115.6	2270.2
Construction work: housing		809.9	772.0	696.0	805.9	1445.8	1568.1	2103.3	2805.0	3819.9
Construction work: other constructions		3953.2	4379.4	5047.3	6144.1	6395.4	7814.4	10457.4	14492.9	15213.9
Other products		444.3	385.4	357.5	443.9	539.5	628.1	710.5	1141.9	1270.0
Total:		8576.8	9814.3	10564.0	12009.4	13971.6	16405.0	20840.8	27918.8	27984.0

Source: National Statistical Office, Eurostat.

expected due to slowing GDP growth and lower tax collections. The sharp rise in the government deficit mostly reflects considerable revisions and measures on the expenditure side such as a substantial increase in social transfers and an increase in public sector wages (EC, 2009, p. 230).

On the other hand, public investment in 2008 was lower than planned. The debt-to-GDP ratio continued to decrease from 17.0 per cent in 2007 to 15.6 per cent in 2008 due to strong nominal growth and the run-down of financial assets.

2.7 Poland

Poland is among the fastest growing economies in Central Europe with an annual economic growth of over 6 per cent. The country has experienced nearly 20 years of growth during its transition from central planning to a market economy. Throughout the 1990s, the country pursued a policy of economic liberalization (Balcerowicz, 2007). In the late 1990s economic growth slowed down and unemployment shot up following the Russian financial crisis in 1998. These trends had, however, reversed by 2003 when healthy growth rates had been achieved and unemployment had fallen. Four years of growth of nearly 5.5 per cent have increased average Polish income and reduced unemployment to 6.7 per cent in 2008 (EBRD, 'Transition Report 2008').

While the Polish banking system was not severely affected by the global economic crisis, economic growth has slowed down due to weakness in Poland's key export markets and domestic investment. Real GDP growth decreased from 6.7 per cent in 2007 to 4.8 per cent in 2008. A further decline to −0.7 per cent was projected for 2009. Though consumer prices have increased as well, this increase was modest in comparison to other EU NMS. The CPI increased from 2.5 per cent in 2007 to 4.2 per cent in 2008 (IMF, 2009c).

Despite some continued systematic problems, Poland has made tremendous overall economic progress over the last decade, and now is ranked twenty-first worldwide in terms of GDP (World Bank, 2009a). With the largest component of its economy being the service sector, and continued forecasts of positive economic growth, Poland is likely to continue to move up in the world GDP ranking (Kenourgios and Samitas, 2009). Amidst the global financial contraction, Poland remained in the best fiscal and financial situation among all new EU countries.[7] Poland has shown more balanced growth with a considerable contribution of private consumption (World Bank, 2009a).

According to the World Bank (2008b), lack of fiscal space, combined with technical and administrative constraints, has also contributed to a slower rate of absorption of EU funds. Environmental commitments and the challenges posed by global warming call for further efforts to improve energy efficiency. The key challenges are to enhance the quality and efficiency of public finances, increase the supply of relevant and skilled labour and strengthen the business environment. Along the road to adopting comprehensive EU standards and practices, further strengthening of public administration capacity and reforming public finances will be essential.

According to European Commission estimates, the general government balance of the Polish economy improved to −2.0 per cent of GDP in 2007, compared to the target of −3.4 per cent set in the November 2006 convergence programme. The main reason was much higher real GDP growth (6.5 per cent) than assumed in the programme (5.1 per cent). The favourable evolution of the labour market and the ceiling imposed by the Hausner plan resulted in lower social transfers (EC, 2008a, p. 254). In addition, higher inflation contributed to lower expenditure ratios for such items as compensation of public sector employees, which are budgeted in nominal terms. Government investment was lower by 0.5 per cent of GDP because of the slower absorption of EU funds. Overall, total expenditure was lower by 1.3 per cent of GDP. On the revenue side, despite cuts, social contributions were higher by about 0.5 per cent of GDP than projected in November 2006 thanks to much higher employment and wage growth. The revenue from indirect taxes also turned out to be higher. As a result of a lower deficit, the 2007 general government debt declined to 45.4 per cent of GDP, 4.5 percentage points lower than projected in November 2006.

From a more recent perspective, the general government deficit had increased to 3.9 per cent of GDP in 2008. The result is significantly higher than the planned deficit of 2.5 per cent stated in the Convergence Programme in March 2008. The reason for the deterioration in the government balance is explained by stimulation measures such as the reduction of social contributions, an increase in personal tax relief for families, a generous indexation of pensions and social benefits and the consequences of the financial crisis (EC, 2009, p. 242). The government debt was registered at 47.1 per cent of GDP, which is 3 percentage points higher than projected in the March Convergence Programme.

Since accession to the EU, public investment increased from 3.4 per cent of GDP in 2004 to 4.1 per cent in 2007, while private investment also increased from 14.6 per cent to 17.6 per cent during the same period. The volume of total public investment increased by 55.2 per cent during this period. The share of investment in total government expenditure increased from 7.9 per cent in 2004 to 9.8 per cent in 2007. The largest part of the public investment was attributed to the economic affairs section following the COFOG classification. The share of this category increased from 36 per cent of total public investment to 44 per cent from 2004 to 2007, and the growth rate in this category was 92 per cent. The largest share in this category was invested in the transport sector: this share constituted 96 per cent of all public investment into economic needs in 2007. Transport equipment has doubled since 2004 due to both public and private investment in the transport sector. Among the main categories in the economic affairs section, the gross fixed capital formation by the government in the transport sector increased by 94 per cent, or almost doubled from 2004 to 2007. Public investment in the fuel and energy sector doubled and in the communication sector it more than tripled during the same period. Public investment in volume increased in all the categories except Housing and Community Amenities, which in fact decreased by 22 per cent from 2004 to 2007.

Education is the second-largest category of public investment in Poland, though its share decreased slightly from 13 per cent of total government investment in 2004 to 11 per cent in 2007. There was, however, a growth in investment in this category by 28.5 per cent. The largest categories in the education sector for public investment were primary and tertiary education in 2007. The growth in public investment in tertiary education has increased by 24 per cent since the country's accession. The highest growth has been registered, however, for government investment into secondary education. Fixed capital increased by almost 72 per cent in this sector of Education in Poland during the 2004–2007 period.

Among other categories, environmental protection accounted for almost 7.3 per cent of total public investment in 2007. The highest growth was registered for the recreation, culture and religion sector, where the volume of government investment in fixed capital more than doubled. Table 6.11 shows the volume of public investment in the main categories by the COFOG classification.

2.8 Romania

Romania joined the European Union on 1 January 2007. Recent economic developments show that economic growth has been very strong in Romania, with GDP growth of 6 per cent in 2007. The rapid economic growth was boosted by the rise of domestic demand due to a credit boom. Inflation in Romania was decreasing steadily until 2006 (EBRD, 2008a). Headline HICP inflation was recorded at below 4 per cent in early 2007 but started increasing later in the year partly because of a sharp upward trend in agricultural prices, following both the severe drought in the summer of 2007 and trends in world market prices (EC, 2008b).

Table 6.11 Public investment by category in Poland

Variable	COFOG code/ Measure	2002	2003	2004	2005	2006	2007	2008
Public investment	% of GDP	3.5	3.4	3.4	3.5	3.9	4.2	
Private investment	% of GDP	15.3	14.9	14.7	14.8	15.7	17.4	17.5
Public investment:								
General public services	GF01	2105.0	2752.3	2399.4	2455.1	2702.0	3672.0	
Defence	GF02	1806.0	995.4	922.6	964.3	1037.0	1032.0	
Public order and safety	GF03	728.0	1235.6	1443.8	1761.8	1846.0	2486.0	
Economic affairs	GF04	10141.0	10154.7	11138.4	12866.0	17279.0	21388.0	
Environment protection	GF05	2657.0	2752.6	3077.3	3247.4	3501.0	3530.0	
Housing and community amenities	GF06	3549.0	3350.5	3648.9	2859.3	2849.0	2845.0	
Health	GF07	1422.0	1498.7	1928.5	2428.3	2928.0	3250.0	
Recreation, culture and religion	GF08	1390.0	1458.4	1783.8	1697.2	3108.0	3808.0	
Education	GF09	3589.0	3499.7	4121.5	4407.4	4737.0	5290.0	

Table 6.11 (continued)

Variable	COFOG code/ Measure	2002	2003	2004	2005	2006	2007	2008
Social protection	GF10	457.0	381.0	554.9	530.2	832.0	832.0	
Total:		27 844.0	28 078.9	31 019.1	33 217.0	40 819.0	48 133.0	
Gross fixed capital formation by 6 asset types (current prices):								
Products of agriculture, forestry, fisheries and aquaculture		−334.0	145.0	96.0	468.0	90.0	521.0	−527.0
Metal products and machinery		45 142.0	45 240.0	49 398.0	53 676.0	61 576.0	73 454.0	79 040.0
Transport equipment		13 686.0	14 036.0	16 370.0	17 221.0	21 309.0	26 971.0	28 895.0
Construction work: housing		22 948.0	22 511.0	24 016.0	26 636.0	29 529.0	35 668.0	41 964.0
Construction work: other constructions		64 270.0	65 430.0	70 956.0	75 526.0	88 328.0	107 523.0	120 573.0
Other products		5 760.0	6 396.0	6 322.0	5 653.0	7 476.0	9 592.0	10 990.0
Total:		151 472.0	153 758.0	167 158.0	179 180.0	208 308.0	253 729.0	280 935.0

Source: National Statistical Office, Eurostat.

The recent global financial turmoil has had its effect on the Romanian economy through indirect channels as the country's financial system remained relatively stable due to its limited exposure to 'toxic assets'. The economy has, however, faced constraints on external finance, decreasing FDI, declining external demand for Romanian exports and increased exchange rate volatility (National Bank of Romania, 2008). Though real GDP followed a positive growth trend in 2007 and 2008, there was projected a sharp decline in GDP of −4.1 per cent in 2009 (IMF, 2009c). Furthermore, there was an increase in consumer prices of 7.8 per cent in 2008. This increasing tendency will not persist, however, due to economic recession.

Unemployment in Romania decreased from 6.1 per cent in 2007 to 4.1 per cent in 2008. (EBRD, 2009). Though there is a possibility of deterioration in employment levels, it is not going to be a critical issue for the Romanian economy due to the low current level of unemployment. Moreover, an increase in unemployment would bring some relief to wage increase pressures (National Bank of Romania, 2008). The labour market in Romania has a relatively low activity rate in comparison to the EU average with high unemployment rates for the age groups of 15–19 years and 20–24 years, a high percentage of early retirement from the formal labour market and significant employment in the agriculture sector with work relationships that are not subject to taxation (Government of Romania, 2007).

The general government balance has deteriorated significantly over the recent period, with the deficit rising from 1.2 per cent of GDP in 2005 to 2.5 per cent of GDP in 2007. Both the revenue- and expenditure-to-GDP ratios have gradually increased in the past few years (EC, 2008b). The general government debt was reduced from 25 per cent of GDP in 2002 to 13 per cent of GDP in 2007, while modest increases were foreseen for 2008 and 2009 (EC, 2008a, p. 259). There are, however, important changes in the realizations and projections related to the government balance due to the global financial crisis. The government deficit was 5.4 per cent in 2008, which is more than two times higher than planned in the budget rectification in March 2008. The main reason for such deviation is weak budgetary planning and execution, which resulted in substantially higher-than-planned current spending. Moreover, a sudden drop in government revenue has contributed to this outcome (EC, 2009, p. 261).

Recent financial turmoil and large domestic and external imbalances made its necessary for Romania to request external multilateral financial assistance in March 2009. In this context, the government planned important fiscal adjustments to decrease the government budget deficit. On the expenditure side, a recruitment freeze and the reduction of various bonuses in the public sector, cuts in expenditures for goods and services and subsidies and limiting pension increases were envisaged. On the revenue side, measures aimed at eliminating certain tax deductions and allowances, in particular for company cars and the depreciation of revalued assets. The government also planned an increase in public expenditure to support the economic recovery (EC, 2009, p. 261).

Table 6.12 shows the level of public investment by the COFOG categories in Romania from 2002 to 2007. The public investment as a percentage of GDP has increased steadily in Romania from 1.9 per cent in 2000 to 5.7 per cent in 2007, while private investment in fixed capital increased from 17 per cent to 24.8 per cent during the same period. The volume of public investment had increased by 31 per cent in 2007. The share of public investment in total government expenditure has been increasing since 2002 in Romania. In 2007 this share was 15.4 per cent.

The share of the government's investment on economic needs was almost 49 per cent in total public investment in 2007. It increased by 43.2 per cent in comparison to 2006. The share of education in public expenditure was 16 per cent of total investment in 2007, and the growth of public investment in this sector has increased by 46 per cent from 2006. The largest share of government investment in education in Romania was attributed to tertiary education in 2007, and constituted 31.4 per cent. The shares of primary and secondary education were 27.2 per cent and 28.5 per cent, respectively.

2.9 Slovenia

The economy of Slovenia has been growing steadily since the country's accession to the European Union in 2004. Economic growth was at a particularly high level for 2006 and 2007, when GDP growth in real terms was 5.9 per cent and 6.8 per cent, respectively (EBRD, 2009). Slovenia became the first among the new EU members to adopt the euro in January 2007. The successful economic performance of the country was aided by favourable initial conditions and generally sound macroeconomic and income policies. The major objective of the monetary authorities after the adoption of the euro remains controlling inflation. The country is considered to be one of the most successful examples of transition from a centrally-planned system to a market-oriented economy. In 2007 the GDP per capita in PPP was 25 755 USD. The main factors that have contributed to such strong economic growth are good external conditions and strong investment activity.

GDP growth has been stimulated by the implemented reforms, particularly in the field of taxation. The membership in the EU has also positively

Table 6.12 Public investment by category in Romania

Variable	COFOG code/ Measure	2002	2003	2004	2005	2006	2007	2008
Public investment	% of GDP	3.5	3.6	3.1	3.9	5.2	5.6	
Private investment	% of GDP	17.9	18.0	18.7	19.9	20.5	24.5	26.4
Public investment by COFOG category:								
General public services	GF01	531.2	485.8	461.8	837.7	746.8	668.6	
Defence	GF02	489.7	615.6	663.7	1319.9	1039.9	655.7	
Public order and safety	GF03	449.5	562.4	727.6	878.9	1272.4	531.9	
Economic affairs	GF04	1 227.0	1 816.3	1 921.1	3 538.4	7 943.8	11 373.7	
Environment protection	GF05	127.2	86.6	67.0	118.3	323.2	624.8	
Housing and community amenities	GF06	741.6	1 664.5	2 355.8	2 573.0	2 737.5	3 481.9	
Health	GF07	597.5	734.7	456.9	690.5	512.9	1 185.1	
Recreation, culture and religion	GF08	114.4	178.5	162.2	199.2	437.6	817.3	
Education	GF09	741.5	678.0	541.8	897.2	2 526.5	3 696.3	

Table 6.12 (continued)

Variable	COFOG code/ Measure	2002	2003	2004	2005	2006	2007	2008
Social protection	GF10	91.3	119.9	116.7	114.9	133.1	195.8	
Total:		5110.9	6942.3	7474.6	11168.0	17673.7	23231.1	
Gross fixed capital formation by asset type (current prices):								
Products of agriculture, forestry, fisheries and aquaculture		108.0	253.6	456.7	175.8	164.4	347.0	
Metal products and machinery		10840.6	14314.5	16298.4	20843.3	25838.4	35566.1	
Transport equipment		4491.3	7187.9	10638.9	12887.3	17465.3	23573.7	
Construction work: housing		2329.7	3376.7	3858.4	5911.8	6122.5	10143.9	
Construction work: other constructions		12592.1	15674.3	20168.9	26558.2	35092.8	51774.9	
Other products		2004.8	1689.6	2429.0	2150.2	3588.6	4239.7	
Total:		32366.5	42496.6	53850.3	68526.6	88272.0	125645.3	164264.4

Source: National Statistical Office, Eurostat.

affected the external trade of the country. The export growth was 12.5 per cent in 2006 and almost 13.8 per cent in 2007 (EBRD, 2009). The economy of Slovenia is dependent on its foreign trade. According to the Statistical Office of Slovenia, the majority of Slovenia's export is consumed by EU countries. The current account balance has improved as a result of increasing exports and a changed composition of imports by economic purpose.

The global financial crisis started to affect the Slovenian economy only at the end of 2008. The banking system of Slovenia was significantly affected as the global financial turmoil caused a lack of confidence and a considerable decrease in interbank lending. Economic growth remained high in the first half of 2008, at 5.6 per cent. It decreased to 3.9 per cent in the third quarter of 2008 and was negative in the last quarter of the year. The main driver of economic growth was domestic spending as growth in exports decreased from 13 per cent in 2006 and 2007 to 8 per cent in the first half of 2008 (Bank of Slovenia, 2008, pp. 7–8). Thus, the growth of real GDP was only 3.5 per cent in 2008 and was projected to fall further to −2.7 per cent in 2009 (IMF, 2009c).

In the context of the current crisis and to deal with its consequences, the government of Slovenia has adopted a fiscal stimulus package to support economic activity and promote faster recovery. IMF assessments predicted that these measures would increase the government deficit to −4.2 per cent in 2009 (IMF, 2009f). The fiscal stimulus package is broadly in line with the preceding priorities in the fiscal policy of the country. It comprises wage subsidies, subsidies to companies (including for R&D), elimination of the payroll tax and reducing corporate tax rates.

The expenditures of the government of Slovenia on gross fixed capital formation are shown in Table 6.13. Public investment as a percentage of GDP has slightly increased in Slovenia from the time of the country's accession to the EU. It increased from 3.5 per cent in 2004 to 3.7 per cent in 2007, while private investment increased from 20.3 per cent to 23.8 per cent during the same period. The share of investment also increased in total government expenditure from 7.5 per cent to 8.8 per cent during the same period. The growth constituted almost 37.5 per cent during the period 2004–2007. Public expenditure on capital formation increased by more than 11 per cent in 2007. The largest part of the 32.7 per cent of government investment was attributed to general public services in 2007, while the share of economic affairs investment was 20.7 per cent in the same year. Public investment in the economic activity sector has increased by 78 per cent since Slovenia's accession to the EU. In 2007 the growth of public investment into economic needs was 35.5 per cent. Both public and private investment in transport equipment has increased since 2004. Gross fixed capital has increased by half in the transport sector due to this investment.

Table 6.13 Public investment by category in Slovenia

Variable	COFOG code/ Measure	2002	2003	2004	2005	2006	2007	2008
Public investment	% of GDP	3.0	3.2	3.5	3.2	3.7	4.3	4.4
Private investment	% of GDP	19.9	20.6	21.5	22.3	22.9	23.5	24.6
Public investment:								
General public services	GF01	2710	266.0	337.0	298.0	408.0	422.0	
Defence	GF02	32.0	66.0	78.0	36.0	82.0	71.0	
Public order and safety	GF03	31.0	39.0	31.0	25.0	47.0	71.0	
Economic affairs	GF04	100.0	122.0	149.0	165.0	197.0	267.0	
Environment protection	GF05	7.0	12.0	16.0	13.0	12.0	11.0	
Housing and community amenities	GF06	19.0	29.0	34.0	34.0	49.0	57.0	
Health	GF07	78.0	80.0	80.0	71.0	96.0	108.0	
Recreation, culture and religion	GF08	45.0	51.0	48.0	52.0	58.0	64.0	
Education	GF09	90.0	117.0	131.0	198.0	179.0	182.0	

Social protection	GF10	24.0	34.0	33.0	21.0	31.0	37.0	
Total:		695.0	816.0	938.0	914.0	1 159.0	1 290.0	
Gross fixed capital formation by asset type (current prices):								
Products of agriculture, forestry, fisheries and aquaculture		32.6	29.4	29.4	33.7	31.9	30.8	28.9
Metal products and machinery		1 714.4	1 940.1	2 077.1	2 231.5	2 617.0	2 844.4	3 072.0
Transport equipment		473.3	566.0	722.3	658.7	884.4	922.1	921.4
Construction work: housing		718.9	718.2	867.4	1 095.8	1 222.9	1 474.4	1 722.7
Construction work: other constructions		2 065.0	2 458.5	2 708.0	2 945.2	3 097.2	3 841.4	4 475.0
Other products		328.0	303.2	347.9	356.5	388.7	458.3	522.4
Total:		5 332.2	6 015.4	6 752.1	7 321.3	8 242.1	9 571.3	10 742.4

Source: National Statistical Office, Eurostat.

While public investment in all the sectors by the COFOG classification has increased since the country's accession to the EU, gross fixed capital formation has declined for defence and environmental protection needs.

Public investment in education grew by 39 per cent during the period 2004–2007. The largest growth of 50 per cent in government investment into education was registered in 2005, while in 2007, this investment only increased by 1.8 per cent. The shares of investment of the government in primary, secondary and tertiary education in 2007 were 35.4 per cent, 41.6 per cent and 18.3 per cent, respectively. The expenditures of the government of Slovenia on gross fixed capital formation are shown in Table 6.13.

2.10 The Slovak Republic

The Slovak Republic was established in January 1993 and since 1998 major structural reforms have been introduced in the country to support the transformation from central planning to a market economy. The labour market was made more flexible, the social benefits system became less generous and more targeted, the tax system was simplified, a funded pension pillar was established and state ownership was reduced. These reforms were aimed at increasing incentives to work, employment and investment. GDP growth accelerated gradually from 4.2 per cent in 2003 to 8.3 per cent in 2006 and peaked at around 10.4 per cent in 2007 (EBRD, 2007). The country almost doubled its automobile production in 2007 and is now the world's largest automobile manufacturer in per capita terms (EBRD, 2008b).

The global financial crisis has affected the Slovak economy as well. Real GDP growth was 6.4 per cent in 2008 and was projected to fall to −2.1 per cent in 2009. The average inflation rate in 2008 reached 3.9 per cent, reflecting the developments of global fuel prices and prices for agriculture products (NBS, 2008).

The overall unemployment level has been decreasing recently and was estimated at 11 per cent in 2007 (EBRD, 2007). An increase in the retirement age had a positive impact on employment rates for the elderly segment of the labour force (55–66 years), while young people continue to face serious problems on the labour market. Stronger public policies might be necessary to resolve the problems of long-term and youth unemployment as insufficient education and training seem currently to be the biggest obstacles to finding employment. Public expenditure on education in Slovakia amounted to 4.2 per cent of GDP in the period of 1999–2003 and was below the EU27 level of 5.1 per cent of GDP (EC, 2008a, p. 264).

The IMF mission from May 2009 states that the main challenge for fiscal policy in the coming years will be to achieve a reduction in the government deficit and to improve the quality of public finances. The consequences of the global financial crisis made it necessary for the Slovak government to undertake special measures, such as a fiscal stimulus package, in late 2008 and the beginning of 2009. The stimulus measures comprised a reduction in taxation and subsidies, an improvement in the liquidity of the corporate sector and incentives to accelerate the use of EU funds. The general government deficit is projected to be about 5 per cent of GDP, and could be larger in the case of negative shocks to growth (IMF, 2009d).

Public investment as a share of GDP has slightly decreased in Slovakia since its accession to the EU. It declined from 2.4 per cent in 2004 to 1.9 per cent in 2007. Table 6.14 contains data on government expenditure on gross fixed capital formation by the main COFOG categories. The volume of public investment, however, increased by 6.8 per cent during that period. In 2007 the largest share of public investment was attributed to economic activity, which accounted for 28.1 per cent of total public investment. The second most important category of the COFOG classification was housing and community amenities that accounted for 19.2 per cent of public investment. The government expenditure on fixed capital formation in the economic sector generally declined by about 24 per cent from 2004 to 2007. This indicator increased, however, by 7.9 per cent from the end of 2006 to the end of 2007. Among the activities in the economic sector, investment in transport equipment increased by 60 per cent from 2004 to 2007. This number comprises, however, both public and private investment. In 2007, the total investment in transport equipment was about 8.2 per cent.

Public investment in education has increased by 8.3 per cent since Slovakia became a member of the EU. The fastest growth was registered in 2005, when government investment in education increased by 32 per cent. This investment, however, decreased in 2006 and 2007.

2.11 Cyprus

Cyprus is an island divided into the Southern area controlled by the Cyprus Government and the Northern Turkish Cypriot-administered area. The Greek Cypriot economy is prosperous but highly susceptible to external shocks. In 2008 it was classified by the IMF as amongst the 32 advanced economies of the world (IMF, 2008g). Unstable economic growth rates over the 1990s reflected the country's dependence on the tourist sector that is largely influenced by political instability on the island and economic fluctuations in Western Europe.

The years 2007 and 2008 were characterized by the overheating of the economy of Cyprus. The major reasons were increasing credit, strong real

Table 6.14 Public investment by category in Slovakia

Variable	COFOG code/ Measure	2002	2003	2004	2005	2006	2007	2008
Public investment	% of GDP	3.3	2.5	2.4	2.2	2.0	2.0	
Private investment	% of GDP	25.1	22.9	22.2	24.9	24.7	24.5	23.0
Public investment by COFOG classification:								
General public services	GF01	150.4	106.2	110.3	153.3	215.3	143.5	
Defence	GF02	18.2	6.5	7.9	14.5	21.5	26.3	
Public order and safety	GF03	116.5	58.1	81.5	106.0	107.3	144.4	
Economic affairs	GF04	400.5	377.0	422.4	251.5	300.7	324.4	
Environment protection	GF05	53.4	49.1	43.0	62.2	65.1	61.6	
Housing and community amenities	GF06	141.7	133.7	117.2	166.4	206.9	221.9	
Health	GF07	85.2	110.6	113.6	35.6	31.9	18.2	
Recreation, culture and religion	GF08	77.3	58.8	53.9	66.7	102.4	72.6	
Education	GF09	115.6	95.6	95.6	126.7	110.5	103.5	

Social protection	GF10	46.2	44.8	35.3	47.5	43.6	36.7	
Total:		1205.2	1040.4	1080.8	1030.2	1205.3	1153.1	
Gross fixed capital formation by asset type (current prices):								
Products of agriculture, forestry, fisheries and aquaculture		445.2	374.5	431.0	497.8	312.7	511.2	503.5
Metal products and machinery		3505.4	3598.9	4030.0	5080.9	4414.0	4559.9	5219.9
Transport equipment		1316.7	1268.5	1030.1	1168.8	1527.4	1654.9	1831.7
Construction work: housing		1232.8	1234.3	1281.5	1448.5	1288.2	1446.8	1560.9
Construction work: other constructions		3212.6	3104.6	3580.9	4283.9	6432.3	6832.5	6720.0
Other products		361.1	469.8	482.5	609.5	614.2	1091.1	879.6
Total:		10073.7	10050.5	10836.0	13089.5	14588.8	16096.5	16715.6

Source: National Statistical Office, Eurostat.

wage growth, low levels of unemployment, rising FDI in the property market and a good business climate. The country seems to be withstanding the impact of the global financial crisis reasonably well (IMF, 2009e). Real GDP growth slowed down to 3.7 per cent in 2008, which is much higher than the average growth rate in advanced economies and New EU Member States in the same year. The GDP growth rate was projected to decline further to 0.3 per cent in 2009, which is a very good indicator as the rest of the European region on average suffered a severe economic decline (IMF, 2009c).

The country has seen a deteriorating current account deficit over the 2007–2008 period. This is related to the changing structure of Cypriot exports and imports. As the country gained market share in financial services, it has lost its comparative advantage in the manufacturing and tourism sectors (IMF, 2009e). There was also a sharp increase in consumer prices from 2.2 per cent in 2007 to 4.4 per cent in 2008. Rising inflation rates are explained by a large and positive output gap, higher prices for oil and food, and higher wages. Consumer prices were, however, projected to fall to 0.9 per cent in 2009 (IMF, 2009c).

The economy of Cyprus might start feeling more of an impact of the financial crisis as it is a small open economy and largely depends on the economic situation in its trade partners who are the UK, Greece and Russia. Moreover, the main sectors of the economy, construction and financial services, are already affected. In terms of structural reforms, there should be measures taken to improve competitiveness in order to enhance economic growth and assist the recovery (IMF, 2009e).

Fiscal adjustment plays a very important role in strengthening macroeconomic stability. Cyprus managed to convert its fiscal deficit into a surplus in 2007. The country was doing rather well with a government budget surplus of 3.4 per cent of GDP in 2007. The surplus was maintained into 2008 but declined to 1 per cent of GDP, which is higher than was projected in 2007. This is explained by high government revenues, lower interest payments and a good result in 2007 (EC, 2009, p. 226). The surplus achieved might turn unsustainable due to the fact that fiscal consolidation has depended largely on temporary factors such as a property price boom and a revaluation of assets. There are important expenditure-side factors related to the launched pension reform. The growing pension spending, despite increased contributions, does not reflect the ageing-related increases (IMF, 2009e). The general government debt decreased from 59.4 per cent in 2007 to 49.3 per cent in 2008 reflecting the planned reduction of deposits with the central bank, a primary surplus and a positive growth effect (EC, 2009, p. 226).

Public investment as a percentage of GDP declined in Cyprus starting from 2004, the year of the country's accession to the EU, to 2007, while the percentage of private investment increased slightly from 14.7 per cent to 18.5 per cent during this period (EC, 2008, p. 234). The level of public investment dropped by 10 per cent in the same period. The data show, however, that this decline had taken place in 2005, and afterwards there was an upward trend in the evolution of public investment. In 2007, public expenditure on gross fixed capital formation grew by almost 7 per cent. The largest share of public investment is attributed to general public services, housing and community amenities and economic sector developments. It is, however, important to note that the government invested less in economic activities in 2007 by more than 40 per cent than in 2004. In 2007, public investment in the economy was 16 per cent of total public investment. The transport sector has benefited the most from public investment in 2007, when the share of investment in transport in total investment in economic activities was 57 per cent. Communication sector investments accounted for a relatively modest share in investments into economic needs. Its share was only 0.4 per cent. Total investment (private and public) in transport equipment grew by 3 per cent in 2007. The agricultural sector, forestry, fishing and hunting received 22.1 per cent of the total economic investment of the government in 2007. The government expenditure on gross fixed capital formation in the transport and communication sectors dropped by 40 per cent and more than 70 per cent, respectively, from 2004 to 2007. The investment in environmental protection constituted a share of 3 per cent in the total public investment in 2007, and it had increased by 12 per cent since 2004.

The share of public investment in education was 12.6 per cent in 2007. Since 2005, the government of Cyprus has been steadily increasing its investment expenditure on education. In 2007, the growth of public investment in education was 20 per cent. The major recipients of public investment in education are tertiary education and education non-definable by level with shares of 43.6 per cent and 46.2 per cent, respectively. The share of the expenditure of the government on gross fixed capital formation in total public expenditure was 6.9 per cent in 2007 in Cyprus. The general information on public expenditure on gross fixed capital is shown in Table 6.15.

2.12 Malta

A favourable geographic location and a productive labour force are important economic advantages of Malta. This economy produces, however, only 20 per cent of its food needs, has limited freshwater supplies, and has no domestic energy sources. Malta is dependent on foreign trade,

Table 6.15 Public investment by category in Cyprus

Variable	COFOG code/ Measure	2002	2003	2004	2005	2006	2007	2008
Public investment	% of GDP	3.0	3.4	4.0	3.1	3.0	2.9	
Private investment	% of GDP	15.0	14.2	14.9	16.1	17.6	19.1	20.4
Public investment by COFOG classification:								
General public services	GF01	73.8	87.3	114.1	101.6	101.3	161.9	
Defence	GF02	0.3	0.3	0.4	0.3	0.3	0.5	
Public order and safety	GF03	10.7	13.3	16.8	12.8	13.4	17.3	
Economic affairs	GF04	83.2	102.1	130.1	97.5	103.7	75.4	
Environment protection	GF05	8.2	8.9	12.4	15.3	13.8	14.0	
Housing and community amenities	GF06	61.5	73.0	95.0	82.3	82.9	90.2	
Health	GF07	34.2	42.1	53.6	40.1	42.7	15.2	
Recreation, culture and religion	GF08	16.8	19.2	25.6	25.9	24.8	28.1	
Education	GF09	38.2	47.1	60.0	45.0	48.0	58.0	

Social protection	GF10	0.3	1.0	0.2	0.2	0.2	0.0	
Total:		327.2	394.3	508.2	421.0	431.1	460.6	
Gross fixed capital formation by asset type (current prices):								
Products of agriculture, forestry, fisheries and aquaculture		3.3	3.4	3.1	5.1	2.1	2.2	2.9
Metal products and machinery		476.9	519.4	627.9	622.8	678.3	791.4	972.3
Transport equipment		245.7	116.3	122.2	109.3	174.4	164.7	189.9
Construction work: housing		620.9	750.9	931.7	1123.1	1252.1	1414.9	1492.9
Construction work: other constructions		632.7	671.1	709.2	747.4	869.2	1130.8	1368.5
Other products		5.3	6.0	5.0	−8.4	−1.9	−3.8	−0.9
Total:		1984.7	2067.1	2399.1	2599.3	2974.1	3500.3	4025.6

Source: National Statistical Office, Eurostat.

manufacturing (especially electronics), tourism and financial services. The level of Maltese GDP per capita, 23 200 USD, is above the middle of the list of European Union countries.

The economy of Malta has managed the first waves of the crisis relatively well due to the absence of exchange rate risk and limited exposure to structured financial products, a traditional retail funding model, and conservative lending policies (IMF, 2009g). The IMF projected growth contraction of around 2 per cent in 2009 and a modest recovery in 2010. Consumer prices decreased from 3.6 per cent in 2007 to 1.6 per cent in 2008 and deflation was projected for 2009. Unemployment actually decreased from 6.4 per cent in 2007 to 5.8 per cent in 2008. However, a reverse tendency was projected for 2009 (IMF, 2009c). Being a small open economy, Malta is also dependent on the economic situation in its main trade partners and global shocks.

In 2007, the general government deficit in Malta was estimated at 1.8 per cent of GDP, against a target of 2.3 per cent of GDP in the 2006 update of the convergence programme (EC, 2008, p. 247). The main measures presented in the 2008 budget include a reform of the personal income tax regime (more favourable personal income tax bands effective in 2008), increases in the amount of cash benefits granted to children as well as improved social entitlements given to specific social groups including pensioners and first-time property buyers. In 2008, however, the general government deficit is estimated to have reached 4.7 per cent of GDP, against a target of 1.2 per cent of GDP in the November 2007 stability programme (EC, 2009). The reasons are mainly lower tax revenue and lower-than-expected absorption of EU funds.

Public investment as a share of GDP increased from 3.9 per cent in 2004 to 4.0 per cent in 2007. At the same time private investment decreased from 17.2 per cent to 15.8 per cent in the same period. The volume of public investment has increased by 22.1 per cent since Malta's accession to the EU. The share of expenditure on gross fixed capital formation in total government expenditure was 9.5 per cent in 2007. The largest share of government investment expenditure was in the health sector with 80 per cent of the total investment in 2007. Economic activity is the second most important sector to receive public investment. Government investment in the economic sector increased by 22.3 per cent during the period from 2004 to 2007. The priority economic sector is transport where the government invested 73 per cent of its economic sector investment in 2007. The communication sector received only 0.2 per cent of the investment in this category, and 6 per cent was invested in the energy sector. Overall public investment in the transport sector has increased by 51.7 per cent since 2004. In 2007, the government invested about 6 per cent more than the previous year into the transport sector. Total investment (public and private) into transport equipment has more than doubled since the country's accession to the EU. Public investment in the energy sector almost doubled during the period after accession. A significant growth of government investment was registered for environmental protection. Public investment on environmental purposes increased more than four times during the period 2004–2007.

The share of education in total public investment was 9 per cent in 2007, as seen in Table 6.16. This sector has been receiving a gradually increasing amount of government investment since 2004. The level of public investment into education increased by more than 50 per cent during that period. The most important share of public investment in education is attributed to secondary education, which constituted a share of 63.8 per cent in total investment in education in 2007. Primary and tertiary education shares were 22.4 per cent and 9.1 per cent, respectively. Moreover, the government has increased its investment twice in the secondary education sector in comparison to 2004, while investment in primary and tertiary education has declined. The public investment in Malta is shown in Table 6.16.

3. CONCLUSION

This chapter presents the major economic developments and recent trends in the macroeconomic policy design of the NMS of the European Union. In particular, the overall macroeconomic situation, fiscal reforms and public finance developments are discussed for each Member State. A particular emphasis is made on the developments in public investment into different sectors of economic activity and on a background analysis of and information on the economic developments in the NMS of the EU.

The analysis of aggregated data reveals that most of the new EU Member States have experienced strong positive economic growth over the period 2005–2007. The highest real GDP growth in 2007 was registered in Latvia, Lithuania and Slovakia, 10.5 per cent, 9.8 per cent and 8.8 per cent, respectively. The budget discipline in the newly acceded economies has been rather good over the recent period. Hungary, Poland and Slovakia have, however, experienced deficits more than 3 per cent of GDP in 2006, and Hungary was the only country with government debt exceeding 60 per cent of GDP over the recent period. The tax systems in the new members are characterized by a lower direct tax share on the total in comparison to old members. Reforms of the public finances in the NMS are aimed at sustaining stable government finance positions and further alleviating the direct tax burden through reforming the tax

Table 6.16 Public investment by category in Malta

Variable	COFOG code/ Measure	2002	2003	2004	2005	2006	2007	2008
Public investment	% of GDP	4.2	4.8	4.0	4.8	4.0	3.8	2.5
Private investment	% of GDP	12.0	14.9	15.3	15.0	16.1	16.0	13.2
Public investment:								
General public services	GF01	13.7	15.1	31.7	20.5	17.9	23.5	13.9
Defence	GF02	0.8	5.5	11.3	9.8	2.2	−0.9	1.8
Public order and safety	GF03	4.1	4.9	2.6	3.2	2.5	3.2	4.9
Economic affairs	GF04	37.4	50.8	35.4	56.5	42.1	42.6	25.1
Environment protection	GF05	7.2	8.8	3.9	10.1	15.2	23.0	30.8
Housing and community amenities	GF06	2.5	2.5	1.9	1.0	2.1	2.1	6.0
Health	GF07	67.6	71.0	62.4	97.3	95.0	79.4	26.5
Recreation, culture and religion	GF08	8.5	8.5	7.8	6.2	3.0	5.6	5.9
Education	GF09	27.1	34.0	12.8	16.6	15.4	19.5	22.2

Social protection	GF10	6.4	5.8	3.4	4.9	6.2	4.7	4.7
Total:		175.2	206.8	173.2	226.1	201.5	202.7	141.8
Gross fixed capital formation by asset type (current prices):								
Products of agriculture, forestry, fisheries and aquaculture		3.5	4.7	4.7	3.9	4.4	3.6	2.8
Metal products and machinery		277.6	281.1	275.3	283.7	306.5	285.0	277.3
Transport equipment		−131.0	49.4	33.0	34.0	66.2	86.8	37.9
Construction work: housing		174.1	182.4	204.5	235.8	264.0	314.9	239.5
Construction work: other constructions		319.6	293.0	280.0	325.9	301.3	278.2	230.2
Other products		51.5	50.7	64.2	58.6	83.1	108.0	108.0
Total:		695.3	861.3	861.8	942.0	1025.5	1076.6	895.7

Source: National Statistical Office, Eurostat.

systems. The inflation rates measured by HICP in 2007 were rather high in some countries. The highest rate of more than 10 per cent was registered in Latvia, while the average inflation rate in the EU27 was 2.4 per cent. Unemployment rates were among the highest in Hungary, Poland and Slovakia, where they exceeded the average rate in the EU.

The role of the government in investing into different sectors in NMS has been growing over the last several years. The volume of public investment and its share of GDP have been on average increasing steadily in the new EU members. The sectors that benefited the most from the public investment in NMS are transport systems, general government services, housing and community amenities and education. Education is considered to be a highly prioritized sector with a special emphasis on higher education. The formation of qualified specialists and the encouragement of young people to continue education constitute a long-term investment into a country's competitiveness. The recent trends in public investment into gross fixed capital formation are presented in the present report for each NMS country.

Previous favourable developments in the new EU members have, however, been replaced by less optimistic outcomes as the financial crisis in 2008 began affecting the real economy in full force in 2008. The NMS have faced two major shocks: the recession in the high-income countries that had an adverse effect on the external demand for exports, and a reduction in capital inflows into the region coupled with lower domestic demand. The crisis has affected all the NMS economies but this impact varies across the countries because macroeconomic imbalances had different magnitudes in these countries at the beginning of the crisis, and each NMS had a different degree of integration in the trade, capital and labour markets of the EU.

According to IMF and World Bank estimates, real GDP in the emerging European economies was projected to contract by about 3.7 per cent in 2009 and recover to about 1 per cent in 2010 (see Table 6.17). The Baltic countries are expected to suffer the most severe contraction. In the first quarter of 2009, the reduction in GDP ranged from 18 per cent in Latvia and 16 per cent in Estonia, to 3.5 per cent in Bulgaria and 3.4 per cent in the Czech Republic (IMF, 2009c). The average unemployment rate in the ten NMS (excluding Malta and Cyprus) is projected to increase from 6.5 per cent in 2008 to 10.4 per cent in 2010. In Malta and Cyprus the unemployment rate was projected to increase from 3.7 per cent and 5.8 per cent in 2008 to 4.3 per cent and 7.6 per cent, respectively (World Bank, 2009b).

In view of the global economic uncertainty, global spending on capital goods and durables has declined sharply. This has curbed foreign direct investment and hurt manufacturing in the NMS. In early 2009, industrial

Table 6.17 Recent macroeconomic forecasts (as percentage of GDP in case of current account and fiscal balances)

		Real GDP growth			Inflation			CA Balance			Fiscal balance		
		2008	2009	2010	2008	2009	2010	2008	2009	2010	2008	2009	2010
Bulgaria	WEO	6.0	−2.0	−1.0	12.0	3.7	1.3	−24.4	−12.3	−3.6	na	na	na
	EC	6.0	−1.6	−0.1	12.0	3.9	3.6	−24.8	−18.8	−17.2	1.5	−0.5	−0.3
Czech	WEO	3.2	−3.5	0.1	6.3	1.0	1.6	−3.1	−2.7	−3.0	−1.5	−4.1	−4.2
Republic	EC	3.2	−2.7	0.3	6.3	1.1	1.6	−3.1	−3.2	−3.3	−1.5	−4.3	−4.9
Estonia	WEO	−3.6	−10.0	−1.0	10.4	0.8	−1.3	−9.2	−6.5	−5.4	na	na	na
	EC	−3.6	−10.3	−0.8	10.6	0.6	0.5	−9.1	−1.1	−3.1	−3.0	−3.0	−3.9
Latvia	WEO	−4.6	−12.0	−2.0	15.3	3.3	−3.5	−13.2	−6.7	−5.5	na	na	na
	EC	−4.6	−13.1	−3.2	15.3	4.6	−0.7	−13.6	−1.5	−1.9	−4.0	−11.1	−13.6
Lithuania	WEO	3.0	−10.0	−3.0	11.1	5.1	0.6	−11.6	−4.0	−5.3	na	na	na
	EC	3.0	−11.0	−4.7	11.1	3.6	−0.4	−12.2	−1.9	0.7	−3.2	−5.4	−8.0
Hungary	WEO	0.6	−3.3	−0.4	6.1	3.8	2.8	−7.8	−3.9	−3.4	na	na	na
	EC	0.5	−6.3	−0.3	6.0	4.4	4.1	−8.4	−5.0	−4.8	−3.4	−3.4	−3.9
Poland	WEO	4.8	−0.7	1.3	4.2	2.1	2.6	−5.5	−4.5	−3.9	na	na	na
	EC	4.8	−1.4	0.8	4.2	2.6	1.9	−5.3	−4.7	−3.7	−3.9	−6.6	−7.3
Slovakia	WEO	6.4	−2.1	1.9	3.9	1.7	2.3	−6.3	−5.7	−5.0	−2.2	−2.9	−2.9
	EC	6.4	−2.6	0.7	3.9	2.0	2.4	−6.8	−7.5	−7.1	−2.2	−4.7	−5.4
Slovenia	WEO	3.5	−2.7	1.4	5.7	0.5	1.5	−5.9	−4.0	−5.0	−0.3	−4.2	−3.7
	EC	3.5	−3.4	0.7	5.5	0.7	2.0	−6.1	−4.6	−4.4	−0.9	−5.5	−6.5
Romania	WEO	7.1	−4.1	0.0	7.8	5.9	3.9	−12.6	−7.5	−6.5	na	na	na
	EC	7.1	−4.0	0.0	7.9	5.8	3.5	−12.3	−7.4	−6.1	−5.4	−5.1	−5.6

Source: World Bank EU 10 Regular Economic Report. The table is prepared on the basis of the European Commission (EC) and World Economic Outlook (WEO) forecast.

production contracted between 20 per cent and 30 per cent in Estonia, Latvia, Hungary, the Slovak Republic and the Czech Republic (World Bank, 2009b). The export-oriented manufacturing sector – in particular, machinery, automobile, transport and electric equipment, but also labour-intensive industries such as textiles and clothing – has been affected the most. Exports have declined in the NMS due to a fall in demand in importing countries. The value of exports fell by 37 per cent in February 2009 in comparison with February 2008. There is a decline in domestic demand due to the credit crunch, a collapse in equity markets, weakening housing markets and the deteriorating situation in the labour market. This has reduced households' wealth and income. Consumption growth was negative in the last quarter of 2008 in Estonia, Hungary, Latvia, Lithuania and Romania.

While none of the NMS had fiscal deficits of more than 3 per cent of GDP in 2007, in 2008 five countries had a deficit above 3 per cent of GDP: Hungary, Latvia, Lithuania, Poland and Romania. The NMS' deficits were projected to increase further in 2009. The major factor that would cause an increase in the deficit is sharp rises in public expenditures. The collapse of fiscal revenues, the fiscal support of the financial sector and public spending on unemployment benefits and pension systems are imposing large pressure on government budgets. The European Commission projections showed that the public debt in the NMS would increase from 37 per cent in 2008 to 46 per cent in 2010. A number of these countries are taking measures to limit public sector wages and employment, cut spending on operations and maintenance, postpone investments and reduce subsidies. Rising pressures on fiscal policy, a decline in external funding and the critical situation in the banking systems have stipulated the need for some countries to ask for external assistance from international organizations. Hungary and Latvia have received IMF support to sustain their balance of payments. Other countries have smaller exposures to Western short-term capital (IMF, 2009c).

The economy of Cyprus was hit by the global financial imbalances as well, although the negative impact was less severe than in other new members. The economy of Cyprus is still projected to grow with growth rates above the average in Europe. The IMF estimated the GDP growth to be 0.3 per cent in 2009 and 1.1 per cent in 2010 (IMF, 2009e). The economy of Malta has also managed the first waves of the crisis relatively well due to the absence of exchange rate risk and limited exposure to structured financial products, a traditional retail funding model, and conservative lending policies (IMF, 2009g). The IMF projects growth contraction of around 2 per cent in 2009 and a modest recovery in 2010.

The global financial distress thus has had a negative impact on all the

Member States of the European Union and in particular has posed a risk to further progress in the convergence process of the new EU members. Future economic developments will mainly depend on successful measures to maintain financial stability to regain the credibility of the foreign investors, rational fiscal policies with the support of growth-enhancing public investments and social networks and the economic situation in the region's major economic partners. Therefore, public investment plans should be amended and reconsidered in view of the pressure of the crisis situation. An emphasis should be made on a better coordination of the economic policies within the EU in the sphere of banking supervision to enhance the coordination of active banking groups in the region to achieve sustained financial integration (World Bank, 2009b).

NOTES

* We would like to thank Asel Isakova and Nargiza Maksudova for meticulous research assistance. We acknowledge helpful comments and suggestions from Chiara Del Bo, Massimo Florio, and participants at the Milan European Economy Workshop, June 2009.

1. The Czech Republic, Estonia, Hungary, Latvia, Lithuania, Poland, and Slovakia joined the EU on 1 May 2004; Romania and Bulgaria joined on 1 January 2007. Cyprus and Malta, which joined the EU on 1 January 2008, are covered only briefly and excluded where applicable due to the size and the effect of their economies within the integration.
2. The EU27 group consists of the following countries: Belgium, Bulgaria, the Czech Republic, Denmark, Germany, Estonia, Ireland, Greece, Spain, France, Italy, Cyprus, Latvia, Lithuania, Luxembourg, Hungary, Malta, the Netherlands, Austria, Poland, Portugal, Romania, Slovenia, Slovakia, Finland, Sweden, the United Kingdom.
3. The EU15 group contains following countries: Belgium, Germany, Ireland, Greece, Spain, France, Italy, Cyprus, Luxembourg, Malta, the Netherlands, Austria, Portugal, Slovenia, Finland.
4. COFOG – Classification of the functions of the government – is the provision by Eurostat of first- and second-level government expenditure data.
5. Source: European Commission 2009, Budget Law of Estonia, Supplementary budget of February 2009.
6. Parex Bank is Latvia's second largest bank and the largest domestically owned bank.
7. The Group of New EU Member States consists of the following countries: the Czech Republic, Bulgaria, Estonia, Hungary, Latvia, Lithuania, Poland, Romania, Slovenia, Slovakia, Cyprus, Malta.

REFERENCES

Balcerowicz, E. (2007), 'The impact of Poland's EU accession on its economy', Center for Social and Economic Research CASE report 335, accessed at SSRN: http://ssrn.com/abstract=1015782.

Bank of Slovenia (2008), *Annual Report*, Ljubljana: Bank of Slovenia.

Bivol, A. (2009), 'Bulgarian economy with good chance of growth in 2009 – World

Bank', *The Sofia Echo*, accessed at: www.sofiaecho.com/2009/02/22/679565_bulgarian-economy-with-good-chance-of-growth-in-2009-world-bank.

Bruha, J., Podpiera, J. and Polak, S. (2007), 'The convergence dynamics of a transition economy: the case of the Czech Republic', International Monetary Fund working papers, 07/116, pp. 1–48, accessed at SSRN: http://ssrn.com/abstract=986813.

Campos, N. and Jolliffe, D. (2007), 'Earnings, schooling, and economic reform: econometric evidence from Hungary (1986–2004)', *The World Bank Economic Review*, **21**(3), pp. 509–526, accessed at SSRN: http://ssrn.com/abstract=1146046.

Cekota, J., Gönenç, R. and Yoo, K. (2002), 'Strengthening the management of public spending in Hungary', in *OECD Economics Department Working Papers 336*, Paris: OECD.

CERGE-EI (2008), *Czech Republic 2008: Strong Currency, No Rush Toward the Euro*, Prague: CERGE-EI, ISBN 978-80-733-176-1.

CIA (2008), *The World Factbook 2008*, Washington, DC: Central Intelligence Agency, accessed at www.cia.gov/library/publications/the-world-factbook/index.html

Czech Statistical Office (2001), *Statistical Yearbook of the Czech Republic 2000*, Prague: Czech Republic.

Dimova, R. (2003), 'The impact of structural reforms on employment growth and labor productivity: evidence from Bulgaria and Romania', William Davidson Institute Working Paper 600, accessed at SSRN: http://ssrn.com/abstract=432080.

European Bank for Reconstruction and Development (EBRD) (2007a), *Transition Report 2007*, ISSN 1756-9028.

EBRD (2007b), 'Transition report 2008', ISSN 1356-3424.

EBRD (2008a), 'Economic overview of Romania', EBRD country page, accessed at: www.ebrd.com/country/country/romania/econo.htm.

EBRD (2008b), 'Economic Overview of the Slovak Republic', EBRD country page, accessed at: www.ebrd.com/country/country/slovakia/econo.htm.

EBRD (2008c), 'Hungary strategy overview', accessed at: http://www.ebrd.com/about/strategy/country/hungary/index.htm.

EBRD (2009), 'Transition Report 2009', EBRD, ISSN 978 1 898802 31 0.

European Commission (EC) (2007), *Final Recommendation for a Council Opinion in accordance with the first paragraph of Art. 9 of Council Regulation (EC) No 1466/97 of 7 July 1997 on the Convergence Programme of Bulgaria, 2006–2009 (presented by the Commission)*, 7/3/2007, SEC (2007) 290, Brussels: Commission of the European Communities.

EC (2008a), *Public Finances in EMU – 2008*, Brussels: Directorate-General for Economic and Financial Affairs, European Economy.

EC (2008b), *Convergence Report 2008*, European Economy, 3-2008, Brussels: Commission of the European Communities.

EC (2009), 'Public finances in EMU – 2009', Directorate-General for Economic and Financial Affairs, Commission Staff working document, provisional version, 5/2009.

Eurostat News Release (2008), 'Taxation trends in the EU: EU27 tax ratio at 39.9% of GDP in 2006, Strongest year-on-year increase in ten years', DG TAXUD, accessed at http://epp.eurostat.ec.europa.eu/pls/portal/docs/PAGE/PGP_PRD_CAT_PREREL/PGE_CAT_PREREL_YEAR_2008/PGE_CAT_PREREL_YEAR_2008_MONTH_06/2-26062008-EN-AP.PDF.

Friedrich, P., Gwiazda, J. and Nam, Ch. (2003), 'Development of local public finance in Europe', Center for Economic Studies and ifo working paper series 1107, accessed at SSRN: http://ssrn.com/abstract=486065.

Government of Romania (2007), *The 2007–2010 Convergence Programme*, Bucharest: Government of Romania.

Granlund, P. (2008), 'Regulatory choices in global financial markets: restoring the role of aggregate utility in the shaping of market supervision', Bank of Finland research discussion paper, 1/2008, accessed at SSRN: http://ssrn.com/abstract=1092858.

Iinskas, J., Cornelius, P. and Treigiene, D. (1995), 'Trade policies and Lithuania's reintegration into the global economy', International Monetary Fund working paper, 95/138, pp. 1–50.

International Monetary Fund (IMF) (2007a), 'Bulgaria: 2007 Article IV Consultation – staff report; public information notice on the Executive Board discussion; and statement by the Executive Director for Bulgaria', IMF country report 07/389.

IMF (2007b), 'Statement by IMF Mission to Latvia on 2007 – Article IV consultation discussions', press release 07/87.

IMF (2008a), 'Czech Republic: 2007 Article IV Consultation – staff report; public information notice on the Executive Board discussion; and statement by the Executive Director for the Czech Republic', IMF country report 08/39.

IMF (2008b), 'IMF Article IV Consultation for Estonia: conclusions of the mission', IMF staff report, accessed at: www.imf.org/external/np/ms/2008/051908.htm.

IMF (2008c), 'Hungary: letter of intent, and technical memorandum of understanding', accessed at: www.imf.org/external/np/loi/2008/hun/110408.pdf.

IMF (2008d), 'Statement by an IMF staff mission to Hungary', press release 08/321.

IMF (2008e), 'Republic of Lithuania: 2008 Article IV Consultation – staff report; staff statement; public information notice on the Executive Board discussion; and statement by the Executive Director for the Republic of Lithuania', IMF country report 08/141.

IMF (2008f), 'Republic of Lithuania: selected issues', IMF country report 08/140.

IMF (2008g), *World Economic Outlook*, Washington, DC: IMF

IMF (2009a), 'Hungary – stand-by arrangement – interim review under the Emergency Financing Mechanism', IMF country report 09/21.

IMF (2009b), 'Republic of Latvia: request for stand-by arrangement – staff report; staff supplement; press release on the Executive Board discussion; and statement by the Executive Director for the Republic of Latvia', IMF country report 09/3.

IMF (2009c), *World Economic Outlook*, Washington DC: International Monetary Fund.

IMF (2009d), 'Slovak Republic: 2009 Article IV consultation – staff report; and public information notice on the Executive Board discussion', IMF country report 09/221.

IMF (2009e), 'Cyprus: 2009 Article IV consultation – staff report; public information notice on the Executive Board discussion; and statement by the Executive Director for Cyprus', IMF country report 09/225.

IMF (2009f), 'Czech Republic: 2008 Article IV consultation – staff report; staff statement; public information notice on the Executive Board discussion; and statement by the Executive Director for Czech Republic, IMF country report 09/122.

IMF (2009g), 'IMF: Malta – 2009 Article IV Consultation, concluding statement of the mission, June 2009', accessed at www.imf.org/external/np/ms/2009/062209a.htm.

Kenourgios, D. and Samitas, A. (2009), 'Financial development and economic growth in a transition economy: evidence for Poland', *Journal of Financial Decision Making*, **3**(1), 35–48.

Kočenda, E. Kutan, A. and Yigit, T. (2006), 'Pilgrims to the Eurozone: how far, how fast?', *Economic Systems*, **30**(4), 311–27.

Kočenda, E., Kutan, A. and Yigit, T. (2008), 'Fiscal convergence in the European Union', *North-American Journal of Economics and Finance*, **19**(3), 319–30.

Kovacs, Janos Matyas (ed.) (2003), 'Small transformations: the politics of welfare reform – East and West', Münster–, Hamburg–, Berlin and London: LIT Publishing.

Maiväli, M. and Lubenets, N. (2007), 'Managed vs. free wage-setting in Finland and Estonia: optimizing outcomes', *Economic Analysis from the European Commission's Directorate-General for Economic and Financial Affairs*, **4**(10).

Ministry of Finance of Latvia (2005), *Macroeconomic Development of Latvia*, accessed at: www.am.gov.lv/data/visit/08-ekonomika.pdf.

Ministry of Finance of the Czech Republic (2009), *Fiscal Outlook of the Czech Republic*, Prague: Department for Financial Policies.

Nam, Ch. and Parsche, R. (2001), 'Municipal finance in Poland, the Slovak Republic, the Czech Republic and Hungary: institutional framework and recent development', Center for Economic Studies and ifo working paper series 447.

National Bank of Romania (2008), 'Romania in the context of global financial crisis: an overview', presentation of the governor, Bucharest, accessed at: http://194.102.208.22/En/Prez/E20081210Guv.pdf.

National Bank of Slovakia (NBS) (2008), 'Annual Report 2008', Bratislava, accessed at www.nbs.sk/_img/Documents/VS%5CVSNBS08A.pdf.

Organisation for Economic Co-operation and Development (OECD) (2007), 'Economic survey of Hungary', accessed at www.oecd.org/document/63/0,3343,en_2649_34569_38601087_1_1_1_1,00.html

Polackova, H., Shatalov, S. and Zlaoui, L. (2000), 'Managing fiscal risk in Bulgaria', World Bank policy research working paper 2282.

Rahman, J. (2008), 'Current account developments in NMS of the European Union: equilibrium, excess, and EU-Phoria', International Monetary Fund working paper 08/92.

Rosenberg, Ch. (2008), 'EU membership: a post-accession boom but new policy challenges presentation at International Monetary Fund', Office for Central Europe and Balitics, 18th Economic Forum in Krynica, accessed at: http://www.imf.org/external/CEE/2008/091008.pdf.

Tang, H., Zoli, E. and Klytchnikova, I. (2000), 'Banking crises in transition economies: fiscal costs and related issues', World Bank policy research working paper 2484.

Uctum, M., Thurston, T. and Uctum, R. (2006), 'Public debt, the unit root hypothesis and structural breaks: a multi-country analysis', *Economica*, **73**(289), 129–56.

World Bank (2002), 'Republic of Latvia public expenditure review', World Bank report 22392-LV.

World Bank (2008a), 'World Bank: data and statistics: country groups', accessed at http://web.worldbank.org/WBSITE/EXTERNAL/DATASTATISTICS/0,,cont

entMDK:20421402~pagePK:64133150~piPK:64133175~theSitePK:239419,00.html.
World Bank (2008b), 'Poland – public finance management, employment, and private sector development programmatic policy loan project', programmatic policy loan document, World Bank Report, 46439-PL.
World Bank (2009a), *World Development Report 2009: Reshaping Economic Geography*, Washington DC: the World Bank Group.
World Bank (2009b), *EU10 Regular Economic Report*, Washington DC: the World Bank Group.

Tax Legislation of Slovenia:

Zakon o dohodnini (ZDoh-2), Ur.l. RS, št. 117/2006 (Personal Income Tax Act, Official Gazette of the Republic of Slovenia, No. 117/06).
Zakon o davku na izplačane plače (ZDIP), Ur.l. RS, št. 108/05 (Payroll Tax Act, Official Gazette of the Republic of Slovenia, No. 108/05).
Zakon o davku od dohodkov pravnih oseb (ZDDPO-2), Ur.l. RS, št. 117/2006, 90/2007, 56/2008, 76/2008, 92/2008, 5/2009 (Corporate Income Tax Act, Official Gazette of the Republic of Slovenia, No. 117/2006, 90/2007, 56/2008, 76/2008, 92/2008, 5/2009).

PART III

Investment, structural change and regional policy

7. Structural change in New Member States (1995–2005): shift–share analysis of productivity growth and its determinants

Aleksandra Parteka*

1. INTRODUCTION

The pace of economic growth and productivity upgrading related to the structural change in EU New Member States (from now on NMS), and in Central and East European Countries (CEECs)[1] in particular, has been a crucial issue since the beginning of the system transformation in the early 1990s (for an overview see Kornai, 2006). Aggregate data (GGDC[2], 2008) show that average levels of macro productivity in these countries still remain well below the EU-15 standards (in 2006 average productivity in CEECs amounted to only 45 per cent of EU-15 average level). In this context, quality upgrading of economic structures and the rise in productivity can be seen as necessary elements of the eventually successful catch-up process between NMS and EU-15 living standards.

The theme of structural change and quality upgrading in NMS gained importance especially in the context of the process of European integration and the division of economic activity across European countries (Boeri, 2000; Landesmann and Stehrer, 2003; Kaminski and Ng, 2005; Crespo and Fontoura, 2007). It has been argued that there are substantial differences in industrial upgrading and competitiveness on world markets among Central and East European Countries (Dulleck et al., 2005; Hotopp et al., 2005).

The main aim of this chapter is to propose an empirical framework for the measurement and assessment of the last developments in NMS seen from the perspective of a structural change and quality upgrading. We fit our analysis among empirical studies of the reallocation of resources (in our case, the labour force) across sectors and its relation to productivity developments; leaving aside the analysis of shifts between agriculture, manufacturing and services or analytical approaches in line with neoclassical multisector growth models and evolutionary theories of structural change. We present ten NMS (NMS-10) in a comparative setting with respect to former EU-15 countries; due to data availability the analysis has to be restricted to the years 1995–2005. Still, to our knowledge there is no other study that presents patterns of a structural change and its determinants for almost all members of the enlarged EU in the decade of rapid East–West integration.

The scope of the research is twofold. Firstly, we aim at assessing the speed and the direction of a structural change process in our sample of countries. In particular, we want to determine if productivity growth associated with a structural change has been driven by intra-sectoral efficiency improvements or rather by inter-sectoral effects linked to labour reallocation. Secondly, we intend to determine the forces driving the whole process, focusing on the role played by the initial level of development and productivity, human capital, R&D, public spending, trade and other country-specific factors.

The research is structured as follows: in Section 2, following the introduction, we provide the background for our analysis, presenting both theoretical motivations and existing empirical contributions on structural change and its determinants. In Section 3, we present the data and emerging empirical evidence on the pace of a structural change and patterns of productivity upgrading in NMS-10 and in EU-15 countries. Section 4 is dedicated to the exploration of the role played by country-specific factors in influencing productivity growth and structural change process. Finally, the fifth section concludes.

2. THEORETICAL AND EMPIRICAL BACKGROUND

Structural change can be understood as a process characterizing changes in the composition of economic structure and is usually analysed in the context of productivity growth.[3] The simplest approach to the study of a structural change, in the spirit of Kuznets and Kaldor, focuses on the shifts of labour and value added between three basic sectors: agriculture, manufacturing and services: the typical tendency along the path of growth is the movement from the primary sector (agriculture) to manufacturing and then to the tertiary sector (services), resulting in rising overall productivity. Multisector growth models (for example Romer, 1990; Grossman and Helpman, 1991; Aghion and Howitt, 1992) provide a useful extension of the three-sector approach by considering a larger number or a continuum of sectors: the expansion of the number of goods produced or the rise in their quality eventually causes total factor productivity growth. Evolutionary theories (for example Dosi and Nelson, 1994), instead, see economic growth process as highly dynamic and far from equilibrium paths, with structural change being a consequence of innovations, occurring in heterogeneous industries with different intensity.

Theoretical literature on endogenous growth points towards a direct relationship between qualitative aspects of economic structures and the pace of growth (Grossman and Helpman, 1991). Indeed, empirical findings confirm that industrial structures and their changes through specialization dynamics are strongly related to successful development (Fagerberg, 2000; Peneder, 2003); the link between structural change and growth has also gained interest in recent studies (Bonatti and Felice, 2008). Consequently, it is important not only to measure the speed of the structural change process, but also understand the forces lying behind productivity growth and quality upgrading as important factors which may speed up (or slow down if a negative scenario prevails) the catch-up process.

Endogeneous growth theory underlines the role of research capacity and human capital as important determinants of productivity growth, facilitating the transfer of knowledge and ideas across countries. International technology spillovers, promoting rapid productivity growth, are likely to be more successful if so-called 'absorptive capacity' (Nelson and Phelps, 1966) is strong. In this respect, both domestic R&D stock (Cohen and Levinthal, 1989) and human capital (Benhabib and Spiegel, 1994; Hanushek and Kimko, 2000) should be considered as factors influencing productivity developments and structural change. As far as international trade is considered, empirical evidence confirms that it exerts positive effect on productivity (Frankel and Romer, 1999; Alcala and Ciccone, 2004) through improvements in productivity associated with so-called 'learning from exporting' (improvements in efficiency level as firms enter into export markets, gaining new knowledge and expertise, see Wagner, 2007) or technology transfer through imports (Eaton and Kortum, 2001). One should take into account the position of trade partners: for example it has been shown that a country that imports goods from technological leaders receives more technology and experiences stronger effect on productivity than a country that imports mainly from the followers (Keller, 2000).

Additionally, the role of public spending in economic growth has been put forward by various streams of economic literature. The importance of government spending in an endogenous growth framework was introduced in a seminal contribution of Barro (1990) which was followed by a vivid debate on the public spending–growth/productivity nexus (among others: Hansson and Henrekson, 1994; Devarajan et al., 1996; Agell et al.,

1997; Bucci et al., 2009). From the point of view of quality upgrading and productivity growth, components of public expenditure promoting better quality of human capital and investment climate should favour positive structural change and the movement towards more skill-intensive sectors, eventually contributing to economic growth through endogenous mechanisms (Aghion and Howitt, 1998). The efficiency of the public sector has been put forward as one of the important aspects of economic transformation in NMS (Alfonso et al., 2006).

Our analysis is related to the empirical studies on the reallocation of labour accompanying the structural change process that apply a decomposition of productivity growth (shift–share analysis) to industry level data. Overall productivity growth is split into effects that can be attributed to intra-industry (intra-sectoral) efficiency rise and inter-industry (inter-sectoral) effects, reflecting the impact of labour reallocation. The so-called 'structural bonus hypothesis' states that in the course of growth, factors of production (labour, capital) shift to more productive industries. On the contrary, according to Baumol's (1967) view, structural change can have a negative impact on aggregate growth if employment shares shift away from progressive industries to those with a lower pace of productivity growth. Fagerberg (2000) found that in a sample of 39 countries analysed through the years 1973–1990, the within-sector component dominated, while the importance of inter-industry shifts in driving productivity growth was rather small. Productivity growth was stronger in those countries where the structural change was associated with an expanding electronics industry. Timmer and Szirmai (2000) analysed the case of four Asian countries over the period 1963–1999 and found no support for the structural bonus hypothesis. Similarly, Peneder (2003) found that in the case of the EU-15 countries (various years across the 1980s and 1990s), the USA (1987–1997) and Japan (1990–1999), the within-sector effects of productivity growth dominated over the contribution of inter-industry movements to productivity growth and there was no unambiguous tendency of labour reallocation to favour industries with high productivity performance. To the best of our knowledge no study addresses this issue in the case of EU New Member States.

3. METHODOLOGICAL SETTING

3.1 Data

As far as the data is concerned, we use several sources. For the assessment of productivity the findings draw on the industry level data from EU KLEMS Growth and Productivity Accounts database (released March

2008).[4] Data for NMS are obtainable only for some more aggregated sectors, thus for the purpose of our study we construct a restricted dataset composed of 27 sectors (consistent with the NACE Rev.1), including 18 market economy industries, five market services sectors and four non-market services.[5] The composition of our country set[6] and time span adopted are influenced by data availability. Unfortunately, reliable and comparable statistics concerning NMS prior to the year 1995 are unavailable (except for Hungary for which the data is available since 1992); hence, throughout the analysis we focus on the period of time 1995–2005.

Additional country-specific variables used in the analysis aimed at finding the determinants of productivity growth and structural change process come from various sources.[7] GDP, GDP per capita and population statistics come from PWT 6.2.[8] Secondary and tertiary enrolment rates are calculated with data on enrolment from UNESCO and population data from PWT 6.2. R&D variables, as well as the ratios of exports and imports in GDP come from the World Bank's *World Development Indicators* 2008. Total employment and the share of employment in agriculture are taken from EU KLEMS. The inflation rate and overall openness ratio (exp + imp as percentage of GDP) come from PWT 6.2 combined with Eurostat data. All the remaining trade statistics (trade/value added (VA), share of trade from different partners' groups) are calculated with UNComtrade data on trade and EU KLEMS data on value added. Finally, Eurostat is the source of all the statistics on public spending (overall and by function).

3.2 Measurement of Structural Change

3.2.1 Speed of overall structural change

In order to compare the speed of overall sectoral restructuring at the level of countries we use the indicator of Lilien (1982, p. 787),[9] defined as:

$$\Psi_{jT} = \left\| \left[\sum_{i=1}^{n} \frac{EMP_{ijT}}{TEMP_{jT}} (\Delta \log EMP_{ijT} - \Delta \log TEMP_{jT})^2 \right]^{1/2} \right\| \tag{1}$$

where i refers to sectors, j to countries, T to time period; EMP denotes sectoral employment and $TEMP$ is total employment. If we compare two countries, the one with the higher value of this indicator has gone through a more rapid process of employment reallocation across sectors during time period T than the other country. Due to data availability, we calculate Ψ for 1995–2005 and for five-year subperiods within the years 1995–2005 for NMS-10 and (for comparison) for EU-15 countries.

In general within the years 1995–2005 the speed of structural restructuring was positively related to the process of economic development in

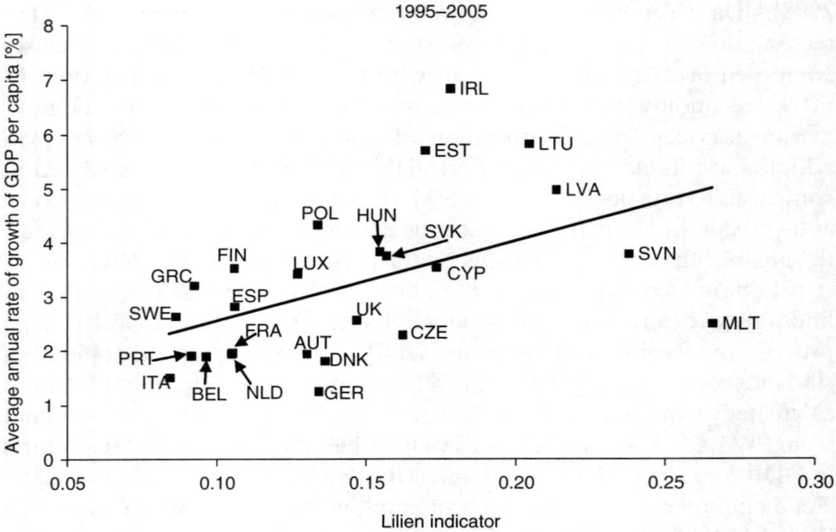

Note: Lilien indicator of economic restructuring calculated with employment data (27 sectors) from EU KLEMS; average annual rate of GDP per capita growth from PWT 6.2. Line refers to the regression line.

Source: Own elaboration.

Figure 7.1 Economic restructuring and economic growth (NMS-10 and EU-15, 1995–2005)

our sample of EU countries (Figure 7.1). The highest speed of economic restructuring characterized New Member States (mainly the Baltic States, Slovenia and Malta).[10] Among the EU-15 countries the noticeable exception was Ireland – a dynamically changing economy both in terms of GDP per capita growth and the ongoing economic restructuring. In order to have a direct comparison between the speed of structural change in 'Old' and 'New' Member States in Table 7.1 we report the values of the Lilien indicator for the two groups of countries.[11] Looking at the single countries, it turns out that the speed of structural adjustments varied not only across EU countries, but also across time periods. Within the NMS-10, among countries that went through major employment reallocation in the late 1990s rather than between the years 2000–2005 we can find the Czech Republic, Estonia and Latvia. Lithuania, Malta, Slovakia and Slovenia registered major structural changes in the twenty-first century, while in Cyprus, Hungary and Poland the structural transformation was rather an even process throughout the years 1995–2005. As far as EU-15 countries

Table 7.1 Pace of structural change in NMS-10 and in EU-15 (Lilien indicator, 1995–2005)

	Ψ T_1 1995–1999	Ψ T_2 2000–2005	Ψ T 1995–2005
CYP	0.08	0.08	0.17
CZE	0.10	0.06	0.16
EST	0.15	0.06	0.17
HUN	0.08	0.08	0.15
LTU	0.08	0.16	0.20
LVA	0.15	0.08	0.21
MLT	0.07	0.20	0.27
POL	0.06	0.06	0.13
SVK	0.06	0.11	0.16
SVN	0.08	0.18	0.24
Average NMS-10	0.09	0.11	0.19
AUT	0.05	0.07	0.13
BEL	0.04	0.05	0.10
DNK	0.06	0.07	0.14
ESP	0.05	0.06	0.11
FIN	0.05	0.06	0.11
FRA	0.05	0.05	0.11
GER	0.07	0.06	0.13
GRC	0.04	0.07	0.09
IRL	0.09	0.09	0.18
ITA	0.04	0.04	0.08
LUX	0.07	0.07	0.13
NLD	0.05	0.05	0.11
PRT	0.04	0.05	0.09
SWE	0.04	0.06	0.09
UK	0.05	0.10	0.15
Average EU-15	0.05	0.06	0.11

Note: Lilien indicator of economic restructuring calculated with employment data (27 sectors) from EU KLEMS.

Source: own elaboration with EU KLEMS.

are concerned, the indicator reveals some cross-country heterogeneity, with Greece, Italy, Portugal and Sweden characterized by the slowest sectoral reallocation of the labour force[12] while the most rapid structural adjustments within the EU-15 group between 1995 and 2005 took place in the UK and in Ireland.

3.2.2 Structural change and labour reallocation

Structural change process can evolve in different directions, depending if resources (labour force) shift between sectors/industries, generating productivity growth (in the case of the confirmed structural bonus hypothesis) or if major productivity changes take place within them. In order to quantify these phenomena we apply a shift–share analysis of productivity growth in order to assess the importance of intra-industry and inter-industry job reallocation, as well as structural adjustments on productivity growth.

Total labour productivity growth is broken down into three terms (Fagerberg, 2000, p. 401), namely: contributions to productivity resulting from inter-industry movements (static and dynamic shift effects) and productivity developments within sectors (intra-industry effect):

$$\left(\frac{\Delta P_{jT}}{P_{t_0}}\right) = \sum_{i=1}^{n}\left[\underbrace{\frac{P_{ijt_0}\Delta s_{ijT}}{P_{ijt_0}}}_{\substack{\text{static shift}\\ \text{effect } \Phi_{stat}}} + \underbrace{\frac{\Delta P_{ijT}\Delta s_{ijT}}{P_{ijt_0}}}_{\substack{\text{dynamic shift}\\ \text{effect } \Phi_{dyn}}} + \underbrace{\frac{s_{ijt_0}\Delta P_{ijT}}{P_{ijt_0}}}_{\substack{\text{intra}\\ \text{effect } I}}\right] \tag{2}$$

where P denotes labour productivity in terms of value added (in constant euro, 1995 =100) per hour worked, s is the employment share of a given sector in total country employment, i refers to sectors, j to countries and T denotes time period (t_0, t), so that $\Delta P_T = P_t - P_{t_0}$ and so on. The first term (static shift effect) reflects the ability of a country to move resources (employment) towards higher productivity activities. The second interaction term (dynamic shift effect) is positive if fast-growing sectors (in terms of productivity) increase their share in total employment, and thus measures the ability to move towards industries with rapid productivity growth.[13] It is negative if industries with fast growing productivity do not manage to maintain their shares in total employment. The third term (intra effect, denoted as I) measures the contribution from productivity growth within single industries. The shift effects, from now on denoted as Φ_{dyn} and Φ_{stat} respectively, for dynamic and static shifts, are crucial here, as they measure the quality upgrading of a given country and its ability to move towards more advanced sectors. We will denote total shift effect as $\Phi = \Phi_{dyn} + \Phi_{stat}$.

In Table 7.2 we present the results of the shift–share decomposition for NMS-10 countries within the years 1995–2005 (overall and in the two subperiods), along with analogical results for EU-15 countries. On average, overall growth of value added per hour worked that took place between 1995 and 2005 in NMS-10 was more than double that in EU-15 countries (59.5 per cent versus 22.2 per cent). In both groups of countries productivity growth was mainly due to intra-industry developments while

Table 7.2 Decomposition of labour productivity change, NMS-10 and EU-15, 1995–2005*

	T_1 = 1995–1999				T_2 = 2000–2005				T = 1995–2005			
	Total change	Shift effect		Intra effect	Total change	Shift effect		Intra effect	Total change	Shift effect		Intra effect
		static	dynamic			static	dynamic			static	dynamic	
	$\Delta P/P$	Φ_{stat}	Φ_{dyn}	I	$\Delta P/P$	Φ_{stat}	Φ_{dyn}	I	$\Delta P/P$	Φ_{stat}	Φ_{dyn}	I
CYP	14.0	4.6	0.1	9.3	11.1	0.7	−0.1	10.7	30.2	6.6	0.9	22.8
CZE	−0.5	2.1	−0.1	−2.5	51.5	0.3	−0.4	51.6	62.5	2.4	−0.2	60.3
EST	69.0	5.4	1.5	62.1	19.6	0.8	−1.2	20.0	111.5	7.0	−2.7	107.2
HUN	−26.2	0.5	−0.1	−26.6	37.7	2.4	−2.4	37.7	4.4	4.1	−3.0	3.3
LTU	59.2	−1.1	−2.6	62.9	48.0	4.2	−2.5	46.3	176.1	1.5	−13.9	188.5
LVA	28.3	3.1	−1.4	26.6	18.4	−0.8	−3.0	22.2	90.4	4.2	−10.1	96.3
MLT	21.0	2.2	−0.2	19.0	−0.7	2.7	−0.5	−2.9	30.7	7.2	−2.6	26.1
POL	−13.6	1.1	−0.7	−14.0	31.6	0.4	−2.3	33.4	31.3	3.2	−5.8	33.9
SVK	2.9	1.9	−2.6	3.6	44.2	0.4	−4.0	47.8	59.4	0.4	−9.9	68.9
SVN	−3.6	10.4	−4.5	−9.4	5.0	4.7	−0.9	1.2	−1.7	22.1	−13.9	−10.0
Total NMS-10	15.1	3.0	−1.1	13.1	26.7	1.6	−1.7	26.8	59.5	5.9	−6.1	59.7
AUT	8.8	1.5	−1.2	8.4	6.1	−0.6	−0.8	7.5	19.2	2.1	−4.3	21.4
BEL	5.5	0.7	−0.5	5.3	5.3	−0.4	−0.5	6.2	12.1	1.0	−2.5	13.6
DNK	1.5	−0.2	−0.5	2.2	6.9	0.6	−0.6	6.9	11.5	0.9	−2.2	12.8
ESP	0.4	2.2	−1.4	−0.4	3.9	2.9	−1.4	2.4	4.5	7.8	−7.0	3.7
FIN	11.4	−0.9	−0.2	12.5	12.2	−1.6	−1.7	15.6	30.2	−1.1	−2.7	33.9
FRA	7.3	−0.5	−0.5	8.2	7.2	0.0	−0.4	7.6	19.0	−0.2	−1.9	21.2
GER	8.6	3.6	−1.1	6.1	8.8	0.4	−0.4	8.7	21.5	5.0	−2.9	19.5

Table 7.2 (continued)

	T_1 = 1995–1999				T_2 = 2000–2005				T = 1995–2005			
	Total change	Shift effect		Intra effect	Total change	Shift effect		Intra effect	Total change	Shift effect		Intra effect
		static	dynamic			static	dynamic			static	dynamic	
	$\Delta P/P$	Φ_{stat}	Φ_{dyn}	I	$\Delta P/P$	Φ_{stat}	Φ_{dyn}	I	$\Delta P/P$	Φ_{stat}	Φ_{dyn}	I
GRC	8.5	−0.9	−0.4	9.7	16.1	7.2	−1.5	10.4	30.5	9.4	−1.6	22.7
IRL	19.7	2.1	0.9	16.7	14.6	−1.2	−2.8	18.6	43.0	2.1	−5.7	46.5
ITA	1.2	−0.4	−0.5	2.1	1.1	−0.6	−0.6	2.3	5.0	−1.0	−2.5	8.6
LUX	2.9	1.9	−1.7	2.7	2.0	−1.4	−0.4	3.7	6.2	2.6	−3.8	7.4
NLD	6.8	−1.0	−0.2	8.0	8.5	−1.0	−1.0	10.5	18.6	−1.6	−2.2	22.4
PRT	12.3	1.2	−0.6	11.7	4.5	−1.6	−1.6	7.7	19.6	0.8	−5.6	24.4
SWE	17.3	−0.8	−0.3	18.4	12.9	−1.5	−4.2	18.6	43.8	−0.7	−6.8	51.2
UK	37.6	−0.7	−0.4	38.7	−3.0	−0.3	−1.1	−1.6	47.8	−0.8	−3.0	51.6
Total EU-15	10.0	0.5	−0.6	10.0	7.1	0.1	−1.3	8.3	22.2	1.8	−3.6	24.0

Note: labor productivity measured as value added (in constant terms) per hour worked; * multiplied by 100.

Source: own elaboration with EUKLEMS data.

inter-industrial structural change contributed very little (static shift effect, Φ_{stat}) or even negatively (dynamic shift effect, Φ_{dyn}) to overall growth of labour efficiency. In the whole period within the NMS-10 group total growth in productivity was the highest in the Baltic States. The movement of the labour force towards higher productivity industries was relatively strong in Slovenia, but it was partly cancelled out by strong negative dynamic shift effect.

The dynamics of productivity changes appears to differ in the two subperiods.[14] Looking at total change in productivity levels, on average in NMS-10 labour productivity rose more rapidly in the second subperiod ($\Delta P/P$ equal to 26.7 per cent within 2000–2005 compared to 15.1 per cent in 1995–1999) while in EU-15 labour productivity growth was smaller than in NMS-10 and rather higher in the earlier subperiod (7.1 per cent within 2000–2005 compared to 10.0 per cent in 1995–1999). In both subperiods the overwhelming part of total productivity growth in both groups of countries can be accounted for by intra effect (I). It means that both in the years 1995–1999 and 2000–2005 changes in value added per hour worked were due mainly to positive developments (rising productivity) within single sectors while shift effects have played a much less important role. On average (total EU-15 and NMS-10 values) the contribution of the static shift effect (Φ_{stat}) has been positive which reflects some ability to move employment towards higher productivity activities. Contrastingly, the average interaction term (Φ_{dyn}) is negative, both for the NMS-10 and EU-15 groups and in both subperiods. It may be a sign of the lack of ability of EU countries to reallocate resources (labour force) towards sectors with rapid productivity growth. The support for the 'structural bonus hypothesis' in the 1995–2005 period is weak in the case of NMS-10 and even weaker in the case of EU-15 countries.[15]

However, again, each of the country groups is composed of countries with different productivity dynamics. Focusing on NMS-10 (upper panel of Table 7.2) we may note that in the first subperiod productivity change was particularly high in Estonia and Lithuania where total productivity levels in 1999 were 69 per cent and 59.2 per cent, respectively, higher than in 1995. In the second subperiod the Czech Republic and again Lithuania were the most successful in promoting productivity growth ($\Delta P/P$ equal to 51.5 per cent and 48 per cent, respectively). Hungary, Poland and Slovenia registered productivity decline between 1995 and 1999 (considerable especially in the two former countries) while Malta was the only NMS where productivity per hour worked dropped (but only by 0.7 per cent) between 2000 and 2005.

The static shift effect was in most cases low but positive, thus the share of advanced sectors in total employment in NMS-10 must have increased.

Slovenia is an example of a country where shift to more advanced industries was noticeable (but within the first time period such a positive effect was flattened down by negative productivity developments within industries). The ability to move the labour force towards fastly growing (in terms of productivity) sectors in NMS-10 was rather scarce (the dynamic shift effect was negative or negligible). Comparing NMS-10 to EU-15 countries it is clear that shift effects contributed to overall productivity change rather in the former countries (in many EU-15 economies not only the dynamic, but also the static shift effects were negative).

Note that the overall result of shift–share analysis, which points out that movements of the labour force between sectors (shift effects) have contributed rather little (or even negatively) to EU countries' productivity growth, is not a contradiction to the evidence on quite rapid process of a structural change which took place in the same countries (section 3.2.1). The results, put together, indicate that even though NMS-10 and EU-15 economies have gone through labour reallocation processes (more rapid in NMS), in the years 1995–2005 within-sector developments, rather than inter-sectoral movements, have contributed positively to the productivity growth process.

4. DETERMINANTS OF PRODUCTIVITY GROWTH AND STRUCTURAL CHANGE PROCESS

Drawing on the results presented in the previous section, we pass to the assessment of the role that various country-specific factors have played in the structural change process analysed. We link overall productivity growth and its inter- and intra-sectoral components revealed through shift–share analysis (2) with country-specific characteristics possibly influencing the process:

$$Y_{jT} = \alpha + \beta X_{jT} + D_T + \varepsilon_{jT} \tag{3}$$

where j refers to countries and T to time period (we use five year averages). Y denotes productivity growth and its components, structural change effects included, which enter into the estimation alternatively, so that $Y = \{\Delta P/P, \Phi_{stat}, \Phi_{dyn}, I\}$, X represents country-specific characteristics which are divided into several groups. First of all, we consider the basic country-specific factors characterizing countries': initial level of productivity (important from the point of view of beta convergence growth), economic development level, human capital, economy size, R&D stability and trade (we consider different groups of partners

– world, EU-15 and NMS-10 – in order to check if the choice of trade partners is important for productivity changes). The results are presented in Table 7.3. Secondly, we draw attention to the role played in promoting productivity growth by public spending and its components (results in Table 7.4). We consider total public spending as a percentage of GDP, consisting of spending on: general public services, defence, public order and safety, economic affairs, environment, housing and community, health, recreation, culture and religion, education and social protection.[16] In order to isolate the importance of single factors and given possible collinearity problems, we include each of the explanatory variables separately (along with time period dummy D_T accounting for business cycle effects and time specificity) in univariate fixed effect (FE) estimations (fixed effects are aimed at capturing the importance of all other country-specific characteristics).

First of all, it turns out that the whole process of productivity growth ($\Delta P/P$) has been guided by a beta-convergence type mechanism (a negative relationship between the initial level of productivity and GDP per capita). The contribution of the static shift effect (reflecting the ability to move resources towards higher productivity activities) in productivity growth was also negatively related to the initial and contemporary development levels (thus quicker in EU countries at lower stages of development, as revealed in the previous sections), while there is a significant negative correlation between initial productivity levels and subsequent intra-industry productivity growth (I). Most of the other factors related to human capital, economy size, R&D, economy structure or stability are not statistically significant. Interestingly, productivity growth is not significantly linked to human capital *per se*, but the major share of hours worked by highly educated workers in all economy results is a negative factor in the process of shifting labour towards sectors with fast-growing productivity (Φ_{dyn}). On the contrary, trade openness has had a positive impact on overall and intra-sectoral productivity growth but a major share of exports and imports in GDP is a negative determinant of the static shift effect, measuring the ability to move towards higher productivity activities. The nature of the partners' group is important: the major ratio of trade with EU-15 affected productivity developments positively (overall and within-sectors) while the bigger relation of imports from NMS-10 to the reporter's VA are among the negative determinants of both the static and dynamic shift effects.

In Table 7.4 we report separately the results of univariate estimations (3) obtained from measures of government spending (aggregate and by function). Government spending as a whole does not result in being a significant determinant of productivity growth or any of its components.

Table 7.3 Estimation results – productivity growth and structural change versus country-specific factors (EU-25, 1995–2005)

	Total change	Shift effect (Φ)		Intra effect
		static	dynamic	
	$\Delta P/P$	Φ_{stat}	Φ_{dyn}	I
Initial productivity				
Initial GDP per hour worked (real euro 1995)	−2.16***	0.06	−0.12	−2.75**
	(−2.87)	(−0.53)	(−1.26)	(−2.74)
Development level				
GDP per capita (real euro 1995)	−5.03*	−0.52**	−0.23	−4.28
	(−1.78)	(−2.24)	(−0.84)	(−1.41)
Initial G DP per capita	−4.58*	−0.47*	−0.14	−3.97
	(−1.72)	(−1.74)	(−0.55)	(−1.42)
GDP per capita (squared)	−0.07	−0.01	0.00	−0.06
	(−1.47)	(−1.55)	(−0.16)	(−1.30)
Human capital				
High-skilled HC (share of hours worked in total economy by high-skilled persons engaged)	−2.92	0.12	−0.64**	−2.40
	(−0.79)	(−0.39)	(−2.37)	(−0.65)
Secondary enrolment rate (% of population)	−4.01	0.11	0.12	−4.24
	(−1.09)	(−0.25)	(−0.67)	(−1.16)
Tertiary enrolment rate (% of population)	2.24	0.41	−0.35	2.18
	(−0.43)	(−0.47)	(−0.88)	(−0.41)
Size				
Population (mln)	−0.01	0.00	0.00	−0.02
	(−1.21)	(−1.49)	(−1.35)	(−1.35)
GDP (cons US$ 2000)	−72.02	5.12	3.60	−80.79
	(−0.99)	(−0.84)	(−1.11)	(−1.13)
Total employment (mln)	−9.04	0.55	0.28	−9.88
	(−1.34)	(−1.26)	(−1.41)	(−1.45)
R&D				
R&D spending (% GDP)	−12.74	0.94	−0.36	−13.33
	(−0.67)	(−0.58)	(−0.30)	(−0.71)
Researchers (per mln inhabitants)	−6.30	−0.08	−0.32	−5.90
	(−0.93)	(−0.10)	(−0.66)	(−0.86)
Structure				
Share of emp. in agriculture (%)	−4.49	−18.98	6.51	−4.37
	(−0.55)	(−0.18)	(−0.16)	(−0.52)

Table 7.3 (continued)

	Total change $\Delta P/P$	Shift effect (Φ) static Φ_{stat}	Shift effect (Φ) dynamic Φ_{dyn}	Intra effect I
Stability				
Inflation rate (%)	−1.03	−0.10	0.02	−0.96
	(−0.69)	(−0.65)	(−0.36)	(−0.63)
Trade				
(exp + imp) as % of GDP	0.67**	−0.04	0.00	0.71**
	(−2.46)	(−1.57)	(−0.20)	(−2.74)
exp as % of GDP	2.22**	−0.16**	0.03	2.36**
	(−2.52)	(−2.10)	(−0.68)	(−2.67)
imp as % of GDP	2.64**	−0.15*	0.02	2.77***
	(−2.78)	(−1.96)	(−0.55)	(−2.89)
exp to EU25 as % VA	2.14**	−0.04	−0.01	2.18**
	(−2.59)	(−0.38)	(−0.08)	(−2.66)
imp from EU25 as % VA	2.56**	−0.05	0.00	2.62**
	(−2.22)	(−0.38)	(−0.05)	(−2.25)
exp to EU15 as % VA	2.27**	−0.04	−0.02	2.33**
	(−2.64)	(−0.39)	(−0.29)	(−2.75)
imp from EU15 as % VA	3.03**	0.00	0.02	3.02**
	(−2.33)	0.00	(−0.16)	(−2.33)
exp to NMS10 as % VA	3.88	−0.33	0.21	3.99
	(−0.31)	(−0.39)	(−0.57)	(−0.32)
imp from NMS10 as % VA	0.00	−1.04*	−0.48*	1.52
	0.00	(−2.01)	(−1.98)	(−0.25)

Note: period dummy included, OLS FE univariate estimations with 5-year averages, BEL and LUX aggregated robust standard errors, t-statistics in parentheses; $*p < 0.10$, $**p < 0.05$, $***p < 0.01$

Source: own elaboration.

However, when we analyse the impact of separate components of public spending (divided by function), it is clear that especially spending on public order, safety, social protection and education, directly influencing human capital quality, plays an important role in promoting productivity growth. In particular, these categories of government expenditure are related positively with within-sectors productivity upgrading.

Table 7.4 Estimation results – productivity growth and structural change versus public spending (EU-25, 1995–2005)

	Total change	Shift effect (Φ)		Intra effect
		static	dynamic	
	$\Delta P/P$	Φ_{stat}	Φ_{dyn}	I
Gov. spending				
Total government spending as %GDP	−1.17	−0.04	0.10	−1.22
	(−0.74)	(−0.16)	(−0.98)	(−0.76)
Gov. spending by function (%GDP)				
General public services	0.41	−0.95**	0.48*	0.89
	(−0.11)	(−2.42)	(−1.9)	(−0.23)
Defence	8.25	2.31	0.21	5.75
	(−0.47)	(−1.12)	(−0.24)	(−0.31)
Public order & safety	24.12*	−0.49	0.01	23.62*
	(−1.84)	(−0.29)	(−0.01)	(−1.79)
Economic affairs	1.05	−0.04	−0.36**	1.45
	(−0.27)	(−0.07)	(−2.68)	(−0.38)
Environment protection	6.52	−0.29	−0.44	7.26
	(−0.14)	(−0.06)	(−0.11)	(−0.16)
Housing and community	−4.70	−1.64*	0.65	−3.70
	(−0.54)	(−1.77)	(−0.64)	(−0.43)
Health	2.36	1.27**	−0.14	1.24
	(−0.24)	(−2.12)	(−0.43)	(−0.12)
Recreation, culture & religion	10.89	(−0.28)	0.48	10.70
	(−0.43)	(−0.17)	(−0.32)	(−0.42)
Education	18.26*	0.72	−0.04	17.59*
	(−1.98)	(−1.22)	(−0.07)	(−1.93)
Social protection	6.92***	−0.06	0.00	6.98***
	(−2.82)	(−0.13)	(−0.00)	(−2.97)

Note: period dummy included, OLS FE univariate estimations with 5-year averages (48 obs.), BEL and LUX aggregated robust standard errors, t-statistics in parentheses; $*p < 0.10$, $**p < 0.05$, $***p < 0.01$

Source: own elaboration.

5. CONCLUSIONS

This chapter has focused on the latest developments in ten New Member States (presented *vis-à-vis* EU-15 countries), seen from the perspective of structural change and quality upgrading of their employment structures. In particular, we have used recently released disaggregated labour statistics, allowing us to analyse the process of labour reallocation and productivity changes associated with inter- and intra-industry structural change.

We find that since the mid-1990s NMS have gone through a rapid process of sectoral restructuring. Looking at the single countries it turns out that the speed of structural adjustments varied not only across countries, but also across time periods. Within the NMS-10 group among countries that went through major employment reallocation in the late 1990s rather than between the years 2000–2005 are the Czech Republic, Estonia and Latvia. Lithuania, Malta, Slovakia and Slovenia registered structural changes mainly after the year 2000, while in Cyprus, Hungary and Poland labour market transformation was rather an even process throughout the years 1995–2005.

However, despite rapid economic restructuring, the tendency for labour reallocation towards sectors with higher productivity has been rather weak in NMS-10 (but still stronger than in EU-15 countries). We have applied a shift–share analysis of productivity growth in order to assess the importance of intra-industry and inter-industry patterns on productivity growth. It turns out that it was mainly driven by the intra effect, signifying rising productivity within sectors, but labour reallocation played a much less important role.

The results, put together, indicate that even though NMS-10 and EU-15 economies have gone through a labour reallocation process (more rapid in the former group of countries), within-sector developments, rather than inter-sectoral movements, have contributed positively to the labour productivity growth process in the years of East–West EU integration. We notice a very scarce ability of reallocating the European labour force towards developing industries with higher rates of productivity. Such a conclusion is in line with what other authors have found for other samples of countries and time periods.

As far as the determinants of productivity growth accompanying the structural change process are concerned, we indeed find a set of variables characterizing our sample of EU countries that result in being positively related to the rise in labour efficiency. The productivity growth process (overall and intra-sectoral) has followed a path similar to the beta convergence type mechanism. Trade openness appears to be an important stimulating factor, but major stimulus seems to have been given through trade with EU-15 countries. Last but not least, government spending on education, public order, safety and social protection results in being related positively to the productivity growth.

NOTES

* Gdansk University of Technology, Faculty of Management and Economics; Narutowicza 11/12, 80-233, Gdansk, Poland; aparteka@zie.pg.gda.pl. The author is grateful for comments on an earlier draft to Massimo Florio, Gianfranco de Simone and Giulia Felice. The usual disclaimer applies.

1. Namely: Bulgaria, Czech Republic, Estonia, Hungary, Latvia, Lithuania, Poland, Romania, Slovenia and Slovak Republic.
2. Groeningen Growth Development Centre (www.ggdc.net).
3. See Krüger (2008) for a recent survey of literature on productivity and structural change.
4. www.euklems.net. See O'Mahony and Timmer (2009) for an overview of the database.
5. *Market economy industries*: Food, beverages and tobacco; Textiles, leather and footwear; Wood and products of wood and cork; Pulp, paper, paper products, printing and publishing; Coke, refined petroleum and nuclear fuel; Chemicals and chemical products; Rubber and plastics; Other non-metallic mineral products; Basic metals and fabricated metal products; Machinery, n.e.c.; Electrical and optical equipment; Transport equipment; Manufacturing n.e.c., recycling; Post and telecommunications; Agriculture, hunting, forestry and fishing; Mining and quarrying; Electricity, gas and water supply; Construction. *Market services*: Transport and storage; Renting of machinery and equipment and other business activities; Wholesale and retail trade; Hotels and restaurants; Financial intermediation. *Non-market services*: Real estate activities; Public admin and defence; compulsory social security; Education; Health and social work.
6. NMS-10: CYP – Cyprus, CZE – Czech Republic, EST – Estonia, HUN – Hungary, LTU – Lithuania, LVA – Latvia, MLT – Malta, POL – Poland, SVK – Slovak Republic, SVN – Slovenia. EU-15 (as a reference set): AUT – Austria BEL – Belgium, LUX – Luxembourg, DNK – Denmark, ESP – Spain, FIN – Finland, FRA – France, GER – Germany, GRC – Greece, IRL – Ireland, ITA – Italy, NLD – ,Netherlands, PRT – Portugal, SWE – Sweden, UK – United Kingdom.
7. Summary statistics of all variables are not shown here due to space constraints but are available upon request.
8. Penn World Table 6.2. (available at: www.pwt.econ.upenn.edu).
9. Originally, Lilien applied this indicator to measure the implications of labour reallocation on the rate of unemployment in the US economy from the late 1970s to the early 1980s.
10. Note that it is highly plausible that the major part of a structural change in the remaining NMS from Central and Eastern Europe took place in the early 1990s – unfortunately with the data at our disposal we can only trace the developments since 1995 onwards.
11. Even though there is no benchmark value of the indicator (it rather serves for making comparisons across countries and/or time periods), the values of the Lilien index that we obtain for single countries are in line with existing evidence concerning EU-15 countries (ECB, 2004, p. 23).
12. Greece, Italy and Portugal registered also the lowest pace of a structural change of their economic structures within the period 1970–2005.
13. Of course, the dynamic shift effect can also be positive if both changes (in productivity and in the share) are negative.
14. The values concerning periods T_1 and T_2 do not sum to those obtained for the period

1995–2005 because the two 5-year decompositions are based on border values from the years 1995 and 1999 (T_1), 2000 and 2005 (T_2), while the decomposition for the whole period uses values for the years 1995 and 2005.

15. It is in line with the results obtained by Fagerberg (2000), Timmer and Szirmai (2000) and Peneder (2003) described in Section 2. Additional evidence concerning EU-15 countries for the years 1970–2005 (available upon request) confirms that also in the long run productivity growth was driven by efficiency gains within sectors while the impact of labour shift to sectors with higher productivity levels was much less pronounced and all EU-15 countries but Luxembourg failed to draw productivity gains from a dynamic shift effect.
16. The levels of total government spending (as a percentage of their GDP) are still rather low in NMS when compared to EU-15 standards. On average NMS-10 in 1995 spent around 6 per cent less of their GDP on public expenditure than EU-15 economies and in the course of time (between 1995 and 2005) total public spending with respect to GDP declined. The differences between GDP levels between NMS-10 and EU-15 economies result in huge differentials between the amount of government spending in euros per inhabitant. NMS-10 countries spent on average around five times less per each inhabitant that was spent in EU-15 countries. The highest levels of public expenditure per person are typical for rather high income NMS-10, namely: Cyprus, Slovenia and Malta. However, as GDP grew in NMS-10, total government expenditure rose by around one-fourth if we consider effective spending per person.

REFERENCES

Afonso, A., L. Schuknecht and V.Tanzi (2006), 'Public sector efficiency: evidence for New EU Member States and emerging markets', European Central Bank Working Paper, 581.

Agell, J., T. Lindh and H. Ohlsson (1997), 'Growth and the public sector: a critical review essay', *European Journal of Political Economy*, **15**(2), 359–66.

Aghion, Philippe and Peter Howitt (eds) (1998), *Endogenous Growth Theory*, New York: The MIT Press.

Alcala, F. and A. Ciccone (2004), 'Trade and productivity', *Quarterly Journal of Economics*, **119**(2), 613–46.

Barro, R.J. (1990), 'Government spending in a simple model of endogenous growth', *Journal of Political Economy*, **98**(5), 103–26.

Baumol, W. (1967), 'Macroeconomics of unbalanced growth: the anatomy of urban crisis', *The American Economic Review*, **57**(3), 415–26.

Benhabib, J. and M. Spiegel (1994), 'The role of human capital in economic development. Evidence from aggregate cross-country data', *Journal of Monetary Economics*, **34**(2), 143–73.

Bonatti, L. and G. Felice (2008), 'Endogenous growth and changing sectoral composition in advanced economies', *Structural Change and Economic Dynamics*, **19**(2), 109–88.

Boeri, Tito (ed.) (2000), *Structural Change, Welfare Systems and Labor Reallocation: Lessons from the Transition of Formerly Planned Economies*, Oxford: Oxford University Press.

Bucci, A., M. Florio and D. La Torre (2009), 'Transitional dynamics in a growth model with government spending, technological progress and population change', UNIMI – Research Papers in Economics, Business, and Statistics, economics working paper, 28.

Cohen, W.M. and D.A. Levinthal (1989), 'Innovation and learning: the two faces of R&D', *Economic Journal*, **99**(397), 569–96.

Crespo, N. and M. Fontoura (2007), 'Integration of CEECs into EU market: structural change and convergence', *Journal of Common Market Studies*, **45**(3), 611–32.

Devarajan, S., V. Swaroop and H. Zou (1996), 'The composition of public expenditure and economic growth', *Journal of Monetary Economics*, **37**(2), 313–44.

Dosi, G. and R. Nelson (1994), 'An introduction to evolutionary theories in economics', *Journal of Evolutionary Economics*, **4**(3), 153–72.

Dulleck, U., N. Föster, R. Stehrer and J. Wörz (2005), 'Dimensions of quality upgrading. Evidence from CEECs', *Economics of Transition*, **13**(1), 51–76.

Eaton, J. and S. Kortum (2001), 'International technology diffusion', *Journal of International Economics*, **40**(3), 537–70.

European Central Bank (ECB) (2004), 'Sectoral specialization in the EU. A macroeconomic perspective', ECB occasional paper series 19.

Fagerberg, J. (2000), 'Technological progress, structural change and productivity growth: a comparative study', *Structural Change and Economic Dynamics*, **11**(4), 393–411.

Frankel, J. and D. Romer (1999), 'Does trade cause growth?', *American Economic Review*, **89**(3), 379–99.

Grossman, Gene M. and Elhanan Helpman (eds) (1991), *Innovation and Growth in the Global Economy*, Cambridge, MA: The MIT Press.

Hanushek, E. and D. Kimko (2000), 'Schooling, labour-force quality and the growth of nations', *American Economic Review*, **90**(5), 1184–208.

Hansson, P. and M. Henrekson (1994), 'A new framework for testing the effect of government spending on growth and productivity', *Public Choice*, **81**(3–4), 381–401.

Hotopp, U., S. Radosevic and K. Bishop (2005), 'Trade and industrial upgrading in countries of central and eastern Europe', *Emerging Markets Finance and Trade*, **41**(4), 20–37.

Kaminski, B. and F. Ng (2005), 'Production disintegration and integration of Central Europe into global markets', *International Journal of Economics and Finance*, **14**(3), 377–90.

Keller, W. (2000), 'Do trade patterns and technology flows affect productivity growth?', *World Bank Economic Review*, **14**(1), 17–47.

Kornai, J. (2006), 'The great transformation of Central Eastern Europe', *Economics of Transition*, **14**(2), 207–44.

Krüger, J. (2008), 'Productivity and structural change: a review of the literature', *Journal of Economic Surveys*, **22**(2), 330–63.

Landesmann, M. and R. Stehrer (2003), 'Evolving competitiveness of CEECs in an enlarged Europe', *Rivista di Politica Economica*, **92**(1–2), 23–87.

Lilien, David M. (1982), 'Sectoral shifts and cyclical unemployment', *Journal of Political Economy*, **90**(4), 777–93.

Nelson, Richard R. and E.S. Phelps (1966), 'Investment in humans, technological diffusion, and economic growth', *American Economic Review*, **56**(1–2), 69–75.

O'Mahony, M. and M.P. Timmer (2009), 'Output, input and productivity measures at the industry level: the EU KLEMS database', *Economic Journal*, **119**(538), F374–F403.

Peneder, M. (2003), 'Industrial structure and aggregate growth', *Structural Change and Economic Dynamics*, **14**(4), 427–48.

Romer, Paul M. (1990), 'Endogenous technological change', *Journal of Political Economy*, **98**(5), 71–102.
Timmer, M. and A. Szirmai (2000), 'Productivity growth in Asian manufacturing: the structural bonus hypothesis examined', *Structural Change and Economic Dynamics*, **11**(4), 371–92.
Wagner, J. (2007), 'Exports and productivity: a survey of the evidence from firm-level data', *The World Economy*, **30**(1), 60–82.

8. Structural funds business support and employment growth in manufacturing: perspectives for the New Member States

Luigi Moretti*

1. INTRODUCTION AND MOTIVATION

The Structural and Cohesion Funds (SCF) are the European Union's (EU) financial instruments for the achievement of social and economic cohesion through the reduction of disparities between the levels of development of the regions (art. 130a-b Treaty of European Union). The SCF finance and support a variety of investments affecting regions' business environment and capital endowment through a variety of channels. For instance, the SCF can potentially create better public infrastructure, improve workforce skills and the capacity to adapt, help the reconversion process of declining industries, or improve the availability of funds to increase productivity and production capability through R&D and direct business support. Overall the SCF account for almost two thirds of the EU budget, and one of the main areas of expenditure is business support (about one fifth of the overall funds allocation across EU-27 in 2007–2013); this is the financial scheme geared to directly assist large business organizations, small and medium enterprises and the craft sectors, and the adoption of research technology, development and innovation activities (RTDI).

This chapter illustrates the impact of SCF business support on manufacturing performance in a sample of regions belonging to the eight New Member States from Central and Eastern Europe that joined the EU in 2004 (NMS-8) and, in particular, it has the aim of extending the analysis proposed by Florio and Moretti (2009), who investigate the relationship between SCF expenditure in business support and employment growth. In their analysis, they exploit cross-industry variation for a sample of German, Italian and Spanish regions and take advantage of detailed SCF thematic expenditure data at the regional level. They examine the hypothesis that business support financed through SCF might have differential effects on the reallocation of production activities and employment across industries, sustaining the growth of those industries with higher growth potential or consolidating the distribution of business activities across manufacturing industries. To this end, they ask whether SCF business support contributes to a convergence process, with smaller industries (in terms of employment share) growing faster than others. They find a positive relationship between funds and employment growth for those industries that are initially smaller in size. This implies that less established sectors – that is, new ones, or niches residual to firms' selection in old activities – gain more from business support.

Florio and Moretti (2009) also test whether SCF stimulate or dampen employment in industries with different growth opportunities, in addition to contributing to the reallocation of employees between different sized industries within a region. They assume that firms within an industry have similar growth opportunities (relative to firms operating in other industries) and that firms' growth opportunities influence their investment decisions. Hence, if SCF business support creates a better business environment for the exploitation of this potential, we should expect the advantage for those industries with higher growth opportunities to be greater when they are located in regions that receive higher support. The authors find a positive relationship between SCF business support and employment growth in industries with higher growth opportunities.

In this chapter, we re-estimate the relationship between the ratio of SCF business support to region's GDP and employment growth in manufacturing industries using the model specification and the dataset of Florio and Moretti (2009), and we employ it as our benchmark scenario. Then, assuming that the estimated relationship can be applied to a sample of regions belonging to NMS-8 during the programming period 2007–2013 and given the specialization of the manufacturing industries in each NMS-8 region, we run a sensitivity analysis by raising the average annual SCF business support to GDP ratio of 0.15 percentage points in all the NMS-8 regions. This exercise can give us a picture of the regions and industries that are more responsive to the SCF business support. Nevertheless, we focus on short-run, rather than long-run effects of business support on the reallocation of economic activities and employment across industries and its contribution to the processes of regional converge and competitiveness that are the overall goals of the EU Regional Policy in both EU-15 and NMS-8 regions.

A more direct analysis of the effectiveness of SCF business support on NMS-8 regions would require the passing of some additional years before allowing us to identify their potential effects, but NMS-8 received

Table 8.1 SCFs business support during the programming period 2007–2013

Share of SCFs business support in country's total SCFs (%)				Average annual SCFs business support to GDP ratio (%)			
EU-15		NMS-8		EU-15		NMS-8	
Austria	43.8	Czech Rep.	15.3	Austria	0.03	Czech Rep.	0.28
Belgium	28.4	Estonia	19.3	Belgium	0.03	Estonia	0.41
Denmark	36.8	Hungary	13.9	Denmark	0.02	Hungary	0.32
Finland	36.3	Latvia	15.7	Finland	0.05	Latvia	0.32
France	22.1	Lithuania	16.2	France	0.02	Lithuania	0.31
Germany	29.6	Poland	16.0	Germany	0.05	Poland	0.29
Greece	9.3	Slovakia	10.7	Greece	0.10	Slovakia	0.19
Ireland	20.9	Slovenia	22.9	Ireland	0.01	Slovenia	0.30
Italy	21.6			Italy	0.06		
Luxembourg	32.0			Luxembourg	0.01		
Netherland	19.5			Netherland	0.01		
Portugal	21.2			Portugal	0.32		
Spain	23.1			Spain	0.10		
Sweden	36.6			Sweden	0.03		
UK	31.7			UK	0.03		

Source: Author's elaboration of DG Regio and Eurostat data. GDP data are for 2007.

SCF only from 2004. However, applying the estimated impact of SCF business support on manufacturing employment growth obtained for Germany, Italy and Spain (during the period 2000–2006) is a useful exercise to analyse the potential effects on NMS-8 regions and industries.

SCF expenditure in business support is a larger share of the total funds allocation in EU-15 countries compared to NMS-8, since in the latter countries SCF expenditure is mainly concentrated on investments in basic infrastructures. However, business support as a share of country's GDP is much greater in NMS-8 and is likely to increase in the future for NMS-8 as their needs will move from basic infrastructure to alternative stimuli to the productive environment to achieve the EU Regional Policy objectives (see Table 8.1). Thus, the analysis of the effects of SCF capital grants to business activities becomes particularly relevant for these countries as capital grants will contribute to increase the sources of firms' external finance and will have a direct impact on the entrepreneurs' decisions to expand their businesses and workforce.

The rest of the chapter is structured as follows. In Section 2 we briefly review the empirical evidence on the effectiveness of SCF. In Section 3 we present the estimation of the benchmark scenario and the approach to the sensitivity analysis on NMS-8. In Section 4 we show the main results, while Section 5 concludes.

2. BRIEF REVIEW OF THE EMPIRICAL EVIDENCE

Although in the last two decades a large number of studies have focused on the effectiveness of the SCF, the debate is still quite open, as the empirical results do not point in a unique direction. Most of the evidence focuses on the contribution of SCF to the convergence process, using aggregate data at the regional and country level.[1] To cite some examples, Boldrin and Canova (2001) look at the dynamics of cross-regional income per capita and productivity during the period 1980–1992 and show that SCF net recipient regions did not perform significantly differently from the other regions; while, Garcia-Solanes and Maria-Dolores (2002) find that SCF have significant effects on convergence both at the regional and country level. Others find more ambiguous evidence. For instance, Ederveen and Gorter (2002) find that SCF contribute to the economic growth of lagging regions if one assumes that each region grows towards its own steady state level of GDP per capita, but this effect becomes negligible or even negative if one assumes that each region within a country will convergence to the same steady state.

Some authors look at different aspects of the relationship, such as the presence of non-linear effects across the programming periods. For instance, Puigcerver-Peñalver (2007) shows that SCF have positive effects on the growth process of Objective 1 regions, but these effects are greater during the first programming period (1988–1993); by contrast, Fiaschi et al. (2009) show that, although on average SCF have significant effects on growth, their impact is greater in the second (1994–1999) and third (2000–2006) programming periods.

Others try to take advantage of more advanced econometric techniques to explore the relationship. For instance, Dall'Erba and Le Gallo (2008), using spatial econometric techniques to account for spatial spillover between regions, show that a convergence process between EU regions is taking place, but that SCF have no impact on it. Becker et al. (2008) build a quasi-random experiment and find positive growth effects of Objective 1 funds but no employment effects.

Some other authors look at whether SCF effects are conditional on regions' characteristics. Ederveen et al. (2006) show that SCF are effective only if the institutional quality of the recipient economy is sufficiently high; while Beugelsdijk and Eijffinger (2005) find that SCF have contributed to the reduction of interregional disparities within EU-15, and that countries with higher levels of corruption do not benefit less in terms of economic growth from the SCF. Finally, Cappelen et al. (2003) show that SCF have positive effects on the growth and productivity of poorer regions, even if there are diverging factors at play. In fact, they point out that growth of poorer regions is hampered by an unfavourable industry structure and lack of R&D. In order to maximize the advantages from EU funds, addressing these issues should be a key objective of a supporting policy.

Only a relatively small number of studies look at industry-level effects (in particular, macroeconometric model simulations used by the EU Commission for country impact evaluation).[2] However, looking at the differential effects across sectors could shed light on differences in terms of gains from SCF intervention, which might be concealed in more aggregated analyses. This is particularly important when the object of analysis is the effectiveness of capital grants to business activities, as it is likely that, due to their intrinsic characteristics (such as size, level of development, dependence from sources of external finance, capacity of R&D adoption and growth potential), industries might react to the availability of business support in different ways.

3. ESTIMATION STRATEGY

3.1 Model Estimation

In this work we first re-estimate the differential effects of the SCF business support to GDP ratio on industries with different initial share of employment and growth opportunities in a sample of German, Italian and Spanish regions, using the model specification and a reduced version of the dataset proposed by Florio and Moretti (2009). Then, we employ these estimates as a benchmark scenario and run sensitivity analysis on NMS-8 regions.[3]

Florio and Moretti (2009) stress the potential problems of establishing a causal relationship using macro-level data, given the availability of SCF data for a programming period only. However, they are confident that the estimation of a model including variables controlling for the several dimensions (industry, region and country) can assure the identification of the real effects of SCF business support.

Their decision to focus on the regions of only three countries is mainly due to the fact that many EU-15 regions received a small amount of business support as a share of their GDP, which would potentially create identification problems. Furthermore, they want to preserve a high level of variation in terms of the business support to GDP ratio as well as the level of economic development between the regions included in the sample. The regions of these three countries had both these characteristics. In fact, they had a high number of Objective 1 regions, that is, a high number of lagging-behind regions receiving a larger amount of SCF relative to the size of their economy, and invested relatively large shares of business support from total SCF financing in both Objective 1 and Objective 2 regions.

The estimated model looks as follows:

$$EmGr_{i,r} = \beta_0 + \beta_1{*}Sh_{i,r} + \beta_2{*}BS_r + \beta_3{*}BS_r{*}Sh_{i,r} + \beta_4{*}BS_r{*}GO_i$$
$$+ \beta_5{*}GO_i + \beta_6{*}R_r + \gamma{*}I_i + \rho{*}C_c + \varepsilon_{i,r} \qquad (1)$$

where ($EmGr_{i,r}$) is the compounded annual growth rate of persons employed in industry *i* and region *r* between 2000 and 2006. Beyond the main term of interest (BS_r) (that is, average annual business support financed by SCF during the period 2000–2006 as a share of the initial GDP in region *r*), the model specification includes the initial share of employment ($Sh_{i,r}$) of industry *i* in the total manufacturing of region *r*, taken at the beginning of the period of analysis, to control for an industry convergence trend. The regional indicators (R_r) (that is, the region's *r* (log of the) GDP in PPS and the (log of the) per capita GDP in PPS), measured at the beginning of the period of analysis, control for the size of the regional economy as well as the trend in regional convergence. We also include industry fixed effects (*I*), to control for those industry-specific factors common across regions and countries (such as raw material price shocks or the level of technology), as well as country fixed effects (*C*), since the decision to expand business activities and to hire additional employees is influenced by country-specific factors (such as the regulation and legislation involved in hiring or firing employees).

The SCF business support to GDP ratio (BS_r) enters the specification as a single term and as part of two interaction terms. The first interaction term ($BS_r{*}\ Sh_{i,r}$) checks for the effects of the business support to GDP ratio on employment growth of different sized industries. After controlling for both constitutive terms of the interaction, a negative and statistically significant sign for the coefficient β_3 indicates that the SCF capital grants to business activities support a convergence process between manufacturing industries within a region, with smaller industries growing faster than larger ones.

The second interaction term (BS_r*GO_i) checks for the presence of differential effects of the business support to GDP ratio on those industries that are exogenously experiencing higher growth opportunities. Since growth opportunities are typically not observable, the test is built upon the assumption that firms operating in the same industry respond similarly to exogenous shocks (for example changes in demand and in factor prices, resulting in changes in industry growth opportunity), independently of the region (and country) in which they operate. Thus, an industry-specific measure of growth opportunity can be computed for a benchmark sample and then interacted with the SCF variable of interest (BS_r).

This test is similar to Fisman and Love (2004), who assume that exogenous shocks create new opportunities for growth in some industries, and show that higher level of financial development is crucial for the exploitation of these industries' growth.

The measure of growth opportunities proposed by Florio and Moretti (2009) is defined as the median firm average real growth rate of sales for each industry in a benchmark economy, with the EU-15 countries (excluding Germany, Italy and Spain, which are the countries under analysis) acting as a benchmark economy. Then, they create a dummy variable (GO_i) that takes on 1 if the industry growth opportunity indicator is above the median (of the industry-specific distribution of the same indicator) and 0 otherwise.[4]

Thus, if SCF business support contributes to the faster growth of employment in those industries that in the EU-15 are experiencing higher growth rates (that is, they have more growth opportunities), we would expect to find a positive and statistically significant β_4 coefficient for the interaction term (BS_r*GO_i).

Using a reduced version (12 manufacturing industries) of Florio and Moretti's dataset we obtain the following estimated coefficients:[5]

$$\begin{aligned} EmGr_{i,r} = {} & (\hat{\beta}_0 = 0.017) + (\hat{\beta}_1 = -0.071)*Sh_{i,r} + (\hat{\beta}_2 = 0.005)*BS_r \\ & + (\hat{\beta}_3 = -0.258)*BS_r*Sh_{i,r} + (\hat{\beta}_4 = 0.031)*BS_r*GO_i \\ & + (\hat{\beta}_5 = -0.027)*GO_i + (\hat{\beta}_6 = -0.004)*GDP_r \\ & + (\hat{\beta}_7 = -0.031)*GDPpc_r + \gamma*I_i + \rho*C_c + \varepsilon_{i,r} \end{aligned} \tag{2}$$

These estimation results are very similar to those obtained with 14 manufacturing industries by Florio and Moretti (2009), confirming again the robustness of the model specification. Again all estimated coefficients are statistically significant at the 1 per cent, 5 per cent or 10 per cent levels, except the single term of business support to GDP ratio (BS_r).[6]

Table 8.2 Summary statistics by industry for a sample of NMS-8 regions

NACE	Obs	*GO*	Share of employment in region (%)			
			Mean	SD	Min	Max
DA	39	0	15.05	6.04	7.26	31.21
DB	39	0	8.44	4.85	1.99	29.32
DD	39	1	6.11	3.87	1.65	19.61
DE	39	0	5.47	3.62	2.39	20.02
DG	39	0	3.36	1.84	0.70	7.56
DH	39	1	5.28	1.77	2.18	10.47
DI	39	1	5.20	2.44	1.52	14.98
DJ	39	1	13.56	5.40	6.29	32.27
DK	39	1	9.19	3.22	4.08	17.40
DL	39	0	11.54	5.81	3.07	25.24
DM	39	0	7.90	5.61	2.06	26.48
DN	39	1	7.00	3.49	2.57	19.85
Total	468		8.18	5.44	0.70	32.27

Note: *GO* is an indicator that is equal to the average firm sales real growth rate for the median firm of each industry *i* from a sample of EU-15 countries during 2000–2006. A dummy variable is built and takes the value 1 when the industry is above the median and the value 0 when is below the median of the distribution of this indicator (source: BvD Amadeus). Share of employment in region is the share of number of persons employed in industry *i* in region *r* to the total number of persons employed in manufacturing in region *r* in 2006 (source: Eurostat).

3.2 Sensitivity Analysis

The aim of this chapter is to show the sensitivity to the SCF business support of regions and industries in NMS-8. To this end, we assume that the relationship between the SCF business support to GDP ratio and employment growth estimated with equation (1) for a sample of German, Italian and Spanish regions in 2000–2006 holds in NMS-8 in 2007–2013. Thus, we use the estimated parameters of equation (2) and apply them to the manufacturing industries structure of NMS-8 regions to show how the regions and industries are responsive to a uniform increase in the SCF business support to GDP ratio. In particular, we use Eurostat–Regio data for 2006 to capture the structure of regional manufacturing in NMS-8 and compute the relative size of each industry ($Sh_{i,r}$), while we assume that the same exogenously determined high-growth opportunity industries (GO_i) maintain their relative growth potential in 2007–2013.[7]

Suppose that in NMS-8 regions during the period 2007–2013 for some reason the average annual SCF business support to GDP ratio increased in any region by 0.15 percentage points. Thus from equation (2) the partial effect of business support to GDP ratio on employment growth of industry i in region r is:

$$\begin{aligned} &\textit{impact on the employment growth of industry i in region r} \\ &\quad = (\beta_2 + \beta_3 * Sh_{i,r} + \beta_4 * GO_i) * \Delta BS_r \\ &\quad = [0 + (-0.258 * Sh_{i,r}) + (0.031 * GO_i)] * 0.15 \end{aligned} \tag{3}$$

The industries that would benefit the most are those with smaller initial size and higher growth opportunity. At the same time, the regions with highest benefit are those where the smaller-sized as well as the higher-growth opportunity industries have a higher weight on the total regional manufacturing compared to those regions where the smaller-sized and the high-growth opportunity industries account for a smaller share of the regional manufacturing.

To summarize the impact of the region's SCF business support to GDP ratio on manufacturing employment growth at the regional, country and country-industry levels, we compute weighted averages of equation (3) for any region, country, or country-industry combination. The weights are the share of each industry's employment in the relevant region, country and country-industry. In particular, considering that $(x_{i,r})$ is the value of employment in industry i and region r, we compute the following estimated impacts:

$$\begin{aligned} &\textit{impact on the employment growth of region r} \\ &\quad = \sum_i \left[\frac{x_{i,r}}{\sum_i x_{i,r}} (\beta_2 + \beta_3 * Sh_{i,r} + \beta_4 * GO_i) * \Delta BS_r \right] \\ &\quad = \sum_i \left[\frac{x_{i,r}}{\sum_i x_{i,r}} [0 + (-0.258 * Sh_{i,r}) + (0.031 * GO_i)] * 0.15 \right] \end{aligned} \tag{4}$$

$$\begin{aligned} &\textit{impact on the employment growth of country c} \\ &= \sum_{r \in c} \left\{ \frac{\sum_i x_{i,r}}{\sum_{r \in c} \sum_i x_{i,r}} \sum_i \left[\frac{x_{i,r}}{\sum_i x_{i,r}} (\beta_2 + \beta_3 * Sh_{i,r} + \beta_4 * GO_i) * \Delta BS_r \right] \right\} \\ &= \sum_{r \in c} \left\{ \frac{\sum_i x_{i,r}}{\sum_{r \in c} \sum_i x_{i,r}} \sum_i \left[\frac{x_{i,r}}{\sum_i x_{i,r}} [0 + (-0.258 * Sh_{i,r}) + (0.031 * GO_i)] * 0.15 \right] \right\} \end{aligned} \tag{5}$$

impact on the employment growth of country c and industry i

$$= \sum_{r \in c} \left[\frac{\sum_{r \in c} x_{i,r}}{\sum_{r \in c} \sum_{i} x_{i,r}} [(\beta_2 + \beta_3 * Sh_{i,r} + \beta_4 * GO_i) * \Delta BS_r] \right] \quad (6)$$

$$= \sum_{r \in c} \left[\frac{\sum_{r \in c} x_{i,r}}{\sum_{r \in c} \sum_{i} x_{i,r}} [0 + (-0.258 * Sh_{i,r}) + (0.031 * GO_i)] * 0.15 \right]$$

4. RESULTS

From equation (4) we obtain a measure of the impact on each region that equals the weighted average of business support to GDP ratio estimated effect on the industries' employment growth. Figure 8.1 shows the weighted average effects according to four clusters of regions corresponding to the quartile ranges of the distribution of the measure of the impact. We observe that the two clusters including the regions with higher impact are located in the Czech Republic (except Central regions), Western and Southern Poland, along the Czech–Polish–Slovak border, Slovenia and Estonia.

The increase in SCF business support might have a negative weighted impact on employment growth, since in region *r* the relative weight of larger-sized industries and low-growth opportunity industries (which would grow slower) might be so high that it more than compensates for the positive impact of business support on smaller-sized industries and high-growth opportunity industries. However, our results show that only in a few regions would an increase of business support have an average negative impact on employment growth. In all the other regions the weighted average of the impact of an increase of SCF business support is positive.

Equations (5) and (6) summarize the impact of the increase in the SCF business support to GDP ratio at country and industry-country levels using the relevant weights. The results show that the weighted average impact at the country level of a uniform increase of the business support to GDP ratio in any region does not have negative effects for any country, and the countries that would benefit the most are Slovenia and Estonia, followed by the Czech Republic, Poland, Slovakia, Lithuania, Latvia and Hungary.

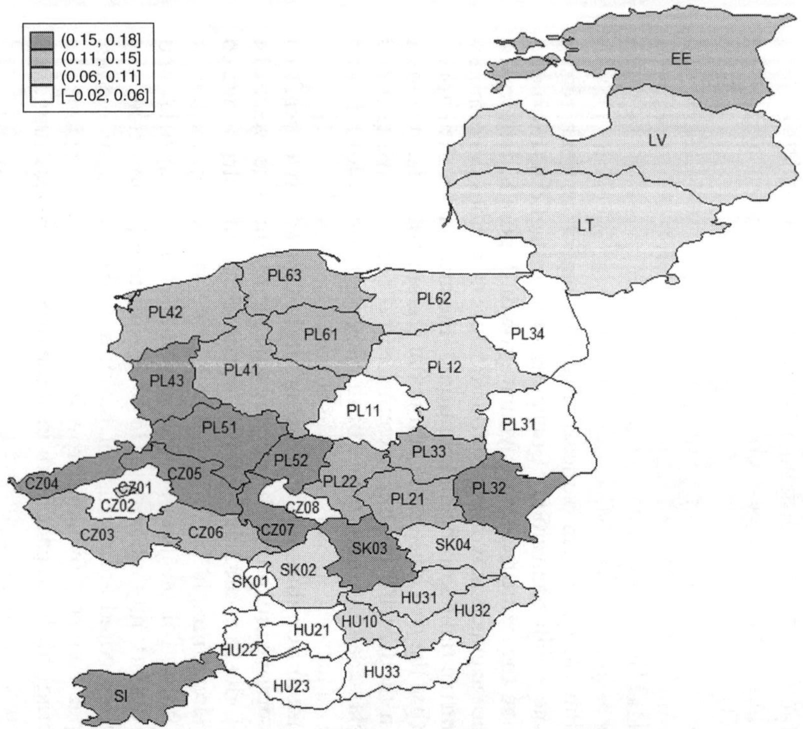

Source: Own elaboration.

Figure 8.1 *Weighted average of the impact on region's average annual employment growth in manufacturing (%) of an increase of 0.1 percentage points of average annual of SCFs business support divided by region's GDP (2007–2013)*

As expected, the manufacturing industries that would contribute most to the employment growth are similar among countries. In fact, in our model the effect of business support is conditional on the initial relative size of the industries, which are relatively similar in many regions, as well as on an indicator of industry growth opportunities, which enters the model exogenously and does not have regional variation. In particular, in NMS-8 the industries which would benefit the most are the machinery and equipment (DK), rubber and plastic products (DH), other manufacturing (DN), basic metals and fabricated metal products (DJ), other non-metallic mineral products (DI), and wood and wood products (DD).

If we look for a correlation pattern between the estimated effects and the regions' and countries' initial GDP per capita or GDP growth (during the years just before the beginning of the programming period 2007–2013), we observe that most of the NMS-8 regions that according to our analysis would gain the most from an increase of SCF business support are not necessarily those with higher GDP per capita or with higher growth performance at the aggregate level. For instance, within the Czech Republic it seems that the regions that would gain the most from business support are both those with initially lower GDP per capita and lower growth performance. This might suggest a higher sensitivity of the lagging-behind regions to an increase in the SCF business support to GDP ratio. However, for instance in Poland, the most growing and richest regions have a higher sensitivity to an increase in SCF business support.

All in all, a uniform increase of business support as a share of GDP in all the NMS-8 regions would not support the convergence process at the regional level, but it would have country-specific paths of contribution to economic performance.

5. CONCLUSION

This chapter extended a recent work by Florio and Moretti (2009), who show that business support financed through SCF has a greater and positive impact on the economic performance of smaller-sized and higher-growth-opportunities industries. We use the model specification of their work and re-estimate the coefficients on a sample of German, Italian and Spanish regions. Finally, assuming that the relationship holds in NMS-8, we run a sensitivity analysis by increasing the SCF business support to GDP ratio to show the regions, industries and countries that, given their manufacturing sector structure, would gain the most from this type of investment.

The results indicate that the regions that have a higher sensitivity to a uniform increase in SCF business support to GDP are located in the Czech Republic (Central regions), Western and Southern Poland, along the Czech–Polish–Slovak border, Estonia and Slovenia. Those regions have an industrial composition of the manufacturing sectors that allows the exploitation of the greater advantages from higher capital grants. Thus averaging the effects at country-industry level, not surprisingly, we find that within the eight countries analysed similar industries are the most responsive to SCF business support.

Clearly, this chapter does not aim to provide conclusive estimations of the impact of SCF business support in NMS, but simply shows the different sensitivity of industries and regional economies to an increase in SCF capital grants, which is likely to take place in NMS-8 from the next programming periods. We show that regardless of the aim of this type of public investment (that is, contributing to economic cohesion through support to lagging-behind regions or stimulating the growth of economies already in a higher growth path), industry-specific effects should be taken into account seriously and should be followed by differential increases in SCF capital grants as a share of GDP between regions.

NOTES

* The views expressed in this chapter are exclusively the author's. The usual disclaimer applies. luigi.moretti@unifi.it.

1. See, for example, Funk and Pizzati (2003) for a collection of contributions about SCFs effectiveness.
2. See Beutel (1995) for a description and application of an input–output model for SCFs impact evaluation. See also Treyz and Treyz (2003) for an application of the REMI policy evaluation model and a review of macroeconometric models used for the SCF' impact evaluation.
3. See Florio and Moretti (2009) for descriptive statistics of their dataset (a sample of 14 manufacturing industries for 70 regions belonging to Germany, Italy and Spain) and discussion on their model specification. From their original dataset we drop data for manufacturing of leather and leather products, and manufacturing of coke, refined petroleum products and nuclear fuel, due to the high number of missing data for those two industries in NMS-8 regions. This is to avoid potential problems when we run sensitivity analysis on the sample of NMS-8 regions. We are confident that this choice does not change the simulation results much as these two industries represent very small shares of manufacturing in most of the NMS-8 regions. For the rest of the missing values in different industries and regions we used the number of persons employed for 2005 (only for the food industry in Lithuania we use data for 2004).
4. Florio and Moretti (2009) use a dummy variable (rather than a continuous variable) to avoid potential measurement errors that might derive from the computation process and data cleaning described above. They are confident of the industry ranking of this indicator, thus a dummy variable may be appropriate. See Florio and Moretti (2009) for details about the Bureau van Dijk's Amadeus firm-level dataset used to construct this indicator.
5. Regression statistics: R^2 = 0.45, Obs. = 761. All independent variables have been

rescaled around their mean values to reduce multicollinearity problems. See Florio and Moretti (2009) for robustness checks and a discussion on endogeneity issues.
6. This term is not significant in Florio and Moretti (2009) either.
7. See Table 8.2 for summary statistics by industry for the sample of NMS regions.

REFERENCES

Becker, Sascha O., P. Egger, M. Von Ehrlich and R. Fenge (2008), 'Going NUTS: the effect of EU Structural Funds on regional performance', Center for Economic Studies and ifo working paper series 2495.

Beugelsdijk, M. and S.C.W. Eijffinger (2005), 'The effectiveness of Structural Policy in the European Union: an empirical analysis for the EU-15 in 1995–2001', *Journal of Common Market Studies*, **43** (1), 37–51.

Beutel, Jan (1995), 'The economic impacts of the Community Support Frameworks for the Objective 1 regions 1994–99. Methodology of the dynamic input–output model', report to the European Commission.

Boldrin, M. and F. Canova (2001), 'Inequality and convergence in Europe's regions: reconsidering European regional policies', *Economic Policy*, **16** (32), 205–253.

Cappelen, A., F. Castellacci, J. Fagerberger and B. Verspagen (2003), 'The impact of EU regional support on growth and convergence in the European Union', *Journal of Common Market Studies*, **41** (9), 621–44.

Dall'Erba, S. and J. Le Gallo (2008), 'Regional convergence and the impact of European Structural Funds over 1989–1999: a spatial econometric analysis', *Papers in Regional Science*, **87** (2), 219–44.

Ederveen, S. and J. Gorter (2002), 'Does European Cohesion Policy reduce regional disparities?', CPB discussion paper 15.

Ederveen, S., H.L.F. de Groot and R. Nahuis (2006), 'Fertile soil for Structural Funds? A panel data analysis of the conditional effectiveness of European Cohesion Policy', *Kyklos*, **59** (1), 17–42.

Fiaschi, D., A.M. Lavezzi and A. Parenti (2009), 'Productivity dynamics across European regions: the impact of Structural and Cohesion Funds', University of Pisa Dipartimento di Scienze Economiche (DSE) discussion papers 2009/84.

Fisman, R. and I. Love (2004), 'Financial development and intersectoral allocation: a new approach', *Journal of Finance*, **59** (6), 2785–807.

Florio, M. and L. Moretti (2009), 'The effect of business support on employment in manufacturing: evidence from the EU Structural Funds in Germany, Italy, and Spain', University of Milan Department of Economics, Business and Statistics departmental working papers 2009-33.

Funk, Bernard and Lodovico Pizzati (eds) (2003), *European Integration, Regional Policy and Growth*, Washington, DC: The World Bank Publications.

Garcia-Solanes, J. and R. Maria-Dolores (2002), 'The impact of European Structural Funds on economic convergence in European countries and regions', in W. Meeusen and J. Villaverde (eds), *Convergence Issues in the European Union*, Cheltenham, UK and Northampton, MA, USA: Edward Elgar Publishing, pp. 334–58.

Puigcerver-Peñalver, Mari C. (2007), 'The impact of Structural Funds Policy on

European regions' growth: a theoretical and empirical approach', *European Journal of Comparative Economics*, **4** (2), 179–208.
Treyz, F. and G. Treyz (2003), 'Evaluating the regional economic effects of Structural Funds programs using the REMI Policy Insight Model', paper presented at the Fifth European Conference on Evaluation of the Structural Funds, Challenges for Evaluation in an Enlarged Europe, Budapest, June 2003.

9. Infrastructure investment opportunities in the EU New Member States: the role of regional policies

Emanuela Sirtori and Silvia Vignetti

1. INTRODUCTION

Infrastructure development is a priority on policy agendas in the EU and worldwide. Governments at different levels (supra-national, national, regional and local) invest a large share of their funds for infrastructure projects in transportation, energy production, telecommunications, water and sanitation. It is estimated that half of public investment in the EU member states is for infrastructure, the largest proportion being in the Cohesion Countries and New Member States (NMS).[1]

Investment needs in basic infrastructures are still very high, especially in lagging-behind regions and countries. A recent OECD study estimates that, in order to cope with infrastructure investment needs to 2030, annual investments in transport, energy, water and telecommunications should be roughly equal to 2.5 per cent of world GDP (OECD, 2007).

Traditionally, different endowments in basic infrastructures (as well as other ingredients such as factors of production, natural resources and technology) between regions or countries have been seen as the cause of disparities in economic performance. Justification of public funding for infrastructure stems from the expectation that they foster economic growth by enhancing factor productivity, and promote convergence in income distribution and living standards.

Literature shows that although this holds true at an aggregate level (at the country level and with an aggregate measure of infrastructural endowment, see for example Aschauer, 1989; Barro, 1990, and other papers cited by Del Bo in a earlier chapter), if the regional dimension, typologies of infrastructures and conditions or nature of investments are considered, a different picture emerges. Evidence is not conclusive on this point, also due to the lack of homogeneous data at the regional (NUTS2[2]) and sectoral/industry level. In terms of data availability, the most comprehensive picture can be gathered for transport. In this field, many studies show for example that different effects in terms of regional growth are recorded if core/peripheral or urban/rural typology of regions are encountered.

This chapter contributes to this debate by providing a descriptive analysis of the infrastructure gaps in the NMS at the national and (as far as possible) regional level for some infrastructure sectors (transport, telecommunications, environment and energy) and discussing policy challenges in the light of the potential offered by the Structural Funds. The analysis shows that wide gaps do exist between the EU Member States and that regional gaps in the NMS are not wider than those in some EU15 countries; in other words, the greatest divergence can be detected not in the extent of regional gaps, but in the national averages, with the first being significantly lower than the latter.

The chapter is organized as follows: in the second section a literature review on the conceptual models related to infrastructure and growth, the regional disparities in the EU and the Cohesion Policy actions and funding of infrastructure at the national and regional level are presented. In section 3 the current infrastructural endowments in the NMS are discussed and, as far as possible, broken down at the regional level, in transport, telecommunications, environment and energy. Conclusions are drawn in the fourth and final section.

2. INFRASTRUCTURE AND REGIONAL DISPARITIES IN THE EU

2.1 Theoretical background

A vast literature shows that, at an aggregate level, infrastructures are a key driver of economic growth.[3] In theoretical growth models infrastructural endowments are a growth factor of the aggregate stock of capital (either private or public) in the aggregate production function.[4] Different channels of influence, either direct or indirect, link infrastructure endowment to economic growth, mainly through productivity effects on the other factors (more efficient transportation services enable entrepreneurs to cut production costs, access to broadband connections improve the performance of human capital and so on).

However, evidence is often mixed in terms of magnitude and direction of effects. Infrastructures have different natures, features and operate in different market conditions.[5] The quality and maintenance of infrastructural investment, the way infrastructures are managed and priced, or the level of maintenance cost over capital expenditure are also relevant aspects influencing the final effects on growth.

Andraz and Pereira (2007) suggest that, even if infrastructures financed by public investments are public goods which become available simultaneously to all industries, their marginal effect is different for each industry. They estimate that, at the aggregate level, public investments that occurred in Portugal between 1976 and 1998 positively affected output and employment and crowded in private investment. However, through separate models the authors find out that some industries actually benefited the most from public investments. These were Construction, Transportation and Finance, both in absolute terms and relative to their size.

The complexity of the relationship between infrastructure and economic development is confirmed also if considering the impact of the trans-European transport network (TEN-T). An analysis carried out by TRT (2006) highlights that the local impacts of the TENs network are highly differentiated across regions and measures the effects in terms of cohesion (GDP growth and employment) in the short (2005–2015), medium (2005–2030) and long period (2005–2050). While the most developed European Central countries (France, Germany and the Benelux) benefit immediately from the TENs, effects are uncertain for the peripheral and less developed areas: they are expected to be positive by 2030 for Greece, Ireland and Eastern Europe countries and no real advantages are estimated in the short or longer terms for Finland, Sweden and Italy.

Location theory and new economic geography place an emphasis on the divergence forces of agglomeration effects and spatially unequal distribution of resources. According to this approach, regional features do matter in shaping the effects of infrastructures, which may even be detrimental for poor or peripheral regions, as TRT and other contributions on transport and telecommunication projects suggest (De Rus et al., 1995; Martin, 1997). The argument is that basic transport infrastructure not only increases the accessibility of core regions from peripheral ones (better access to input factors for firms from peripheral regions for example) but the opposite also occurs, with negative effects on peripheral regions being exposed to higher competition (firms from core regions can now supply peripheral entrepreneurs with local supply being crowded out).

Again, the results of a simulation model by Spieckermann and Wegener (2006) applied to South East Europe confirms the need for a spatially-differentiated transport policy which adopts a differentiated development model according to the phase of development of each country and region. Such a strategy would imply strengthening existing or emerging polycentric structures (disregarding the economically most successful large agglomerations), in the already highly-developed and urbanized EU15, through the improvement of accessibility of medium-level central places and compensating for the accessibility deficits of rural and peripheral regions. However, in the still-urbanizing EU12, accession countries and Western Balkans, it may be justified, over a transition period of 10–15 years, to enhance the growth dynamics of these countries via fast and efficient transport connections between their capital cities and the major agglomerations and economic centres in Western Europe.[6] Similar results (but for high/low-density regions) are found also by Rothengatter and Schaffer (2004), who consider also the quality of the transport system.

The link between infrastructure and growth performance at the regional level is particularly relevant in the framework of the EU cohesion policy, whose aim is to reduce regional disparities by promoting convergence mainly in terms of regional per capita GDP (the distance of regional GDP from the EU average being the basis for eligibility to different priorities of Structural Funds). However, evidence on the effectiveness of Structural Funds support to infrastructure for promoting regional growth is still debated. Despite several empirical works confirming a positive link between infrastructure and regional growth (see, among others, Biehl, 1986; Rapún et al., 2000; Basile et al., 2001) some others are rather critical on the potential of Structural Funds in reducing disparities in regional income levels in the long run (see Boldrin and Canova, 2003; Puga, 2002). These contributions focus mainly on regional disparities in the EU27 and how to reconsider regional policies in the light of agglomeration forces affecting the uneven distribution of growth effects.

2.2 Regional Disparities in the NMS

The accession of Estonia, Latvia, Lithuania, Poland, the Czech and Slovak Republics, Hungary and Slovenia in 2004, and Romania and Bulgaria in 2007, former transition economy countries, inevitably increased the differences inside the European Union, under a cultural, social, political and economic point of view. These countries are characterized by a higher rate of inflation, and lower levels of GDP per capita. As a consequence, the whole Union's average of GDP per capita fell by around 7 per cent in 2004 and by 10 per cent in 2007, compared to the average of the EU15 in the same year (Eurostat data). Between 2005 and 2008, among the NMS, Slovenia had the highest average of per capita GDP, corresponding to 88.86 per cent of the EU27 average, but still below the average of the Old Member States (124.22 per cent of the EU27 average). The most recent members, Romania and Bulgaria, have the lowest value: respectively 40.4 per cent and 37.13 per cent of the EU27 average.

The NMS have a potential growth that is estimated at around 4 per cent per year for the next decade. Real GDP growth between 2005 and 2008 shows clearly that the NMS contribute at raising the EU average, that is around 3.8 per cent. The highest value is registered in Slovakia, with an average growth close to 8 per cent. Only Hungary, after a period of growth at 4 per cent, in 2007 and 2008 experienced a rate lower than 1 per cent, reducing its average and placing it close to the level of the Old Member States (2.46 per cent).

These high growth rates suggest that a catching-up process is underway. However, at the regional level the picture can be quite different, since some regions grow faster than others. In particular, some regions of Bulgaria, Hungary, Poland and the Slovak Republic in the period 2003–2005 have grown much more slowly than the others and they are placed below the total European average. The growth rate in these countries is driven by some specific fast-growing regions, with others lagging behind. In all cases, the capital city is located in regions with the highest growth, while the most peripheral areas are the least developed ones.

An analysis of the variance (ANOVA[7]) inside each European country shows the highest variability of the GDP growth between 2003 and 2005 in Bulgaria (6.4 per cent), Slovakia (3.7 per cent), Hungary (2.4 per cent) and Romania (2.3 per cent); Poland and the Czech Republic have a reduced internal growth variability, that is similar to the Old Member States' (OMS) regions (below 1.5 per cent). The comparison of the whole group of the NMS to the OMS highlights that the GDP growth variance of the first is higher (respectively 3.17 per cent and 1.27 per cent). The F-test rejects the hypothesis that the groups' (countries') averages are the same, which means there is a significant[8] difference among the countries' average GDP growth: actually, for example, the gap between the Italian and the Slovak growth rate is higher than 7 percentage points.

Also considering the GDP per capita distribution, regional gaps can be detected, with the NMS being below the European average of EUR 20 670.37 per capita (PPS), with few but predictable exceptions: in the Czech Republic, Hungary and the Slovak Republic the regions corresponding to the areas where the capital cities of Prague, Budapest and Bratislava are placed stand out from the others. This confirms that in the New EU Member States, the level of development and wealth is widely differentiated among the regions: in Bulgaria, for example, some regions grow very fast, at more than 7 per cent, dragging the national growth and contributing to raising the total European average, while others are almost stagnant. It is worth pointing out that higher national averages of per capita GDP correspond to higher regional gaps within the country: Bulgarian regions have the lowest per capita GDP and there is no significant difference among them, while the Czech Republic, that has higher per capita GDP, also has the deepest regional gaps.

The ANOVA confirms that among the NMS, Slovakia and the Czech Republic have the greatest regional variability in terms of GDP per capita PPS, followed by Hungary. However the variance in the OMS group is bigger than in the NMS. Per capita GDP in Bulgaria and Poland, that is among the lowest in the whole of Europe, is less differentiated among their regions. As with the GDP growth, the F-test rejects the hypothesis of significant similarities among the groups (countries).

What emerges from this simple analysis is that development gaps in Europe are present both at the national, between the OMS and the NMS, and at the regional levels, between each country's regions: the GDP growth is more variable in the group of the NMS, while per capita GDP variability is higher in the Old EU countries. However, even if in some cases the regional divergences are big, the distances at country level are even bigger, both for GDP growth and per capita GDP.

2.3 Infrastructure and EU Cohesion Policy

The structural Funds budget for the period 2007–2013 is around EUR 350 billion; it accounts for more than one-third of the total EU budget and it is its fastest-growing component. EUR 70 billion are addressed to the Cohesion Fund, which supports transport and environment projects (including energy) in countries with a per capita GDP below 90 per cent of the EU average. While the Cohesion Fund is planned and managed at the national level, the other financial instruments (European Regional Development Fund, ERDF and European Social Fund, ESF) are regional tools.[9]

Notwithstanding the emphasis placed by the Lisbon strategy on the so-called soft measures, such as support to R&D activities, innovation, technology transfer and entrepreneurship, filling in the infrastructure gaps is still considered a top priority, especially for lagging-behind regions, NMS and accessing countries. As put forward in the EC new growth and jobs agenda 'growth and jobs are determined by framework conditions such as the endowment of infrastructure of various kinds – physical, in the form of transport and telecommunication networks, human, in the form of the skills and know-how of the work force, and social, in the form of care and other support services' (European Commission, 2007, p. 60).

A large share of the Cohesion Policy budget is spent on infrastructure, especially transport (road, rail, waterway, airport, port and urban transport) and environment (energy, water, sewage and waste treatment). Less significant in financial terms at an aggregate level, but still noteworthy in some regions, are telecommunications (telephone, broadband networks,

ICT) and social infrastructure (health and education). Major efforts in infrastructure development are concentrated in the NMS. In the period 2007–2013 half of the total Structural Funds were directed towards the NMS, which dedicate 60 per cent of total expenditure to infrastructure programmes. In the previous programming period (2000–2006), a much lower amount of Structural Funds was assigned to these countries since they joined the EU only in 2004.[10] Nevertheless, the share going to infrastructure is higher than what the other members received (37 per cent versus 26 per cent) (DG Regio data). These data confirm the EU commitment to promoting development and growth, especially in the lagging-behind countries, in order to achieve economic, social and territorial cohesion. Poland is the country that receives the largest amount of Structural Funds, being programmed to receive over EUR 65 billion in 2007–2013, 61 per cent of which is directed to the infrastructure sectors. The prevalence of infrastructure investment on other sectors is peculiar to the NMS.[11] Apart from Poland, also Bulgaria, Estonia, Hungary, Latvia, Malta, Romania and Slovakia address more than 60 per cent of their total Structural Funds to infrastructure. Among the Old Member States, Spain, Italy, Germany and Greece receive the largest amount of funds (more than EUR 20 billion), but only Greece dedicates more than 60 per cent of EU funds to the infrastructure sector (the other shares are respectively 47 per cent, 38 per cent and 23 per cent).

In the period 2000–2006, the share of Structural Funds allocated to the NMS was only 37 per cent. However, if we also consider the Cohesion Funds, the total funds exceed EUR 48 355 million, of which 78 per cent is dedicated to infrastructures.

3. INFRASTRUCTURAL ENDOWMENT IN THE NEW EU MEMBER STATES

The present section describes the European infrastructural gaps at country and, whenever the data are available, to regional level. This kind of gap, even if not completely, contributes to explaining the differences in per capita GDP. The analysis will focus on infrastructure capacity in three sectors: transport, telecommunications and environment (environment protection and energy). The descriptive analysis of the transport, telecommunications and environment infrastructure endowment has two objectives:

1. illustrating the existing investment needs and the actual allocation of EU funds in the most important infrastructure sectors;

2. carrying out an illustrative analysis on the infrastructure endowment, comparing the extent of cross-country divergences with the regional gaps in the NMS and in the OMS.

3.1 Transport

Transport infrastructures have always been one of the biggest components of government investment in Europe. In the period 2000–2006, more than EUR 47 billion were committed by the European Commission only for transport infrastructures through the European Regional Development Fund (ERDF) and the Cohesion Fund (CF), from a total of EUR 157 billion (DG Regio data). In the current period the amount has risen significantly: the programmed investments of Structural Funds between 2007 and 2013 amount to more than EUR 75 billion for transport, 50 billion of which (67 per cent) is directed to the NMS. In all the New Members, transport is the field that receives the highest share of funds from the total of infrastructures, ranging from 56 per cent in Poland to 42 per cent in Latvia; the only exceptions are Estonia and Hungary, where transport infrastructures occupy the second places (after the environmental sector), but still with a high share: respectively 40 per cent and 36 per cent of total infrastructural SF funds.

The Commission recognizes the need to optimize the transport system in order to meet the demands of enlargement and suitable development, from an economic, social and also environmental point of view. In 2001, the European Commission set clear policy guidelines to govern transport infrastructure investment up till 2010 (EC, 2001), which include:

- improving quality and safety of all the transport modes;
- paying attention to environmental protection, reducing noise and pollution;
- promoting inter-modality;
- building the trans-European transport network and improving access to outlying areas.

After the accession to the EU and the elimination of borders, in the Eastern European Countries new traffic patterns and national priorities appeared. There is a considerable need for transport investment in the New EU Members, in terms of rehabilitation of the existing network, upgrading or new construction. The infrastructures are generally in bad conditions, due to both lack of periodic maintenance and also the absence of renewal and replacement of assets reaching the end of their economic life.

ESPON (2005), in its evaluation study on European transport services and network, calculates the multimodal potential accessibility indicator for all the regions of the European Union. This indicator is a measure of transport infrastructure endowment and it takes into account roads, railways, ports and airports infrastructures. The results show that in 2001 regions with clearly above EU average accessibility were mainly located along the so-called Blue Banana.[12] There are also highly accessible regions in other countries, such as Madrid, Barcelona, Glasgow, Copenhagen, Oslo, Rome and Naples. Their accessibility is ensured above all by airport connections. In the OMS many regions with a very low accessibility level, with no good access to an international flight service, are also present. As far as the NMS are concerned, nearly all regions have below average accessibility, with the exception of the capital cities' regions. Again, international airports seem to play an important role in multimodal accessibility in Europe, especially for the regions with the capital or other main cities.

Analysis of the 2007–2013 allocation of Structural Funds in the transport sector highlights that priority in the transport sector has been given to promote the trans-European transport (railways and motorways) network, while in the NMS the Commission also funds national, regional and local roads.

Yet, the full exploitation of the benefits coming from trans-national corridors and the internal transport network may be prevented by the existence of regional infrastructure gaps inside each country and urbanization differences.

3.1.1 Motorways and roads

Jevčák and Keereman (2008) report that in the NMS there are on average around 30 per cent fewer roads per square kilometre than in the OMS. Motorways represent only 1 per cent of total road infrastructures, half the share of the rest of Europe.

The motorway network is generally more developed in the OMS. The lengths of motorway related to the total surface of the country reaches its highest value in Benelux and Germany. All the NMS have fewer kilometres of motorways respective to their area. Poland and Romania, which have the largest territory among the NMS, are placed at the bottom of the ranking, and also smaller countries like the Czech Republic and Slovakia have relative few motorways. Slovenia is the only exception, being placed above both the European and the EU15 average, mainly because of its peculiar geographical position: situated at the border of Italy, Austria, Hungary and Croatia, Slovenia is the natural 'bridge' between Western and Central Europe and the Balkans; hence, a good motorway network is required to transport people and freight throughout the continent. In addition, its small size contributes to raising the density indicator.

Apart from geographical reasons, in general it can be pointed out that while in the OMS almost every city is connected by motorways, in the NMS motorways link a limited number of centres, usually those where productive activities are concentrated. In Poland this is particularly clear: three separate high-speed roads serve the cities of Cracow and Legnica in the South, Poznan and Lodz in the Centre, and Grudziadz and the principal port of Danzig in the North.

The same can be referred from the other NMS: during the pre-accession period, the length of motorways increased but they were concentrated in a few areas, either around capital cities or in transit routes to the west. In the Czech Republic there is a road concentration around Prague and in Jihovychod in the South, at the border of Austria and Slovakia. In Romania, virtually all the motorways are in the surroundings of Bucharest.

The infrastructure endowment of primary and secondary roads is more homogeneous. Apart from Malta, Belgium and the Netherlands, where the road density is very high (respectively 9.8, 4.7 and 3.2 km/km^2) mainly for geographical reasons (small dimensions and central location in the Union), most of the NMS have a road network as dense as the other European members, with an approximate average of 1.5 km/km^2). There is not a clear distinction between the Old and the NMS, indicating that the European road transport gap is mainly a motorway matter, at least under the density perspective. If we consider the quality of roads, in the NMS these are generally poor, suffering a lack of maintenance over many years (EC, 2004; European Investment Bank, 2000). Most of the investment activity in Bulgaria and Romania, for instance, took place in the 1970s and 1980s and backlog of maintenance is particularly acute in certain case.

To sum: even if some countries seem to have made some efforts to increase their road and motorway networks (namely Hungary and the Czech Republic), taking advantage of the Structural Funds, on the whole the quantity and quality of the road infrastructure in NMS is still below the standards of the rest of the EU.

A regional analysis of the NMS at the NUTS2 level and the ANOVA show the existence of the widest transport infrastructure gaps in the Czech Republic, Hungary, Romania and Slovakia. The case of Slovakia is particularly visible and pronounced: the region of Bratislava has got the highest density of motorways in the NMS (0.05 km/km^2) but it is also largely above the EU15 and EU27 averages (around 0.02 km /km^2). However, the Slovakian variance is exceeded by Germany, the United Kingdom, the Netherlands, Austria, Portugal and Spain. The variance in the group of the 15 OMS is much higher than in the NMS group. This suggests that, even if in the NMS regional gaps do exist in the density of road transport, these gaps are not in general deeper than those in the OMS.

The density distribution of other roads is more homogeneous in the NMS regions, like at the national level. They are all below the EU15 and EU27 average (around 1.5 km/km^2) with few cases of outsiders: the region of Slaskie in Poland, near Cracow, has 2 km/km^2 of roads, and the region of Bucharest in Romania has the national highest density not only in motorways but also in other roads, with 5.60 km/km^2 of roads. Among the New members, Romania has the highest variance, but this value is lower than the variability in Austria and in the United Kingdom: in particular, the United Kingdom's density of roads has a variance that is more than double that of Romania. Again, the variability in the group of the NMS is lower than in the OMS. The F-test rejects the hypothesis that the national average density of motorways and roads are similar.

To sum up, the data show generally underdeveloped motorway and road networks in the New EU Member States with respect to the Union average and a strong relation between the density of transport infrastructure in physical terms, especially motorways, and the economic importance of a region within a single country.

Since it could be expected that the infrastructural endowment depends not only on the territorial dimension but also on the degree of urbanization,[13] the ANOVA has been repeated after comparing the transport endowment to the regional population size and the main results do not change: as expected, motorways and other roads are more concentrated in the urbanized regions of all the European countries.

3.1.2 Railways

Railways are a significant mode of transport in the South-Eastern European countries. They provide key connections to neighbouring countries, particularly towards the West of Europe. Rail density, related to the country area, is generally high, as compared to the EU15 and EU27 average and, unlike road transport, no clear gap between Western and Eastern Europe can be highlighted. While Estonia has got a low railway density, the Czech Republic occupies the highest ranking, even above Belgium and Germany. Hungary, Slovakia, Poland and Slovenia are above the European average, too. However, the overall standard of the rail network in the New Member Countries is poor and reflects decades of low investments (European Investment Bank, 2000; ECORYS, 2005). The proportion of electrified railway lines and double-track lines is below the EU27 average (42 per cent for the three Baltic countries, the Czech Republic, Hungary and Romania; Slovenia and Slovakia are close to the EU27 average, while Poland and Bulgaria are even above the EU15 average of 53 per cent, with respectively 59 per cent and 68 per cent of electrified rail lines of the total. The highest values correspond to countries where, in the last years, recent investments in the railways sector have been taking place.

The European Commission is supporting investment in order to improve the railway quality and to promote the creation of an intermodal transport network, since improvements in the road network, which are undoubtedly required, will tend to further encourage the use of the car, leading to increased congestion and environmental pollution.

From the ANOVA for the rail sector a lesser degree of dispersion emerges with respect to the motorways and other roads. In Bulgaria, Hungary and Slovakia no internal gaps in the density of railway lines are shown. In Poland, Romania and the Czech Republic, the regions of Slaskie, Bucharest and, above all, Prague have a greater density of train lines; higher than not only the other NMS but also the whole of Europe. The concentration of transport is higher in correspondence with the national productive centres: the urbanization indicator is positively linked to the density of railways in Europe and especially in the NMS. In general, there is a significant difference among the national density of railways (confirmed by the F-test), with variability in the NMS group higher than in the rest of Europe.

To summarize, from the description of the investment needs in the transport sector, it emerges that:

1. the New European Member States have motorway and road network densities lower than the rest of Europe, while their rail networks are relatively more developed;
2. inside the NMS there are regional differences in the density of motorway and railway infrastructures, which mainly reflect the level of urbanization and productivity of a region, while the other kinds of roads are more homogeneously spread over the national territory;
3. the inter-regional transport gaps within the NMS are not systematically higher than those in the OMS.

3.2 Telecommunications

Investment in telecommunications services in Southeastern Europe are needed both to extend the service towards universality and also to modernize and upgrade the quality of existing services.

The ICT sector not only is the second largest economic sector and a major generator of new jobs and business worldwide, but it also forms the basis of the emerging global 'knowledge economy', seen as the main driver of economic growth in the twenty-first century. The modern infrastructures can generate new business opportunities in local environments, can increase the competitive abilities of existing lines of business and create new lines and better-paid jobs and can have a positive effect on the local community's awareness of development and business opportunities. At least in principle, improving the level of telecommunication infrastructures can be a determinant factor in reducing the gap between the developed and less-developed areas in each country. Rural, peripheral and outermost regions can exploit the opportunities that ICT offers to reduce the problems of remoteness from which they suffer.

Technological innovations, especially wireless telecommunications and the Internet web base, supported by policy reform, are rapidly making ICT affordable and accessible to all nations and regions. The European Union assists the NMS in developing and using the telecommunication and information technology sector (Skoric, 2006) by:

- building ICT infrastructures (telephone and broadband networks) and expanding ICT access for under-served populations,
- promoting legal, policy and regulatory reform to foster liberalization of telecommunications,
- promoting competition and private investment,
- supporting the ICT services and applications for citizens and businesses, especially small and medium enterprises (SMEs).

Moreover, in the Czech Republic (the only one among the NMS) the Structural Funds are also directed towards the promotion of the trans-European information and communication technologies.

The analysis of the allocation of Structural Funds for the 2007–2013 programming periods shows that Slovakia and Poland are the New Member Countries addressing the highest percentage (15 per cent and 9 per cent) of Structural Funds to the information society sector, corresponding to about EUR 11 million and EUR 37 million.

However, as in the transport sector, in ICT a number of evident regional disparities can also be listed in terms of communication infrastructures, affordability of access to networks, quality of ICT services and Internet usage (EC, 2004). These disparities can be specified at three levels: between West and East Europe, with the NMS having a generally lower rate of penetration of new technologies; between the NMS, where the ICT development levels are different, with Romania far below the average; and within single countries, between urbanized and peripheral areas.

Telecommunication services and accessibility to the ICT network can be measured by the number of main telephone lines and the number of mobile subscriptions in relation to the population size. In the NMS, the number of fixed lines is below the EU27 average of 39 per cent and the EU15 average of 46 per cent, varying from 19 per cent in Romania to 35 per cent in Estonia. Bulgaria, which joined the Union in the same year as Romania, has a better telephone access, around 31 per cent. These values, which are relative to 2006, have risen significantly since the 1990s and it is reasonable to think that this growing trend is coming to an end, as the mobile lines develop (Dvornik and Sobolic, 2007).

Indeed, in 2006 the number of subscriptions to cellular mobile services as a percentage of population does not show evidence of any marked discrepancy in Europe. Estonia, the Czech Republic and Lithuania have a higher share of mobile subscriptions than the EU15 and EU27 averages (both around 107 per cent), respectively of 110 per cent, 124 per cent and 139 per cent. Bulgaria is at the EU27 average while the other NMS have a lower share of mobile subscriptions, but still at high levels (more than eight people from ten), similar to some of the most developed countries, such as France, Belgium and Germany. The extensive use of mobile telephones in some degree offsets the use of fixed lines.

In Slovenia, Estonia and Slovakia, 60 per cent of households with members aged 16–74 years have Internet access, between EU15 (66 per cent) and EU27 (58 per cent) averages. The remaining NMS are still lagging behind, with a share between 45 and 50 per cent; the percentage is much lower in Romania and Bulgaria (less than 30 per cent). These generally low proportions in part reflect the technical difficulty of gaining access to the Internet in these countries. The extent of the increase, however, may well depend on both the spread of broadband and the services available on the Internet. Although the proportion of households with access to the Internet may not have a direct impact on economic performance, indirectly it tends to reflect the technical abilities of people and their receptiveness to the new technology, both of which can be important in economic development (EC, 2004).

The number of enterprises having access to the Internet, instead, can be considered more directly related to economic performance, since the Internet allows undoubted advantages, like the reduction of communication costs and opportunities deriving from e-commerce. Ninety-six per cent of Slovenian enterprises have access to the Internet, a value that is among the highest in Europe and above the EU15 and EU27 average (91 per cent and 88 per cent in 2008); since 2004, Romania, Bulgaria, Hungary and Latvia have significantly increased the share of enterprises using the Internet, but they are still placed below the average, between 67 per cent and 92 per cent. Slovakia experienced the fastest growth (35 per cent), moving from the bottom to the top of the European ranking in only four years.

Eurostat offers few telecommunication indicators at the regional level: since these are indicators of accessibility, they only indirectly refer to telecommunication infrastructures.

The analysis of the variance shows that the highest variability in accessibility in Europe is in Romania (63.9 per cent), while the lowest one is in Slovakia (4.7 per cent): this is determined not only by the scarce number of regions into which it is divided, but also by recent investments to enlarge the Internet access over the territory. The variable in the other NMS has a high variance too (27.8 per cent in Bulgaria, 36.7 per cent in Hungary and 46 per cent in the Czech Republic[14]), similar to the one in some OMS, like the United Kingdom (58.3 per cent), Spain (41.8 per cent), Italy (33.1 per cent) and Portugal (31 per cent). There are significant cross-country differences among the percentage numbers of households with Internet access. However, within each group (NMS and OMS) the variance is similar.

Eurostat (2009), in addition to the North–South and latitudinal patterns of Internet access, highlights the existence of a third pattern at the regional level: households in urban regions tend to have higher Internet access rates than households living in rural regions. At the EU27 level, 65 per cent of households in densely populated areas have access to the Internet, against only 51 per cent of households in thinly populated regions. This is confirmed by the analysis of indicators: the regions of Prague (Czech Republic), Bucharest (Romania), Budapest (Hungary) and Bratislava (Slovakia) are above their national average, and for the two former regions the gap is significant.

3.3 Environment

The Lisbon Strategy emphasizes the importance of achieving sustainable development as a factor to make Europe the most dynamic and competitive knowledge-based economy in the world, with more and better jobs, greater social cohesion and respect for the environment. Infrastructures that help environmental improvement and protection are unanimously considered by the European countries as an important element in regional development for several reasons (EC, 2004). In the NMS, the environment protection sector[15] usually receives the second largest amount of funding by the European Commission, behind the transport sector. The only two exceptions are Estonia and Hungary, whose share of Structural Funds for environment protection (on the total of infrastructure investments) are respectively 36 per cent and 40 per cent, more than for transport (32 per cent and 36 per cent).

The broad objectives of the Member States' Environmental Strategy or Investment Plans include: ensuring the quality and quantity of the drinking water, reducing the creation of waste, and lowering industrial and private emissions of pollution to water, land and air. The Drinking Water Directive (98/83/EC), the Urban Waste Water Treatment Directive (91/271/EEC), the Landfill Directive (99/31/EC) and the Directive on Electricity Production from Renewable Energy Sources (2001/77EC) drive the investments related to water supply, waste water treatment, municipal solid waste management and renewable energy sources. Actually, these are the subsectors to which the 2007–2013 allocation of Structural Funds gives priority both in the Old and in the New Member States

The European Commission (EC, 2004) reports that water is scarce and in a number of regions the amount of clear water abstracted annually is at or above critical levels, so threatening local eco-systems, agriculture, electricity generation and tourism. Progress has been made in respect of water supply. In 2007, Hungary and Bulgaria abstracted around 800 m^3 of fresh surface and ground water per capita, like Italy and Spain. The Czech Republic and Romania abstracted lower amounts (respectively 190 and 275 m^3 per capita), but the big challenge is Poland, where, even though the water demand is expected to increase, its supply is only around 300 m^3 per capita, below the EU27 average, approximately 550 m^3/year/per capita (Eurostat data). In Romania only 49 per cent of the total population is connected to the public water supply, in Lithuania and Estonia the share is 76 per cent,[16] in Poland and Slovakia it amounts to 86 per cent; only Bulgaria, the Czech Republic and Hungary have more than 90 per cent of the population connected to the public water supply.

As for the infrastructures in the water sector, most of the projects related to wastewater treatment are driven by the need to comply with the EU Directives. The Urban Waste Water Treatment Directive requires investments to create new sewage treatment plants and to upgrade the quality of the existing ones. The implementation of such projects will contribute to the reduction of surface water pollution from municipal wastewater, to the extension of wastewater services in urban and rural areas, and to the construction, renovation and upgrading of wastewater plants, pumping stations and sewerage networks. In countries where the production intensity has fallen and the treatment efficiency increased, such as Poland, Latvia and Estonia, a decline in the volume of wastewater requiring treatment can be expected. In the other NMS, like Slovakia, obsolete public utility networks and facilities will need to be replaced or upgraded to comply with the EU performance criteria.

The investments related to Municipal Solid Waste cover initiatives for the expansion and building of waste collection and sorting facilities, composting sites, incineration plants and for the upgrading of the existing landfills. The Landfill Directive, but also the directives[17] on packaging waste, end-of-life vehicles, incineration of hazardous waste, waste electrical and electronic equipment set objectives and benchmarks.

Among the NMS, Estonia has the highest level of municipal waste collected (536 kg per capita); in line with the EU27 average (524 kg per capita). These values are expected to rise due to the increase in quantity of development-related waste, that is construction and demolition waste, and of household waste, as a consequence of rising incomes and the creation of wealth. The need to expand the overall capacity of waste collection must face also the need to upgrade or close non-compliant landfills and of investing in waste sorting, treatment and recycling activities.

Finally, implementation of Directive 2007/77/EC has been a key driver behind the development of electricity produced from renewable energy sources. Investments in this sector vary across the Member States, depending on the particular natural potential for renewable resource. The objectives set by the directive concern the increase of the capacity for the production of heat and electricity from renewable energy sources, increase of the utilization of waste heat and energy saving, increase of public and industrial energy efficiency, decrease of energy consumption for heating and replacement of fossil fuels with green energy sources.

Figure 9.1 presents an overview across EU27 for the share of electricity produced from renewable energy sources in total electricity consumption, distinguishing between electricity generated from pumping in hydropower plants and other renewable energy sources. In 2002, Latvia, Slovenia and Slovakia had the highest share of renewable energy sources of electricity consumption (EC, 2005), respectively amounting to 48 per cent, 32 per cent and 20 per cent. The greatest part relates to electricity generated from pumping in hydropower plants. The other NMS' share is below 9 per cent and below the EU27 average of 12.7 per cent. The European Commission (EC, 2005) states that the likelihood of meeting national targets by 2010 differs between Member States: while Slovenia is considered likely to meet its target through extensive use of biomass and wind power, Poland is very unlikely to meet the 7.5 per cent target.

4. CONCLUDING REMARKS

The objective of this chapter was twofold: from one side, identifying the typologies and extent of gaps existing in the EU Member States, particularly in the NMS, both in GDP and in infrastructure endowment; from the other, giving a concise descriptive analysis of the infrastructural investment needs in the New EU Member States.

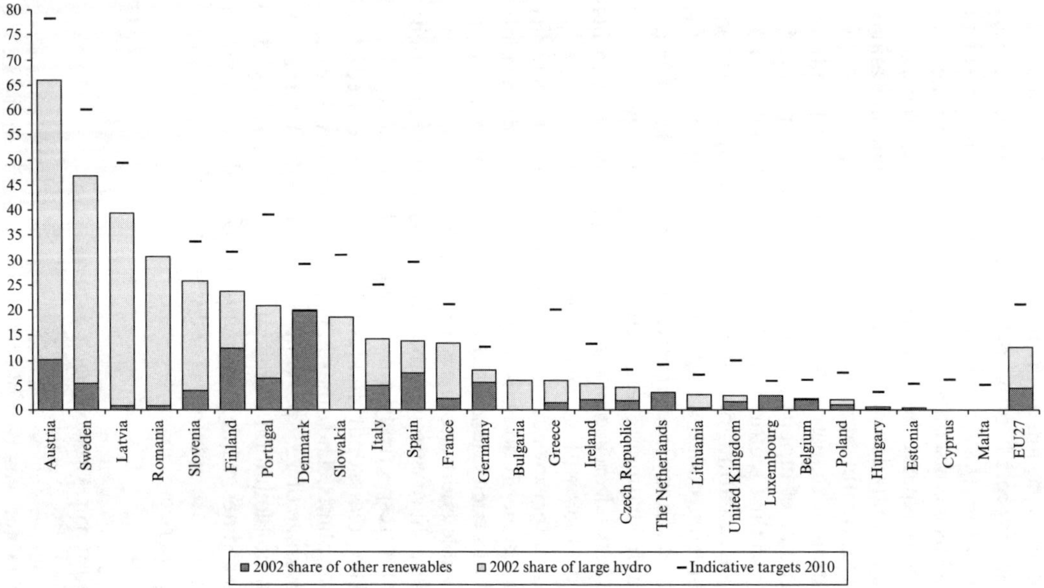

Note: The electricity directive (2001/77/EC) defines renewable electricity as the share of electricity produced from renewable energy sources in total electricity consumption. The latter includes imports and exports of electricity. The electricity generated from pumping in hydropower plants is included in total electricity consumption but it is not input as a renewable source of energy.

Source: European Environment Agency.

Figure 9.1 Share of renewable electricity in gross electricity consumption in the EU27 in 2002 (%; includes 2010 indicative targets)

Wide gaps exist between the OMS and the Central and Eastern European countries, in terms of GDP growth, per capita GDP, and the density of road, railway, telecommunication and environment infrastructures. While the NMS are growing faster than the European average, their per capita GDP and level of infrastructure is below the EU average.

The analysis of the variance shows that internal gaps are present, between the urbanized capital cities' regions and the peripheral and rural areas of each country. The internal divergences in the NMS are not deeper than those in the OMS, while the cross-country variability is much more significant. This suggests that, on average, the infrastructure endowments in all the European members is not homogeneous at the regional level; yet, the density and quality of such endowments is significantly higher in the Western countries and limited in the Eastern ones.

These results hold true at the same time for per capita GDP, and the transport and telecommunication infrastructures. As far as the environment (environment protection and energy) sector is concerned, the NMS have still much to do to comply with the EU Directives in the fields of water supply, wastewater treatment and renewable energy. However, since regional data are not available, conclusions over the kinds and level of regional gaps cannot be derived.

From a preliminary, illustrative and not comprehensive review of the allocation of Cohesion Policy funds for the period 2007–2013, it emerges that higher priorities have been given to the allocation of Structural Funds in the NMS to the transport and environment sectors, by promoting the trans-European transport network[18] and the use of renewable energy sources.[19] The findings of the present study could be further developed, by comparing the types and extent of regional and national gaps with the actual allocation of Structural Funds at the sectoral and sub-sectoral levels, in order to verify whether they are consistent with the intention to favour convergence in Europe.

NOTES

1. Up to 2 per cent of GDP on average in the period 2000–2005 (see EIB, 2000). As a matter of comparison in China, Thailand and Vietnam total infrastructure investment exceeds 7 per cent of GDP (see World Bank, 2008).
2. Eurostat and other European Union bodies use three levels of Nomenclature of Territorial Units for Statistics, also called NUTS, to refer to macro-regional (NUTS1), regional (NUTS2) and district (NUTS3) level in each member states.
3. For a comprehensive literature review of infrastructure and growth see Gramlich (1994) for theoretical foundations and Straub (2008) for a survey on empirical works.
4. The other factors being labour, non-infrastructural capital stock, technology, institutions and environment. This traditional model implies that infrastructures are pure

public goods, while other formulations consider that rather services produced by infrastructures are included in the production function. For a comprehensive literature review of infrastructure and growth see Gramlich (1994) for theoretical foundations and Stroub (2008) for a survey on empirical works. See also Butten (1998), Del Bo (2009), Del Bo and Florio (2008).

5. For example, the public good nature of some types of infrastructure is relevant to detect if public capital is cause or effect of development (see Biehl 1986).
6. After that period, however, the risk of the over-dominance of these cities will have to be reduced by a shift in the focus of transport investments first to medium-sized cities and later, as in the OMS, to rural and peripheral regions.
7. The ANOVA calculates and compares the variance between and within different groups, which, in the specific case, are the European countries and their regional sub-divisions, and it tests (through a Fisher Test) whether the means of different groups are significantly different. The analysis of variance is carried out only on countries with regional divisions (NUTS2): among the NMS there are Bulgaria, Czech Republic, Hungary, Poland, Romania, Slovakia; among the OMS Austria, Belgium, Denmark, Finland, France, Italy, Netherlands, Spain, Sweden, United Kingdom are considered.
8. The level of significance is 1 per cent.
9. This was less so in the period 2004–2006 for the EU12, when the decentralization process was still at a very early stage. Practically this meant that, for example in Poland, Structural Funds funded seven different Operational Programmes (planning documents setting priorities and implementation procedures) all of them managed at the national level. They focused on: business competitiveness, human resources, transport, food sector and rural development, fisheries, the integrated regional programme and technical assistance. In the period 2007–2013 the situation is different: in Poland four programmes are managed at the national level (innovation, infrastructure and environment, development of Eastern Poland and technical assistance), and 16 at the regional level.
10. Before 2004 a large share of funds came from the instruments of pre-accession.
11. The only exception is Greece which, even if it is an Old Member country, still gives much importance to infrastructures.
12. Term coined by Roger Brunet in 1989. It indicates a corridor stretching approximately from the North-West of England to Milan, passing by the Benelux countries and the Rhine's basin.
13. An indicator has been elaborated by the authors, which classifies the NUTS2 regions into four groups, according to the percentage of population living in sizeable cities or rural and peripheral areas.
14. NUTS2 data are not available for Poland.
15. The list of the European fields of intervention (EC Regulation No. 1083/2006) splits the 'Environment protection and risk' sector from the 'Energy' sector. We use this distinction also to analyse the allocation of funds, since they both are referred to under the general category of Environment.
16. A similar share applies also to Latvia, even if official data are missing.
17. An indicator has been elaborated by the authors following Applica et al. (2008), which classifies the NUTS2 regions. Directive 94/62/EC, Directive 2002/96/EC, Directive 94/67/EC, Directive 2002/96/EC.
18. In Objective 2 countries, instead, in 2007–2013 eligibility is given only to funding access to the trans-European corridors.
19. No clear priorities can be detected in telecommunications.

REFERENCES

Andraz, J.M. and A.M. Pereira (2007), 'Public investment in transportation infrastructures and industry performance in Portugal', College of William and Mary Department of Economics working paper 45.

Applica, Ismeri Europa and Wiiw (2008), 'Ex post evaluation of Cohesion Policy Programmes 2000–2006 financed by the European Regional Development Fund in Objective 1 and 2 regions', work package 1, task 5, final report, accessed at http://ec.europa.eu/regional_policy/sources/docgener/evaluation/expost2006/wp1_en.htm.

Aschauer, D.A. (1989), 'Is public expenditure productive?', *Journal of Monetary Economics*, **23**, 177–200.

Barro, R.J. (1990), 'Government spending in simple model of endogenous growth', *Journal of Political Economy*, **98**(5), S103–25.

Basile, R., S. De Nardis and A. Girardi (2001), 'Regional inequalities and cohesion policies in the European Union', ISAE Istituto di Studi e Analisi Economica working paper 23, Rome.

Biehl, D. (1986), 'The contribution of infrastructure to regional development', report produced by the Infrastructure Study Group for the European Community, Brussels.

Boldrin, M. and F. Canova (2003), 'Regional policies and EU enlargement', Centre for Economic Policy Research discussion paper 3722.

Button, K. (1998), 'Infrastructure investment, endogenous growth and economic convergence', *The Annals of Regional Science*, **32**(1), 145–62.

De Rus, G., C. Romàn and L. Trujillo (1995), 'Convergencia en infraestructuras de transporte', *Economistas*, **64**, 563–70.

Del Bo, C. (2009), 'Recent advances in public investment, fiscal policy and growth', University of Milan Department of Economics, Business and Statistics departmental working papers 2009-25.

Del Bo, C. and M. Florio (2008), 'Infrastructure and growth in the European Union: an empirical analysis at the regional level in a spatial framework', University of Milan Department of Economics, Business and Statistics departmental working papers 2008-37.

Dvornik, D. and D. Sabolic (2007), 'Telecommunication liberalization and economic development in European countries in transition', *Technology in Society*, **29**(4), 378–87.

ECORYS (2005), *Strategic Evaluation on Transport Investment Priorities under Structural and Cohesion Funds for the Programming Period 2007–2013*, synthesis report, 2005.CE.16.AT.014, Rotterdam, accessed at: http://ec.europa.eu/regional_policy/sources/docgener/evaluation/rado_en.htm.

ESPON (2005), '*Accessibility, transport and communication network – thematic study of INTERREG and ESPON activities*', final report, accessed at http://archive.interact-eu.net/download/application/pdf/1068941.

European Commission (EC) (2001), *European Transport Policy for 2010: Time to Decide*, COM(2001)370, 12/09/2001, *white paper* accessed at: http://ec.europa.eu/transport/strategies/doc/2001_white_paper/lb_com_2001_0370_en.pdf.

EC (2004), *A New Partnership for Cohesion – Convergence, Competitiveness, Cooperation*, third report on economic and social cohesion, February 2004, Brussels.

EC (2005), *Strategic Evaluation on Environment and Risk Prevention under Structural and Cohesion Funds for the period 2007–2013*, Directorate General Regional Policy Synthesis report 2005.CE.16.0.AT.016.

EC (2007), *Growing Regions, Growing Europe – Fourth Report on Economic and Social Cohesion*, May 2007, Brussels.

European Investment Bank (2000), 'Basic infrastructure investments in South-Eastern Europe – regional project review', Regional Funding Conference for South-Eastern Europe, 29–30 March 2000, Brussels, available at: http://ec.europa.eu/enlargement/archives/seerecon/infrastructure/documents/bii_see.pdf.

Eurostat (2009), 'Information society', in *Eurostat Regional Yearbook 2009*, Luxembourg: Office for Official Publications of the European Communities, accessed at: http://epp.eurostat.ec.europa.eu/cache/ITY_OFFPUB/KS-HA-09-001/EN/KS-HA-09-001-EN.PDF.

Gramlich, E. (1994), 'Infrastructure investment: a review essay', *Journal of Economic Literature*, **32**(3), 1176–96.

Jevčák, A. and F. Keereman (2008), 'Challenges for public investment in New EU Member States', in Gerd Schwarts, Ana Corbacho and Katja Funke (eds), *Public Investments and Public–Private Partnership – Addressing Infrastructure Challenges and Managing Fiscal Risks*, Washington, DC: IMF Publications.

Martin, P. (1997), 'Can regional policies affect growth and geography in Europe?', *World Economy*, **21**(08), 757–74.

Organization for Economic Co-operation and Development (OECD) (2007), 'Infrastructure to 2030 volume 2 – Mapping policy for electricity, water and transport', accessed at http://www.oecd.org/dataoecd/61/27/40953164.pdf.

Puga, D. (2002), 'European regional policies in light of recent location theories', Centre for Economic Policy Research discussion paper 2767.

Rapún, M., C. Gil and P. Pascual (2000), 'Infrastructure and growth in the European regions', ERSA conference paper ersa00p309.

Rothengatter, W. and A. Schaffer (2004), 'The impact of transport infrastructure and other immobile production factors on regional competitiveness', Transportation Research Board annual meeting paper 06-0868.

Skoric, M. (2006), 'Culture and communication technology development in Central and Eastern Europe: revisiting the "fault line" thesis', paper presented at the annual meeting of the International Communication Association, Dresden International Congress Centre, Dresden, Germany, 16 June.

Spieckermann, K. and M. Wegener (2006), 'The role of transport infrastructure for regional development in South East Europe', *SEER South-East Europe Review for Labour and Social Affairs*, (01), 51–61, accessed at: www.boeckler.de/pdf/seer_2006_01_spiekermann_wegener.pdf.

Straub, S. (2008), 'Infrastructure and growth in developing countries: recent advances and research challenges', World Bank policy research working paper 4460, Washington, DC.

Trasporti e Territorio srl (TRT) (2006), *The Impact of Trans-European Networks on Cohesion and Employment*, final report of the study IP/B/REGI/ST/2005_105 requested by the European Parliament's Committee on Regional Development, accessed at: www.trttrasportieterritorio.it/. . ./European. . ./The%20Impact%20of%20Trans-European%20Networks%20on%20Cohesion%20and%20Employment.pdf.

World Bank (2008), *The Growth Report – Strategies for Sustained Growth and Inclusive Development*, Commission on Growth and Development, accessed at www.growthcommission.org/index.php?Itemid=169&id=96&option=com_content&task=view.

Index